Perversion and Modern

How did nerves and neuroses take the place of ghosts and spirits in Meiji Japan? How does Natsume Sōseki's canonical novel *Kokoro* pervert the Freudian teleology of sexual development? What do we make of Jacques Lacan's infamous claim that because of the nature of their language the Japanese people were unanalyzable? And how are we to understand the re-awakening of collective memory occasioned by the sudden appearance of a Japanese Imperial soldier stumbling out of the jungle in Guam in 1972? In addressing these and other questions, the essays collected here theorize the relation of unconscious fantasy and perversion to discourses of nation, identity, and history in Japan.

Against a tradition that claims that Freud's method, as a Western discourse, makes a bad fit with Japan, this volume argues that psychoanalytic reading offers valuable insights into the ways in which "Japan" itself continues to function as a psychic object. By reading a variety of cultural productions as symptomatic elaborations of unconscious and symbolic processes rather than as indexes to cultural truths, the authors combat the truisms of modernization theory and the seductive pull of culturalism. This volume also offers a much needed psychoanalytic alternative to the area studies convention that reads narratives of all sorts as windows offering insights into a fetishized Japanese culture. As such, it will be of huge interest to students and scholars of Japanese literature, history, culture, and psychoanalysis more generally.

Nina Cornyetz is Associate Professor of Interdisciplinary Studies at New York University, USA.

J. Keith Vincent is Assistant Professor of Japanese and Comparative Literature at Boston University, USA.

Perversion and Modern Japan: Psychoanalysis, Literature, Culture
Edited with Introductions by Nina Cornyetz and J. Keith Vincent
Routledge Contemporary Japan Series

Perversion and Modern Japan

Psychoanalysis, literature, culture

**Edited by Nina Cornyetz
and J. Keith Vincent**

To Jon

An academic book - but
a thoroughly enjoyable read, I felt.
After all, what better combination
is there other than sex, literature
and Japan?
I hope you enjoy it anyway.
A hopelessly belated happy
birthday — hope 2012 is a great
one for you.
Love Hannah
xxx

Routledge
Taylor & Francis Group

LONDON AND NEW YORK

First published 2010
by Routledge
2 Park Square, Milton Park, Abingdon, Oxon OX14 4RN

Simultaneously published in the USA and Canada
by Routledge
711 Third Avenue, New York, NY 10017

Routledge is an imprint of the Taylor & Francis Group, an Informa business

First issued in paperback 2011

Typeset in Times New Roman by
Swales & Willis Ltd, Exeter, Devon

British Library Cataloguing in Publication Data
A catalogue record for this book is available from the British Library

Library of Congress Cataloging-in-Publication Data
Perversion and modern Japan : psychoanalysis, literature, culture / edited by
Nina Cornyetz and J. Keith Vincent. — 1st ed.
p. cm.
1. Deviant behavior— Japan. 2. Psychoanalysis and literature—Japan. I. Cornyetz,
Nina. II. Vincent, J. Keith, 1968-
HN723.5.P47 2009
302.5"42095209045—dc22

2008054938

ISBN13: 978-0-415-69143-7 (pbk)
ISBN13: 978–0–415–46910–4 (hbk)
ISBN13: 978–0–203–88042–5 (ebk)

Contents

Figures

Contributors

Jonathan E. Abel is Assistant Professor of Comparative Literature and Asian Studies at Pennsylvania State University. He is completing a book that examines the archival essence of censorship from literary examples in the collections of the Japanese Imperial Publishing Police and of the United States' Civil Censorship Detachment. His articles have appeared in *Japan Forum, Comparative Literature Studies, Asian Cinema,* and *Nation, Language, and the Ethics of Translation.* He is also co-translator of Azuma Hiroki's *Otaku: Japan's Database Animals* (Dōbutsu-ka suru posuto modan: otaku kara mita Nihonshakai).

Carl Cassegard is Associate Professor of Sociology at Gothenburg University, Sweden. He has lived in Kyoto for five years and is currently engaged in researching Japanese social movements and the transformation of the discourse of Leftist activists in response to the changes in Japanese society during the 1990s. His most recent publication is *Shock and Naturalization in Contemporary Japanese Literature* (Global Oriental, 2007), in which he discusses four Japanese writers – Kawabata Yasunari, Abe Kōbō, Murakami Haruki, and Murakami Ryū – with the help of the concepts of shock and trauma.

Nina Cornyetz is Associate Professor of Interdisciplinary Studies at the Gallatin School, New York University. Her publications include *The Ethics of Aesthetics in Japanese Cinema and Literature: Polygraphic Desire* (Routledge, 2007), "The meat manifesto: Ruth Ozeki's performative poetics," *Women and Performance,* 2001, and "Amorphous identity, disavowed history: Shimada Masahiko and national subjectivity," *Positions,* 2001.

Irena Hayter teaches modern Japanese literature and film at the University of Leeds. She recently completed a doctoral dissertation on modernism, narrative, and ideology in 1930s fiction (focusing on the works on Takami Jun, Ishikawa Jun and Dazai Osamu) at the School of Oriental and African Studies in London. Her interests include psychoanalytic theory, Marxist conceptualizations of ideology, and historicist approaches. She has published on Okuizumi Hikaru and the cultural politics of post-bubble Japan (*Proceedings of the Association for Japanese Literary Studies,* Vol. 5).

Christopher Hill is Associate Professor at Yale University, where he teaches modern Japanese literature and culture. He is the author of *National History and the World of Nations: Capital, State, and the Rhetoric of History in Japan, France, and the United States*, an interdisciplinary study of the writing of history in the late nineteenth century (Duke University Press, 2008). He is working on a book-length study of the dissemination of literary naturalism around the world in the late nineteenth and early twentieth century.

Dawn Lawson is New York University's East Asian Studies Librarian and a student in its PhD program in East Asian studies. Her interests include translation, narrative voice, and the history of the novel in Japan and Korea. Lawson recently digitized Nanette Twine's English translation of Tsubouchi Shōyō's *Shōsetsu shinzui*, and she is the co-translator, with J. Keith Vincent, of Saitō Tamaki's *Japan's Beautiful Warrior Girls: A Psychoanalysis [Sentō bishōjo no seishin bunseki]*, forthcoming from University of Minnesota Press.

Margherita Long is Assistant Professor in the Department of Comparative Literature and Foreign Languages at the University of California, Riverside. Her essay here is adapted from *This Perversion Called Love: Tanizaki, Feminist Theory, Freud*, forthcoming from Stanford University Press. In addition to her work on Tanizaki, she has published two pieces on Nakagami Kenji – an essay called "Nakagami and the denial of lineage: On maternity, abjection, and the Japanese outcast class" (*Differences*, Summer 2006), and a *zadankai* with Asada Akira, Karatani Kōjin, Tsushima Yūko, Watanabe Naomi, and Aoyama Shinji, called "Nakagami and the 'End of Kindai Bungaku'" (*Waseda Bungaku*, November 2004). Currently, she is working on a book of feminist essays about anime. The first appeared as "Malice@Doll: Konaka, specularization, and the virtual feminine" (*Mechademia* 2, Fall 2007).

Yutaka Nagahara is Professor of Japanese economic history at Hōsei University and a committee member of the Institute of Comparative Economic Studies. He is the author of *The Emperor System and Peasants* (in Japanese, 1989) and others. He is a regular contributor to many leftist journals as well as literature and poetry journals in Japan. He is also a translator of Slavoj Žižek, Alain Badiou, and others.

Kazushige Shingu is a psychiatrist and Professor at the Graduate School of Human and Environmental Studies, Kyoto University. He is the author of many books and papers on clinical psychiatry and psychoanalysis, including *Being Irrational: Lacan, the Objet a and the Golden Mean,* translated and edited by Michael Radich (Gakuju Shoin, 2004) and "Japanese myth, Buddhist legend, and the structural analysis of clinical dreams in relation to the mourning process," *The Letter: Lacanian Perspectives on Psychoanalysis* 37(Summer 2006): 93–113.

Bruce Suttmeier is Associate Professor of Japanese at Lewis & Clark College in Portland, Oregon. He is the author of several articles on postwar memory, trauma, and visual culture. His ongoing research continues his exploration of

1960s visual culture, particularly how technology affects notions of representation and experience. He is currently working on a manuscript exploring 1960s cultural responses to the emerging predominance of images as events, as modes of experience and as forms of communication.

J. Keith Vincent is Assistant Professor of Japanese and Comparative Literature at Boston University. His recent publications include "Haiku kara shōsetsu e: Meiji teki homososhiaritii no shūen" [From haiku to the novel: the end of Meiji homosociality] in *Jendā kenkyū no furontiya* vol. 5, Sakuhinsha, 2008 and "A Japanese Electra and her queer progeny" *Mechademia* 2, Fall 2007. His partial translation of Book 5 of Natsume Sōseki's *Bungakuron* appeared in *Theory of Literature and Other Critical Writings*, Columbia, 2009. His chapter for this volume is adapted from a manuscript in progress entitled *Two-Timing Modernity: Homosocial Narrative in Modern Japanese Fiction.*

Gavin Walker is a doctoral student in East Asian Literature at Cornell University, and works on Marxist theory, postcolonial studies, theory of translation, and postwar literature and film. His recent publications include "The filmic time of coloniality" in *Mechademia* 4: *War/Time* (forthcoming), and "On the 'End': Mishima Yukio and the double dislocation of literature," in *Proceedings of the Association for Japanese Literary Study* vol. 9, 2008. He is currently translating Uno Kōzō's *Capital and Socialism* and other selected writings.

Ayelet Zohar is an artist, independent curator, and cultural researcher, specializing in the visual culture of contemporary East Asian art (Japan and China). Zohar is currently working as a post-doctoral Japan Fund fellow at Freeman Spogli Institute, Stanford University. She has a PhD in Fine Art (theory and practice) from the Slade School of Fine Art, University of London (2007). In 2005, Zohar curated a large-scale exhibition of contemporary Japanese photography and video art entitled *PostGender: Gender, Sexuality and Performativity in Contemporary Japanese Art* for the Tikotin Museum of Japanese Art, in Haifa (Israel). A new publication exploring issues raised by the exhibition is edited by Zohar, and is forthcoming from Cambridge Scholars Press, 2009.

Introduction

Japan as screen-memory: psychoanalysis and history

Nina Cornyetz and J. Keith Vincent

> Creative writers are valuable allies and their evidence is to be prized highly, for they are apt to know a whole host of things between heaven and earth of which our philosophy has not yet let us dream.
>
> Sigmund Freud, *Delusions and Dreams in Jensen's* Gradiva

> For Freud, the nation and the individual are equal disguises for a struggle, a dismemberment, which always returns to the scene from which it is erased; and the novel is the theoretic instrument of this analysis . . . . By a device customary to Freud at important turning-points in his analyses, he ultimately authorizes his conception, not by proofs, but by the quotation which shapes his thought. It is a poem; that is writing where truth is supported by nothing other than writing's relationship to itself, its beauty. The authorizing poem is a fragment, one of Schiller's aphorisms:
>
> > What will live of the poem's immortal
> > must darken in this life
> >
> > Michel de Certeau, The Freudian novel

The diverse collection of essays in this book have two things in common: they all discuss some aspect of Japanese culture, and they all do so with the aid of some form or offshoot of Freud's psychoanalytic method. Depending on the reader's perspective, we recognize that one or another of these criteria might seem somewhat arbitrary. Why just Japan? some might ask. If the point is to explore the application of psychoanalysis to culture, then why not open the inquiry up to other cultures as well? Or, Why the focus on psychoanalysis? If the point is to produce more knowledge about "Japan" then why not subject it to scrutiny through the lenses of multiple methodologies? These are entirely reasonable questions, and ones that we have asked ourselves many times in the process of editing this book.

Limiting the scope of the book to Japanese culture was of course partly a result of the fact that both of its editors happen to be specialists in Japanese literature; and the emphasis on psychoanalysis likewise reflects our own interest and expertise in this area. But beyond this coincidental convergence of institutional situatedness and intellectual interest, we felt very strongly that there was something potentially both salutary and exciting in thinking psychoanalytically about "Japan" within the context of Western Japan studies. Not only does Freud's method offer us many useful tools for analyzing cultural phenomena, some of which will be discussed below, but it is in the nature of psychoanalytic reading since Freud to include methodological self-reflection as an integral part of the analysis itself. And this self-reflexive aspect of psychoanalytic reading is particularly valuable for scholars in Japanese studies who are saddled with the historical legacy of area studies. Like other branches of area studies, the Japan "field" is characterized by extraordinarily overdetermined relations between its practitioners and their "object." Unlike the traditional 19th century disciplines such as English and European national literatures and history, the study of literatures and cultures outside the West had to wait for the postwar period, and then emerged only as a result of the perceived need to "know our enemies" in an atmosphere of Cold War paranoia. Since the 1950s area studies programs throughout the United States have produced knowledge in multiple disciplines about strategically identified geographical "areas." But this knowledge tends to remain ghettoized in area studies departments and only rarely feeds back into the mainline disciplines. This is a result not only of continuing Eurocentrism in academia, but also of the isolating effects of the organization of area studies departments according to nation state, as well as, in the case of Japan studies, an insistence on Japanese cultural uniqueness that is underwritten not only by many Japanese scholars themselves but also by the funding priorities of Japanese government entities that are charged with propagating Japanese culture abroad. The vast amount of knowledge produced outside Japan about Japan thus remains suspended in a curious limbo, jealously guarded by its producers, like a fetish that compensates for their lack of access to the "larger" scholarly community. As Harry Harootunian and Masao Miyoshi put it, employing a striking metaphor that Freud would have had a field day with, "More than fifty years after the war's end American scholars are still organizing knowledge as if confronted by an implacable enemy and thus driven by the desire either to destroy it or marry it."[1]

Of course virtually any object of study is capable of inspiring powerful feelings of hate, love, and ambivalence, depending on the psychic disposition of the scholar in question. But in the case of those who study Japan, these relations are clearly overdetermined by historical and institutional circumstances going far beyond what any individual's experience can encompass. Understanding how "Japan" has been constructed not just as an object of study, but also as an object of *fantasy,* is one of the goals of this book. We will have more to say about this later, but for now it is enough to note that while some of the essays included here, such as those by Bruce Suttmeier and Nina Cornyetz, tackle this question head-on, in others it is addressed implicitly by employing psychoanalysis to understand the construction of other sorts of fantasy objects, such as the national past, the maternal body, or the phallus as the unique guarantor of non-psychotic subjectivity. Jonathan Abel, for example, uses a discussion of the way women's underwear in Japanese porn works to both conceal and to signify the object of male heterosexual desire as a means of discussing the ambivalent status of "Japan" itself as the object of Japanese studies. "If the continued survival of Japanese Studies in the U.S. rests no longer on U.S. government grants to prevent future wars," he writes, "[and] no longer on the continued belief in a threatening economic powerhouse, but rests on Japan's 'gross national cool' (as recent claims have been made), then nothing could be cooler than Japanese porn."

Rather than preview the contents of this volume here, we have devoted the remainder of this introduction to a discussion of the history of psychoanalysis in Japan and what we consider to be the primary advantages of the psychoanalytic method as applied to Japanese studies. But before we move on to that section, a word on the other key word in our title: "perversion." As the short list of topics already mentioned might have suggested, many (although not all) of the essays collected here deal with various forms of "perverse" sexuality. Those that are not overtly sexual have to do with perversions of other types such as the perversion of narrative, of politics, and language. But even without perusing its table of contents, we have both been amused at how many people, upon hearing the title of this book, smile knowingly and say some version of, "Ah yes. Those Japanese are very perverse!" as images of girls in school uniforms, "love hotels," and sadomasochistic porn seem to dance in their heads. This image of Japanese people as somehow more "perverse" than us (as a reaction, so the theory seems to go, to an excessively repressive social order) is fascinating in its own right for the work it does (thanks to all those *New York Times* articles about weird Japan) in shoring up our sense of our own normalcy. But our choice of perversion as an organizing rubric for this volume was motivated not by any sense that Japan is any more perverse than the next country, but rather by Freud's understanding that the status of the "normal" as *the normative* rather than the natural can best be understood by taking the perversions seriously. "Thus the extraordinarily wide dissemination of the perversions forces us to suppose," he famously wrote, "that the disposition to perversions is itself of no great rarity but must form a part of what passes as the normal constitution."[2] If the perverse is an inherent part of the normal rather constituting some alien and deficient *outside* to it, its analysis is all the more crucial as a way of understanding how subjects come into existence, identities are formed, and histories written.

Psychoanalysis comes to Japan

Psychoanalysis was first introduced to Japan in a series of articles published in 1912, just seventeen years after Freud had first used the term "psychoanalysis" to describe his method of psychological interpretation.[3] The next year saw the publication of three articles by the psychiatrist Morooka Son in the *literary* journal *Eniguma*. These comprised the seven-part "Dreams of an unmarried woman" translations of Otto Rank, appended by a comment on Morooka's own use of psychoanalytic dream interpretation, "Introduction of the literature abroad," which interpreted a 1909 European novel in relation to Freud's work on incest, and "Concerning the volume of Nowaki of the *Tale of Genji*," which used Freudian theory to read the canonized classic, *The Tale of Genji*.[4]

Although other early proponents of psychoanalysis in Japan took the opposite position, Morooka introduced psychoanalysis as an analytic methodology theoretically valuable on its own merits, rather than as a strictly medical or psychological therapy for the treatment of neuroses. This was markedly unlike the history of the reception of psychoanalysis in the United States, where the medicalization of psychoanalysis divested it from its originally broader cultural applications.[5] In the 1920s, Freud gave up on his attempt to convince leading American psychoanalysts that "the spirit of psychoanalysis was not medical."[6] Joseph Schwartz notes, "In Europe, the high-cultural appeal of psychoanalysis took it far beyond narrow medical circles. In Britain, France, Germany and Austria many of the most distinguished early practitioners were lay analysts drawn to psychoanalysis from the disciplines of literature, philosophy, law, pedagogy and natural science . . . . The situation in the United States was quite the reverse. Here psychoanalysis developed almost exclusively as an extension of medical practice by doctors trained in psychiatry and neurology."[7]

In Japan, throughout the first half of the twentieth century four men in particular, Marui Kiyoyasu, Kosawa Heisaku, Ohtsuki Kenji and Yabe Yaekichi, three of whom studied abroad with followers of Freud, worked tirelessly alongside many less well known others to establish psychoanalytic training institutes and clinics, have these recognized by Freud's International Psychoanalytic Association (IPA), originate psychoanalytic journals, and make available Japanese translations of Freud's writings. Several of them sought and received Freud's enthusiastic endorsement of their activities. These pioneers of the psychoanalytic movement in Japan included professionals in the fields of psychiatry and medicine, and lay practitioners – a practice supported by Freud but disparaged by American psychoanalytic circles, as noted above.

It was nonetheless an uphill battle to spearhead a psychoanalytic movement in Japan. As Christopher Hill demonstrates in his contribution to this volume, psychiatric approaches to psychology were already incorporated into universities as fields of study and research. On the one hand, psychoanalysis was denigrated as the irrational and insufficiently scientific, hence inferior competitor to psychiatry.[8] On the other hand, culturalist theories of Japanese uniqueness critiqued psychoanalysis from the more or less opposite perspective – claiming it needed to be nuanced by Buddhism or other "Eastern" sensibilities or traits to suit the Japanese temperament.

It was, and still is frequently asserted that Japan and psychoanalysis make a poor fit. We use the vague term "poor fit" because the notion that psychoanalysis is ill-adapted to Japanese culture takes myriad and sometimes contradictory forms. It may take the form of scientism, or it may appear within the huge volume of literature on "Japanese-ness" (*Nihonjinron*). *Nihonjinron* discourse is wide and varied, insisting on a special uniqueness to Japanese culture, temperament and sensibility, which distinguish the Japanese people not only from Westerners of all nations, but also from other Asians such as Chinese or Koreans.[9] This resistance to psychoanalysis, whichever camp it claims allegiance to, comes from Japanese scholars themselves as well as from non-Japanese Japanologists, and has existed since psychoanalytic theory was first introduced to Japan.

Morita Masatake insisted that Zen Buddhism be the foundation of a "Japanese" therapy. Later, Doi Takeo would further insist on another sort of Japanization of psychoanalysis to suit the model of "indulgence" (*amae*) in Japanese culture. Even Kosawa, one of the most enthusiastic advocates of the Freudian psychoanalytic movement, coined the term Ajase Complex to relativize the importance of the Oedipal Complex in Japan by prioritizing the relation to the mother. At the same time, it is worth noting that Kosawa turned to Buddhist legend for the origins of the Ajase Complex just as Freud turned to Greek myth to describe the Oedipal Complex, suggesting psychoanalysis's constitutive bond with what might provisionally be called literary narratives.

Most recently, it was Jacques Lacan himself who contended that, because of the structure of the Japanese language, the Japanese were "unanalyzable."[10] When used in Japanese, Chinese characters (*kanji*) generally have multiple potential pro-nunciations, some of which can be traced back to indigenous (pre-Chinese influence) sounds, called "kun" readings, and some that originate in Japanese approximations of Chinese sounds, called "on" readings. In addition, the system of so-called honorifics in Japanese is such that the subject, or oneself, can only be posited in *relation* to its position among others. For example, when "I" refer to myself the word I choose to represent me will differ depending on whom I am addressing, whether in reality or in my imagination. For these reasons, Lacan theorized that for the Japanese, the process of becoming a subject through alienation in language, or the acceptance of the signifier in the place of the subject, is thwarted.[11] Since both Kazushige Shingu and Jonathan Abel take this problematic up directly in their essays included here, we will leave further discussion of this issue in their capable hands.

This perception of a "poor fit" also has roots in far less sophisticated, Orientalist critiques of Japanese culture by non-Japanese. In 1953 the American psychoanalyst James Clark Moloney published a venomous article harshly critiquing Japanese psychoanalysis, concluding that "The goal of occidental psycho-analysis is the freeing of the individual. But in Japan . . . there is no such thing (permissibly, at least) as a true individual who feels, thinks, and acts voluntarily in a self-determined manner."[12] Moloney's assessment of the Japanese "individual" and psychoanalytic practice was the result of two visits to Japan in the 1940s and his reliance on the Japanese Ministry of Education's 1937 infamous nationalist tract, *Kokutai no hongi* (Cardinal Principles of the National Polity) as a text telling the "truth" about Japanese culture.[13] One of Japan's leading proponents of psychoanalysis, Ohtsuki Kenji responded, "Dr. Moloney's references are out of date and biased, presumably because they are mostly from work published during the war . . . It is definitely not a book that should be regarded as a fair representation of Japanese thinking in general."[14] Toward the conclusion of his protest to Moloney's article, Ohtsuki added an eminently rational comment,

No culture or doctrine . . . can avoid reflecting to some extent the specific traits of the country, State, and era of its origin, and Freudian science is no exception to this rule. When it was imported into America it became more or less Americanized; in the same way, when it was imported into Japan, it naturally tended to become gradually Japanified. Is it justifiable to assume that the

American version is an absolute standard and all other modifications per-versions?[15]

We cite this controversy not in order to correct or promote an evaluation of Japanese psychoanalysis as more "true" to psychoanalysis, nor to support Moloney's contention that it is some lesser imitation perverted by Japanese national culture. To the contrary, three issues foregrounded in Moloney's critique and Ohtsuki's response are in fact the central problematics *against which* the essays gathered here argue in favor of *other ways of reading*.

The culturalist critique by Moloney does a number of fascinating things.

First, Moloney's statement completely misses the astute point made by Ohtsuki in the second comment quoted above: for him, American psychoanalysis has become the universalist standard against which any other cultural modifications are deemed "perversions." This is of course an example of gross American provincialism. Indeed, much of American psychoanalysis of the 1950s had been transformed by the rejection of drive theory as Freud had formulated it in favor of "ego psychology" – or a therapy that also focused on the individual's (actual) social, cultural and interpersonal conflicts, thus constituting a first step towards its current "object-relations" and "relational" dispositions.[16] Freud, on the other hand, had written that, "The ego is not master in its own house."[17] As Schwartz put it, "Freud characterized the ego as the rider on the horse of wild directionless drives, located in the mental structure called the id. . . .[However] the ego was now off rather than on the horse."[18] Regardless of whether one feels that ego psychology's attempt to put the rider in control of the horse was an advancement in the field of psychoanalysis as therapeutic tool or not, it must be recognized as an *Americanization* of Freudian theory, that moreover focused on psychoanalysis as putatively *curative*.

Second, in keeping with one effect of ego psychology, Moloney's notion of psychoanalysis as dedicated to a "true individual who feels, thinks, and acts voluntarily in a self-determined manner," strikes us as a decidedly American, and indeed anti-Freudian concept of the subject. As Tim Dean argues, the non-American (Continental) tradition of psychoanalytic thought that originated with Freud is both distinct from and often antithetical to the "various American traditions of psychoanalytic empiricism, which historically have harnessed Freudianism to an ideological project of boosting individualism rather than questioning it."[19] The Freudian subject is first and foremost *split*, and alienated from itself. According to Freud, not only is our ego "lived by unknown and uncontrollable forces,"[20] but in fact consists of conglomerations of introjected others, or objects.

> The character of the ego is a precipitate of abandoned object-cathexis and identification – cases, that is, in which the alteration in character occurs before the object has been given up. In such cases the alteration in character has been able to survive the object-relation and in a certain sense to conserve it. . . .When the ego assumes the features of the object, it is forcing itself, so to speak, upon the id as a love-object and is trying to make good the id's loss by saying Look, you can love me too – I am so like the object."[21]

The ego, however, is only a part of the subject in Freud, which has to be inferred as made up of three coextensive and overlapping components: id, ego, superego. What emerges in the process of *relation* between the co-figured unconscious and conscious components of the mind would be, then, the "subject." The subject is the effect of this process of relation, and not something that exists *a priori*. According to Thomas Ogden:

> The subject in the historical era of psychoanalysis is no longer to be considered coincident with conscious awareness, no longer equated with the conscious, speaking, behaving, "I" (ego).
>
> . . .
>
> To equate Das Ich (the ego of the structural model) with the experiencing "I" is to obscure the generative process of mutual negation and preservation involving ego, id and superego upon which the structural model is based. To make such an equation is to mistake the part (the ego) for the dialectical (negating and negated) whole. Although no single word can carry the requisite multiplicity, ambiguity and specificity of meaning, the term subject seems particularly well suited to convey the psychoanalytic conception of the experiencing "I" in both a phenomenological and a metapsychological sense. The term is etymologically linked with the word "subjectivity" and carries an inherent semantic reflexivity, i.e. it simultaneously denotes subject and object, I and it, I and me. The word subject refers to both the "I" as speaker, thinker, writer, reader, perceiver and so on, and to the object of subjectivity, i.e. to the topic (the subject) being discussed, the idea being contemplated, the percept being viewed, etc. As a result, the subject can never be fully separated from the object and therefore can never be completely centred in itself.[22]

The very notion of the unconscious, of course, means that the subject is split, or *cut off* from as much, if not more, of "him/herself" than s/he is cognizant of. Certainly neither the subject, nor even the ego, as Lacan, or even Freud described them bears much resemblance to Moloney's "true individual who feels, thinks, and acts voluntarily in a self-determined manner."[23]

Third, and most importantly in our opinion, in Moloney's vitriolic attack on Japanese psychoanalysis there is the puzzling and indeed ironic, *literal reading* by Moloney (a psychoanalyst) of the verbatim content of a written text as revealing – un-encoded – an actual "truth" of Japan. Psychoanalytic interpretations, as we understand the methodology, and as we will elaborate at some length below, are ones that take narrative seriously – that is, "at its word," or literally – at the very same time as they recognize that what is articulated may be in a negative, displaced, or somehow "canted" (in other words, "encoded") relation to what it "means."

In the case study "From the history of an infantile neurosis," Freud explains that the onset of anxiety in the patient's childhood was heralded not by an external event, but rather, by a dream he had right around his fourth birthday, "from which he awoke in a state of anxiety."[24] After a short description of the patient's mental status at the beginning of treatment (intermittently confined to sanatoriums for "manic-depressive insanity") and a brief overview of some material from his childhood, Freud embarks on an analysis of the analysand's nightmare.

> *I dreamt that it was night and that I was lying in my bed. (My bed stood with its foot towards the window; in front of the window there was a row of old walnut trees. I know it was winter when I had the dream, and night-time.) Suddenly the window opened of its own accord, and I was terrified to see that some white wolves were sitting on the big walnut tree in front of the window. There were six or seven of them. The wolves were quite white, and looked more like foxes or sheep-dogs, for they had big tails like foxes and they had their ears pricked like dogs when they are attending to something. In great terror, evidently of being eaten by the wolves, I screamed* and woke up.
> (Original emphasis, p. 498)

Apparently the most vivid or powerfully recollected attributes of the dream included the opening of the window and the rapt gaze and motionlessness of the wolves. A few pages into the analysis, Freud reports that the patient realized that the part of the dream in which the window "opened of its own accord," was a distortion of a recollection, and decided that "It must mean: 'My eyes suddenly open.' . . . The attentive looking, which in the dream is ascribed to the wolves, should rather be shifted to him" (p. 505). Freud muses that perhaps the stillness of the wolves is in fact a "transposition or reversal" of what he actually saw: "a scene of violent movement at which he looked with strained attention" (p. 505).

Indeed, as the analysis continues, the dream is analyzed to be the stand-in for the traumatic memory of the "primal scene," or the small child or infant's screen-memory of seeing his parents copulating "*a tergo*." But how does the dream do this, that is, "stand in" for the memory? In place of the opening of the child's eyes, the dream distorts this "opening" to the window, which opens of its own accord. It displaces the act of opening. Likewise, the attentive gaze of the wolves rightfully belongs to the child, who was the one "attentively" looking. Finally, a memory of violent movement is replaced with its obverse, absolute stillness.

And how do Freud and his patient get from the one (the dream as told by the dreamer) to the other (the memory as reconstructed in the analytic sessions)? It is, of course, in the long and rambling process of the patient's associations, and Freud's interpretive promptings, to the (literal) words that construct the telling of the dream. The dream, rendered into a narrative, is thus simultaneously *literally what it is* and yet *not at all what it is literally*.

Moreover, as Freud's own narrative of the analysis continues, we discover that it is determined in fact that the patient was quite young when he witnessed this "primal scene" – as recovered from the dream of the wolves in the tree. The analysand had just turned four years old when he had the dream. However, it seems that he was only one and a half when the actual act of witnessing took place. Freud observes that the child could not have understood what he saw "at the time of the observation. He received the impressions when he was one and a half; his understanding of them was deferred, but became possible at the time of the dream owing to his development" (p. 508, footnote 4). At the time when the patient recounted the dream to Freud he was in his upper twenties. This in turn also contributes meaningfully to the memory of the dream.

> We must not forget the actual situation which lies behind the abbreviated description given in the text: the patient under analysis, at an age of over twenty-five years, was lending words to the impressions and impulses of his fourth year which he would never have found at that time. If we fail to notice this, it may easily seem comic and incredible that a child of four should be capable of such technical judgements and learned notions. This is simply another instance of *deferred action*. At the age of one and a half the child receives an impression to which he is unable to react adequately; he is only able to understand it and to be moved by it when the impression is revived in him at the age of four; and only twenty years later, during the analysis, is he able to grasp with his conscious mental processes what was then going on in him." (pp. 516–17, footnote 1)

What is Freud saying here? An event occured that psychically impacted the subsequent sexual development and neurotic symptomology of his patient, but this event itself was only understood by the patient after he had reconstructed the memory at a later age. In addition, the memory was repressed and retrievable only in the form of a distorted dream, recalled in the patient's adulthood. The dream is one clue that when interpreted reveals a complex network of associated thoughts and feelings that in turn reveal origins of neurotic symptoms.

However, in the next section of the case study Freud does something rather astonishing. He postulates that the memory of the witnessing of the primal scene may well have been a fantasy that the man had as a child. Perhaps the memory recovered from the dream in fact never constituted a scene, only an imaginary version of one. Freud contemplates how the child might have seen animals copulating and perhaps retroactively constructed a memory in which the actions of the animals are made to "overlay" a memory of awakening in his parents' room. Freud goes so far as to argue that "these scenes from infancy are not reproduced during the treatment as recollections, they are the productions of construction" (p. 523).

Even more striking is Freud's next assertion, which is that *it does not matter to the analysis whether or not these memories,* constructed either from dreams or existing as normal "memories" of childhood, *are real.* "It is also a matter of indifference in this connection whether we choose to regard it as a primal scene or as a primal phantasy" (p. 603, footnote 1). In other words, because what is important to the psychoanalysis is the psychic material *encoded within* the memory, or the patient's mental processes and not the retrieval of some literal truth or event, it is virtually inconsequential to determine if the memory "really happened" or not.

It is important that the above be clear. While it may indeed matter enormously to society, and to juridical proceedings, whether or not a memory of what we now might call child abuse actually physically occurred, for the *analysis* what matters is the psychic material that is retrieved, and not proof that an event – be it sexual abuse of a child or the witnessing of parental coitus – occurred.

Above we have used the word "screen memory" to describe the analysand's recollection of the primal scene. It is not only primal scene memories, however, that constitute what Freud called "screen memories."[25] These memories are often of such mundane and apparently trivial events that the reason for their retention is puzzling. Why would someone bother to remember, for example, a banal garden scene from early childhood in which nothing really happens? Freud's explanation is that the screen memory is the result of a compromise between two opposing psychic forces: the attempt to remember an important experience, such as a death, or an illness, etc., and a resistance to such recollection. What one remembers is something closely associated with the repressed memory; this way both resistance to memory and desire to remember are in a sense satisfied. This explanation, of course, is the result of the material recovered in the analytic free-association to the memory. "And since the elements of the experience which aroused objection were precisely the important ones, the substituted memory will necessarily lack those important elements and will in consequence most probably strike us as trivial" ("Screen memories," p. 307). In these sorts of screen memories, fantasies are "projected" onto one another, and childhood memories are constructed "almost like works of fiction" ("Screen memories," p. 315).

It is, however, also entirely possible that the scenes viewed by the individual in his or her memory are "genuine." If so, the scene recalled, Freud observes, has been selected "from innumberable others of a similar or another kind because, on account of its content . . . it was well adapted to represent the two phantasies. . . A recollection of this kind, whose value lies in the fact that it represents in the memory impressions and thoughts of a later date whose content is connected with its own by symbolic or similar links, may appropriately be called a '*screen memory*'" ("Screen memories," pp. 315–16).

What Freud is postulating about screen memories parallels what he postulated about memories retrieved from dreams: they may or may not be "real" memories, but that is inconsequential to the psychoanalytic inquiry. Because the screen memory, whether consisting of an entirely fantastical event, or of a puzzlingly banal actual scene from childhood, is important only in relation to the suppressed and symbolic associations that can be teased out of it.

> Scenes from early infancy, such as are brought up by an exhaustive analysis of neuroses. . . are not reproductions of real occurrences, to which it is possible to ascribe an influence over the course of the patient's later life and over the formation of his symptoms. It considers them rather as products of the imagination, which find their instigation in mature life, which are intended to serve as some kind of symbolic representation of real wishes and interests. ("Infantile neurosis," p. 521)

What we think we are remembering are in fact inventions that owe their existence to thoughts and feelings *in the rememberer's present.* In all the complex processes of constructing the memory, relating the memory, and analyzing it, *time is not linear.* In some instances a screen memory of childhood is constructed to express suppressed thoughts and feelings that occurred subsequent to the scene recalled in the memory (whether the scene was real or not). In others it is the suppressed thoughts or affects of an earlier "event" (real or fantasized) that is expressed in the memory in coded form. Indeed, a screen memory

> will also be formed from residues of memories relating to later life as well . . . Some of these screen memories dealing with events later in life owe their importance to a connection with experiences in early youth which have remained suppressed. . . . A screen memory may be described as "retrogressive" or as having "pushed forward" according as the one chronological relation or the other holds between the screen and the thing screened-off. ("Screen memories," p. 320)

Time in its conventional sense no longer exists here. There is no "past" event distinct and discrete from the present. Memory then is falsely "fixed" and more accurately represents a process of what one might call *rewriting.* (Freud's teleology of passage through three psychosexual stages – from oral to anal to genital maturity – can be understood similarly as a "bad" or imperfect teleology, because strictly speaking one never outgrows any of the previous stages, which continue to coexist alongside genital maturity to varying degrees within all individuals, animating our choices unconsciously.)

Freud points out the obvious: in most childhood scenes that we remember, in which the rememberer him/herself "appears," "the subject sees himself in the recollection . . . as an observer from outside the scene would see him. . . . such a picture cannot be an exact repetition of the impression that was originally received. For the subject was then in the middle of the situation and was attending not to himself but to the external world" ("Screen memories," p. 321). The appearance of the subject as an "object among other objects" (p. 321) indicates that the memory has been reworked or even "falsified" (p. 322). Even more astonishing perhaps, Freud presses this theory further, to argue that what he has postulated about memory in relation to faithfulness to actual events, and to linearity, is not true only of "screen memories." The distinction between "screen" memories and other childhood memories may be a false one, because

> It may indeed be questioned whether we have any memories at all *from* our childhood: memories *relating to* our childhood may be all that we possess. Our childhood memories show us our earliest years not as they were but as they appeared at the later periods when the memories were aroused. In these periods of arousal, the childhood memories did not, as people are accustomed to say, *emerge*; they were *formed* at that time. And a number of motives, with no

concern for historical accuracy, had a part in forming them, as well as in the selection of the memories themselves. ("Screen memories," p. 322)

Freud is no longer talking specifically about neurotics or hysterics whose memories of childhood are distorted by psychic processes, but is here theorizing a way of thinking about *everyone's* memories of childhood. The very structure of memory is precisely the same for neurotics suffering from "pathological mental conditions" as it is for all individuals recollecting their childhood ("Screen memories," p. 303). Thus all (early) memory operates by the same structural rule of faithfulness *not to a literal truth or event but to the psychic processes of repressed thoughts and affects*. This is the case regardless of whether the memory is "accurate" (the event remembered happened) or not (the event remembered never happened). *What Freud is saying, then, is that memories, whether retrieved through dreams or not, are never either true or untrue, but are both (and neither) simultaneously and constitutively.* Psychoanalysis allows for the interpretation that *narratives are not always what they are*, while the forms of articulation in which they appear are essential to a rewriting, or reading, of other significations encoded within the manner, form, and literal words of that narrative. The specificity of numbers, or names, for example, are important clues to "reading" dreams (or memories), but may not even represent *accurately* the number (or exact name) that they have encoded, and to which they have a *symbolic* relation.[26] It is this sort of reading – or one that is attentive to the *literal* narratives under discussion at the same time as it puts into question the relation of those narratives to *what they mean* – that we are considering the core of a psychoanalytic methodology shared by the various essays gathered together in this volume.

To return briefly to Moloney's comments about Japan and psychoanalysis, one final way in which it provides us with a model *against which* we position this collection of essays can be found in his culturalist notion of the difference between Japan and the USA, that also informs the notion that psychoanalysis is ill adapted to Japan. This culturalism projects a fantasy of some fixed, homogeneous thing named "Japanese culture," culled in large part from written texts, onto the peoples of a modern nation-state in classical Orientalist fashion. The very construction of something called "Japanese culture" *in general* is of course dependent on a number of factors. It can only exist in negative relation to the equally imaginary postulation of something like "Western culture" or "Chinese culture," which are "co-figured" against what they are not.[27] It also relies on the elision of those cultural factors that, for example, replicate ones found in the "West," or "China" in favor of emphasizing attributes that are putatively uniquely "Japanese." It disregards historical rupture in favor of continuity, and ignores regional variations that might weaken the claims to "uniqueness" and homogeneity. In other words, it represents one dominant way of organizing the fragments of past events into a coherent, recognizable, and relatively unitary nationalized narrative of history. In addition, it links relatively temporally recent cultural dispositions, social mores, and all manner of ways in which lives are currently lived with historical antiquity, and erases the evidence of their modern invention.[28] Japan is of course "really" both like and unlike China, Korea, or any other Asian nation, and like and unlike the United States or whatever one might mean by "the West." Moreover, the rupture of modernity is simultaneously acknowledged and denied in Japan's own national narratives.[29] Area studies in the USA and elsewhere, however, are economically and otherwise dependent on the insistence on both radical difference from the "West" *and* its historical "traditions" as the core to "knowledge" about East Asia.[30]

As we discussed in the beginning of this essay, aside from the use of a psychoanalytic methodology this volume has a second criterion for the inclusion of essays, which is of course their relation to "Japan." As we also discussed, this is both a capitulation to and an attempt critically to engage the existing academic organization of area studies. With the help of Moloney's counter-example, we can now also say that when we write the word "Japan," we intend to bring the same sort of methodology – a reading that is simultaneously attentive to the literal and to the encoded nature of articulation to any "truth" or faithfulness to event (history, culture) – to the issue of culturalism. And in fact we believe that the modern notion of a homogeneous thing called Japan, that is then imagined to modify all and myriad cultural productions within a certain bounded geographic area, or by an imagined community of like-minded individuals wherever they might physically be, is no less "constructed" than memory as we have described it above. For us, then, "Japan" first and foremost signifies a psychic object constructed by fantasy, regardless of its sociopolitical *materiality* as a modern nation-state. What constitutes this imagined community of Japan is of course nonetheless indebted to unconscious and encoded motivations as well as capitalist and national interests. And it is also indebted to the establishment of a modern, cause and effect narrative of history.

Chris Hill notes that in Meiji, as Chinese sovereignty waned to Western dominance and imperialism, Japanese intellectuals had to reconsider "existing ideas of history . . . they needed a new way to place Japan in the world, geographically and historically."[31] This was part and parcel of Japan's modernization process, and included rewriting conventions of telling stories about the past in service to a new concept of linear, progressive time and to the nation. In the 1880s, historians Kume Kunitake and Shigeno Yasutsugu began the modern historical project of trying to separate myth from history, or to discern a truth about the past unembellished by narrative or fiction.[32] As Hill has shown, this was a temporal and spatial recoding of community in the endeavor to place Japan as a nation-state within its global context as well as to define itself within modernity and capitalism *and* trace something exceptional to its historical past.

> The task was not simple in an archipelago with strong local sensibilities, a range of dialects, and patterns of political jurisdiction that bore little resemblance to regional boundaries, and where individuals were as likely to identify themselves by their occupation as by a putative bond to an emperor whom few had ever seen . . . The government's decision in 1869 to resume compiling annalistic political histories reflects its expectations that historical writing would contribute to the project.[33]

However, state-sponsored attempts to compile new histories divested of myth were apparently thwarted because it turned out that "the historical tales and many other accounts that the state had hoped to use" were "fraught with inaccuracies and often based on legends and myths."[34] Royal genealogies did not tell the story of "Japan," but that of Imperial lineage. War tales mixed "fact" with legend. With the Meiji-period recognition that the first Japanese Emperor Jimmu, a direct descendent of the *kami* according to the "historical" chronicle *Kojiki*, was in fact mythical, new histories renarrated those origins with reference to "ancient ancestors." Stefan Tanaka notes wryly, "Interestingly, Japan now is older under the rational and secular approach than that through the *Kojiki*. Which is more mythical?"[35]

As Benedict Anderson showed some time ago the imagined communities of premodern societies were organized around religious communities and dynastic realms that had no relation to modern nation-state notions of belongingness.[36] Accordingly, the stories that were told about the past had different agendas than those of modern capitalist nation states. As a matter of fact, there was no idea of "history" severed from "literature," nor distinctions between "national" literatures such as "Japanese literature" and "Chinese literature."[37] The newly established Meiji discipline of national literary studies, *kokubungaku* "took those texts that were of questionable historical status and gave them a literary status as exemplary texts that described the spirit of the people of the nation."[38] And so the modern separation of "history" and "literature" was established in Meiji, dedicated to inventing a cause and effect timeline of "Japanese" conventions and events that could provide the modern nation-state with a narrative of national origins. Historical discourse would be one of the major means historians, novelists, and social theorists used to "suture the disjunction between the national particular and the systemic universal."[39]

As late as 1964 Japanologist Ivan Morris wrote a book detailing "life" in Heian (794–1185) Japan, *The World of the Shining Prince*. However, this "history," which is dedicated in part to the oxymoronic attempt to disentangle Heian "Japan" from "China,"[40] turns out to have been largely culled from works of literature written in Heian, most often the *Tale of Genji*.[41] That is, this description of Heian life does not consider the possibility that (prose) literature may have depicted idealized, or otherwise *elaborately* embellished fictions rather than chronicled life as it was truly lived.[42] Rather than establish a "history" of how lives were lived on the basis of Heian literary texts, one might interpret the relationship between text and "real life" as decidedly less coterminous. Rein Raud, for example, postulates that

> the entire life of non-divergent Heian courtiers ideally consisted in following pre-established patterns, moving along a set of trajectories, and emulating true-to-essence preconceived experiences that *nobody had actually had*. The situation is similar to that of the romantic girl, a heroine of a European novel who lives in the world of (other) novels, as well as her modern descendants, who project imaginary relationships with rock or movie stars onto real relationships with young men who simultaneously indulge in similar fanatasies.[43]

Raud directs our attention to the danger of seeking history in literature when our goal is to invent a narrative about how real life might have been lived in all its materiality (and even ideology). Perhaps texts such as Morris's actually tell us more about 1960s British Japanology and its imaginings of a Heian past, than they do a "truth" of Heian. Accordingly, Edward Carr suggested, "Before you study the history, study the historian . . . [and] before you study the historian, study his historical and social environment."[44]

More importantly, even when it can be established that an event occurred at a particular moment in the past (a "truth"), the recording of that event cannot be severed from some agenda that deemed it memorable, while countless other events have of course never been commemorated, and hence do not exist as narratives of the past.[45] Even our excavated objects – artifacts – are shards of materiality around which we have woven elaborate narratives. Today, of course, we recognize that the new linear, causal and essentially narrative history that was to "tell the truth" about the past divested of myth, superstition and legend is equally constructed. That events happened and people lived and died with various and differing impacts on events does not negate the fact that all our histories are constructed narratives with a point of view in service to larger epistemologies. The ordering of data into coherent narratives is a way of narrativizing events through a process of distancing, both spatially and temporally.

What historiography often leaves out, even in its recognition of the constructedness and subjective nature of what is deemed to be "history," is the psychoanalytic understanding that meaning is not co-extensive with expression (or that the motivation for action might be *encoded* in some aspect of its activation, and not necessary literally as articulated). Freud, to the contrary, postulated the existence of a punitive societal "superego," arising out of the primarily *unconscious* ambivalence and guilt felt by civilized humans over the *metaphoric* murder of the primordial father, and the introjection of restrictive mores on sexuality and aggression.[46]

Indeed, history, argues Adam Phillips, ideally would share a structural relationship with psychoanalysis. "The personal past – re-presenting itself as dream, as screen-memory, as symptom or slip, as desire or repeated action – from a psychoanalytic point of view comes, as Mark Phillips says history writing should come, "as a family of related genres, rather than (as customarily) a simple unitary one."[47] What emerges as "the past" (history) is a set of fragmentary "data" which with the help of the psychoanalyst (historian) become narratives about the individual's personal (national) "history" that may take the place of an earlier narrative of that same "history." A. Phillips refers to the resistance to making conscious the fragments of a traumatic past as resistance to "having a history."[48]

In other words, like the psychoanalytic understanding of the constructedness of a personal, individual history, that owes more to the psychic significance of past events *as they are remembered and as they signify something in encoded form about the present*, our national histories likewise are constructs deeply referential in oblique and otherwise encoded ways to the current historical moment. Japanese "history," one might claim, is the "screen-memory" of the modern Japanese nation-state. And the psychic object of "Japan today" is like the Freudian subject – or a *construct* that emerges in the co-figured conscious and unconscious *relations* between Japan, its past, and other nation-states.

When psychoanalytic inquiry is combined with a historiographic awareness of the constructedness of historical and/or national narratives something other than the question of "what really happened," or "the truth of Japan today" may be put to the side in favor of readings that, as we have already elaborated in some detail, are both more and less literal. And what we might learn – or uncover – from reading "Japan" as a constructed narrative of a psychic object, is not "truth" or "untruth," but something else about cultural imaginaries and desires.

This positioning must constitutively refuse the area studies convention that seeks to read narratives of all sorts – be they literary, cinematic, historical, or even simply cultural texts – as "windows" (transparent or opaque) offering insights into something we call "Japan," or as culturalist imaginings. We want to extend this spirit – of reading with a different motive than one of uncovering a "truth" or "untruth," and moreover, one that takes texts of all sorts literally, while understanding that literalness may register itself in various canted relations to what we conventionally consider "the literal" – to our use of psychoanalytic methodology in relation to a set of texts that for one reason or another may be called "Japanese." We want to read narrative (whether historical, cultural, or literary) as processes of *rewriting* that have a *symbolic encoding* to another level, or layer, of signification than what lies on the surface level of articulation.

Finally, we have attempted to pay tribute to the original breadth of psychoanalysis which, as discussed in the opening of this introduction, was not a methodology limited to therapeutic uses, or pathologizing/medicalizing discourses, but had a wide application in literature, culture, philosophy, law and other fields. Most of the essays in fact position psychoanalysis as an interpretive methodology to elucidate something about other "constructed narratives" (be they cinematic, historical, literary, or cultural texts), rather than to diagnose something in Japanese culture, literature, or film, that ostensibly should be "cured," or marks the presence of a pathology.

As noted earlier, we have opted to not preview the book here, but to preface each individual chapter with a short introduction. In closing, however, we want to note that while this introduction has almost exclusively restricted its elucidation of a psychoanalytic methodology to a close reading of Freud's "Screen Memories" and "From the History of an Infantile Neurosis," this is not to suggest that the essays included herein are all strictly, or even marginally, *Freudian*. This introduction has devoted itself to Freud's notions of the psyche, the psychoanalytic methodology, and memory because it is this *foundation* from which any number of post-Freudian psychoanalytic theories have sprung forth, including some that have taken an anti-Freudian turn in the end, or which encompass serious critiques of Freud. Accordingly, for example, included among the essays gathered here are those more Irigarayian, Lacanian, Derridean, or Deleuzian than Freudian, one focused on affect theory, and another that critiques the phallocentrism of both Lacan and Freud. Our criteria for inclusion in this volume has overwhelmingly been more the *type of reading* that we have described above, than direct application of Freudian theory.

Notes

1. H. D. Harootunian and Masao Miyoshi (2002) "Introduction: The 'afterlife' of area studies," in H. D. Harootunian and Masao Miyoshi (eds) *Learning Places: The Afterlives of Area Studies*, Durham: Duke University Press, pp. 1–18, esp. 10.
2. Sigmund Freud (1995) *"Three essays on the theory of sexuality* (1905)", in James Strachey (ed.) *The Standard Edition of the Complete Psychological Works of Sigmund Freud*, Vol. 7, London: Hogarth Press, p. 171.
3. Peter Gay (1960) "Sigmund Freud: A brief life" (1989) in James Strachey (ed.) Sigmund Freud, *The Ego and the Id*, Joan Riviere (trans.) New York: W. W. Norton, p. xv.
4. Taketomo Yasuhiko (Winter 1990) "Cultural adaptation to psychoanalysis in Japan, 1912–52," *Social Research* 57(4): 955–6.
5. Joseph Schwartz (1999) *Cassandra's Daughter: A History of Psychoanalysis,* New York: Viking, pp. 144–92.
6. Ibid., p. 175.
7. Ibid., p. 144.
8. Taketomo, pp. 958–9.
9. See Harumi Befu (2001) *Hegemony of Homogeneity: An Anthropological Analysis of Nihonjinron*, Melbourne: Trans Pacific Press.
10. Jacques Lacan (2004) *"Postface au Seminaire X1,"* and *"Avis un Lecteur Japonais,"* both in J. A. Miller (ed.) *Le Séminaire de Jacques Lacan* 11, Paris: Editions du Seuil, pp. 503–7; 497–500.
11. Jacques Lacan (2004).
12. James Clark Moloney (1953) "Understanding the paradox of Japanese psychoanalysis," *The International Journal of Psycho-Analysis* 34: 302.
13. Available in translation as Robert King Hall (ed.) (1949) *Kokutai no hongi: Cardinal Principles of the National Entity of Japan,* John Owen Gauntlett (trans.) Cambridge MA: Harvard University Press.
14. Ohtsuki Kenji (1955) "The misunderstanding of Japanese psycho-analysis: A protest against the views expressed by Dr. J. C. Moloney," *The International Journal of Psycho-Analysis* 36: 205.
15. Ibid., 206.
16. Schwartz, pp. 189–92. This debate in psychoanalysis actually predates American ego psychology, and can be seen in nascent form in Adler's attempt to relativize Freud's instinctual (drive) theory with individual agency. William Alanson White, one of the first psychiatrists in America to embrace psychoanalysis also insisted on the importance of *human relations* to relativize drive theory. See Schwartz, "First Splits," pp. 93–129 and "Expanding the Frontiers," pp. 144–69, for more.
17. Sigmund Freud (1958) "A difficulty of psychoanalysis," in Sigmund Freud, *On Creativity and the Unconscious: Papers on the Psychology of Art, Literature, Love, Religion*, New York: Harper and Row, p. 9.
18. Schwartz, pp. 189, 190. See Freud's illustration of the ego as a "hat" askew on the id in his (1960) *The Ego and the Id*, James Strachey (ed.) Joan Riviere (trans.) New York: W. W. Norton, p. 18.
19. Tim Dean (2000) *Beyond Sexuality*, Chicago: University of Chicago Press, p. 2.
20. Freud (1960), *The Ego and The Id*, p. 17.
21. Ibid., p. 24.
22. Ogden, Thomas H (1992) "The dialectically constituted/decentred subject of psychoanalysis I: the Freudian subject," *International Journal of Psycho-Analysis* 7 3: 519, 522.

23. Moloney, p. 302.
24. Sigmund Freud (1959) "From the history of an infantile neurosis," in *Collected Papers* 3, New York: Basic Books, p. 497. Hereafter, pagination appears parenthetically in text following quotations.
25. See Sigmund Freud (1962) "Screen memories," in James Strachey (ed.) *The Standard Edition of the Complete Psychological Works of Sigmund Freud* 3, London: The Hogarth Press, pp. 303–22. Hereafter, pagination appears parenthetically in text following quotations.
26. On numbers, see, for example, Sigmund Freud (1953) *The Interpretation of Dreams*, James Strachey (trans. and ed.) New York: Avon Books, pp. 449–53.
27. See Naoki Sakai (1997) *Translation and Subjectivity: On Japan and Cultural Nationalism*, Minneapolis: University of Minnesota Press, esp. "The problem of 'Japanese thought.'"
28. See Stephen Vlastos (ed.) (1998) *Mirror of Modernity: Invented Traditions of Modern Japan*, Berkeley: University of California Press, for specific examples.
29. See Christopher L. Hill (2009) for an excellent discussion about the creation of a complex national narrative that simultaneously establishes modernity as a rupture with the past, and yet particularizes and essentializes something distinctly "Japanese" through reference to an imagined "Japan" of antiquity: *National History and the World of Nations: Japan, France, and the United States in the Second Imperial Wave*, Durham, NC: Duke University Press.
30. See Rey Chow (1993) *Writing Diaspora: Tactics of Intervention in Contemporary Cultural Studies*, Bloomington and Indianapolis: Indiana University Press.
31. Hill, p. 51.
32. Stefan Tanaka (2004) *New Times in Modern Japan*, Princeton: Princeton University Press, pp. 78–82.
33. Hill, p. 53.
34. Tanaka, p. 79.
35. Ibid., p. 125.
36. Benedict Anderson (1983) *Imagined Communities: Reflections on the Origin and Spread of Nationalism*, London: Verso.
37. See Tanaka, pp. 111–43. It was only in Meiji that the study of the classics shifted from one which encompassed literature and "stories of the past" (history) and included Chinese and Japanese language texts to separate departments of "Japanese history," "Chinese literature" and "Japanese literature."
38. Tanaka, pp. 139–140.
39. Hill, p. 42.
40. See Thomas LaMarre (2000) *Uncovering Heian Japan: An Archaeology of Sensation and Inscription*, Durham: Duke University Press, on how Heian writings were intertwined with so-called Chinese and Korean counterparts.
41. Ivan Morris (1964) *The World of the Shining Prince: Court Life in Ancient Japan*, New York: Knopf. See LaMarre on the imbrication of Heian with the "Middle Kingdom."
42. This is not to claim that Morris didn't at all acknowledge some possibility of fictionalization, but his very objective was at its core based on a belief that literature of any era must "reflect" reality.
43. Rein Raud (1999) "The lover's subject: its construction and relativization in the Waka poetry of the Heian Period," in *Proceedings of the Midwest Association for Japanese Literary Studies 5: Love and Sexuality in Japanese Literature,* Summer: 74.
44. Edward Carr (1961) *What is History?* New York: Vintage, p. 54.
45. Ibid.
46. See Sigmund Freud (1950/1961) *Totem and Taboo*, James Strachey (ed. and trans.) New York: W. W. Norton; and *Civilization and its Discontents*, James Strachey (ed. and trans.) New York: W. W. Norton. Human civilization, he argued, depended upon the

murder of the tyrannical, all powerful father of the tribe or clan, by a group of "brothers." (*Civilization and its Discontents*, p. 93). However, we must remember that this "murder" is neither literal nor symbolic, but both and neither at the same time. Fear of paternal reprisal gives rise to guilt, which speaks to the profound ambivalence at the core of patricide – the sons who killed their father in order to establish a society of "equals" after all loved their tyrannical father as deeply as they hated him.

47. Adam Phillips (2004) "Close-ups," *History Workshop Journal* 57: 144. The quote is from Mark Salber Phillips (2000) *Society and Sentiment: Genres of Historical Writing in Britain*, Princeton: Princeton University Press, p. 343.

48. Ibid., p. 142. See also Mark Salber Phillips (2004) "Distance and historical representation," *History Workshop Journal* 57: 123–41.

1 Introduction

Bruce Suttmeier:
Speculations of murder . . .

When Freud set out, in *Moses and Monotheism,* to argue that Moses was not a Jew but an Egyptian and that the Jewish people themselves had murdered him, he was not being provocative, nor was he unaware of the likely response. "To deny a people," he wrote, "the man whom it praises as the greatest of its sons is not a deed to be undertaken lightheartedly – especially by one belonging to that people. But," he continued, "No consideration, however, will move me to set aside truth in favor of supposed national interests."[1] While the historical accuracy of what Freud called his "historical novel" has been largely discounted, his goal in writing it, described by one critic as the introduction of "impurity and secondariness into the heart of Jewish cultural identity"[2] still stands as a superb example of how the psychoanalytic method can be used to combat nationalist historiography. Indeed it is not just Jewish cultural identity, but the very notion of "cultural identity" itself, along with "supposed national interests" that are Freud's real targets in *Moses and Monotheism.* And, paradoxically, in his attempts to uncover the rotten truth behind them, Freud may have been acting as an exemplary son.

Bruce Suttmeier's account of the case of Yokoi Shōichi, a Japanese soldier straggler from the Second World War, who emerged from the jungles of Guam in 1972, performs a similar operation on the myths of postwar Japanese identity. Yokoi was first greeted as a hero whose extraordinary survival skills and tenacity in the jungle supplemented popular narratives of the Japanese people's resilience in wartime. But there was also something uncanny about his habit of referring to "his Majesty the Emperor" that served as an uncomfortable reminder of a past the nation would rather have forgotten. When stories began to circulate about his possible murder of two fellow soldiers, they brought with them a flood of unwanted memories.

If the Japanese people were just getting comfortable thinking of themselves primarily as victims of the war, Yokoi's return forced them to remember not only the atrocities committed by the Emperor's army, but also their own eagerness to forget. His astonishing ability to survive and face hardship reminded them how spoiled and complacent they had become. And at the same time Yokoi's repeated revisions and retractions of his own memories of life in the jungle played out as an acute spectacle of the same protracted struggle the whole country had long been engaged in to reconcile wartime experience with a postwar world. Suttmeier's analysis of this "unsettling, symptomatic eruption of the past into the present" in the early 1970s is all the more relevant in today's Japan where a resurgent nationalism threatens to repress the past in the interest of an emperor-centered "monotheism" of its own.

Notes

1. Sigmund Freud (1939) *Moses and Monotheism*, Katherine Jones (trans.), New York: Vintage.
2. Eric Santner (Spring 1999) "Freud's 'Moses' and the Ethics of Nomotropic Desire," *October* 88: 7.

1 Speculations of murder

Ghostly dreams, poisonous frogs and the case of Yokoi Shōichi

Bruce Suttmeier

[A]lmost every part [of the text] came to include obvious gaps, awkward repetitions, and tangible contradictions – signs that tell us things we were never meant to know. The corruption of a text is not unlike a murder. The problem lies not in doing the deed but in removing the traces of it.

Sigmund Freud, *Moses and Monotheism*

The dead heroes and ghosts he sees are probably illusions.

(from a January 30, 1972 report on Yokoi Shōichi by Dr Koyama, Guam Memorial Hospital)[1]

Yokoi a murderer

On February 2, 1972, thousands of people stood on the viewing decks of the Tokyo International Airport, holding small Japanese flags, watching as a DC8 plane from Guam touched down and taxied toward them. Tens of millions more reportedly watched the scene on TV.[2] As the door to the plane opened, the excited crowd roared with deafening cheers, waving their flags and shouting for its inhabitants to emerge. But when the first figures emerged onto the gangway, reporters at the scene noted, the "shouting abruptly ceased." The first two men out of the plane, black-suited and grim-faced, carried two boxes wrapped in white cloth, the remains of two soldiers who had died in the Guam jungle eight years earlier. A moment later, a frail-looking man in a dark suit leaned forward and gingerly stepped onto the gangway. "The shouting broke out again as if in one huge voice," the reporters wrote, growing louder as the man, waving and bowing, his hands trembling, his voice cracking, passed just yards away from the assembled onlookers (Figure 1.1).[3]

The frail figure, the object of this thunderous reception, was Yokoi Shōichi, the Japanese soldier found in the jungles of Guam nine days earlier, an army straggler who after hiding for 28 years, living in a 13-foot hole dug among the roots of a bamboo grove, had emerged as an odd, intriguing remnant of Japan's imperial past. Consular officials in Guam had marveled at his initial appearance, the long straggly beard and unkempt hair, the tattered clothes fashioned out of pago-tree bark, the anachronistic speech filled with the idioms and ideas of imperial Japan. The next day, his hair cut and his face shaven, he had the first of two press conferences,

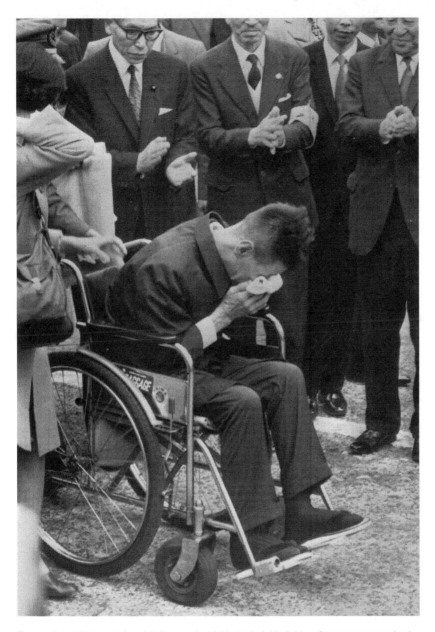

Figure 1.1 "Homecoming," February 2, 1972: Yokoi Shōichi, a former sergeant in the
Imperial Japanese Army, weeping with emotion as he is applauded on his
arrival in Tokyo after hiding in the jungle of Guam for 28 years, 31 years
after he had left Japan to do his military service. (Photograph by
Keystone/Getty Images.)

detailing his unit's utter defeat in 1944, his retreat, with several other soldiers, into the jungle, his struggle to procure food and shelter, his leaving of the larger group in 1946 with his comrades Shichi Mikio and Nakahata Satoshi, his final separation, after discord and temporary splits, from these two in 1960, and their death in 1964, the beginning of his eight years of complete isolation.[4]

This chapter examines the return of Yokoi, exploring, in particular, the speculation that his comrades Shichi and Nakahata, whose remains returned in those cloth-covered boxes, did not die in 1964 of accidental food poisoning but instead were murdered by Yokoi himself. This speculation was but a small aspect of the enormous, frenzied media attention that followed Yokoi's discovery in 1972, but it offers an intriguing entry into the story of his uncanny return, a narrative of obsession and suspicion, of uneasy celebrity and unwelcome memories, a narrative where dreams of dead comrades and displaced confessions unsettled the public's fascination with this former soldier in the emperor's army.

Throughout this chapter, my interest in these speculations lies less in the factual, verifiable circumstances of the two men's demise and more in the *psychical* ground upon which speculation of their death flourished; or, to use the psychoanalytic terms that will inform my study, less in the "material truth" of their death and more in the "historical truth" enabled by such an investigation. As defined by Freud in *Moses and Monotheism*, "historical truth" is a form of truth that "brings a return of the past," a "distorted," "delusional" truth that is "spectral, fantasmatic," it references an event that may never have happened, but that is, nevertheless "more real than reality."[5] It is a form of truth that finds in both specters and speculation, in both Yokoi's intrusive dreams and the nation's obsessive fascination with his return, a revelatory mode of truth-telling. The lineaments of this speculation – an imperial soldier perpetrating murderous violence – were not completely unprecedented in the postwar period, of course, but what the Yokoi case so incisively illustrates is how violence by Japanese soldiers during the war, so long unacknowledged and denied, so long resisted and repressed, so long displaced by the synecdochal Japanese victim, nevertheless returns in distorted, belated ways, a return attended to in obsessive, over-intensified forms. What is revealed through Yokoi's return, through this unsettling, symptomatic eruption of the past into the present, is the "hauntedness" of postwar Japan, to use Derrida's suggestive term for the repressed, uncanny figures from history that return to disturb everyday life.[6] What is addressed, in all the speculation, is the revisitation of the ghosts of the past, the unconscious conjuring up of spirits long thought put to rest.

If Yokoi was a murderer . . .

In the first few days following Yokoi's discovery, as he rested in a Guam hospital, comments concerning his comrades came up frequently, in his outlining of their early survival together, in his brief mention of their split, in his description of discovering their bodies in early 1964, and most often, in his repeatedly expressed desire to pray for "the dead soldiers who were under me."[7] (Yokoi was the oldest, and the ranking figure in the group.) As Yokoi told the tale, in 1964, four years after a dispute over food rationing had forced him to set off on his own, the two had visited him, as they had done a few times a year, but this time they complained of stomach pains. Ten days later, he said, he went to see them and found them dead, "nothing but bones." Tests of their remains suggested they had died of poisoning, and officials, as well as Yokoi himself, suggested that they died from accidentally eating a particular species of frog.[8]

This early talk of his comrades culminated on January 28, four days after his discovery and the day officials recovered the skeletal remains of the two in their cave. During that evening's press conference in the Guam hospital, after an initial statement noting how good he felt, how much stronger he was ("I'm well enough to go home tomorrow"), he was asked whether he was having any dreams. He responded, "Last night I had a kind of crazy dream . . . I was being attacked by ghosts and my head got like this [he pressed his head with both hands] . . . But it was not a dream. I can't sleep at all . . . My eyes are open. It seems to be writing, just like in a newspaper. 'Why are you alive and going home? Are you going to go and leave me here?' I see these words in front of me."[9] After several more questions on other topics, he headed back to his room, by all reports strong and in good spirits. But the next morning, hospital officials announced that Yokoi would not be meeting with the press until further notice. He had "broken down" in his room that night, collapsing into a "state of depression," unable to sleep, his body drenched in sweat, his mind disturbed by ghostly visions of departed comrades.[10]

The dreams, his nurse Kimiko Murphy told reporters, featured ghosts whose faces "seemed somehow familiar, yet he saw them first in his dreams." They were all Japanese soldiers, all of them wore expressions of suffering. "You are the only one left alive," they would call out in voices that "seemed squeezed out of the throat."[11] His interpreter and closest companion during his time in the Guam hospital, Edward Tsutsui, later elaborated, explaining that

> every time Yokoi opened his mouth he talked about the "souls of his men" (*buka no rei*). During those first several nights, he was so troubled by these spirits that he did not get a bit of sleep. I asked the doctor if he would give Yokoi some sleeping pills, and though he gave him so much that he said any more would be harmful, Yokoi was still unable to fall asleep.[12]

Within a week, speculation surfaced in several magazines that his two comrades had not died accidentally but had been murdered, deliberately poisoned by Yokoi himself. The intrusive dreams themselves became a significant source for stoking this suspicion. "It's only natural that he is emotionally troubled by the death of his comrades," one weekly wrote, but as the veterans they interviewed explained, Yokoi's dreams were extremely unusual and even "odd." Hearing of Yokoi's dreams, one military man who served on Guam, Mr A, shook his head and noted, "I saw over and over again comrades being killed, but I've never once been troubled by their spirits [appearing in dreams]. My friends in the war tell me the same thing."[13] The press noted the timing of the dreams, coinciding with the recovery of his comrades' remains, and they quoted the "spirits of his subordinates" speaking to Yokoi, telling him that "you can't go home by yourself. We were killed."[14] Other elements of the story started to seem increasingly significant: their simultaneous death; their accidental ingestion of poison (which was at odds with "the extreme care they had always taken with food")[15]; their becoming "mere skeletons" in ten days, as Yokoi had attested; the items belonging to the dead found in Yokoi's hole; not to mention the awkwardness and distrust that was said to characterize Yokoi's relations with his comrades.[16] Yokoi's own words after his discovery were scrutinized as well, such as his distraught comments in the hospital to his childhood friend Oshika Toshio. "Can I have betrayed my war buddies?" he lamented, asking questions that others had begun raising as well. "Have I even once done something cowardly that would turn them against me?"[17]

The Japan that greeted Yokoi in 1972 was in a prosperous, pacifist mood, its enormous reconstruction efforts having largely eliminated the pervasive poverty and widespread destruction that had characterized its early postwar years. With its acclaimed hosting of the 1964 Tokyo Olympiad, and, just before Yokoi's discovery, the wildly popular Osaka EXPO '70 (Asia's first World's Fair), Japan was extolling its postwar accomplishments to both domestic and international audiences, pressing official themes such as "progress and harmony" to distance itself from its own history of war and disaster.[18] But as several scholars have demonstrated, this temporal and psychical distance from the war existed alongside an uncanny fascination with reminders of the traumatic past, an attraction to those occasional glimpses of the traumatic past erupting into the present.[19] Yokoi's emergence in 1972, as the historian Yoshikuni Igarashi has observed, spurred an unprecedented amount of news coverage, and prompted in the public a variety of reactions and remembrances. "Many former soldiers," he argues,

> saw themselves in the emaciated figure of Shōichi, who was merely an ordinary man from a rural community. Some bereaved relatives of fallen soldiers superimposed the images of their beloved sons or brothers over his. The younger generations who had no personal experiences of the Asia Pacific War cast a curious gaze on the man who had been imprisoned by the wartime social mores.[20]

To this list might be added those who glimpsed in Yokoi an image of the despised (and defeated) imperial soldier, a figure feared both for his wartime actions and for his actions following repatriation: extensive "looting and lawlessness" spurred by feelings of entitlement and frustration, of resentment and hopelessness.[21] Rarely was such an image overtly invoked, especially early on, since in the extensive and varied coverage, the favored form of reference involved awe at Yokoi's endurance and self-reliance, for his astonishing survival skills (which contrasted so starkly with the pampered youth of the day). And yet, he was frequently referred to as "somebody 'special'" with all the ambiguity encompassed by that word. As one commentator notes, his experience generated much empathy and admiration, "yet at the same time his weirdness – the term '*kimyō*,' ['curious,' 'queer,' 'strange'] was also used constantly – kept him at arm's length."[22] This weirdness was often attributed in large part to his military training, his indoctrination in the wartime ideologies of loyalty and self-sacrifice. Immediately after the war, the Japanese public had learned a great deal about its military men abroad, due to

> a steady flow of information concerning the shocking range of atrocities committed by the imperial forces in China, Southeast Asia, and the Philippines, as well as against Allied prisoners generally. As a result, many ex-servicemen found themselves regarded not just as men who had failed disastrously to accomplish their mission, but also as individuals who had, it was assumed, participated in unspeakable acts.[23]

Though the public's attention to such matters had substantially waned in the ensuing two decades, it is noteworthy that just months before Yokoi's discovery, the well-known journalist Honda Katsuichi had published his explosive report on the 1937 Nanjing Massacre, a ten-part newspaper chronicle of the Japanese army's atrocities that "seized national attention."[24] His account of the staggering scope of the killing generated intense debate, most strikingly (and controversially) in his descriptions of "killing contests," widespread rapes, and death tolls in the hundreds of thousands.[25] Such reminders clearly played into perceptions of the skinny old soldier and "instant celebrity" then appearing on TV screens and magazine covers across the nation in early 1972.

Yokoi himself exacerbated such ominous connotations a few months after his return. Pained by the letters that questioned his motives for staying in hiding, that accused him of "cowardice," "inaction," and a "selfish desire for self-preservation," he insisted to the press that he had not known the war was over, contradicting his statements made in the days following his discovery.[26] He went on to say that throughout his time on Guam he had never given up fighting the war and that, in fact, as he confessed to several reporters, he had killed two native villagers several years before his discovery.[27] When this revelation appeared in the media, it drew a sharp and immediate negative reaction from the peace-minded Japanese populace. There was widespread condemnation of the murders, and the brisk commercial industry that had arisen around Yokoi showed a sharp dip in sales (evidenced by the tourist buses, once a daily fixture bringing thousands of people by his childhood home, dropping the site from their schedule).[28] After seeing the negative reaction to this story, Yokoi immediately backtracked, saying that it wasn't actually he who had killed the men, but rather, it was his subordinates, Shichi and Nakahata, who had committed the murder.[29]

Yokoi, the nation and speculations on wartime behavior

When evaluating, or even just considering, historical hearsay such as Yokoi murdering his comrades, we run up against the question not only of truth and its availability but of the sheer relevance of such speculation: What is the point of rehearsing these possibilities? And more provocatively, what is the epistemological value in considering psychoanalytic symptoms in constructing such speculative historical narratives? That is to say, what role should dreams and parapraxes, mechanisms of repression and displacement, play in the cultural historian's reconstruction of the past? And how might we understand the public's interest in such possibilities? What is such speculation ultimately in the service of – preparing the ground for historical contingencies or fostering mere historical titillation?

Such questions can be profitably explored through consideration of Sigmund Freud's late work *Moses and Monotheism* and the recent body of scholarship that has arisen around it, scholarship that wrestles with how (or even whether) to take seriously Freud's wildly, even embarrassingly, speculative reconstructions of the primal origins of monotheistic religion.[30] Freud's work, to summarize his well-known argument, insisted that Moses was actually an Egyptian priest, a fervent monotheist who imposed his short-lived, monotheistic cult on the oppressed Semitic tribe then living in Egypt. Moses led the group out of bondage, but his demanding, rigid form of spiritualized, imageless monotheism soon spurred resentment, leading to a violent mob revolt and, eventually, to Moses' murder, a murder whose memory was then repressed. The biblical Moses, Freud continues, was a different man, a Midian priest encountered later by the wandering Israelites, a priest whose volcanic deity, Yahweh, became endowed with the universal and spiritual qualities of the earlier Egyptian god. The priest's identity became fused with that of the slain Moses, and the memory of Moses' murder and its attendant guilt remained repressed among the Jews, the memory re-emerging, in a very disguised form, with the crucifixion of Christ and the rise of Christianity. Freud's ultimate ambition here is to argue that all of Judeo-Christian religious tradition is contingent upon this original murder, that it arises from the repression, guilt and collective obsessional neurosis associated with it, and most significantly, that these ancient events perpetually manifest themselves in the rituals, prohibitions, self-accusations and self-denials of monotheism's various doctrines and practices.

As nearly all commentators have noted, the work contains stark and "self-evident inadequacies" in its historical and sociological claims.[31] But given that its "basic premises, presuppositions and arguments have nearly all been rejected or radically modified even within the psychoanalytic community," why has this particular work of Freud's garnered such attention of late? Why has this, of all his works, "been enjoying the most widespread scholarly interest"?[32] And more pertinent to my argument, what might it offer the scholar investigating issues of historical speculation, the persistence of memory, and the way both individuals and societies remain haunted by the past?

A useful approach to these questions lies in taking seriously Freud's distinction in *Moses* between "material truth" and "historical truth," between Freud's differentiation between, on the one hand, what is manifest and literal in an historical event (material truth) and, on the other, what is "distorted" and "decipherable" upon an event's reexamination in the present (historical truth).[33] Freud saw substantive, verifiable material truth, a form of truth for which "objective evidence" is available, as ineffective in understanding the traumatic past. Historical truth, he argued, renders the way in which the past – regardless of whether it is materially true or false – is appropriated and made the past of the present.[34] In historical truth, Freud posits a truth that "brings a return of the past," a truth that psychoanalysis enables us to uncover amid the materially false, distorted claims of the event.[35] In his view, historical truth is the story of Moses' origin and murder, a narrative that better explains the distinctive, compulsive character of the Jewish people, a truth, in other words, that unearths and unmasks the dynamics of monotheistic thought and its influence on modern civilizations. What consideration of such truth allows, Freud argues, is the emergence of an historical claim that is unverifiable but that demonstrates, precisely because of the claim's absence in the archives, how a horribly traumatic event often can be recovered only through its traces, through its belated reverberations in the present. Our entertaining of such an historical claim – it might also be called a counter-history – is an invitation to interpretation, Freud suggests. It is an exegetical exercise that allows us to understand the elements of trauma, violence, repetition, and irrational binding that plague history, and that, more importantly, continue to shape (and haunt) our present. Ultimately, as Eric Santner reminds us, "historical truth pertains to 'events' that do not properly take place; they can only be constructed through interpretation of the behavior of 'matter' in the world."[36] The concept of "historical truth" demands a kind of "interpretative historiography," which inevitably registers the haunted nature of such reconstructions. In a formulation surely infuriating to most historians, Freud argues that it is precisely in present symptoms, read through our understanding of psychoanalytic dynamics, that allow us to grasp the truth – the unarchived, unregistered truth – about the past.

In Yokoi's case, we are presented with a counter-history of murder: a murder of two comrades that must be repressed, a murder that produces guilt and haunted dreams, a murder that gets "confessed" as the murder of two native villagers and then gets blamed on Shichi and Nakahata, the victims themselves. This historical truth we must note, is visible less in any physical evidence (that is, the bodies and their surroundings in the cave),[37] but rather, is discernible in the voices speaking long after the event took place, in the voices of returned soldiers who questioned Yokoi's innocence, in the "confession" of the killing voiced by Yokoi himself, and most forcefully, in the spectral voices of his dead comrades.

The group of fellow returned soldiers began speaking soon after Yokoi's return to Japan. In stories appearing in late February, they described a figure at odds with the innocuous survivor-image then prevalent in the press. Of all the groups left on Guam, one stated, "the trio of Yokoi, Shichi and Nakahata were the least compatible." While Shichi and Nakahata were young and close in age, the older Yokoi didn't fit in as well. He was "a sullen, moody figure," the ranking soldier in an atmosphere where rank was no longer observed.[38] As Minagawa Bunzō, a soldier rescued from Guam in 1960 added,

> Practically all the military atmosphere that had been there before had now fallen away from us; all sense of rank had disappeared . . . A man might have been a corporal or a sergeant, but now, as far as we ourselves were concerned, he became nothing more nor less than a fellow human being.[39]

This clearly infuriated Yokoi, for as he himself said, describing his reasons for splitting with Shichi and Nakahata, "I was the ranking officer. Whether it was two against one or ten against one, we should have followed my opinion. But ten years ago, I could no longer get them to listen to what I said . . . That's when I decided that I had to set off on my own."[40] After Yokoi's "confession" of killing the villagers a few months after his return, the criticisms of him increased significantly both in frequency and in volume.

Another set of voices belonged to the spirits appearing before Yokoi, disturbing his sleep, haunting his dreams. What Yokoi was doing as he described his comrades appearing before him is a kind of haunted apostrophe, a summoning up of his comrades, a throwing of voice and life into them. It is an act of ventriloquism, as Barbara Johnson termed it in her well-known work on apostrophe, one that summoned up the dead in a kind of desire for their presence, their life.[41] To apostrophize is, in essence, to will a state of affairs into being, to call upon those absent to bend themselves to one's desire.[42] For Yokoi, this unconscious desire to have the dead speak is insistent and unremitting during his hospitalization in Guam and beyond. They crowd into his psyche and disturb his sleep. Their repeated questions to him – "Why are you alive and going home? Are you going to go and leave me here?" – form accusations of abandonment and register Yokoi's guilt toward his own survival and rescue. Such troubled thoughts are visible in the awakened Yokoi's questions to his childhood friend after a night of such dreams: had he "betrayed [his] war buddies," had he "done something cowardly"?[43] The ghosts suggest much the same when they ask him *why* he is alive, thus, implicitly asking him *why* they are not. As Freud himself had discovered, such visions exist in the first place because people are unable or unwilling to recall into consciousness what lies archived in their unconscious.[44] A person's story of suffering, he noted, was inextricable from his or her symptomatology, and the symptom is ultimately itself a kind of story; or at least, a story awaiting acknowledgment.[45] Of course, any interpretative framework here should accommodate the reality and range of survivor guilt, a response found in victims and victimizers alike. But that said, spectral visits are expressions of material in the psyche of the perceiver, legible in displaced and condensed forms, operating through the mechanisms of resistance and repression, and so we must take seriously the force and intrusiveness of his dreams, the power of their disruptiveness, and inquire into the nature of this spectral return.

Some of this can be gleaned in Yokoi's own voice "confessing" the murder, a few months after his discovery, of two native villagers on Guam. On the afternoon of May fourth, about four months after his return to Japan, Yokoi was speaking to reporters at his home when he began talking about an incident that had happened "about eight years ago." "I was out searching for food," he said, "when I came upon two native villagers, out on patrol, and I shot them with my rifle, killing them both."[46] He continued to speak about it for about an hour, detailing how he was out with Shichi and Nakahata at the time, searching for federico nuts, and how he had suddenly come upon the two local men, shot them, and left their bodies lying there in the jungle.[47] When the news hit the airwaves that afternoon, the outrage and shock of the public forced Yokoi to respond, and he released a statement that very night, "I was mistaken in my earlier comments, for I had meant to say that it was

Nakahata and Shichi who killed the two villagers . . . this is all a story I heard from them."[48] The revisions continued. It was actually 12 or 13 years ago, he stated (not eight years past – 1964 – which would be years after the group's estrangement and would coincide with the year of Nakahata and Shichi's death). It was not rifles they used to kill the native villagers, but knives, stabbing them to death (which would counter journalists' questions as to how his old, rotted rifle could have been functioning). It was not near the Talofofo river as originally stated, but some distance from there (at a location Yokoi could not specify).[49] The media uproar led to a notice on Yokoi's home the next day – he would not be speaking to the press for at least three months due to "emotional instability" (*seishin fuantei*).[50] The "confession" occasioned increasingly hostile reactions from the public, as well as from fellow soldiers, who now began openly expressing their disdain for Yokoi.[51] Minagawa Bunzō even added the revelation that "when Yokoi was in Guam Memorial Hospital, he blurted out to me suddenly that 'I killed two people.' "[52] But in the following weeks, as journalists and officials in Guam investigated Yokoi's claims, they found numerous inconsistencies and eventually concluded that there was no reason to believe that this incident had ever occurred.[53] After a further flood of negative press, Yokoi "eventually recanted his story."[54]

It is instructive to consider the Freudian notion of historical truth occasioned by this "non-event," the way it repeats, through overdetermined and displaced means, the possible murder of his comrades Shichi and Nakahata. The parallels are many, from the number of dead to the time and location of their killing. Ultimately, what his voicing of this "confession," as well as all the other voices here, attest to is the difficulty, if not impossibility, of Yokoi narrating his jungle experiences within the context of reconstructed, pacifist Japan; that is to say, the difficulty of situating his wartime experiences within a postwar world. The public's revulsion at hearing of the murders, their obsessional, bemused fascination with his tales of ghostly dreams, all such responses speak to the nation's discomfort at the unacknowledged remainders of its own wartime experiences. Throughout the 1950s and 1960s, Japan tied its national identity ever more tightly to its own victimization in the war. Stories of savagery by imperial forces, both against colonial victims and against fellow soldiers, ran counter to the prevailing postwar narratives of victimhood – stories of Japanese suffering, stories focusing on images such as "atomic and fire bombings, repatriation of civilians from Manchuria and Korea, and general privations such as hunger on the home front."[55] As scholars such as Igarashi Yoshikuni and Yoshida Yutaka have shown, stories of Japanese aggression only began re-entering the public consciousness in the late 1960s and early 1970s.[56] For over two decades, the Japanese remembered the war largely through scenes of domestic deprivation and suffering, scenes that acknowledged the horrors of war even as they allayed the central anxieties concerning Japanese wartime activities.

The dominant narrative shaping the early stories of Yokoi's return – the thin, harmless figure possessing miraculous survival skills – clearly followed the conventional, comforting tales of national deprivation and fortitude, a narrative comparable with homefront stories of destitution and indomitable resilience (a characteristic viewed, nostalgically, as having been lost by the 1970s). What the historical truth of murder in the jungle allowed (and indeed forced into the open) was the re-emergence of narratives more painful to consider, narratives involving intra-army brutality and murder, narratives involving atrocities in the colonies in the name of the emperor (as Yokoi said several times while speaking of killing the native villagers, "I killed them using the rifle bestowed on me by the emperor").[57]

We see this re-emergence of troubling wartime memories throughout the early 1970s: in Honda Katsuichi's much-discussed 1971 series of articles on the Nanjing Massacre in the *Asahi shinbun*, in the renewed interest in Japan's military role *vis-à-vis* the ongoing Vietnam War, in events galvanizing nationalist sentiments like the spectacular November 1970 suicide of author Mishima Yukio. As one critic commented a few months after Yokoi's return, "You cannot explain the peculiarity and intensity of the Yokoi boom simply by pointing to the facts. First of all there is the timing . . . Yokoi appeared smack in the middle of this intense period and people just collectively saw in him this image of an older, better age."[58] But the older, better era that people saw in Yokoi, the image of a victimized, resilient Japanese citizen, was increasingly clouded by darker, more threatening scenes that spoke to an aggressive, brutalizing legacy. The victim-consciousness of early postwar Japan was being replaced by the unsettling realization that, in place of suffering Japanese bodies, bodies of colonial victims "came to present the loci of struggles to signify the war loss."[59] The demands to contemplate Japanese colonial aggression grew as scenes from the end of the Vietnam War, scenes of Asian suffering, filled print and televised reports.[60] That people obsessively and fanatically followed Yokoi's story is, in Freudian terms, a kind of uncanny desire for such colonial scenes, a willingness or even eagerness to be haunted by the unacknow-ledged specters of the nation's imperial past.[61] The intense public response to Yokoi's return – one publication had the television ratings for Yokoi's February return to Japan at 80 per cent and "even now [late May], when Yokoi appears on news shows, their ratings jump"[62] – in part follows the nation's fascination with the reanimated spirits of the war, personified in Yokoi's frail figure. Yokoi's return to Japan embodied a return of the wartime repressed, his inspiring tales of survival and fortitude harboring ineradicable, inescapable elements from a more unsettling recounting of the imperial past.

Conclusion: spectral truth

To be a citizen of postwar Japan meant, at some level, to be haunted by the war, by the still unacknowledged crimes and horrendous cruelties perpetrated in the past. Understanding this hauntedness, as Derrida explains in *Archive Fever: A Freudian Impression*, means understanding the part of the truth that "breathes at the heart of the delusion, of the illusion, of the hallucination."[63] The ghosts at Yokoi's bedside signify the *possibility* of Yokoi as a murderer of his comrades, but more indisputably (and significantly), their presence in Yokoi's narrative enabled a collective rehearsal of war-guilt and responsibility. They arrested the attention of the nation with the inassimilable elements of his experience. It is the uncanny nature of his experience and its reverberations in the present that commanded such collective fascination. And it is the spectral attendants themselves that helped to compel the ensuing speculation. Of course, the "material truth" might be that Shichi and Nakahata died accidentally, carelessly or recklessly eating poisonous frogs or nuts. The blameless Yokoi might still, nevertheless, harbor guilt that calls up his ghostly visitors. As one scholar writes, rhetorically questioning the need for Freud's elaborate historical edifice in *Moses*, "must there have been a murder for there to be ghosts in the symbolic machine, or does the symbolic system, the cultural archive, produce specters as a by-product of its own normal functioning; by-products on which 'normality' in some sense depends?"[64]

With its unsettling reminders of a war thought far removed from the newly prosperous nation, Yokoi's return provoked "long and varied analyses." According to the scholar Beatrice Trefalt in her study of Japanese army stragglers, it also prompted "much discussing, soul-searching, explaining, suspecting, surmising, comparing and exclaiming in the press, and certainly also quite a bit of inventing and imagining."[65] Indeed, of all the voices contributing to these discussions – this soul-searching, this invention – the most unsettling voice belonged to Yokoi himself, trying to articulate what was nearly inexpressible in the postwar world. As Yoshikuni Igarashi writes in his illuminating article about Yokoi's experiences up to his death in 1997 (his unsuccessful run for the House of Councillors in 1974, his flourishing career as a media star commenting as an "outsider critic" on contemporary society), Yokoi continued to speak about his experiences, but never was he able to put the memories to rest. After his return to Japan, and even on his deathbed, it was reported, Yokoi was kept awake by nightmares.[66] One of the survivors of the Guam battle, talking to a reporter about Yokoi's return, complained that "Mr Yokoi talks, talks, talks – [look at] that manner [in which he talks]. It is really sad to see him deceiving himself so completely through his own words. We, too [other survivors of the war], continue to lie, while keeping the truth to ourselves and taking it to our graves."[67]

Notes

1. Asahi shimbun tokuha kishadan (1972) *28 Years in the Guam Jungle: Sergeant Yokoi Home from World War II*, San Francisco: Japan Publications, Inc., p. 97.
2. "The Emperor's Last Soldier, Yokoi Shōichi: Five Days in his Homeland" [*Tennō no saigo no heishi, Yokoi san: sokoku no itsukakan*]. (1972), *Sandei mainichi*, February 20, p. 16.
3. Ibid. Igarashi notes that "the airport crowd was far bigger than that which had welcomed the emperor and empress back from their royal tour of Europe in 1971" (207). See Igarashi, Yoshikuni (2002) "Yokoi Shōichi: When a soldier finally returns home," in Anne Walthall (ed.) *The Human Tradition in Modern Japan*, Wilmington, DE: Scholarly Resources, Inc.
4. A transcription of the press conferences can be found in English in Asahi, *28 Years in the Guam Jungle*, San Francisco: Japan Publications, Inc., pp. 9–14 and 36–46.
5. Except where specified, I have used the recent translation of *Der Mann Moses und die monotheistische Religion* titled *Moses the Man and Monotheistic Religion*. In Freud, Sigmund (2004) *Mass Psychology and Other Writings*, translated by J. A. Underwood.

New York: Penguin Books, pp. 167–299. The phrase "brings a return of the past," "distorted" and "delusional" (Strachey's translations) are from SE 23: 130 (Underwood, p. 292). The phrases "spectral," "fantasmatic," and "more real than reality" come from Slavoj Žižek's (2000) discussion of Freud in *The Fragile Absolute – or why is the Christian legacy worth fighting for*, New York: Verso, p. 64. Žižek illustrates this with the story of a disciple and a well-known rabbi, discussing the legend of a prophet's Divine vision. "Is this true? Did it really happen?" asks the disciple. The rabbi responds, "It probably didn't happen, but it *is* true" (Žižek, p. 64, emphasis in original).

6. Derrida, Jacques (1998) *Archive Fever: A Freudian Impression*, translated by Eric Prenowitz, Chicago: University of Chicago Press, see esp. pp. 85–8.

7. Asahi, *28 Years in the Guam Jungle*, p. 12. He was significantly older than the other two (seven years older than Shichi and ten years older than Nakahata).

8. Trefalt, Beatrice (2003) *Japanese Army Stragglers and Memories of the War in Japan, 1950–1975,* New York: Routledge Curzon, p. 115. Also see Asahi, *28 Years in the Guam Jungle*, p. 73. A doctor at Guam memorial hospital, Dr Orlando B. Barrona, announced that the cause of death was due to food poisoning. After studying the two sets of remains, he stated that "federico nuts and toad both contain poison. It appears that the two experienced symptoms of poisoning simultaneously and died after eating them. Combine this with their lack of nutrition and their ingestion of the poison was all the more lethal." See "The 'domestic affairs' of Yokoi and the two comrades with whom he split" [*Yokoi san ga futari no senyū to bekkyo shita "katei no jijō"*] *Shūkan sankei*, February 25, 1972, p. 24.

9. Asahi, *28 Years in the Guam Jungle*, p. 82.

10. Ibid., p. 85.

11. Ibid., p. 87.

12. Tsutsui, Edward G. (1972) "Yokoi spoke only to me: The truth about his surviving alone" [*Yokoi san ga watashi dake ni katatta: hitori ikinokotta shinsō*], *Shūkan gendai*, February 17, p. 22.

13. "The 'domestic affairs'," *Shūkan sankei* February 25, 1972, p. 24.

14. Ibid.

15. Nihei Kizō, a fellow straggler on Guam who was rescued decades earlier, shook his head as he heard of the "food poisoning" death. "That's really strange. Everyone came to know what had poison in it. And Nakahata was one of those guys who was so sensitive to this. One time, we boiled tempura in palm oil, frying up some toad ovaries. We all got serious diarrhea, but he alone was just fine. 'Hey, are you OK,' someone asked and he said, 'Yeah, I'm fine since I didn't have any of it.' We were absolutely furious at him, since he said that he had learned at school to never eat toad ovaries, and that his grandfather had always told him the same thing" ("The 'domestic affairs'," *Shūkan sankei* February 25, 1972, p. 24).

16. "The 'domestic affairs'," *Shūkan sankei* February 25, 1972, p. 24. Also, see Tsutsui, "Yokoi spoke," *Shūkan gendai*, February 17, 1972, pp. 20–1. The items found in Yokoi's underground home that were unmistakably taken from the two were "Shichi's Japanese flag and his thousand-stitch belt, a kind of talisman against harm in which one thousand people put one stitch each" (Asahi, *28 years in the Guam Jungle*, p. 73).

17. Asahi, *28 Years in the Guam Jungle*, p. 87. Also scrutinized were his remarks to a reporter, whom Yokoi reportedly thought was an Army official. Asked about his friends' remains being returned to Japan, Yokoi commented, "I wanted to go home with them. Many things happened. I had the highest rank. Maybe that made the other two keep their distance. (He closed his eyes.) I want to meet their families and hold memorial services as soon as possible," pp. 106–7).

18. The exhibit on national history in the Japan Pavilion famously had "references to the Asia Pacific War . . . carefully erased," the history of the twentieth century "leapt from the Meiji period to the present without bothering to account for what lay between." Igarashi (2000) *Bodies of Memory: Narratives of War in Postwar Japanese Culture, 1945–1970*, Princeton: Princeton University Press, p. 165.

19. A useful discussion of this can be found in Igarashi, *Bodies of Memory*.
20. Igarashi (2002), "Yokoi Shōichi," p. 198.
21. Dower, John (1999) *Embracing Defeat: Japan in the wake of World War II*, New York: WW Norton & Company, Inc., p. 60.
22. Trefalt (2003), p. 119.
23. Dower (1999), p. 60.
24. Daqing Yang (2001) "The Malleable and the Contested: The Nanjing Massacre in Postwar China and Japan," in T. Fujitani *et al.* (eds) *Perilous Memories: The Asia-Pacific War(s)*, Durham: Duke University Press, p. 59. Honda Katsuichi, a journalist for the *Asahi shinbun*, was well known at the time for his award-winning coverage of Vietnam.
25. Ibid.
26. Igarashi (2002) "Yokoi Shōichi," p. 208. Soon after his capture, Yokoi told officials and reporters that he had known the war was over less than a year after surrender, having found a Japanese newspaper in the jungle. But after he heard criticism that his time in Guam was motivated by selfish self-preservation, that he should have died in the war effort, he changed his story. Abruptly, Yokoi began claiming that he had not known the war was over, maintaining this position in all his subsequent interviews (and in his autobiography).
27. This story is outlined in several articles I cite, including "I killed two native villagers" [*Watashi wa futari no genchijin o koroshita*], *Josei sebun*, May 24–31, 1972, pp. 207–9; and "Did he really kill them? The Mysterious Past of Yokoi Shōichi" [*Hontō ni futari o koroshitanoka: Yokoi Shōichi san no misuterii kako*], *Shūkan myōjō*, May 21, 1972, 198–9. Yokoi's autobiography, which reveals remarkably little about his time on Guam, is Yokoi Shōichi, *Asu e no michi*. Tokyo: Bungei shunjū, 1974.
28. "Yokoi, don't make my son out to be a murderer!" [*Yokoi-san watashi no musuko o satsujinsha ni shinaide*], *Bishō*, May 27, 1972 (547), p. 42.
29. "Did he really kill them?" *Shūkan myōjō*, p. 198.
30. Again, although I use the well-known translation of the title given in Strachey's *Standard Edition*, Vol. 23, nearly all other quotes are from *Moses the Man*, translated by J. A. Underwood, 2004.
31. Paul, Robert A. (1996) *Moses and Civilization: The Meaning Behind Freud's Myth*, New Haven: Yale University Press, p. 4.
32. Santner, Eric (Spring, 1999) "Freud's 'Moses' and the Ethics of Nomotropic Desire," *October, Vol. 88*, p. 1. Undoubtedly one reason for the work's recent popularity is the oblique approach to it many scholars have taken, reading it not as a credible contribution to any history or ethnography, but rather "in terms of the cultural pressures that might have made Freud produce such a text," that is to say, historicizing the book as a "document of the tense, conflictual nature of the German-Jewish formation on the eve of its destruction" (Santner, pp. 4–5). The list of important scholars' works on Freud's *Moses* includes Jan Assmann's *Moses the Egyptian*, Edward Said's *Freud and the Non-European*, Yosef Yerulshami's *Freud's Moses*, and Jacques Derrida's *The Post Card* and *Archive Fever: A Freudian Impression*.
33. Freud, *M&M*, p. 292. Strachey's translation translated the two terms as "material truth" and "historical truth," and I follow that convention here. In the new Penguin translation, translator J. A. Underwood uses the terms "substantive truth" and "historical truth."
34. Eric Santner discusses this uncertainty of the event's occurrence, calling such happenings "an event of fantasy – or better, as an *eventful fantasy* embedded in the larger narrative structure" ("Freud's 'Moses,'" p. 27, emphasis in original). He also employs Slavoj Žižek's term "phantasmatic specter," which he describes as forming a "sort of second-order myth 'secreted' or 'encrypted'" in other narratives. It is "spectral rather than symbolic" and "must be reconstructed through structural analysis" of the narrative, p. 28.
35. Freud, *M&M*, p. 292. Again, this is Strachey's translation (SE 23: 130). Underwood renders it with "occasions a recurrence of things past."
36. Santner, "Freud's 'Moses,'" p. 34.

37. Poison was reportedly detected in the recovered remains (poison, attributed to either federico nuts or toads, that skeptics were hard-pressed to believe were mistakenly ingested by the pair). Journalistic eyebrows were also raised over Yokoi's appropriation of Shichi's "thousand-stitch belt," a common talisman sent to soldiers to ward off harm (*Shūkan sankei,* February 25, 1972, p. 24).
38. *Shūkan sankei,* February 25, 1972, pp. 20–3.
39. Minagawa Bunzō (1971) *Guamu-tō jūrokunen* [Sixteen years on Guam], Tokyo: Chōbunsha, p. 52.
40. *Shūkan gendai,* February 17, 1972, pp. 20–1. Yokoi spoke of his distrust of these comrades rescued earlier from Guam, noting that, "There are all kinds of folks that are completely untrustworthy. Minagawa and Itō and those like them cannot be trusted." *Sandei mainichi,* February 20, 1972, p. 22.
41. See Barbara Johnson (1987), "Apostrophe, Animation, and Abortion," in *A World of Difference,* Baltimore: John Hopkins University Press, pp. 184–99. Paul de Man writes of the "latent threat" in apostrophe, that "the fiction of address . . . acquires a sinister connotation that is not only the prefiguration of one's own mortality but of our actual entry into the frozen world of the dead." Quoted in Sanford Budick's (2000) *The Western Theory of Tradition: Terms and Paradigms of the Cultural Sublime,* New Haven: Yale University Press, p. 75.
42. Jonathan Culler (1981) *The Pursuit of Signs: Semiotics, Literature, Deconstruction,* Ithaca: Cornell University Press, p. 139.
43. Asahi, *28 years,* p. 87.
44. Phillips, Adam (1996) *Terrors and Experts,* Cambridge: Harvard University Press, p. 66. In interpreting the significance of Yokoi's visions, we should take heed of Freud's famous footnote added to the 1914 edition of *The Interpretation of Dreams,* where he wrote, "It has long been the habit to regard dreams as identical with their manifest content; but we must now beware equally of the mistake of confusing dreams with latent dream-thoughts." Quoted in Phillips (1996) *Terrors,* p. 73.
45. Phillips, Adam (2006) *Side Effects,* New York: Harper Perennial, p. 44.
46. "Did he really kill them?" *Shūkan myōjō,* May 21, 1972, p. 198.
47. "The stir from Yokoi's jungle confession" [*Mitsurin no himitsu o kokuhakushita Shoicchan no dōyō*]. *Shūkan taishū,* May 18, 1972, pp. 142–3.
48. "The sudden cloud over the Yokoi myth" [*Hayakumo kageri dashita "Yokoi-san shinwa"*], *Shūkan bunshun,* May 22, 1972, pp. 152–3.
49. "Did he really kill them?" *Shūkan myōjō,* May 21, 1972, p. 198.
50. "The sudden cloud," *Shūkan bunshun,* May 22, 1972, p. 152. As one article noted, "The magnitude of the shock for the public came about because his statements about what he did in the jungle had turned him, in an instant, from a 'hero' into a 'killer.' Echoes of this 'murder' remained in people's ears, and criticism, which had been conducted in hushed tones now overflowed as if a dam had been broken." "The sudden cloud," *Shūkan bunshun,* p. 153.
51. As one veteran stated, "He was a coward. A crybaby." Another added, "I thought from the beginning that he was someone trying to keep something hidden." "The sudden cloud," *Shūkan bunshun,* p. 153. The article also quotes numerous residents of Yokoi's town newly disturbed by their "returning hero," speaking to his oddness, his strange behavior. One states, "my children were watching television that night, and one turned to me, saying, 'Shōichi killed someone,' and I had to tell him that it appeared he had." Quoted in "Yokoi, don't . . ." *Bishō,* p. 42. Relatives of Nakahata and Shichi both expressed their anger at Yokoi's accusations, stating that they were extremely "suspicious" of him. *Bishō,* p. 43.
52. Ibid., p. 154.
53. Ibid., p. 154.
54. Igarashi (2002) "Yokoi Shōichi," p. 208.

55. Orr, James J. (2001) *The Victim as Hero: Ideologies of Peace and National Identity in Postwar Japan*, Honolulu: University of Hawaii Press, p. 3. In the years immediately following the war, the vast majority of the Japanese populace had clung to the concept of a reckless military, a concept pushed by Occupation officials and the Japanese government that relieved ordinary citizens, "deceived" into supporting the war, of the burdens of guilt and responsibility. See Orr, p. 14.
56. See Igarashi, *Bodies of Memory*, and Yoshida Yutaka. *Nihonjin no sensōkan: sengoshi no naka no henyō*. Tokyo: Aoki shoten, 1997. Also see Bruce Suttmeier (Winter 2007) "Seeing Past Destruction: Trauma and History in Kaikō Takeshi," *positions: east asia cultures critique* 15: 3.
57. "The stir . . ." *Shūkan taishū*, May 18, 1972, p. 143.
58. Quoted in "The stir . . ." *Shūkan taishū*, May 18, 1972, p. 154.
59. Igarashi (2000) *Bodies of Memory*, p. 203.
60. Suttmeier (Winter 2007), "Seeing past destruction," *positions*, pp. 476–7.
61. The compulsive desire for such scenes stems in large part from the guilt engendered by wartime activity (both national and individual), guilt strenuously repressed in the postwar period, and guilt, most germane to my point, that structures the interminable nature of remembrance itself. The act of remembrance becomes a mode of unpacking, by means of narration, the kernel of "historical truth" manifest in these scenes, the "spectrality" of what seems hidden within. It is this very tropological mechanism, seeing the war *in* uncanny forms, that provides the desired recognition (however unacknowledged and unwelcome) of the transgressions of the past. See Santner (1999), p. 39–40.
62. "The sudden cloud," *Shūkan bunshun*, p. 152. It is instructive to note that the previous set of stragglers, returning twelve years earlier in 1960, had received almost no fanfare and comparatively little publicity. See Trefalt (2003), p. 112.
63. Derrida (1998) *Archive Fever*, p. 87.
64. Santner (1999), p. 25.
65. Trefalt (2003), pp. 111–12.
66. Igarashi (2002) "Yokoi Shōichi," p. 211.
67. Quoted in Igarashi (2002) "Yokoi Shōichi," p. 211.

2 Introduction

Carl Cassegard: Japan's lost
decade and its two recoveries . . .

Freud did not hesitate to extend his theories to the analysis of culture and history. In texts such as *Civilization and its Discontents, Totem and Taboo,* and *Moses and Monotheism,* Freud applied psychoanalytic processes to society in the form of a superego, repression of trauma, and repetition compulsion. It is in this spirit that Carl Cassegard brings Freud's theory of trauma, repetition, and recovery to bear on the cultural landscape of postwar Japan. Fundamental to Freud's theory of trauma and repetition is, of course, the psychoanalytic concept of a psychic temporality in which the past continues to exist in a sort of simultaneity, albeit often an unconscious one, in the present. This is a concept of time that is radically different from a historical one.

At the core of Cassegard's argument is the thesis that recent Japanese anti-war protests, such as the *Korosuna* movement of 2003 and the revival of enthusiasm for the avant-garde were made possible by a process of repetition of traumatic cultural moments with some degree of orientation towards recovery. Focusing his discussion on the art critic Sawaragi Noi, who revised his opinion of Japan from a "bad place" and "closed circle" in the 1960s to a "good place" in which political activism and artistic expression have become possible once again in the 2000s, Cassegard analyzes the process of recovery from three traumatic events in Japanese history after which the future seemed dim indeed: 1945, or the loss of the Second World War, the defeat of the 1960s student protest movements, and the economic depression of the 1990s. Part of this process involves confronting Japan's own "monstrosity" and challenging the "self-evident" nature of Japan's national myths.

2 Japan's lost decade and its two recoveries

On Sawaragi Noi, Japanese Neo-pop and anti-war activism

Carl Cassegard

On 21 March 2003, after the start of the US-led invasion of Iraq, the biggest anti-war demonstration in Japan since the Vietnam War took place in Tokyo.[1] Spearheading the demonstration as it headed towards Ginza was a colourful group of some 300 people, dancing and playing music on sound systems, drums, tambourines or other instruments while shouting or holding placards with the words "Korosuna" [Do not kill]. Among them were the art critic Sawaragi Noi banging a gong, and his friend, the artist and ethnographer Oda Masanori, with a huge bass drum in a strap around his shoulder. *Korosuna* – as this group is called – was organized by Sawaragi in 2003 together with Oda, Yamamoto Yūko and Kudō Kiki.[2] A few days before the demonstration Sawaragi had sent out an e-mail appeal which is noteworthy because of the mention of the artist Okamoto Tarō and *Beheiren* (Citizen's League for Peace in Vietnam), which was a famous Japanese civic movement, active from 1965 to 1974.

> Dear Everybody, I know it comes all of a sudden, but we're starting an anti-war movement. Its name is *Korosuna*. Incidentally, "Korosuna" is adopted from the words of Okamoto Tarō that were posted by *Beheiren* in the midst of the whirlpool of the movement against the Vietnam War in *Washington Post* 1967. To those who feel offended by this e-mail, I truly apologize. To those who feel like giving it a try, please join us! Sawaragi Noi.[3]

Beheiren was notable for its loose and open organization – anybody who wanted to protest against the Vietnam War was welcome to participate regardless of ideological conviction and no membership lists were maintained – which contrasted with the dogmatic stance of many student sects during the same period. In April 1967, it posted a full-page advertisement in *The Washington Post* (Figure 2.1), which conspicuously featured the words "Korosuna" drawn by Okamoto Tarō. During the build-up towards the war in Iraq in early 2003 – when Sawaragi confessed to an "emotional heightening without precedent"[4] – he reports seeing *Beheiren*'s advertisement for the first time and being struck with its spiky and tilted calligraphy. "At Tarō's 'Korosuna', I experienced a shock of such freshness as I have never felt before."[5] His decision to start *Korosuna* was taken shortly afterwards and flags replicating this calligraphy were also used during the demonstration.

Figure 2.1 Full page advertisement in the *Washington Post*, Monday April 3, 1967. "Korosuna" – do not kill.

As the sociologist Mōri Yoshitaka points out, this was the "first large political street demonstration organized by contemporary art critics and artists over the last two decades."[6] The participants included many who, like Sawaragi, were new to political activism. To Mōri, *Korosuna* forms part of the "new cultural movements" that have developed in Japan outside the traditional left since the early 1990s. In contrast to older Leftist movements, which are often felt to be too hierarchical, stiffly organized and ideologically dogmatic, many of the new movements are characterized by a loose, network-like organization, by a great diversity of participants lacking a unified ideological stand, by their use of music and dance, and by an emphasis on "pleasure" and "fun."[7] Mōri links the emergence of these movements to the increasing number of "freeters" in a post-Fordist economy and deregulated labour market. "The central political actors of mass mobilization are now the *freeter* generation, who have not experienced traditional leftist politics."[8]

Intriguingly, however, in certain respects *Korosuna* "repeats" the older movements. When Sawaragi states that there is no need for participants to subscribe to any ideology and that anyone can take part in *Korosuna*'s activities, his words echo *Beheiren*.[9] The high regard he holds for Okamoto, who he clearly views as a predecessor, may come as a surprise to many readers in view of the criticism that he directs against the latter in his *Nihon gendai bijutsu* (*Contemporary Art of Japan*).[10] This is arguably his most famous work, well-known for portraying Japan as a "bad place" and "closed circle" in which the avant-garde artists of the postwar era have made futile attempts to break with earlier traditions while falling back into various forms of traditionalism or nationalism, surreptitiously strengthening what they claimed to be opposing. This portrayal, however, is modified in his recent writings. In his 2003 book, *Kuroi taiyō to akai kani* (*Black sun and red crab*), Sawaragi looks back on the antiwar manifestation of 21 March:

Participating in a street demonstration for the first time since I was born, I made many fresh discoveries . . . Today, the street is undoubtedly one of the few "good places" left where we can reassemble our thoughts and once more move to action.[11]

This chapter is about how Sawaragi arrives at this insight. How does this discovery of the street as a "good place" come about? What happens to his previous portrayal of Japan as a "bad place" and "closed circle"? In what way is this shift connected to his re-evaluation of Okamoto Tarō and how should we understand the presence of the legacy of the 1960s in a movement that in many other respects signalled a break with earlier forms of protest?

Below, I will turn to Freud's theory of trauma, and in particular his discussion of the ambivalent relation between recovery and repetition, to elucidate these questions.[12] Doing so will help us understand not only the sense of closure expressed in the idea of Japan as a "bad place," but also the reawakening of political involvement and the repetition of elements of the past. These questions have broader significance. Sawaragi's writings offer a valuable close-up of the increasing political involvement of many writers and intellectuals in Japan since the mid-1990s – a phenomenon sometimes referred to as the "post-1995" phenomenon.[13] Examples include Karatani Kōjin's founding of NAM (the New Associationist Movement) in 2000 and Murakami Haruki's turn to "commitment" in the mid-1990s – leading to his engagement with the victims of the Tokyo Subway Gas Attack or the Great Hanshin Earthquake. Similarly, Sawaragi has today "returned to Japan" to participate in and wrestle with its history.

Postwar Japan and the concept of trauma

In Japan, the so-called "lost decade", starting with the collapse of the economic "bubble" in 1993, produced a widespread mood of pessimism regarding the future, of impasse or claustrophobic closure. One response to this situation has been the rise of a nationalistic discourse, with clamorous calls for a restoration of national pride. Another response is the budding rise of social protest against neo-liberalism. The influx of neo-liberal "globalization" has therefore had an intriguing effect both of strengthening the nationalistic discourse and of bringing forth an "alternative" political imagination that challenges this discourse. To properly grasp the dynamic relation between these two tendencies it will be helpful to give attention to two facts that contradict the simplistic view that the burst of the economic bubble in the early 1990s was nothing but a catastrophe that plunged the country into despair.

First, the sense of impasse or claustrophobic closure did not start with the period after the burst of the bubble-economy. As has often been pointed out, it forms a recurrent feature in much of the popular culture and literary imagination of the 1970s and 1980s and can to a great extent be seen as a lingering after-effect of the defeat of protest movements of the 1960s.[14]

Second, the "collapse of the Japanese model" in the 1990s was not unanimously viewed as a disaster. Some even welcomed it. Comparing the bubble economy to a maniacal feeling of having conquered the world, the Neo-pop artist Murakami Takashi writes that "when that mirage vanished, we felt relief, as if to say: "That's right, this is what reality looks like."[15] To Karatani the collapse was a breath of fresh air. Looking back in 1997, he writes that he had "felt almost suffocated in Japan during the 1980s," when people were euphoric and Japanese capitalism seemed triumphant.[16] The end of the bubble-economy was not only a trauma, but also had a vitalizing effect, which is manifested in the growth of civil society and political engagement – with NAM, the movement founded by Karatani, being one example.

These facts suggest that apart from the defeat of the "Japanese model" in the early 1990s, we also need to focus on the effects of an earlier defeat, that of the protest movements of the 1960s. Corresponding to these two traumatic events there are two competing ideas of "recovery": the recovery of national self-esteem and economic and political might on the one hand, and the recovery of "civil society" after the defeat of radical activism in the late 1960s and early 1970s on the other. Both conceptions of recovery are often articulated in a way which makes it clear that they are linked to a fundamental sense of discontent or frustration with the "post-war system" of Japan as such – the system forged by the occupation authorities in the wake of the defeat in the Pacific War in 1945 – and we should therefore add that a third trauma, that of "1945," is directly or indirectly at issue in both of these ideas of recovery. The picture that emerges is therefore that of a layer of interacting traumas which are addressed and confronted in varying degrees by nationalists as well as by radical activists.

Freud's concept of trauma is helpful in understanding this situation. When the ego is unable to grasp or fully register the traumatic event, Freud suggests that it is forced to act it out symptomatically in the form of compulsive repetitions in dreams, fantasies or action.[17] Applying this idea to the analysis of "post-apocalyptic" literature and philosophy, James Berger argues that such texts are often pervaded by a desire for another more complete or conclusive catastrophe. Post-apocalyptic representations prevalently "put forward a total critique of any existing social order" since only an "absolute, purifying cataclysm" can make possible an utterly new, perfect world.[18] Berger above all points to the Second World War and the defeat of the counterculture of the 1960s as two traumas that have had these effects, but it is also possible to view the collapse of the "Japanese model" in the 1990s as such a trauma. Thus a well-known sociologist, Ōsawa Masachi, has argued that the attraction voters perceived in Koizumi Jun'ichirō's promises of sweeping neo-liberal reforms in 2000 could be interpreted as a sign of a general wish to repeat this collapse a second time in order to master the trauma retrospectively.[19]

It is important to point out that a trauma is not only accompanied by symptomatic repetitions, but also by an orientation, however slight and imperceptible, towards recovery. Recovery is when trauma loosens its grip. Consciously working through the trauma and verbalizing the loss are often mentioned by Freud as necessary prerequisites for genuine recovery. Otherwise, the patient "is obliged to *repeat* the repressed material as a contemporary experience instead of, as the physician would prefer to see, *remembering* it as something belonging to the past."[20] However, as he also points out in his classic description of the "*fort-da* game," repetitions can also contribute to a retrospective mastering of the trauma. By repeating the experience of the mother's departure retrospectively in the form of a game, the child no longer had to experience it as a passive victim, but could pretend that he had wished it to happen himself. "All right, then, go away!" he pretends to tell the mother, "I don't need you. I'm sending you away myself."[21] Freud's ambiguous attitude towards this game is famous: it is both a symptom of a trauma and an attempt to master it. By turning himself from a passive victim to an active agent, the child makes the trauma more acceptable to consciousness and thereby facilitates a working-through.[22]

Sawaragi's writings provide a good opportunity to study the interaction between the two competing ideas of "recovery" in contemporary Japan mentioned above. Below, I will compare his *Nihon gendai bijutsu* to more recent works, such as *Kuroi taiyō* and *Sensō to banpaku* (2005, *World wars and world fairs*). I will suggest, first, that his idea of a "bad place," which seemingly reflects the sense of closure or deadlock in the late 1990s, is better understood as a remnant of an earlier sense of claustrophobic closure that originates in the defeat of radicalism in the early 1970s. Second, I will argue that a scrutiny of how he relates himself to the two competing orientations towards "recovery" today will help us understand his shift towards political involvement. Just as the shattering impact of the "lost decade" on the "self-complacent space" of Japan made Karatani feel that he could breathe again, it helped Sawaragi discover a "good place" on the street.

Japan as a "bad place"

Nihon gendai bijutsu was written as a series of instalments in the journal *Bijutsu techō* from July 1996 to June 1997 and was published as a book in 1998. At first sight, Sawaragi's description of Japan as a "bad place" and a "closed circle" appear to reflect the then prevalent mood of "deadlock," but a look at how these expressions are used in the text suggest another interpretation.

What does the expression "bad place" mean? In a straightforward sense, Japan is a bad place for art, since art is an imported concept only weakly rooted in Japanese society. Only the "forms" of art are imported – galleries, art historians, museums – while a social stratum supporting art, providing it with social recognition, and a market for art is lacking. However, Sawaragi also uses the term in a more ambitious sense. His point of departure is a claim made by Hikosaka Naoyoshi – a founding father of the avant-garde group *Bikyōtō* – that, beginning with *Gutai* in 1955, the Japanese avant-garde had started to move away from "poiesis" (making) to "praxis" (acting), i.e. from a conception of art emphasizing the production of the art work towards the idea of art as a performance or gesture intervening in society. Sawaragi, however, denies that any transition to praxis in the sense of a radical questioning of the institutional boundaries of art was ever decisively accomplished and states that praxis signifies a task which is still with us.[23]

Sawaragi sees the failure of the avant-garde as rooted in the fact that it attempted to overcome a modernity that was still weak, incomplete and immature. The idea of an "avant-garde" at the forefront of historical progress had rested on an ideology claiming "simultaneity" for Japan with the West while overlooking the historical conditions, the "violence," of the founding of Japan's postwar order through military defeat. To Sawaragi, the idea of Japan as a bad place therefore connotes the repression in public consciousness of a particular layer of memory, an amnesia which was cemented through the "1955-system," the political hegemony of the LDP and the country's dependency on the USA.[24] Not only has this amnesia deprived art of the ability to address existing power relations – from taking the step to praxis – it has also prevented art from approaching modernity in a self-reflexive fashion and changing it from within. Instead art has again and again taken the short-cut of claiming avant-garde status for features of "Japanese" tradition such as Zen, festivals, or *mono no aware*, thus falling back into traditionalism and contributing to a strengthening of national identity. In this way, a vicious circle has emerged in which the avant-garde coexists harmoniously with nationalism.[25]

A clue to where this sense of living in a bad place comes from can be gained by relating Sawaragi's texts to those of his contemporaries. This will also expose still another connotation of the term bad place: that of trauma, and in particular of the traumatic effects of the defeat of the radicalism of the 1960s. We can start by considering why the term "bad place" appears so strange to begin with. Isn't there something paradoxical about designating the "place" in which one is embedded as "bad" in its totality? If it is totally bad, then how could it possibly contain a yardstick reliable enough to make such a value judgement possible? Sawaragi's expression evokes something similar to the "perfectly wrong" worlds depicted by Murakami Haruki. In one of the latter's novels, the difficulty of finding an external standpoint from which to criticize the system is well captured in the following dialogue in which the narrator is warned by his alter ego, the "shadow," about the "Town" in which he is living.

I repeat what I said at the very beginning: this place is wrong. I know it. More than ever. The problem is, the Town is *perfectly* wrong. Every last thing is skewed, so that the total distortion is seamless. It's a whole. Like this –

My shadow draws a circle on the ground with his boot.

"The Town is sealed," he states, "like this. That's why the longer you stay in here, the more you get to thinking that things are normal. You begin to doubt your judgment. You get what I'm saying?"[26]

Despite its seeming perfection, the "Town" is sensed to be somehow "unnatural and wrong." The literary critic Hatanaka Yoshiki has used the theological expression "fallen world" to describe this kind of world, whose falseness can only be vaguely sensed, not clearly realized.[27] To use an expression by Brecht it is a world in which "something is missing" – *etwas fehlt* – which cannot be brought fully to consciousness.

This sense of claustrophobic closure recurs in many of Murakami's earlier writings. "We can go anywhere, and yet we're locked up," another of his narrators reflects while gazing out at Tokyo from a train, "There's no exit anywhere."[28] As has often been remarked, Murakami's cities tend to be mere landscapes, unrelated to the disengaged, introvert spectator.[29] These landscapes are characterized by their lack of outlets for action – they are little more than an indifferent background or setting. Karatani sees the emergence of such landscapes as a corollary of political disillusionment, a withdrawal or retracting of energies that had once sought outlet in political imagination and action. The emergence of landscapes in Meiji-period writers, he argues, was linked to the internalization of libido that followed on the trauma of the suppression of the People's Rights movement in the 1880s. "To speak in Freudian terms, the libido which was once directed toward the People's Rights movement and the writing of political novels lost its object and was redirected inward, at which point 'landscape' and 'the inner life' appeared."[30] To Karatani, the emergence of landscapes implies an extinction of "exteriority," of the ability to transcend "inner life" in order to perceive otherness. When he criticizes the "discursive space" of Japan during the 1980s as "almost totally lacking in exteriority," he implies that the "landscapes" of contemporary writers such as Murakami are the result of a similar suppression.[31]

Indeed, Murakami himself explicitly points to the defeat of the protest movements of the 1960s as the source of the sense of closure. "I didn't think so then, but the world was still simple in 1969. In some cases, it was enough to throw stones at the riot police for people to achieve self-expression. In its own way, it was a good time," one of his protagonists says. In today's "advanced capitalist society," by contrast, even opposition has become part of the system: "A net has been stretched from one corner of society to the other. Outside the net there is another net. We can't go anywhere. If we throw a stone it's deflected and bounces back."[32] In Murakami's world there is no simple way to disentangle oneself and negate the system. Externally applied criticism has become powerless, since the protagonists are themselves enmeshed in and part of the decay and fallenness of the world. To speak with Freud, this can be described as a "melancholic" loss of self. Many commentators have pointed out that such melancholia was an important part of the legacy left by the Japanese New Left, whose self-destructive development into sectarian and militant groups embroiled in infighting left little or nothing to be proud of.[33]

Taking some liberty with Murakami's and Karatani's texts, I would suggest that what they call "exits" and "exteriority" serve as codewords for freedom: not being confined to a single system you possess the freedom to choose and to act. Similarly, what Sawaragi refers to as "praxis" can be understood as the ability to break out of the confines of contemporary art and act back on your wider social and political environment. Much contemporary art, by contrast, has the qualities of a landscape, a spectacle of otherness founded on a foreclosure of memory as well as of opportunities for "praxis." These parallels suggest that the sense of claustrophobia in Sawaragi carries on the legacy of the "exitlessness" or "lack of exteriority" described in the decades following the defeat of radical protest by writers and thinkers like Murakami and Karatani.

That this defeat plays a pivotal role in Sawaragi's thinking is supported by the fact that *Nihon gendai bijutsu* pre-eminently deals with the avant-garde of the 1960s. The book can be considered a form of working through and confronting the legacy of that decade. By contrast, the Neo-pop of the 1990s, as I will discuss later, is assessed by Sawaragi in more positive terms as a "pop of reduction" which challenges the amnesia of postwar art. Far from assessing the 1990s as a decade of "deadlock," then, Sawaragi places hope in the "malicious" use that artists such as Murakami Takashi make of pop culture in order to re-awaken the memory of the violence – the war, the defeat and the submission to the former enemy under the aegis of Cold War ideology – which underlies the "peace" of postwar Japanese history.

World war and world fairs

As Sawaragi himself recognizes in recent texts, the "closed circle" began to crack open in the 1990s. With the end of the Cold War, the postwar political order in Japan, characterized by the long reign of the LDP under the "1955 system," began to fall apart. The Tokyo Subway Gas Attack of 1995 and the neo-liberal policies of the Japanese government along with the resulting gap between rich and poor also served as catalysts in the collapse of faith in the postwar order.[34] At the same time, several of those writers and thinkers who had previously lamented about closure began to find possibilities of action: Just as Murakami Haruki turned to "commitment" and Karatani to political activism, Sawaragi today claims to have discovered a "good place" in Japan. I will now turn to *Kuroi taiyō* and *Sensō to banpaku*, two works written in instalments almost simultaneously between the years 2002 and 2004, to throw light on this shift.

Sensō to banpaku is a book about the World Fair in Osaka 1970, commonly known as Expo '70. The book was written in the context of the world war on terror and the planned World Expo in Aichi outside Nagoya in 2005. Why did Sawaragi choose to focus on the Expo '70? Part of the reason lies in his preoccupation with the defeat of the radicalism of the 1960s. Expo '70 signalled the futility and bankruptcy of the "radicalism" of the avant-garde, which with depressing ease had let itself be recruited for a nationalist project.[35] Okamoto Tarō constructed the very symbol of the Expo (Figure 2.2), an enormous curved statue with three faces called the Tower of the Sun (*Taiyō no tō*). Other famous avant-garde artists included the sculptor Narita Tōru, the psychedelic painter Yokoo Tadanori, architects such as Tange Kenzō, Isozaki Arata and Asada Takashi, members of the *Jikken Kōbō*-group such as the painter Yamaguchi Katsuhiro, the poet and composer Akiyama Kuniharu and the composer Takemitsu Tōru, members of the *Metabolism*-group such as Kurokawa Kishō and Kuritsu Kiyoshi, and many others. "The Osaka Expo," Sawaragi concludes, "was the final settling of accounts of the post-war Japanese avant-garde and its final form."[36]

As many have pointed out, the Expo – with its theme "The Progress and Harmony of Mankind" – was staged as a symbol of the country's "recovery" from the traumas of war. Equally important was the government's wish to defuse the labour and

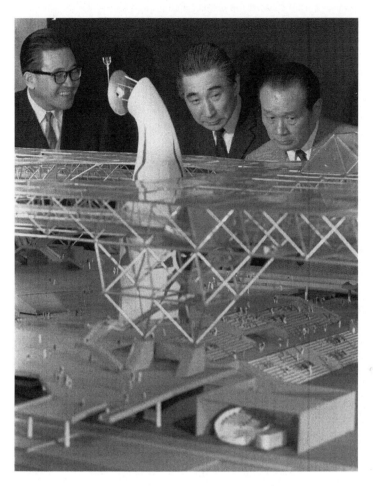

Figure 2.2 Tange Kenzō and Okamoto from Yomiuri Shimbun
  © Yomiuri Shimbun, taken on March 7, 1968 in Ginza, Tokyo.

student unrest which reached its peak with the Anti-Security Treaty unrest in 1960.[37] References to the war in the pavilions were erased, most notably in the exhibit on Japanese history in the Japan Pavilion, which leapt from the Meiji Period to the present without mentioning what lay in between. Yet memories of the lost war stubbornly remained. Sawaragi's aim is to show how the war, while elided, was exactly what was re-enacted in the design and the art of the Expo. In the course of the book, he discovers both lines of *continuity* between the Expo and wartime projects,[38] as well as relations of *causality* between the war and features of the Expo.[39] Third and perhaps most intriguingly, he points to uncanny *similarities* between the war effort and the Expo project. For instance, the Expo art emitted a "strange brightness" similar to wartime propaganda art and totally lacked the usual dark nihilism of the avant-garde.

What on earth, Sawaragi asks, made the avant-garde flock in such large numbers to produce such art? He uses the term "conversion" (*tenkō*) – normally employed for the notorious conversions of socialists and Marxists to conservatism in the 1930s – to describe this phenomenon, which in his view was a repetition of the conversion of pre-war avant-garde artists like Fujita Tsuguji who had turned with enthusiasm to draw propaganda art during the war.[40]

Dadakan and Okamoto Tarō

At first sight *Sensō to banpaku* appears no less totalizing in its view of Japan than *Nihon gendai bijutsu*. The portrayal of Japan as a bad place with an immature modernity in which the avant-garde slips back into nationalism seems unshaken. Despite this appearance, the text of *Sensō to banpaku* is more nuanced than the earlier work. This is evident from how Sawaragi describes the individual responses of artists. He is critical of the so-called Anti-Expo group (*hanpaku*), which in his view replicates the brightness and predictability of Expo art.[41] He has more sympathy for artists and planners such as Isozaki, Kuritsu or Asada who participated in the Expo despite doubts and inner reservations. Neither of these two groups, however, alters the categorical framework of Sawaragi's earlier writings. Neither the direct attempts at negating Expo-art nor the melancholy sense of complicity imply any break with the "circle." It is therefore intriguing to find that in *Sensō to banpaku* he devotes much attention to two artists, who in his view offer the possibility of genuinely stepping out of the "closed circle": Dadakan (Figure 2.3) and Okamoto Tarō.

On 27 April 1970, the Tower of the Sun was occupied by a man wearing a helmet with the signs "Sekigun" (Red Army) who had barricaded himself in the statue's left eye. On the lawn below him a naked man in sunglasses was running around chased by the police. His name was Itoi Kanji, aka Dadakan.[42] A similar stunt had been pulled off on the occasion of the Tokyo Olympic Games, when Dadakan had run naked through the streets pretending to be an Olympic torch-bearer.

In *Nihon gendai bijutsu*, Dadakan is discussed as part of the broader current of Japanese Dada, which Sawaragi sees as enmeshed in traditionalism. Unlike in Europe, where Dada was born out of the shattering of the ideals of culture and civilization after the First World War, in Japan Dada was associated with traditional ideas or practices, such as Zen or festivals, and hence went hand in hand with an affirmation of national culture.[43]

In *Sensō to banpaku*, Japanese Dada is portrayed in a more positive light and Dadakan himself comes forward as a kind of hero – despite still being portrayed as a form of traditionalist. Dadakan sees himself as belonging to a peculiar tradition which goes back not only to Zen – during the war he associated with Zen monks and attended the lectures of Suzuki Daisetsu – but also to the legendary anarchist Ōsugi Sakae and the Great Kantō Earthquake in 1923.[44] Sawaragi seizes on the symbolic role of the earthquake in order to map this tradition. While Dada in the

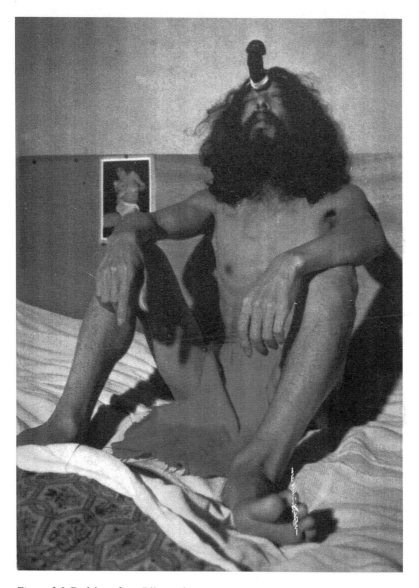

Figure 2.3 Dadakan, from Bijutsu sha.

West was prepared by the First World War, the corresponding experience in Japan was a force of nature, the earthquake.

What Western Dada despaired of most profoundly was the vision of modern man who would eventually plunge back into war no matter how high the ideals he preached. By contrast, what gave substance to Dada in Japan was so to speak a form of nature. That the Japan-made Dada thereafter joined hands with Zen and the "ideal of exposure to the wind,"[45] refused permanent habitation and linked up with a Bashō-like wandering is one of the main differences to Western Dada.[46]

To Sawaragi, then, the Great Kantō Earthquake helps explain the peculiar compatibility of Japanese Dada with native religious traditions. He also points to the millenarian or Utopian symbolism of the earthquake: according to folklore earthquakes are caused by a gigantic catfish (*namazu*), which is also a symbol for the rectification of the world (*yonaoshi*). The echo of the giant catfish, Sawaragi writes, can still be faintly heard in Dadakan's pranks.

> As if opening the lid to the ambivalence of the catfish lurking within the system of the "bright prohibitions" of the Tokyo Olympics and the Osaka Expo, Dadakan's prank of running naked through the city transmitted to the Shōwa Era the far-away overtones of the lost opportunity of a Dadaistic-anarchistic revolution created by the Great Kantō Earthquake.[47]

To Sawaragi, then, Dadakan is part of an anarchistic undercurrent in the Japanese twentieth century, resurfacing at the time of the Expo.

Sensō to banpaku also provides a detailed account of the episode of Dadakan's streaking assault on the Tower of the Sun. Dadakan had been travelling past Osaka in a train when he read about the "Eyeball-man's" occupation of the statue's left eye in a newspaper and decided on the spot to jump off and join him. Sawaragi remarks that the fact that Dadakan – unlike the Anti-Expo group – worked individually and used improvisation made it impossible for the police or the arrangers of the Expo to prevent the assault.[48] This unpredictability gives a clue to Sawaragi's fondness for Dadakan. In the book's final pages, he discusses Lucretius' idea of *clinamen*, the infinitesimally small angle by which falling atoms deviate from a straight fall. Just as *clinamen* to Lucretius represented the possibility of freedom from complete determinism, to Sawaragi it represents the possibility of breaking out of the "closed circle." Dadakan's decision to jump off the train is a perfect example of such irregular and unpredictable behaviour.

So why does Sawaragi, despite his previous criticism of the Dadaists' attempt to link their art to Zen, now have nothing but praise for Dadakan despite the latter's embrace of Zen? Part of the explanation is to be found in the idea of *clinamen* and in Sawaragi's sympathy for forms of activism that escape the rigidity of groups and sects. His budding political involvement may be another part. He and Dadakan have now become brothers in arms. A curious detail is that Dadakan often wore the signs "Korosu na" on his clothes, inspired by Okamoto Tarō's *Washington Post* advertisement.[49]

Okamoto Tarō did not just construct the Tower of the Sun, but was also the "theme producer" of a central part of the Expo site known as the Symbol Zone. This made him an easy target for criticism from the Anti-Expo activists. Okamoto is said to have responded to this criticism by claiming that the Tower of the Sun was "the most Anti-Expo thing there is."[50] Sawaragi too praises Okamoto as "the only one" he approves of among the artists participating in the Expo project.[51] What is the reason for this positive assessment?

The final assessment of Okamoto in *Nihon gendai bijutsu* is critical and in line with Sawaragi's overall argument about the inability of the avant-garde to break open the "closed circle." Okamoto is portrayed as an artist who, after his brilliant early career, himself became a "model" (*kata*) and ended up producing works without tension or critical edge.[52]

Already in this work, however, Sawaragi praised him for his "antipodism" (*taikyokushugi*), his method of creating shocks, or "explosions," through the juxtaposition of seeming opposites. Art, Okamoto insisted, should confront taken-for-granted ideas with their repressed underside. False harmony and "syntheses" should be debunked in favour of exposing contradictions and antagonisms – a stance expressed in his famous statement: "art is an explosion."[53] The way to break out of Japanese tradition was therefore not to imitate the West but to explode the stereotypical images of "Japan" with the help of native and marginal phenomena in today's reality. Using this method, Sawaragi argues, Okamoto was able to upset ready-made categories, such as "Japan" or the "West," and lay bare the "schizo-phrenic" undercurrent of Japanese "reality."[54]

The idea of art as an explosion is explored further in *Sensō to banpaku* and *Kuroi taiyō*. To be sure, Okamoto's antipodism may seem blatantly incompatible with the Expo's theme of "progress and harmony," but in actual fact, Sawaragi asserts, his performance at the Expo represented a perfect realization of the idea of antipodism. Originally, a large part of the central Expo area was to have been covered by a huge "Big Roof" (*dai-yane*), a modernist steel latticework designed by Tange Kenzō that would symbolically unify and harmonize the Expo. Seeing the plans for the roof Okamoto recounts that he was seized by the irresistible impulse to penetrate that roof with an "outrageous thing" (*berabō na mono*). "As against the Expo of technology and modernism," he wrote, "I constructed the very opposite, something outrageous that would look as if it had been there since the dawn of time."[55] This was the origin of his idea of a tower and also explains why the tower looks so angry. Unlike what many critics had believed, the intent behind his participation in the Expo had been subversive.[56]

In Sawaragi's portrayal, Okamoto is almost a mirror-image of Dadakan – a person not belonging entirely to either the Expo- or the Anti-Expo camp. Like Dadakan, he possesses a *clinamen*-like quality of unpredictability and "crookedness." At the end of *Sensō to banpaku*, Sawaragi contrasts this quality to the "straight line" orientation of state-planners. True crookedness, Sawaragi writes, is characterized by unpredictability. The fact that Expo-art in general lacked such crookedness facilitated its appropriation as a propaganda instrument by the state. The Eyeball-man and Dadakan, by contrast, had replied almost by magic to the "outrageous" invitation of the Tower of the Sun. In that moment, Sawaragi writes, the spirit of Ōsugi Sakae was reborn and a moment of anarchy briefly realized.[57]

This interpretation is crowned by the portrait of Okamoto as a radical "nihilist." Only by negating everything in a grand potchlatch-like festival – which he defined as the total exhaustion of all the resources of society without afterthought – could this radical nihility be reached and a new start for society made possible. His hope was that the Expo would become precisely such a festival.⁵⁸ Like Dadakan, Okamoto had tried to infuse art with the millenarian idea of a rectification of the world.

As the idea of "festivals" suggests, Okamoto was a form of traditionalist. To Sawaragi, however, traditionalism *per se* is no longer a cause for criticism. Okamoto's aim was not to strengthen the sense of a unitary national culture, but to pinpoint the things that fall outside this unity and which can be used to challenge it – such as the "crooked" pottery of the Jōmon Period or cultural influences from Oceania and Okinawa. Against the history of the political unit "Japan," he pits the multifarious history of the "Japanese archipelago." The choice of terms here is significant. By eschewing categories such as "Japanese" art, he directs attention to the multiplicity of local traditions and cultural influences that preceded the political unification of the Yamato-state and the Buddhist art sponsored by this state.⁵⁹ Curiously, then, Okamoto's strategy of undermining the "closed circle" by "exploding" it leads back to tradition. Reconnecting to the "schizophrenic" underside of Japan becomes a way of resuscitating the myriad traditions that once existed on the Japanese archipelago, but which were subsequently suppressed, marginalized or forgotten.

The following riddle can now be solved: In *Nihon gendai bijutsu* Sawaragi rejects Japan's avant-garde as caught in a closed circle. His criticism tends to take the form that this avant-garde reverted to tradition and became complicit with nationalism. The riddle is how he is now able to affirm and even praise artists like Okamoto or Dadakan who appear to do *the very same thing*, namely affirm parts of tradition such as Zen or "festivals." The answer can only be that Sawaragi, by studying these artists, has realized that the history of the Japanese archipelago is composed not only of one tradition, but of multiple ones – including traditions that challenge the "closed circle." This has led him to a more differentiated view of history and, significantly, to discover predecessors with whom he feels able to identify.

Instead of proceeding in the negative or deconstructive fashion of *Nihon gendai bijutsu*, Sawaragi's recent works therefore mark a shift towards directly and positively identifying "good" elements in the history of the Japanese archipelago. Through his reading of Dadakan and Okamoto he constructs an alternative tradition of marginal, eccentric forms of art characterized by "crookedness" and "unpredictability." I have shown how in *Sensō to banpaku* he argues that the Expo, with its "brightness" and "straight lines," constituted a form of repetition of the war. Against this tradition, with its cycles of nationalist aspiration and traumatic defeats, he pits a tradition of anarchist and Dadaist protest and equally traumatic defeats stretching from the Jōmon period, via the earthquake and the missed opportunity for revolution in 1923 to the Dadaist pranks of the 1960s.

With this differentiation of "Japanese" history into a plurality of traditions, Sawaragi is able to solve the issue of whether the "trauma" that brings the "closed circle" into being should be understood as primarily that of the defeat in the war of 1945 or that of the defeat of the protest movements of the 1960s. I have traced back Sawaragi's notion of "bad place" to the sense of closure that followed the defeat of the protest movements of the 1960s, but his preoccupation with the repetition of the lost war and wartime art may appear to fit badly with this finding. The ambiguity is resolved in his more recent writings. Rather than talking simply about a single system traumatically affected by either "1945" or the "1960s," the picture emerges of two separate traditions: one tradition identifying with "Japan" and another resisting such identifications by mustering the forces of the "Japanese archipelago." While "1945" was certainly a traumatic setback for the former, the failure of the protests of the 1960s can be understood as a traumatic setback to the latter.

Neo-pop and schizophrenia

One remaining question is to what extent these two traditions are still effective today. In *Sensō to banpaku* Sawaragi argues that the wartime "sacred war-art" has reappeared a third time in today's "Japanimation," i.e. in the more or less explicit fantasies of national redress and the lingering obsession with the lost war and the fascination with apocalyptic imagery modelled on wartime destruction in much popular culture.[60]

Sawaragi is not entirely dismissive of the treatment of the war in popular culture. In particular, subculture fulfilled an important function in preserving the memory of the war, which was repressed in official art throughout the postwar era. He insists, however, on the need for pop not merely to "reflect" but to probe beyond the surface of consumerist life in order to confront it with its traumatic or "schizophrenic" base – a base which is deeply ambiguous and contains the repressed memories of the war and the shame of living in "America's shadow." Confronting it also means confronting "our monstrosity" and putting the "self-evident" character of the nation at stake. He sees hope for such a "pop of reduction" in the "malicious" or anti-cute Neo-pop that emerges in Japan with the end of the bubble-economy.[61]

The artist who perhaps more than anyone takes on the persona of this politically ambivalent pop is the internationally acclaimed Murakami Takashi. Like Sawaragi, he views Japan as a "claustrophobic" space in which discontent is channelled to pop or internalized instead of being expressed in protest. His art therefore "expresses hopelessness." But there is a limit of endurance. "I think there will be a revolution in Japan within fifty years."[62] Significantly, Murakami models himself on the *otaku*, describing them as a form of outcast from mainstream Japan.[63] His criticism of Japanese society goes hand in hand with a nationalist pride in the "deformed" products of this society, and in particular of the *otaku*-subculture. His stance could be described as the nationalism of a self-proclaimed outcast: "I have the misfortune of having been born in Japan," hence he can't help it if his art "stinks of soy sauce," but unlike most contemporary Japanese art, he is not intent on hiding it.[64]

This outcaste nationalism is manifested in Murakami's 2005 exhibition *Little Boy*, which is his most political statement so far. Taking the mushroom cloud as its central image, it points to the link between *otaku* pop and the trauma of 1945. The exhibition catalogue shows a young boy falling from the sky on the front cover, and the laughing giant face of Doraemon "exploding" on the back cover, suggesting how Japan's popular culture was born from the trauma of defeat – "Little Boy" being the name of the bomb dropped over Hiroshima. Sixty years after the war Japan is at peace, he writes, but an unresolved, largely repressed rage remains: "everyone who lives in Japan knows – something is wrong."[65] The American occupation and postwar dependency forced the nation into a kind of infancy.

> Regardless of winning or losing the war, the bottom line is that for the past sixty years, Japan has been a testing ground for an American-style capitalist economy, protected in a greenhouse, nurtured and bloated to the point of explosion. The results are so bizarre, they're perfect. Whatever true intentions underlie "Little Boy," the nickname for Hiroshima's atomic bomb, we Japanese are truly, deeply, pampered children. And as pampered children, we throw constant tantrums while enthralled by our own cuteness.[66]

Murakami's fundamental gesture is to take pride in this "despised" subculture, reclaiming it creatively. True recovery, he seems to believe, can only come from repeating the trauma, appropriating it actively and thereby transforming oneself from victim to perpetrator. This means that the trauma and its symptom, the *otaku*-culture, must be made into a source of pride. Defiantly he declares that "the time has come to take pride in our art, which is a kind of subculture, ridiculed and deemed 'monstrous' by those in the Western art world."[67] This statement echoes Sawaragi's statement in *Nihon gendai bijutsu* that, seen from the West, all Japanese art is marked by the same "deformity" – that of impossibly aspiring to simultaneity with the West – but rather than accepting the West as the "human" norm and Japan as its deviating "monster," what is at stake is to reveal the "monstrosity" of the West itself.[68] Acknowledging his debt to Sawaragi, Murakami agrees enthusiastically: "We are deformed monsters. We were discriminated against as 'less than human' in the eyes of the 'humans' of the West . . . more than ever, we must pride ourselves on our art, the work of monsters."[69]

This is unabashed nationalism, but of an "underdog" kind, which turns the very ugliness of Japan into a source of pride and thereby subverts the conventional nationalist discourse of Japan as a country of refined culture, harmony or beauty. The "outcaste" nationalism of Murakami – which is shared to some extent by Sawaragi – is clearly not to be confused with right-extremism. Both are deeply critical of the Japanese right. Sawaragi points out that siding with Japanese "monstrosity" does not mean embracing the idea of native "authenticity" or cultural essentialism, which – as he himself points out – in its prolongation may lead to fascism. Rather he tries to undermine the "circle" by looking for its myriad inner tensions and contradictions.[70] Nevertheless, rejecting the "post-war" narrative by dissolving it back into its "schizophrenic" undercurrent is a politically ambiguous operation. Sawaragi is aware of the danger that it may lead to a "kind of reversed nationalism."[71] How does he deal with this risk?

Rescuing the forces of repetition for the revolution

The trauma of "1945" plays a large role in Japanese popular culture, but so does that of the "1960s." For instance, it is often asserted that "cute-culture" emerged from the defeat of the protest movements. As some have argued, "cute" can even be seen as a form of rebellion or continuation of protest.[72] This analysis points to how revolutionary impulses after the defeat were not extinguished but became interiorized, or privatized. According to this diagnosis pop-culture is structurally analogous to a state of trauma. Energies unconsciously working towards a political "recovery" may be at work within it, although repressed or hidden from consciousness. The existence of this possibility is crucial to Sawaragi, since it is precisely because of the continuing legacy of the 1960s in Japanese pop, and the strivings for recovery that accompanies it, that he is able to locate a redeeming potential in this pop. Pop-culture, in other words, cannot simply be viewed as caught up in a single trauma, that of the war, but should rather be seen as an arena in which separate forces compete for recovery. This co-existence of competing legacies explains the curious ambiguity of Murakami Takashi, in which the obsession with "1945" co-exists with a longing for "revolution."

The central question for Sawaragi is how to win over the energies of "bad" repetition of nationalist aspiration and its catastrophic failure to the side of the "good" repetition of crookedness and unpredictability. In a central passage of *Sensō to banpaku* he states that the desire to repeat the trauma of the war needs to be transformed from its "nightmarish" guise in pop-culture into a "revolutionary" form, thereby reviving the lost tradition of radicalism. Perhaps ambiguity is indispensable to such a strategy. Realizing the futility of confronting or criticizing the nationalist discourse too directly, he affirms a risky strategy of mimetically closing in on it in the manner of the Neo-pop artists who distort the images of war by mimicking them. These are all artists who are contemporary with the wave of "Japanimation," but still, he seems to imply, able to subvert it or even transform it into a revolutionary art.[73]

Sawaragi's own anti-war activism can be understood as part of this strategy. What he takes recourse to against the danger of a "repetition" of the war is an alternative tendency at work in pop itself – a pop which blossoms forth in music and street demonstrations, the contemporary form of "crooked" resistance. It should be noted that *Korosuna* is no freer from ambiguity than Neo-pop. Concerning the name of the movement, he explains that a deliberate choice was made to avoid fine-sounding words like "peace." "Peace" is a term all too easily appropriated by propaganda and used to justify wars. Instead, he insists on the brutal directness of the words "do not kill." Observers of *Korosuna*'s demonstrations, however, reported rumours that from time to time the chants "Korosuna" (Do not kill!) were modified to "Korose" (Kill!).[74] Shocks, as Benjamin claimed, help us wake up from our nightmares.

As mentioned, a state of traumatization is not only accompanied by symptomatic repetitions, but also by an orientation, however slight, to recovery. How is Sawaragi's shift towards "praxis" and his discovery of a "good" place in Japan related to the problem of recovery? At first sight, *Korosuna*'s use of music and dancing may seem to indicate a mere symptomatic acting out. His insistence on the need to reconnect to the "schizophrenic" undercurrent of history may also suggest a desire to re-encounter and "repeat" the trauma. However, as Freud points out, even repetitions may further recovery to the extent that they facilitate verbalization. The decisive step is when Sawaragi begins to discern a shape in the "noise" of the schizophrenic historic undercurrent, a shape which comes forward as a differentiated view of the alternative traditions existing on the "Japanese archipelago." Identifying such alternatives only becomes possible through distance, through the freedom opened up when the grip of trauma lessens. As his recent works show, the process whereby the plurality of traditions is recognized is a painstakingly conscious and verbal process and can be compared with how in psychoanalysis one needs to confront one's past and recognize its existence in order to recover. In this sense, it is similar to the verbalization stressed by Freud as an indispensable part of recovery. The drastic changes during the 1990s served as a catalyst in this process: in Sawaragi's case they appear to have weakened the sense of "deadlock" rather than strengthening it, a development reflected in the fact that his preoccupation with the "closed circle" in *Nihon gendai bijutsu* has almost vanished in *Sensō to banpaku*.

Sawaragi's discovery of a plurality of traditions may not be significant historiographically so much as for what it says of how he uses history – remakes it, reinterprets it, or "constructs" it. Such "memory," no matter how constructed, takes on historical force, sometimes even rises to the status of myths that inspire action, including political action. Unlike the "bad" traditionalism which he criticized in *Nihon gendai bijutsu*, Sawaragi's affirmation in recent works of marginal traditions on the "Japanese archipelago" is a traditionalism that helps and encourages "praxis." This is why the notion of Japan as a claustrophobically closed "bad place" fades away in recent writings and why he discovers the street as a "good place."

Notes

1. Around 50,000 people participated. The manifestation was organized by *World Peace Now*, which in turn was made up of 50 civic movements, labor unions and other groups (Mōri 2005). Here I would like to express my gratitude to those who have contributed comments to the text – above all Gunhild Borggren, but also my colleagues in Gothenburg and the participants of the NAJS conference in Lund 2007 and the seminar with Professor Alain Touraine in Kyoto 2008.
2. Background information on *Korosuna* can be found in Mōri, Yoshitaka (2005) "Culture = Politics: the emergence of new cultural forms of protest in the age of *freeter,*" *Inter-Asia Cultural Studies* 6(1): 17–29; Sawaragi Noi (June 2003) "Konnichi no hansen undo" (Anti-war movement today), *Bijutsu techō* 55(835): 47–53; Sawaragi Noi (July 2003) "'Atarashii geijutsu' wa naze Iraku shinkō ni hannō shinakatta no ka?" (Why didn't the "new art" react to the invasion of Iraq?), *Gunzō* 58(7): 334–7; Sawaragi Noi (August 2003), "Kono otoko o korosu na" (Do not kill this man), *Gunzō* 58(8): 338–41.
3. Egon (2003) "Kinkyū kikō: Hansen undō 'Korosu na' no yobikake" (Urgent contribution: the appeal of Korosuna), *Web Dengei*. Online. Available at: http//www.indierom.com/dengei/society/korosuna/korosuna.htm (Accessed 28 June 2006).
4. Sawaragi Noi (2003) *Kuroi taiyō to akai kani – Okamoto Tarō no Nihon* (Black sun and red crab: Okamoto Tarō's Japan), Tokyo: Chūō Kōronsha, p. 254.
5. Ibid., p. 255.

6. Mōri Yoshitaka (2005) "Culture = Politics: the emergence of new cultural forms of protest in the age of *freeter,*" *Inter-Asia Cultural Studies* 6(1): 18.
7. See Sharon Hayashi and Anne McKnight (2005) "Good-bye Kitty, Hello War: The tactics of spectacle and new youth movements in urban Japan," *positions* 13(1): 87–113; and Mōri (2005) "Culture = Politics." For examples of how participants distinguish themselves from older forms of activism, see Egon (2003) "3.21 'Korosu na' demo hōkoku" (A report of *Korosuna's* demonstration on 21 March), *Web Dengei.* Online. Available at: http://www.indierom.com/dengei/society/korosuna/korosuna2.htm (Accessed 23 October 2006) or Sawaragi Noi, "Kono otoko o korosu na" (Do not kill this man), *Gunzō* 58(8) August: 338–41.
8. Mōri (2005) "Culture = Politics," p. 26.
9. Sawaragi, Noi (2003) "Konnichi no hansen undō."
10. Sawaragi, Noi (1998) *Nihon gendai bijutsu* (Contemporary Art of Japan), Tokyo: Shinchōsha.
11. Sawaragi, Noi (2003) *Kuroi taiyō to akai kani*, p. 256.
12. I have discussed the problem of the justifiability of the use of psychoanalytic concepts in cultural analysis elsewhere. (See Carl Cassegard (2007) *Shock and Naturalization in Contemporary Japanese Literature*, Folkestone: Global Oriental.) Here, I will simply assume that the use of such concepts is valid, although it is important to stress two points: first, that it is not the various individual thinkers or writers that are the subject of repression, but rather discursive systems, which become affected in a form analogous to what can be seen in cases of individual traumata. Second, I do not employ the concept of trauma in the sense it is used by theorists such as Alexander (2004) or Eyerman (2001), for whom "cultural trauma" is a fully articulated and publicly constructed "memory" that founds or strengthens collective identity. Such a concept is inapplicable to the defeat of Japanese New Left for two reasons: first, here it led to the weakening or disintegration of collective identity. Second, the fact that their concept of "trauma" is discursively constructed makes it difficult to apply to those situations described by Freud where the trauma remains unverbalized. What gets lost in their account is the dynamics of repression and the problematic of the return of the repressed.
13. For discussions of the "post-1995 phenomenon," *cf.* Carl Cassegard (2007) "Exteriority and Transcritique: Karatani Kōjin and the impact of the 90s," *Japanese Studies* 27(1): 1–18; Katō Norihiro (2004), *Murakami Haruki Ierō pēji pāto 2* (Murakami Haruki Yellow Page Part 2), Tokyo: Arechi shuppansha; Murakami Haruki and Kawai Hayao (1996) *Murakami Haruki, Kawai Hayao ni ai ni iku* (Murakami Haruki goes to see Kawai Hayao), Tokyo: Shinchō bunko, pp. 14–24; Otomo Rio, "A Girl with the Amoebic Body and her Writing Machine," paper presented to the 16th Biennial Conference of the Asian Studies Association of Australia, Wollongong, 26–29 June, 2006. Online. Available at: http://coombs.anu.edu.au/SpecialProj/ASAA/biennial-conference/2006/Otomo-Rio-ASAA2006.pdf (Accessed 7 March, 2007).
14. For the traumatic impact on culture of the defeat of the radical movements of the 1960s in Japan, *cf.* Cassegard (1989) "Exteriority and Transcritique"; Maeda Ai, *Toshi no naka no bungaku* (Literature in the midst of the city), Tokyo: Chikuma shobō 324; Strecher, Matthew (1998) "Beyond 'Pure' Literature: Mimesis, formula, and the postmodern in the fiction of Murakami Haruki," *Journal of Asian Studies* 57(2): 354–78.
15. Murakami Takashi (2005) "Earth in my Window," in Murakami Takashi (ed.) *Little Boy: The Arts of Japan's Exploding Subculture*, New York: Japan Society/New Haven, London: Yale University Press, p. 135.
16. Karatani Kōjin (2002) "Japan is interesting because Japan is not interesting," lecture delivered in March 1997. Online. Available at: http//www.karataniforum.org/jlecture.html (Accessed 19 November 2002).
17. Sigmund Freud (1991) *On Metapsychology: The Theory of Psychoanalysis*, translated under the general editorship of J. Strachey, London: Penguin Books, p. 301.

58   *Carl Cassegard*

18. James Berger (1999) *After the End: Representations of Post-Apocalypse*, Minneapolis: University of Minnesota Press, p. 7.
19. Ōsawa Masachi (2002) "'Zettai no hitei'" e no yokubō" (The desire for an "absolute negation"), *Intercommunication* 41: 60–9.
20. Freud (1991) *On Metapsychology*, p. 288.
21. Ibid., p. 285.
22. In *Moses and Monotheism* Freud again acknowledges the possibly therapeutic effect of "symptomatic" repetitions (although he also states that such attempts at a cure must be complemented by "the work of analysis." Sigmund Freud (1964) "Moses and Monotheism," in J. Strachey (ed.) *The Standard Edition of the Complete Psychological Works of Sigmund Freud*, Vol. 23, London: Hogarth Press, pp. 77–9.
23. Sawaragi Noi (1998) *Nihon gendai bijutsu,* pp. 10–14.
24. Ibid., pp. 12–24; *cf.* Sawaragi Noi (2002) *"Bakushinchi" no geijutsu* (The art of "ground zero"), Tokyo: Shōbunsha, pp. 28–9, 73–4, 222.
25. Ibid., pp. 21–2, 29–31, 189, 197–8.
26. Murakami Haruki, *Hardboiled Wonderland and the End of the World* (tr. of *Sekai no owari to hādoboirudo wandārando* by Alfred Birnbaum), New York: Vintage, 1993, pp. 247–8.
27. Hatanaka Yoshiki (1985) "Sekai to hansekai no yume" (The world and the dream of an anti-world), *Bungakukai* 39: 8, 304–5.
28. Murakami, Haruki (1986) *Chūgoku yuki no surō bōto* (Slow Boat to China), Tokyo: Chūkō bunko, 49–51.
29. For example, Maeda (1989) *Toshi no naka no bungaku,* p. 397.
30. Karatani Kōjin (1993) *Origins of Modern Japanese Literature*, Durham & London: Duke University Press, p. 39.
31. Karatani Kōjin (1989) "One Spirit, Two Nineteenth Centuries," in M. Miyoshi and H. D. Harootunian (eds) *Postmodernism and Japan*, Durham: Duke University Press, p. 272.
32. Murakami Haruki (1991) *Dansu, dansu, dansu* (Dance, Dance, Dance), vol. I, Tokyo: Kōdansha bunko, p. 114.
33. Hirai Gen gives a vivid account of the destructive effect that this development had on the self-confidence of the New Left in Japan. Hirai Gen (2005) *Mikkī Mausu no puroretaria sengen* (Mickey Mouse's proletarian manifesto), Tokyo: Ōta shuppan, pp. 13–18.
34. Sawaragi Noi (2002) *Bakushinchi no geijutsu*, pp. 74, 316–18.
35. Ibid., p. 224f.
36. Sawaragi Noi (2005) *Sensō to banpaku* (World wars and world fairs), Tokyo: Bijutsu Shuppansha, p. 68.
37. Yoshikuni Igarashi (2000) *Bodies of Memory: Narratives of war in postwar Japanese culture, 1945–1970*, Princeton & Oxford: Princeton University Press, pp. 16, 132–43.
38. The Expo "repeated" the planned "The 2600-years Jubilee World Exposition," which was planned to be held in 1940 as well as the proposal of a "Greater East Asian Co-prosperity Fair" in 1942.
39. In the case of Asada and Metabolism, Sawaragi argues that the "brightness" of their art originates in the experience of bombed city-ruins. Sawaragi Noi (2005) *Sensō to banpaku*, pp. 26–8.
40. Sawaragi Noi (2005) *Sensō to banpaku*, pp. 62–3, 105.
41. "Anti-Expo" artists included members of groups such as *Bikyōtō* or *Zero Jigen* and other artists associated with Neo-Dada.
42. The man in the tower was baptized the "eyeball man" (*medama otoko*) in the press. His real name was Satō Hideo, a young activist in the *Beheiren* movement. Borggren, Gunhild (2006) "Ruins of the Future: Yanobe Kenji revisits Expo '70," *Performance Paradigm*, Vol. 2.
43. Sawaragi Noi (1998) *Nihon gendai bijutsu*, pp. 178, 181–2.

44. Sawaragi Noi (2005) *Senso to banpaku*, pp. 216–17.
45. The expression "exposure to the wind" (*nozarashi*) has connotations of a naked skull exposed on the ground and is often associated with the classic *haiku*-poet Bashō.
46. Sawaragi Noi (2005) *Senso to banpaku*, pp. 234–5.
47. Ibid., pp. 226–36.
48. Ibid., p. 224.
49. Ibid., p. 223.
50. Quoted in Okamoto Toshiko (2004) "Okamoto Tarō to 'Korosu na'" (Okamoto Tarō and "Do not kill"), interview by Mizuguchi Yoshirō, *Shimin no iken 30 no kai,* No. 86.
51. Quoted in Ozaki Tetsuya (2005) "Korosu na haku" (Do not kill expo), *Out of Tokyo* 108. Online. Available at: http:www.realtokyo.co.jp/japanese/column/ozaki108.htm (Accessed 1 October 2006).
52. Sawaragi Noi (1998) *Nihon gendai bijutsu*, pp. 312, 317–18.
53. Sawaragi Noi (2003) *Kuroi taiyō to akai kani*, p. 11.
54. Sawaragi Noi (1998) *Nihon gendai bijutsu*, pp. 296–9.
55. Quoted in *Taro* (2004) Kawasakishi Okamoto Tarō Bijutsukan, Tokyo: Nigensha, p. 58.
56. Sawaragi Noi (2003) *Kuroi taiyō to akai kani*, p. 191.
57. Sawaragi Noi (2005) *Senso to banpaku*, pp. 281–7.
58. Sawaragi Noi (2003) *Kuroi taiyō to akai kani*, p. 246.
59. Ibid., pp. 118–20.
60. Sawaragi Noi (2005) *Senso to banpaku*, p. 65.
61. Sawaragi Noi (2008) *Nihon gendai bijutsu*, pp. 95–8; Sawaragi Noi (2005) "On the Battlefield of 'Superflat: Subculture and art in postwar Japan,'" pp. 186–207, in Murakami Takashi, ed. *Little Boy: The Arts of Japan's Exploding Subculture*, New York: Japan Society/New Haven, London: Yale University Press, p. 200.
62. Murakami Takashi (2006) "Takashi Murakami," interview by Mako Wakasa, *Journal of Contemporary Art*. Online. Available at: http//www.jca-online.com/murakami.html (Accessed 13 February 2006).
63. Murakami Takashi (2001) *Summon monsters? Open the door? Heal? or Die?*, Tokyo: Kaikaikiki Co. Ltd., p. 137; Murakami Takashi (2006) "Takashi Murakami" interview; Murakami Takashi (2005) "Earth in my Window," pp. 98–149, in Murakami, ed. *Little Boy*, p. 161.
64. Ibid., p. 130.
65. Murakami Takashi (2005) "Earth in my Window," p. 100.
66. Ibid., p. 141.
67. Murakami Takashi (2005) "Superflat Trilogy," in Murakami (ed.) *Little Boy*, p. 161.
68. Sawaragi Noi (1998) *Nihon gendai bijutsu*, pp. 16–17.
69. Murakami Takashi (2005) "Superflat Trilogy," p. 161.
70. Sawaragi Noi (1998) *Nihon gendai bijutsu*, pp. 19–25.
71. Quoted in Murakami Takashi (2005) "Superflat Trilogy," p. 161.
72. Sharon Kinsella (1995) "Cuties in Japan," pp. 220–54, in L. Skov and B. Moeran (eds) *Women Media and Consumption in Japan*, London: Curzon Press, pp. 220–54. Aoyagi, Hiroshi (2003) "Pop Idols and Gender Contestation," in D. Edgington (ed.) *Japan at the Millennium: Joining Past and Future*, Vancouver, Toronto: UBC Press, pp. 144–67.
73. Sawaragi Noi (2005) *Senso to banpaku*, pp. 158, 160.
74. Machida Kō (2003) "Official Machida Kou Website," diary entry for 10 May 2003. Online. Available at: http://www.machidakou.com/diary/diary-200305.html (Accessed 24 June 2007). Ozaki Tetsuya (2003) "Kono sensō, kore kara no sensō" (This war has just begun), *Out of Tokyo* 59. Online. Available at: http//www.realtokyo.co.jp/japanese/column/ozaki59.htm (Accessed 1 October 2006).

3   Introduction

Yutaka Nagahara: The corporeal principles of the national polity . . .

Jacques Lacan wrote: "*The* woman can only be written with the *The* crossed through. There is no such thing as *The* woman, where the definite article stands for the universal . . . A woman is a symptom."[1] For Luce Irigaray, not only does woman "not exist," but as nature she is use-value, and commodified as exchange value between men.[2] Yutaka Nagahara's essay takes these theoretical arguments, among others, as its foundation to show how various tropings of women in national identity function as metaphors for men's "place of departure to which there can be no return." In other words, woman-as-symptom makes possible male self-identity as such, and sexual violence against women is the "origin of social relations." "The Corporeal Principles of the National Polity" traces the fluid and shifting metaphoric uses of gender within national and nationalist imaginaries. Nagahara's primary illustrative texts are the 1937 Japanese Ministry of Education's nationalist tract *Kokutai no hongi* (*Cardinal Principles of the National Polity*), and a *manga* entitled *Nihonjin no wakusei* (*Planet of the Japs*), that reverses the fortunes of the aftermath of the Second World War, depicting the Japanese as the victors and Americans the losers. Employing the term rape both literally and figuratively, and as the monologue between men positioning femaleness as territory as well as mediation, Nagahara shows how the rapes depicted in *Planet of the Japs* – of the Statue of Liberty and of an American woman – "cover up" a *repressed* rape, that of America's rape of Japan as victor of the Second World War and as occupier. Within this framework, Nagahara explores homosociality, homophobia, and women's position as property, her body as territory, and the shifting metaphoric femaleness as interior/border, positing an unconscious homophobia at the core of the Japanese failure to re-act to the historical fact of their *failure* or *loss* of the Second World War (as the symptom) repressed in the mis-labeling of the loss of the war as the "end of the war." The repression of the fact of having raped in the Second World War, alongside having been raped, are hence symptoms that "return."

Notes

1. Jacques Lacan (1982) "God and the *Jouissance* of ~~The~~ Woman," and "Seminar of 21 January 1975," both in *Feminine Sexuality: Jacques Lacan and the école freudienne*, Jacqueline Rose (trans.) New York: W. W. Norton, pp. 144, 168.
2. Luce Irigaray (1985) *This Sex Which is not One*, Catherine Porter and Carolyn Burke (trans.) Ithaca: Cornell University Press.

3 The corporeal principles of the national polity

The rhetoric of the body of the nation, or the state as memory-apparatus

Yutaka Nagahara – translated by Gavin Walker

> L'homme la recherche donc de l'avoir inscrire dans
> le discours, mais comme manque, comme faille.
>
> Luce Irigaray, *This Sex Which is Not One*[1]

The symptom

I would like to exploit the notion of the *symptom* in order to think Japan's so-called postwar, through a close cross-reading of two specifically connected materials – Maruo Suehiro's violent *manga* which bears the aggressive title *Planet of the Jap* and the so-called *Kokutai no hongi* (*Cardinal Principles of the National Polity/National Body*, published in 1937 by the Ministry of Education [Monbushō]). This notion of the symptom, here, is exactly what is paraphrased as follows by Slavoj Žižek when he positively refers to Eric Santner's reading of Walter Benjamin's *Theses on the Philosophy of History*. Žižek quotes from Santner:

> [S]ymptoms register not only past failed revolutionary attempts but, more modestly, past failures to respond to calls for actions . . . They hold the place of something that is there, that insists in our life, though it has never achieved full ontological consistency. Symptoms are thus in some sense the virtual archives of voids – or, perhaps, better, defenses against voids – that persist in historical experience.[2]

Immediately after this quotation, he proceeds to write:

> . . . [A] present revolutionary intervention repeats/redeems the past failed attempts: the "symptoms" – [that is] past traces which are retroactively redeemed through the "miracle" of the revolutionary intervention – are "not so much forgotten deeds, but rather forgotten failures to act, failures to suspend the force of social bond inhibiting acts of solidarity with society's 'others'". . .

With the addition of certain historical connotations, I fully share his standpoint. I would like to retroactively re-member, or re-deem, or re-trieve (in the sense of *retrouver*) the "historical experience," that is, "our" internalized failure to act as well as re-act: our defeat which is other than, yet closely associated with, the defeat of the Japanese Empire in 1945. It is in order for me to be able not only to understand postwar Japan but also to be "responsable de" or "répondre à" the recent anti-Japan movements that emerged throughout the Asian countries as a result of the visits to the Yasukuni Shrine by former Prime Minister Koizumi Junichiro, especially in China and Korea. However, I do not use these French terms without reason; rather, I would like to highlight that retroactive responsibility which haunts us, yet is disavowed. In other words, I would like to draw attention to the fact that, if Jacques Derrida is correct, it is justice which is the last thing that cannot be deconstructed. I move first to the analysis of Maruo's *manga*.

Through the defeat in the Second World War, the "pure" Japanese people wanted to forget the fact that this imperialist, colonialist nation-state called "Japan" was itself so quickly occupied and colonized. This is one of the reasons that they have continued to refer to the events of August 15, 1945 as the "end of the war" rather than as a "defeat." This amnesiac desire is spurred on by homophobia. Of course, it is possible, indeed even necessary, to locate the postwar period in its various continuities with the prewar. But we cannot negate the fact that it was initiated by the discontinuity, or break, of the defeat. Nevertheless, people are forgetting this break, or perhaps more importantly, *re*-remembering it. Such a retrospective *re*-writing of memory, in both a positive and negative sense, is perhaps a description of "history" itself. But we must be aware that precisely because of the characteristics of such a description of history, a "pure" Japanese history that is *re*-remembered on the basis of a "pure" Japanese people will of course be forced into the place of refutation and judgment. And this refutation is placed, indeed it must be placed, not within a so-called "scientific truthfulness" but rather within politicality. Thus, such refutation and judgment must be undertaken by the actual others produced by this impossible "pure" Japanese history on the basis of the impossible "pure" Japanese people. Irrespective of the interior and exterior of this nation-state, this break cannot be forgotten, or to put it more accurately, it was continually questioned by the people of the present day, who recognize that they must not forget it, as they think through these two connected senses of violence that are war and the nation-state. The essential task for me now is to intervene independently in this questioning – that is, precisely within the "postcolonial" condition of the nation-state called Japan.

Let us say that the major function of the mnemo-technics/tectonics of national history is to forget the fact of "having raped" together with the fact of "having been raped." Or perhaps it is a forgetting of "having been raped" with "having raped." This mnemo-technics/tectonics is the essential device through which the national people (*kokumin*) must be granted the status of the "true people" of the history of the state (national history). If only to *re*-state this, it is the desire of the nation-as-state (*kokumin to iu kokka*). I will attempt to think this question through a "reading" of the Ministry of Education's *Kokutai no hongi* (*Cardinal Principles of the National Polity*) from a certain political viewpoint, specifically from the viewpoint of the vulnerability/instability of masculinity. Through this process, I would like to repeat only one political fact.

Before entering into a reading of the *Cardinal Principles*, however, I feel the need to take two detours. The first detour is into the simple but odd vision of the bizarre illustrator Suehiro Maruo's work *Planet of the Jap* (*Nihonjin no wakusei*).[3] This detour appears as a probability. The second detour is a confirmation of the political problematic that supports this vision. This detour appears as a necessity.

The dismal dream of the raped man: three rapes

Adorned with an initial image of a Japanese "man" straddling a tank with pre-cum dripping from the gun barrel (Figure 3.1), *Planet of the Jap* is a parody of *Planet of the Apes*. The story is so obvious, and moreover simplistic, as to not require a "reading."

It is a "dream" in which, after the surprise attacks on Pearl Harbor (December 8, 1941), Japan goes triumphantly from victory to victory, dropping nuclear bombs on Los Angeles (August 6, 1945) (Figure 3.2) and San Francisco (August 9, 1945), and defeats the United States. This phantasmal invasion of the USA begins with a scene in which Tōjō Hideki, just like MacArthur, descends from an airplane

Figure 3.1 Soldier straddling cannon, Maruo Suehiro "*Nihonjin no wakusei*" (*Planet of the Jap*) in Maruo Suehiro, *Paranoia Sutā*, Kawade Shobō Shinsha, 1986, 117–44. Kawade Shobō © Suehiro Maruo.

Figure 3.2 Atomic bombing of Los Angeles, Maruo Suehiro "*Nihonjin no wakusei*" (*Planet of the Jap*) in Maruo Suehiro, *Paranoia Sutā*, Kawade Shobō Shinsha, 1986, 117–44. Kawade Shobō © Suehiro Maruo.

(Figure 3.3), carrying a sword instead of a corn-cob pipe. He lands ready for battle, suggesting at the very outset that he has not yet been victorious.

It must be said that in *Planet of the Jap* two rapes are prepared – one symbolic, the other depicted as a "fact." Their common feature is that they are both first and foremost rapes of the "mother." But these two rapes are animated by the suppression of another rape.

First rape: the destroyed lower body of the Statue of Liberty (Figure 3.4). This destruction of her lower body is depicted in tandem with the destruction of her left hand. In her destroyed left hand is meant to be the sealed Declaration of Independence, of July 4, 1776.

> Long live death!
> The freedom of
> The United States of America
> Like a whore defiled
> By the bubonic plague

Why was it necessary to destroy the Statue of Liberty's left hand? It is the site wherein the "independence" of the USA was declared and signed. To paraphrase Derrida, this is where America itself is located, wherein its origins are declared through the signature, thus the destruction of the left hand is essentially the destruction of the USA as it exists within its own origins.

Why was it necessary to destroy the lower half of the Statue of Liberty's body? Undoubtedly because the Statue of Liberty was made into the

Figure 3.3 Tojo Hideki landing on U.S. soil, Maruo Suehiro *"Nihonjin no wakusei"* (*Planet of the Jap*) in Maruo Suehiro, *Paranoia Sutā*, Kawade Shobō Shinsha, 1986, 117–44. Kawade Shobō © Suehiro Maruo.

Figure 3.4 Destruction of the Statue of Liberty, Maruo Suehiro *"Nihonjin no wakusei"* (*Planet of the Jap*) in Maruo Suehiro, *Paranoia Sutā*, Kawade Shobō Shinsha, 1986, 117–44. Kawade Shobō © Suehiro Maruo.

symbol of the national unity of the United States. Many immigrants passed through her lower body, coming to America to seek freedom and their dreams so-called, and thereby forming the nationality of the United States as a state – "she" was the symbol of this mythology.[4] Consequently, the destruction of her lower body is the symbolic rape of the United States, and at the same time its "feminization." Why did she have to be raped? Because she is a woman. Why did she have to be deliberately "feminized"? Because she appears phallically. But in relation to who? In relation to "Japan."

But this courteous Statue of Liberty is also a prostitute, because she charges admission for people to enter her lower body, and allows them to explore her womb (since "9.11" this has been permanently closed). She is a prostitute who takes money to "open her body."[5] Lauren Berlant explains that in order to construct a framework in which the subject is annexed into the "a priori structures of power," the Statue of Liberty as symbol of the nation is used/exploited, "through the national genitalia of our national prostitute."[6] The lower body, in other words the "national genitalia" of the Statue of Liberty, this nationally-sacred woman/mother who is at the same time a national prostitute, is subjected to a torrent of abuse and degradation about death, the bubonic plague, called a whore, and then is ultimately destroyed, along with the declaration and signature which give this adjective "national" to her genitals. Luce Irigaray states as follows:

> The *prostitute* remains to be considered. Explicitly condemned by the social order, she is implicitly tolerated. No doubt because the break between usage and exchange is, in her case, less clear-cut? In her case, the qualities of woman's body are "useful." However, these qualities have "value" only because they have already been appropriated by a man, and because they serve as the locus of relations – hidden ones – between men. The woman's body is valuable . . . not because its natural assets have been put to use this way, but on the contrary, because its nature has been "used up," and has become once again no more than a vehicle for relations among men.[7]

In speaking of the prostitute, Irigaray shows that in a heteronormative society woman is a commodity, and even if not yet commodified, will sooner or later at some point be commodified, and thereby calls into question the entire rhetoric surrounding the national role of the woman – prostitute, mother, virgin; or say "Immaculate Conception."

The Statue of Liberty, as symbol of the nation-as-state in the United States, is sacralized within her core, and simultaneously accepts defilement and degradation (a symbolic clitoridectomy!). This is the central point of the rhetoric which posits the male co-ownership of the woman through the mediation of her body. But there is a problem here which neither Marvin Trachtenberg nor Berlant touch upon. That is, the question of precisely where it is that "she" receives this defilement and degradation. We can seek an answer in the fact that "she" overlooks Ellis Island, which receives the majority of immigrants, that is, in the fact that she stands at the very boundary, or the edge, of the nation-as-state.

The Statue of Liberty is simultaneously symbolized as sacred internally, while she is critically defiled in the boundary-edge. Through the destruction of the lower body/genitals of this "sacred prostitute," Maruo attempts with a single stroke to depict the drive for revenge against something. We have already seen what this certain something is. But originally, what is rape? It is violence. The masculine noun *viol* is nothing other than rape itself.

The first rape/violence precisely reveals the structure of rape understood in this sense. These various rapes are preceded retroactively by an infinite existence of other rapes from which they are derived. The "conversation" between men which is the repetition of revenge for the majority of rapes, is itself a rape. This conversation is repeated as the rhetorical mediation of the female body as a hidden vehicle owned by the male. The destruction of the raped lower body of the Statue of Liberty is the object of desire of the nation-as-state mediated by the female body.

The object of the second rape is the mother who protects the "home" (Figures 3.5 and 3.6). This mother is violated and degraded before the very eyes of her "husband" (*shujin*) and "son."

While in the midst of this violation, the Japanese soldiers sing a song from the Ministry of Education:

Japan
A good nation
A strong nation
A great nation
Shining
Throughout the world

The mother who protects the home must be raped in front of her husband and son. It is revenge against her husband and his bequeathed (son), an ostentatious violation of his property that is intended to be seen. As the child of the mother, the son is completely, physically destroyed. On the other hand, the husband is not raped, but merely beaten; at least his death is not suggested. Why? Because if he does not see his property violated and degraded, this revenge will not be complete. Property without an owner cannot exist. The men (soldiers) who are supposed to phallically confront each other during the exchange process of war must be present at the scene of the assault on their "property." To put it once more, this mother, as a non-virginal woman who is the property of a certain man, is destroyed as a reproduction device, and pillaged as a territory. The wife/mother as a use-value which prohibits exchange is the territory of the male, the reproduction device of this male. This is precisely why she must be violated before the very eyes of her owner.

Rape. It is a "weapon of revenge" against men, or an "infringement on other men's "property.""[8] Because of this, these two rapes themselves already disclose the following: the rape/defeat of Japan.

The form of the comfortable "big man" (MacArthur) and the uneasy, anxious "little man" (Hirohito) standing side by side was splashed across the top page of every newspaper dated September 29, 1945. This problematic photo, designed to suppress

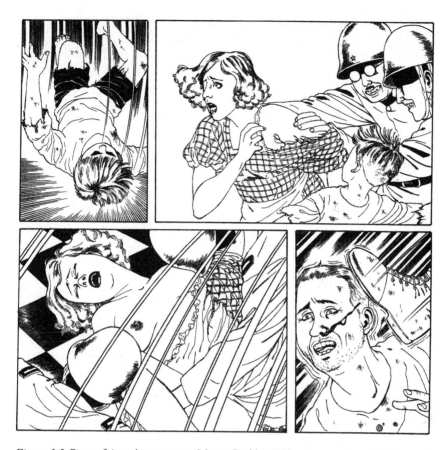

Figure 3.5 Rape of American woman, Maruo Suehiro *"Nihonjin no wakusei"* (*Planet of the Jap*) in Maruo Suehiro, *Paranoia Sutā*, Kawade Shobō Shinsha, 1986, 117–44. Kawade Shobō © Suehiro Maruo.

Figure 3.6 Two frames of rape of American woman, Maruo Suehiro *"Nihonjin no wakusei"* (*Planet of the Jap*) in Maruo Suehiro, *Paranoia Sutā*, Kawade Shobō Shinsha, 1986, 117–44. Kawade Shobō © Suehiro Maruo.

any feelings of strife, is the first page of postwar history. As one of the creators of the *Cardinal Principles of the National Polity*, Kihira Tadayoshi argued, "Japan has never lost even once in battle," that is, he boasts that Japan's virginity was intact,[9] but thus the defeat itself was the "mother who is a virgin," the "mother of god," but at the same time the rape of "the woman who has given birth to the Creator" – as a result the defeat becomes a realization of its own forgetting by those who cannot accept it.[10] Thus control blends together with sexuality, but the point at which it blends together is the point at which the violence of rape comes to a sudden boil.[11]

The feminized United States of America depicted by Maruo, the United States which is dying of the bubonic plague and thus disfigured, this statue of "liberty, the national symbol of the United States," the rape or the destruction of the genitals of this "Statue of Liberty," the national symbol of the United States, the "Great Japanese Empire," and thus the Emperor (*tennō*), the owner of the proper name scrawled on her right arm as it holds aloft the torch, suggests to the abused male, or to the phallic Statue of Liberty, that she has already been raped.

The Japanese soldiers, who continue pillaging while singing of this "good nation," this "strong nation," and this "great nation shining throughout the world" however, are already conscious of themselves as a feminized penis. The drive that spurs on these Japanese soldiers is a mediating "dream of retribution" against the fact of already having been castrated, a fear of being further castrated. Rape desires sacrifice in this crisis of boundaries. In order for the defeat of exchange in peacetime, metaphorized as the "legitimate exchange" or "generative rite" of "matrimony," to be (re)adjusted, the "violent theft" or "dangerous transgression" is required.[12] The essence of the peaceful exchange which makes the woman the mediation of exchange makes the self manifest itself violently in the crisis of the transgression of boundaries. The rhetoric of the conversation between men desires these "social roles imposed on women" as "mother, virgin, prostitute," depending on the circumstances, but the conclusion is always that these women will continue to be the objects of rape/revenge.[13] These social roles are constantly emerging as roles required by the nation-state.

Rape is the male "monologue" surrounding the "invisible woman."[14] But this invisible woman is made invisible precisely through the metaphorical volatility/annihilation of the female body that guarantees the contiguous flow between the metonymically suspended men. Thus even in as much as rape appears as a monologue, it is also the infinite chain of conversations between men that make the female body their mediation, or negotiation. The interlocutor who addresses him when the man speaks to himself is split, another "him." He is, in addressing the (m)other, the *invisible wo*man within the interior – and at the origin – of the split subject, ensuring the continuity of this conversation between men. This *invisible wo*man is the mother, separated here from the son.

The gaze and the decapitation

The anxiety and fear of castration is further depicted in Maruo's work. At the place of execution, we see the decapitated head of MacArthur (Figures 3.7 and 3.8), the

Figure 3.7 The public execution of
General MacArthur, Maruo Suehiro
"*Nihonjin no wakusei*" (*Planet of the Jap*)
in Maruo Suehiro, *Paranoia Sutā*,
Kawade Shobō Shinsha, 1986, 117–44.
Kawade Shobō © Suehiro Maruo.

Figure 3.8 McArthur's beheading, Maruo
Suehiro "*Nihonjin no wakusei*" (*Planet of
the Jap*) in Maruo Suehiro, *Paranoia Sutā*,
Kawade Shobō Shinsha, 1986, 117–44.
Kawade Shobō © Suehiro Maruo.

phallus of the United States of America. Decapitation is castration – it forces us to once again recall the hidden rapes of the past.

At the site of execution, MacArthur is allowed to keep his sunglasses on while he is decapitated. "We'll let you keep the glasses on." In this statement we can see the entirety of postwar Japan. By shielding the eyes of the decapitated person, these sunglasses are a mechanism of concealment for the "pure" Japanese, who prays for relief from the injuries suffered in this dream, from the pain of the memory of being decapitated (castrated). This aggressive phallicism comes to a sudden boil once more through the feminized male, the feminine phallus. The nation's shame/rape (辱), presented by this Emperor-system fascist, is forgotten, and must be purified. Consequently, the object that should be sanctified, obeyed, organized is remembered – negatively recalled (*souvenir*) – as what Nietzsche termed "reaction."

But this dreaming executioner is incapable of looking MacArthur in the eyes. This is because the act of seeing is also an act of being seen – this is the way in which the postwar US–Japan relationship has been instituted. It is this doubled bi-partition through which the gaze is instituted,[15] or the reversibility of the gaze that grounds this "doubled perception"[16] and gives to the dreaming executioner his visible body. The executioner's visible body is what "conditions the gaze itself."[17] MacArthur's eyes make possible the perception of the visible body of the executioner. This is what the decapitator fears in his dream. MacArthur's decapitated head shows us that in fact, this executioner's head has itself already been severed.

The two rapes and the preceding hidden rape that is their genesis. The severed head of MacArthur, the perpetrator of the hidden rape. The refusal of the exchange of gazes between the executioner and the decapitated phallus, MacArthur. In the wake of the decapitation, the proud voice of the executioner accompanies the positionality of the object of orgasmic desire, thus an ejaculation that can never be released and the displeasure and pleasure, anxiety and ecstasy of the executioner (Figure 3.9). Traced around the edges of this dream is the anxiety of castration and revenge for having been castrated. The executioner in this dream deeply feels the sense that it is the male – the nation-state called Japan – who is the already-awake object of rape. It is the rape of the male-as-virgin who has "never once lost in battle."

Figure 3.9 Japanese soldier ejaculating, Maruo Suehiro "*Nihonjin no wakusei*" (*Planet of the Jap*) in Maruo Suehiro, *Paranoia Sutā*, Kawade Shobō Shinsha, 1986, 117–44. Kawade Shobō © Suehiro Maruo.

The dream is nothing more than an attempt to ease the pain he feels upon waking and finding himself once again "fucked over."

Yet there are "two things that cannot be represented" that we must take up here: "death and the female sex." They "need femininity to be associated with death."[18] When Freud identifies the Medusa's power to turn men to stone, a power which nevertheless refuses to be named, the prior violence which grounds this, the repeated first sacrifice, can be represented as rape. What is prior about this prior violence is that the male is already killing her, sacrificing her by turning her into stone.[19] To defend against castration, the decapitator "stiffens himself"[20] with an erection, and massively ejaculates at the same time as he cuts off MacArthur's head. Even though the executioner has shielded himself from MacArthur's gaze, he already has an erection, that is, he has already been turned to stone.

What, and moreover, whom does this dreaming executioner desire? He already sees something and desires someone beyond MacArthur. That is the Emperor (or rather, his image), who appears at the very end, enveloped in flowers (Figure 3.10), a beautiful woman disguised as a man (like Takarazuka). The words that emerge in tandem with the Emperor's appearance paradoxically show us Maruo's bodily comprehension of the nation's defeat. Maruo is laughing when he depicts this dream.

Japan, this raped man. His dark reversed fantasy. One absence exists here, a conspicuous absence. That is the secret within the origin: the fact that while sexual violence against women is the origin of social relations, at the same time, this sexual violence comes to be "omitted" or "erased" from social relations precisely through this violence itself.[21] He is "suspended" between the fantasy of conquest (rape) and the fear of being surrounded or laid siege to (castration).[22] However, is this dark dream not the "suspension" supporting the basis of every nation-as-state? This type of fantasy must be continually cathected into the body in order to give continuity to the nation-as-state, which is originally discontinuous. This type of operation can be confirmed in 1930s Japan. What we will see in the theories of the "national polity/national body" (*kokutai*) that we will examine from here onwards, is the rhetoric of the nation-state in the crisis of the transgression of its boundaries. But it is my duty to perform yet another detour here, to think the question of masculinity while discussing the rhetoric of the woman.

Figure 3.10 Emperor on horse back, Maruo Suehiro "*Nihonjin no wakusei*" (*Planet of the Jap*) in Maruo Suehiro, *Paranoia Sutā*, Kawade Shobō Shinsha, 1986, 117–44. Kawade Shobō © Suehiro Maruo.

T(r)opology of the "Anti-"

At the outset, it is not only that the nation-as-state is imagined (declared)/ "ruled and firmed up" (*shurikosei*)[23] – but precisely because it is, it is continuously, ceaselessly imagined in order to give a semblance of continuity to a history which is originally discontinuous – it is a fantasy that must be conferred and legitimated.[24] In his *Kojiki-den*, Moto'ori Norinaga reads the phrase 天地初発之時 as "the time of the beginning of heaven and earth" (*tenchi no hajime no toki*) and not as "when it first developed." In relation to this, the scholar Morishige Satoshi evaluates him highly, arguing that this is because Moto'ori does not seek "creation" within a notion of "generative origin" but rather in the "beginning of the world on the level of principles" that is, in the sense that Moto'ori discovered the "logical structure of self-awareness."[25] Such a self-awareness and declaration of the level of principles can only actually become a principle by being ceaselessly, and thus, repeatedly and continually imagined. But the problem is not only the question of this sort of mnemonic device, but what must be called its particularized style, the structure of its rhetoric or its persuasiveness.

> They seized her [India] and possessed her, but it was the possession of violence. They did not know her or try to know her. They never looked into her eyes, for theirs were averted and hers downcast through shame and humiliation.[26]

In this one verse, in which the unspeakable domestic violence of the contrast between the manly colonizer and the graceful, chaste colonized, or between the virgin (earth) and her violent deflowering by the rapist is proleptically dramatized, and resounds with cries of obsequiousness and flattery, all the metaphorical-rhetorical operations surrounding imperialism (colonialism) and anti-colonialism, that is, nationalism, are functioning. Plunder = appropriation, rape = violence, body = territory, the eye and the gaze, shyness and humiliation, reconciliation or revenge. In this one verse, these ceaselessly expanding rhetorical sequences are organized and continue to operate.

Sara Suleri quotes this verse from Jawaharlal Nehru, and points out that the homology of "male – subject – colonizer" and "female – object – colonized," and the rhetorical images surrounding the incongruous and widely mobilized dual, hierarchical oppositions of a metonymically suspended and groundless equality,[27] persistently intertwine with and haunt the metaphors of the nationalist resistance strategies of anti-imperialism and anti-colonialism. That is, Suleri critiques the homoerotic complicity of colonizer and colonized, the rhetoric that conceals the events that obscenely materialize in the Malabar Caves – what does this cave, this *grotto* (or *grotesque*) symbolize? It is a warning against the "extremely dangerous zone" of "cultural belonging," a warning against the ease with which gender is brought into the relation of the colonizer–colonized.

Emphasizing her differences with so-called essentialism to cast doubt on Edward Said's definition of cultural identities as "contrapuntal ensembles,"[28] she critiques the structural and fundamental danger inhabiting his rhetorical revisions:

> The common language of imperialism thus perpetuates itself through what seeks to be an opposing methodology, suggesting that the continued equation between a colonized landscape and the female body represents an alteritist fallacy that causes considerable theoretical damage to both contemporary feminist and postcolonial discourses.[29]

The language of imperialism/colonialism and the resistant language of the nationalist "anti-" represent the same crime in as much as they both utilize (exploit) the rhetoric surrounding the female body. It is an exploitation in the sense that it accompanies the language of exchange, and a ceaseless expropriation in the sense that a material (bodily) extraction is concealed. While they are profoundly opposed to each other, precisely in the process of opposition they meet and learn a common language, thereby exchanging and becoming "exchangists" (*échangiste* in the sense of *échangisme*, or "swinging"). This common language is nothing more than the "allegorization" of colonial control through the image of the female body, the symbol of the "female geography" as "map of the world."[30] Through the formation/organization of this discourse in which is crystallized the "geography" of sexuality, the letters of various "national languages," the letters of various languages of the national (body), remain multiply and profoundly inscribed on the female body. On the "earth" (地) the "picture" (図) is drawn. The map (地-図) thus drawn on the female body in fact inverts the female body into the placenta – this "flat cake" – of the "technology of imperial form."[31] This is the moment at which "national language" turns simultaneously towards the exterior and interior of the state, and becomes, for example "Japanese," or "English."

She is the "mother" of the nation as imaginary, but this "she" is merely a womb. She shoulders the burden of reproducing the group boundaries of the nation as imaginary, delineating and transmitting culture. While she is fixed in her existence as a type of collateral for "the privileged signifiers of national difference,"[32] she is always-already being disavowed. As a consequence, this is the site of the feminine, whose body is fragmentarily plundered, dispossessed of experience, and presented with death.

Imperialism (colonialism) and its "anti-" organizes people into "nations" – sometimes completely otherizing them as a heterogeneous or inferior "indigenous" segment of the occupying nation, but even if "merely" internally otherized as heterogeneous or inferior, this process of othering is maliciously concealed within the occupying nation under the rubrics of, for instance, "universal brotherhood" (*isshi dōjin*) or "Japan and Korea as one body" (*naisen ittai*) – simultaneously reducing the female body to a rhetorical/political placenta (nourishment), violently extracting its own concreteness from her. But a further problem is the question of the mechanisms operating in this site of power. The first mechanism is the ideal of the "original" nation; the second is the formation and struggle over the gathering symbols required for its emergence. We should emphasize here the problem contained in the word "symbol" (etymologically "to throw together") itself. That is, the problem of the polymerization between the female body and these uncanny symbols, blazing with the fire of the occupying state, in which we can see that the "outward-looking state" and the "inward-looking state," while seemingly in opposition, are in fact two cooperative directionalities of power.[33]

We must read into the term "symbol" this switch between the sexual, sensual, and destinal gathering (*Versammlung*) of the chance encounter, or "nimble production" – "eating together," "sexual intercourse," the homogeneous "collection, fabrication" of the work (type) – in this mixture of meanings of reproduction. In order for the chance encounter in the boundary to be seen as a destiny, the symbol, which draws along in its wake the nation as gathering, desires "continuity and immutability" in its center, the chaste guardian of "respectability," the "immobile silence" which guarantees the "positive site of national power and fantasy." There is a simultaneous demand for the rhetoric of the female body both in the boundary and in the center in order to symbolize the desire of the nation-as-state. The body of the chaste woman is desired and mediates exchange precisely because it is both fatal and alluring.[34] Thus the common language, while constructing the external and internal other (ecto- and endo- other), simultaneously takes on the role of the forgery of the homogeneity of the nation-as-state.

Thus this rhetoric, from the outset of its formation, ceaselessly demands these symbols sought in and split off from the bi-locational, bi-typical antipodal functions of the "dynamic encounter" in the boundary, and the "immobility and silence" of the center. Despite being pregnant with the crisis of the disintegration of the center/boundary binary, it is at the same time a ceaseless formation-imagination of this binary itself. But this immanent crisis of disintegration is an endless continuation of *différance*, marking the central constituent part of this crisis, that is the female body as mediation, as natural reunion or peaceful exchange.

> Nature could not but be represented by a master metaphor, that of the matrix, the uterus, the mother who gestates only sons, the masculine of the new nation.[35]

Exchange, which takes the female body as mediation, was made into a repeating origin, a numéraire which crystallizes the desire of the nation-as-state, which maintains order or structure,[36] but had to be rearranged by the colonizer into the results (pedagogy, civilization) of the implementation of order to the debased non-order of the "natural excess" and "directionless sexual energy" of the colonized. Thus through this sequence of rhetorical images – plunder = appropriation, rape = violence, body = territory, the eye and the gaze, shyness and humiliation, reconciliation and revenge – the process of mis/re-reading and rewriting the woman secretly proceeds towards a nurturing nature installed in a binary opposition to culture. This is intertwined into an imaginary scenario in which the controller–controlled relationship is symbolized as one of seduction and the satisfaction of sexual desire. But here Radhakrishnan emphasizes that something must have been previously forgotten:

> Nationalist rhetoric makes "woman" the pure and ahistorical signifier of "interiority." In the fight against the enemy from the outside, something within gets even more repressed and "woman" becomes the mute but necessary allegorical ground for the transactions of nationalist history.[37]

The abstracted female as "woman" in capital letters is simultaneously, yet in different sites, assigned both the role of potential or actual sacrificial victim who protects the boundary/edge, and the role of the goddess who fights, who gives relief and care to the center.[38] Thus while the woman is something whose centrality in the nation as discursive formation-organization must be constantly approved, nevertheless this centrality itself is a void space in which, conversely, she can only be approved by being expelled to the edge of the regime, constitution, or political body.

This cyclical mis/re-reading and re-writing of the power differential and the gender differential is a heterosexual intercourse in which the female (body) is erased, absent – that is, it is a homosocial exchange (fraternity). Here the woman's role is as a "pillow," something "shameful/raped" (辱), hidden by a veil. It is this homosociality[39] which coerces people into heterosexuality, which makes them imagine the sexual, sensual "power of the nation."[40] This process, whether conscious or unconscious, is provoked by a coercive heterosexual system which legislates the "appropriateness" of sexual acts in women. It institutes "the crucial distinction" between the nation and its others.[41] This distinction is the struggle and reconciliation between men over the metaphor of the "woman-as-land."[42]

Giving form to the female body as land or territory is "both a politics and a poetics of violence."[43] It is directly tethered to "war."[44] To say that the female body is the focal point of the "reterritorialization" of heterosexual male–female relations in actuality, and at the same time is the site of the fantasy of "deterritorialization,"[45] is to say that the rhetoric surrounding the female body, while actively maintaining the system of heterosexuality which guides the "inward-facing nation-state," at the same time itself, as the drive (*Trieb* 衝動) of the "outward-facing nation-state," signifies the initial urge/impulse (*Drang* 衝迫) for the deterritorialization of the reterritorialized body of the self through the feminization of the other and annexation through phallic rape. This synchronicity between the reterritorialization and deterritorialization of the female body is also a suspension between the "dangerous permeability" of body boundaries and their process of "continual purification," or between the "imperial megalomania" of pillage and the "fear of annexation" which accompanies the anxiety of separation and castration.[46] Thus, precisely because all boundaries must constantly be drawn over and over again, the boundary must be continually declared or signed (that is, "ruled and firmed up," *shurikosei*) over and over again.

Consequently, in this rhetoric, the female body serves as nature – a social/national nature – for the benefit of the male as society. It is nothing more than an "existence to be spoken of,"[47] a placenta for the narrative of the nation as desire. This is shown in the fact that the female body is "internally enclosed within the mode of narrative production, and simultaneously separated from this mode of narrative production." While the female body is a final instance, it is also at the same time located in the outside of this final instance.[48] Thus while this common language appears in the guise of problematizing these central symbols, it ceaselessly forms sensually exposed boundaries and maneuvers through them. It is the symbol of the nation-as-state, which simultaneously desires reterritorialization (endo-colonization) and deterritorialization (ecto-colonization).[49]

Thus the desire of the nation-as-state is held in a "full Nelson." In the first place, through the application of the metaphor of the center to the female body, the nation-as-state comes to be, for the first time, a floating metonymic contiguity. In this contiguity, the boundary-edge is phallically formed-imagined. This boundary-edge is the erect penis, and thus there is the visible transition: center as female, boundary as male. Yet at the same time, this floating metonymic homosocial contiguity requires boundaries that are instituted by the inviolable female body. It functions based on another metaphor, one which images the outline of the nation-as-state. Here the boundary-edge is the hymen exposed to the danger of being deflowered, and we see the invisible transition to the female as boundary, and the male as center.

Thus it is the cross-dressing man (soldier) – the drag queen – who takes up the phallic defense in the edge-boundary. To put it another way, the female is attributed a centrality, but at precisely the same time is robbed of that centrality. So is it the cross-dressed (single) male – the drag king – who is symbolized as the feminine in the center? The female exists neither in the boundary-edge, nor in the center; in fact, the female exists nowhere. The woman and her body are metaphorically, or precisely because they are metaphorical, volatilized and disappearing. Male(ness)/male-sexuality in the form of camaraderie, or the "circle of friends," is metonymically suspended as the nodal point of this metaphor.

However, if we posit that it is the cross-dressing man (soldier) who takes up the phallic defense in the edge-boundary, always, and at the very moment of the actual crisis, what is being commodified as the object of either rape/war or, on the other hand, sexual intercourse/economic exchange, is not being-male but rather being-female.[50] This is because such a drive is cathected into "a fear in men of their own feminization."[51] Therefore, the rhetoric of female(ness)/female sexuality as something that should be chaste and protected must operate in the edge-boundary. Female chastity is simultaneously protected and exhibited by this internal rapist which is the erect penis.

This rhetoric indicates the t(r)opology of the binary opposition between the edge-boundary and the center, in which the center is formed through the invagination of the boundary (penis).The center is the edge-boundary instituted by the invagination of the surface of the female body into the interior.[52] As the female genitalia it lures the gaze, and is accompanied by the fear of gazing – it is a center as edge-boundary, or a center formed through being gazed at far too much.[53] That is to say, while the female body is given form in the center, there is nothing there to stare at it. This is precisely because even though the female body is given form in the center, it is also at the same time erased. But the male, as if possessed, tries to peek at this center, where nothing can be seen. While the essence of the center is given in this focal point, one male who cannot "come out" of this center as "closet" exists here. Men are possessed by peeking into this center. Consequently, they are obsessed with peeking at themselves. This is the formation of the center through the masturbatory gaze – panopticism. Cross-dressing, which disturbs the established order, is its symptomatic, double-edged appearance.[54]

Thus in the rhetoric and politics of the nation-as-state, while the woman seems omnipresent everywhere, she is in fact volatilized and disappearing. On the other hand, the male cross-dresses, hiding his body, but is always-already existent (or pre-existent), idly playing with this rhetoric/politics in camaraderie with his friends. At its roots is the desire for homosocial metonymic contiguity.[55] The guarantee of the legitimacy of the rule of the male-as-nation is based on this sacralization/erasure of woman. The "violence engendered in representation" – or "non-representation" as proxy or substitute – manifests its violent essence precisely by being en-gendered.[56]

Therefore, Hélène Cixous and Catherine Clément write:

> She is in the shadow. In the shadow he throws on her; the shadow she is. Kept
> at a distance so that he can enjoy the ambiguous advantages of the distance,
> so that she, who is distance and postponement, will keep alive the enigma, the
> dangerous delight of seduction, in suspense, in the role of "eloper," somehow
> "outside." But she cannot appropriate this "outside" (it is rare that she even
> wants it); it is his outside: outside on the condition that it not be entirely out-
> side, the unfamiliar stranger that would escape him. So she stays inside a
> domesticated outside.[57]

Here however, the metaphorical erasure of woman which corresponds to the man's
metonymic expansion towards the nation is a device working to keep her fixed to
the "lethargic, maternal land." The "feminine patria" which "belongs to the father"
maintains the systematically formed-organized phallic desire of the nation-as-
state.[58] This is the dynamics of complicity – does this not directly show us the
structure of the rhetoric (politics) of the coerced or institutionalized conspiracy?

The institutionalization of the coerced conspiracy

No functioning state apparatuses are neuter/neutral. "State desire" is by nature
always-already patriarchal and gendered masculine. But the problem is not simply
this fact alone, but rather the fact that the "counter desire" to the masculine state
desire, that is the rhetoric/politics surrounding the "anti-," is not gendered feminine.[59]

Doris Sommer points out that "femaleness is vulnerable not only because it is
victimized by men but because it can be complicitous with them."[60] But this
observation is still inaccurate. Certainly, the basis and institutionalization of the
discourse of "ruling and firming up" (*shurikosei*) which fragmentarily
rhetoricalizes the female body ought to be problematized. The problem is that
femaleness is made vulnerable precisely by the discursive and non-discursive
institutionalized conspiracy of heterosexuality. What has to be problematized is
the fact that "the feminine is as much a part of the masculine system as the neuter."[61]
Suleri's critique, Segwick's concept of homosociality, and indeed Marjorie Garber's
notion of cross-dressing, are all converged at this point.

Without even mentioning Michel Foucault, we can say that power never exists
without an object. If we posit that power (the subject) and "authority are in some
sense conferred by those who obey it,"[62] then in a general sense, the rhetoric/politics
surrounding the "anti-" cannot escape from this structure of complicity. The (desire
of) the nation-as-state is not merely a "phantasmagoria." Rather, it is an endless
institutionalization of difference by means of a violently en-gendered class
opposition, a series of "historical practices through which social difference is both
invented and performed" through the medium of the female body.[63] This
rhetoric/politics surrounding the female body is concretized in relation to the
"exchanges and transfers of power" which take place between the "male warriors"
on the front lines and the central "logistical spouses,"[64] and is quite obviously

demonstrated in the period of the formation of the modern nation-state, its crises and wars, that is, in the crises and revenges for the transgression of boundaries in the relationship of violator and violated.[65]

This rhetoric mediated by the female body, in which is displayed the desires of the nation-as-state, hangs over the meaning of the existence of the rhetoric of "resistance and binary politics" that surrounds every single internal or external transgression of boundaries. Female(ness)/female sexuality as center is imaged in a void, if only to form the rhetorical placenta which manifests difference in the boundary-edge. The (single) man, through the cross-dressed physical body, practically invades and occupies the center, which is the invagination of this boundary-edge (penis). Through this image, the men (soldiers) phallically gaze at each other in opposition in order to substantially defend their own security in the center. In the midst of this, woman is metaphorically volatilized and disappearing, while the male (nation-as-state) continually conspires metonymically (contiguously). The passionately, sensually seen (single) male exists as the tangible embodiment which declares, signs, and transmits the unbroken Imperial lineage (万世一系), without "coming out" from these intimately related processes, from this "closet," from the "vagina" (*mihoto*) of the woman made shadow, from the imperial portrait (御真影). Any political statement which aims at the disintegration of the rhetoric of this institutionalized conspiracy must itself be narrated politically.

The body and power: the burden of sex(uality)

In other words, I still cannot easily distance myself from this rhetoric/politics surrounding the female body, nor will I simply try to do so. As Rosi Braidotti has stated, "the proliferation of discourses about the mother's body and female sexuality is symptomatic of the crises of the masculine social contract and its self-legitimating discourses,"[66] and my starting point is precisely a symptomatic investigation of the crises of these "self-legitimating discourses." Karl Marx once stated:

> Nations and women are not forgiven the unguarded hour in which the first adventurer who came along could violate them. Such turns of speech do not solve the riddle but only formulate it differently.[67]

Here this problematic discourse has a crucial meaning. We must not merely read into this discourse the notion of an awkward, misogynist Marx. Rather, we must discover here Marx's exhibition of a literary style which eludes this gap. Here we see the political content of the revolutionary movement and its symbols (or the movement-content of politics), the problem of the revolutionary aesthetics which explain the "riddled relations" of "the subjective conditions of historical experience."[68] That is, to summarize my understanding of the issue at stake, it is the clarification and elucidation of the type of power which shoulders the burden of the body and sexuality.[69]

As I stated at the outset of this essay, I would like to try to politically read the mnemo-technics, or mnemo-tectonics of Japanese imperialism through the *Cardinal*

Principles of the National Polity, published in 1937 – or more specifically, through the interpretations of the national polity/national body (*kokutai*) in accordance with their moment, put forward by the authors of a series of commentaries on the *Cardinal Principles*.[70] The problem here is neither that of tracing the views of the state as family and their basis in patriarchal authority,[71] nor is it the exposure of the ideological absurdity of the *Cardinal Principles*.[72] Even less is it a question of whether or not this nation was matrilineal or patrilineal, so on and so forth.

Rather, the problem is attempting to think the rhetoric of self-recognition in the crisis of Japan the nation-state that is actually given in (or actualized as given in) the *Cardinal Principles*. The importance of this problem still stems from the rhetoric/politics of the female body as mediation, in particular from this nation which is crowned by the woman's body, the nation crowned by the confinement of the woman in the household, and from the position of the woman whose single body must shoulder the burden of the "shame/rape" (辱) that crowns the nation, that is, from the blending together of nationalism and sexuality (rape and violence).[73]

The language of the national polity: gift

For Kihira Tadayoshi, who was intimately connected to the production of the *Cardinal Principles*, in contrast to western Europe, "ethnicity (*minzokusei*) and nationality (*kokuminsei*) are identical" in the Japanese case, and thus the national language (*kokugo*), that is the "directives, indeed the truths, which emerge from the place in which the entire nation dwells," as an "objective existence," "conversely outlines the limits of this nationality."[74] Thus, the (cardinal principles of the) national polity is first and foremost delineated by "national language." Here Kihira's exalting exposition of the nation, that is, of the national – in fact, "nationality" is used somewhat interchangeably with "national polity"[75] – as an objective existence delineated by the "national language," or by its "magnanimity,"[76] is aimed at deriving the particularity of what is "national" – in other words, Japan the nation-state – in the "national language."

> In the radical "*kunigamae*" (囗) of the character for "nation" (國), the internal "*kuni*" is applied to its exterior, and signifies distinction. It is applied to it on the horizon, and thus we can see this original meaning of "distinction" in another of its component parts, the radical "*shikigamae*" (弋). But this alone still holds the anxiety of invasion from without, and thus must be protected by a further part of the character, (戈) "*hoko*," that is, axes – in other words, by means of weaponry. Throughout the continents, many specific countries (或) emerge, and separate themselves by touching on each other's borders. Thus the term takes on its typical meaning of "certain, specific" (或), and at the same time, it is yet again productive of an "anxiety" (惑) which must be defended with weaponry. The magnification of this "anxiety" (惑), which has only resulted in struggle since time immemorial throughout Europe, became the basis of ideologies such as socialism and anarchism. Thus, in order to effectively distinguish between "specificity" (或) and "anxiety" (惑), the internal

differentiation is applied to the exterior, becoming the commonly-utilized character "nation" (國).[77]

From the outset it should be mentioned that Kihira's explanation does not demonstrate some independent, original understanding. For example, Tetsuji Morohashi's *Dai kan-wa jiten* gives us a more accurate etymological explanation of this character. But Kihira's point is developed around the argument that "the shifts in the character "nation" themselves are precisely the shifts in the actual nations of the earth." The problem here is related to the interpretations of the national polity put forth by Kihira and the other compilers of the *Cardinal Principles*.

Through this explanation of the character "nation," Kihira tries to show the opposition between the state-ideal of Japan – that is, "harmony" – and that of the various European states, which have been mired in "struggle" as a consequence of the "anxiety" produced by these states' mutually shared borders. This was the gathering point for the rhetoric of the desire of the nation-as-state mediated by the female body. We can perceive what this notion of the "nation" was for Kihira in the following statement:

> *Kuni* ("nation") in the national language perhaps means *kuni* ("environment," 木土), the earth which nurtures vegetation . . . The Emperor unifies and connects it, and through the building of the Imperial Palace (and its surroundings), he immediately became the "Emperor who first cultivated all under heaven" (始馭天下之天皇, *hatsukunishirasu sumeramikoto*).[78]

Thus the "nation" in the national language is the "environment" or "land" which nourishes the growth of vegetation – as we will see later, this is "reproduction" and "nurture," which converges in "cultivation" – in short, the "nation" here is "nature." This view of the state is exactly the theory of the state body (*shashaku tōtai ron*) that was used in policy-making by the agricultural administration authorities, and which was appealed to within the agrarian populism (*nōhonshugi*) of figures in the 1930s like Gondō Seikyō.[79] But this notion of the nation as nature was extremely important for their theories of the national polity, in relation to the legitimacy of the Emperor's rule and its requisite style. The exaltation of the Emperor (*sumera-mikoto*) "who first cultivated all under heaven" (or, "who first ruled the nation," *hatsukuni-shirasu*) in the above quotation is a prime example of this.

In relation to the question of these terms – *shirasu* or *shiroshimesu* (知らす), meaning here "to reign" – Kakei Katsuhiko broadly explains as follows. The Emperor's sovereign right derives from his status as the direct successor to the "heavenly gods" (*amatsukami*) and is expressed in his cooperation with the imperial ancestors, and thus this *"shirasu"* or *"shiroshimesu"* signifies the Emperor's "rule of all under heaven." This *"shirasu,"* in this ruling national language, also signifies "opening the self and receiving all power from the exterior," "seizing power as one's own possession" (*ushihaku*, for something to "belong" to one, territory), thus the rule of the Emperor as "subject of national right" has the sense of an antithetical political style (*buntai*, "literary body": I would also remind readers of its botanical sense). Consequently, the one who rules the "nation," that is "nature" as "environment" or "land," "opens the self" and accepts the other, declaring its legitimacy without yet "possessing" it, "belonging to" it. This is because "national right" is not the "power privately held, seized, or possessed by the Emperor personally."[80]

Kōno Seizō, once the president of Kokugakuin University, sought the "spirit of the founding of the state," the formation of this spirit – this "drive to go onwards"[81] – which had appeared already in the "words and matters" of the age of the gods in the *Kojiki* and *Nihon shoki*, in the self-awareness of this "divine age (*kami nagara*; or *kan'nagara*) when the nation was undeclared" which was given cultural expression in the Nara period, in the "conceited state appellation" of this "nation blessed with the power of language (*kotodama*)."[82]

> In accordance with the various conditions of the nation in different eras, the national and ethnic self-awareness of our nation's people has been evoked and expressed under different names and in varying forms, but precisely as a self-awareness which corresponds to the conditions of the nation, it must be a pure expression and operation of the Japanese spirit.[83]

According to Kōno, this "*kami nagara*" does not merely mean "divine, while" or "as if divine." He states that in this phrase "*kami nagara*, the *kami* signifies the heavenly gods, in particular Amaterasu-ōmikami, and the *na* corresponds to the particle *no*, which signifies possession. *Gara* is a term that means the manifestation of the original characteristics of all certain things, and thus signifies the expression of essence." Consequently, *kami nagara* means the manifestation of the "essence of Amaterasu-ōmikami."[84] Thus, Kōno explains, this divine though undeclared nation which emerged in the Nara period implies the "national essence" (*kunigara*) which negates "description," in other words debate, explanation, appellation, and so forth, or the "national character . . . whose divinity none dare challenge."[85]

Kihira rearranges this undeclared operation of the essence of the imperial ancestor Amaterasu-ōmikami as prior, and to that extent, this affirmative spirit of obedience comes first, and thus "their divinity is prior, and the fact that it is 'undeclared' follows," thereby becoming the "undeclared gods." Here Kihira contrasts this with Descartes' *cogito*, arguing that "it is because you 'follow' the gods, that the gods themselves come to exist here."[86] Here obviously Descartes' *cogito ergo sum* (or "I think therefore I am," "Je pense donc je *suis*") is switched into "I think therefore I follow" ("Je pense donc je *suis*"). Thus, "opening the self and receiving all power from the exterior" is nothing more than the manifestation of "following in succession."

The *Cardinal Principles of the National Polity* explain the "origin" as follows: "Our nation was founded when its Founder, Amaterasu-ōmikami, handed the Oracle to her Imperial Grandson Ninigi-no-mikoto and descended to Mizuho-no-kuni at Toyoashihara."[87] In this story of the descent to earth of the imperial grandson, "the reason that Emperor Jimmu succeeded to the imperial throne was not the decision of the Emperor himself, but rather that he accepted this succession by obeying the oracle of Amaterasu-ōmikami," and the "hi" (日) in the term "throne" (*hitsugi*, 日嗣)

"respectfully indicates Amaterasu-ōmikami herself."[88] Thus Amaterasu-ōmikami plays a complex and flexible role throughout the *Cardinal Principles*.

As we have already seen, Amaterasu-ōmikami, who is the direct "origin" of the nation, that is, the "Imperial Ancestor" (Ōji-no-mikoto), although appearing in various forms, as shown in the "operations" underlying the period or state of the "nation," embodies the "national language" as objective existence, nature as environment, land. Thus Kihira's notion of "nation," this nation whose legitimacy is guaranteed by the Imperial Ancestor, Amaterasu-ōmikami, is precisely nature as environment or land. This nation is undeclared, opening itself in the center to receive all power from the exterior, a nation "blessed by the power of language (spirit of the word: *koto-dama* 言－霊)." Kihira attempts to interpret this nation through the development of the following rhetorical chain (or politics/rule as merely "affairs," etiquette): Amaterasu-ōmikami = female body = environment, land = "nature" = "nation." Kihira simply summarizes the distension of this metaphorical chain below:

> The Imperial Ancestor Amaterasu-ōmikami is already honoring the gods in Takamagahara. Thus it cannot be understood as something that could be called religious. That is, it is the final event of the end of the dwelling in harmony between man-nature-gods.[89]

The goddess Amaterasu-ōmikami is already worshipping (obeying/organizing) the gods in Takamagahara – submitting and being submitted. But this is not a religious existence. "She" is not a religious entity, but an actual/substantial (*jitsuzaiteki*) one. This actuality, or this discursive *substantia*, is metamorphosized or incarnated as nature, and this nature itself is discursively – through the national language – formed and organized. This nature is literally the nation itself. Consequently, this "she" who guarantees to the Emperor the legitimacy of his rule, dwells in the environment/land as a nature which is substantialized – or, in fact she *is* these things (substantially). This "harmony between man-nature-gods" is nothing other than what reveals the structure of this notion of nation.

Here the Emperor ex-ists (*extase*) as a "harmonious whole," a Trinity-form of man-nature-god. This is the sense in which he is the *arahitogami*, a god that appears before one's eyes. The Emperor therefore, cannot make "her" (the Imperial Ancestor) nature (land, environment) his possession, that is, her body as territory. This is because "she" is the entity which gives legitimacy to the Emperor, this Imperial Ancestor as goddess. When Kakei states that "from time immemorial there has never been in the Empire an offensive notion such as that which says that the Emperor *must* be the subject (主体－臣民) of national sovereignty," he means that it is "offensive" to the heavenly gods to imagine that the reigning Emperor alone could "possess" such sovereignty.[90]

Thus the Emperor is the successor who declares the unbroken imperial line, the one who "reigns/consumes" (*shiroshimesu*; 知ろし食す) in relation to the "nation" as nature. Through "eating together"/"sexual intercourse" (性交) with the heavenly gods, the Emperor declares/signs the stalemate of his rule – he is a mediator or container which transfers it in succession. What is acting here is, indescribably, the opening of the self in the center, this nature which accepts all power, the "encoding" of the "earth's body" as the "body of infinite womanhood."[91] It is the Emperor who each time (re)deciphers and (re)encodes this coding itself. "A transaction between great male gods" thus inscribes/ enters/records the female body as "the earth as sacred geography."[92] It is impossible to seize/possess the harmony of man-nature-gods. Thus it cannot be ruled. Yet its harmonious cycle can only be explained precisely by being ruled (by being known and consumed, *shiroshimesu*). This is what, directly and initially, gives foundation to the nation as nature, a gift given by Amaterasu-ōmikami.

As an aside, Kihira understands this gift as the "Japanese" principle of "opening of the self," – "union" or the economy of production = reproduction – which would supposedly stand in diametrical opposition to the unilateral exploitative acts of the principle of exchange behaviors (exchange/giving-taking, *yari-tori*) in Western individualism.[93] Kihira negates the concept of society, and determines social relations as the nation-*qua*-household/family (国 - 即 - 家),[94] but this stemmed from his exaltation of the fact that every social (state) relation, including sexual relations, is dominated by this "exchange (giving-taking)" as (impossible) gift. But the beginning of such (impossible) exchange relations must therefore already be initiated by the origin-al hit of this gift, this nature which issues forth from the Imperial Ancestor, that is, the nation. It is declared in self-awareness, in the "moment of the beginning of heaven and earth." Thus it constantly continues to be declared/signed, and must be incessantly, continuously imagined. Consequently, this exchange (giving-taking) is guaranteed through the initial moment of giving, but through what medium is this "giving" given continuity? The medium/container of the Emperor, this Emperor who is secured through the female body, through the institutionalization of the female body. Moreover this (impossible) exchange is instituted through the separation that occurs in the process of the realization of value of this giving-taking, and the fatal leap that accompanies it. Precisely because of this, the separated moment of doing is made into something which must unilaterally secure its fatal leap, while the moment of taking must be maintained.

Kihira states as follows: "just as the two gods Izanagi and Izanami, after their initial failure to give birth to the land, established and unified the organization of male and female, the virtue of protection must in the main be understood as something female. Indeed it is only through this primary virtue of the woman that eternal constancy can be given to the household/family and the nation."[95] This is nothing more than an expression of approval for the system of patriarchal authority and the notion of the family state. But yet again the point that must be validated here is the female body which mediates this institutional, endless *différance* of "giving," the securing of the "eternal constancy" of the "household/family" and "nation" precisely through this doing. Here the trinity-form "man-nature-gods" is substituted with the trinity-form "household-nature-nation" (家-自然-国) – thus it is not the nation itself, but the "state" (国-家), the *qua* in the "nation-*qua*-household" (国-即-家), in other words, nature. But at any rate, what anchors these three terms is nothing other than the gift of the (body of the) woman.

Kihira desparately declares that "since ancient times, Amaterasu-ōmikami has been understood to be female, but at the same time established the positions "male" and "female" themselves, and thus it can be accepted as something reciprocal."[96] Here, beyond the precondition of giving legitimacy to the Emperor, Amaterasu-ōmikami is reaffirmed as a goddess, the nation founded on the basis of "position," the "organization of male and female." The Emperor-system, which functions within this "organization of male and female" – heterosexuality and patriarchal authority – must correctly position Amaterasu-ōmikami, or the woman in capital letters, who confers legitimacy on the Emperor's rule. For Kihira, it was the logic of "ruling and firming up" (*shurikosei*) in the *Kojiki* which for him explicates the "logic of the formation of the nation as the logic of "production," "unification", as the formation of the nation begun not by Kuni-no-toko-tachi no Mikoto, as in the *Nihon shoki*, but more profoundly, by Ama-no-minaka-nushi no Mikoto" that formed the basis of the production of the *Cardinal Principles*.[97] Consequently, the major precondition for this is Amaterasu-ōmikami's guarantee of the Emperor's legitimacy, and thus Amaterasu-ōmikami herself, or indeed the location of woman here, is an exceptionally complicated problem. This was the crucial thematic for Kihira in relation to the contemporary of the total war system at the time – indeed it was the most crucial thematic of the *Cardinal Principles* itself. We can see that this thematic was articulated through the abstract harmonious circuit "man-nature-gods," and further through the trinity-form "household-nature-nation." But in order for this to be incessantly interpreted, ceaselessly imagined, nature and its eternality had to be given in actuality. The logic of "ruling and firming up" (*shurikosei*) had to (re)interpret the numerous problems related to the woman. Now, let us turn to the *Kojiki* itself.

As previously mentioned, the passage which describes "the two gods Izanagi and Izanami, who, after their initial failure to give birth to the land, established the organization of male and female" is well-known. The sexual union of Izanagi and Izanami, standing on the island of Onogorojima, which they created (ruled and firmed up) through the coagulation of salt (female genitals) on the "jewel-spear of Heaven" (male genitals) as they stirred the waters "until they became thick and glutinous," is considered a failure, since the children produced are "not good because the woman spoke first" (leaving aside the interpretation of the leech-child Ebisu).[98] After reorienting themselves in the divination ceremony around the heavenly pillar, the two gods give birth to the environment and land of Ōyashimaguni. After birthing this nation, it becomes the placenta, thereby allowing the birth of the gods to continue onwards.

Thus this placenta as Ōyashimaguni is already emerging as nature, that is, as environment and land. The corporealized woman, or the female body as nature already exists: Ōyashimaguni as territory, as placenta.

Further, there is the story of Amaterasu-ōmikami's birth. In this continuation of the birth of the various gods, she does not yet appear. Before this is possible, one thing must happen: the first murder of the woman-mother – the beginning of the murders of many women. In the process of the sequence of the births of the various gods produced by Izanagi and Izanami, Izanami gives birth to the Hi-no-kagutsuchi no kami, the god of burning fire, and "through giving birth to this child, her august private parts were burnt . . . and at length she divinely retired into death."[99] Subsequently, Izanagi journeys to the Land of Hades (*Yomi-no-kuni*) to beg for the return of Izanami, and violates Izanami's prohibition – "Look not at me!" – and thus is narrated the tale of his cursed escape.

After Izanagi manages to escape, he performs a ritual purification – later I will examine the relation of this "ritual purification" to the wartime ideology of the "eight corners of the world under one roof" (*hakkō ichiu*) – and in this ceremony of purification, Amaterasu-ōmikami is born from his left eye. She is, through the burning of her genitals and death through fire – fire as consciousness and simultaneously fire as the uncanny center of the unconscious household – a goddess who is born, after the symbolic murder of Izanami and her expulsion to Kegarehashiki-kuni, and after Izanagi's ritual purification of the degradation and uncleanness he encountered, not as a result of sexual relations between them; rather Amaterasu-ōmikami is a goddess who is born solely from the male god Izanagi. Because the fragmented female body as placenta is already functioning here, woman is excluded. But while woman is excluded, this "silent substratum" reproduces the social order. It consists in the "murder of the mother."[100]

For Kihira, this state (国家) was not the nation, but rather had to be the nation-*qua*-household/family (国-即-家). But it is instituted precisely through the woman's unilateral "giving," that is, through the (impossible) gift. Kihira writes:

> The duty of the woman . . . It is not a phenomenon limited to the Japanese to call out the name of one's mother, or to see the image of the mother when in the throes of agony, or at the moment of certain death. But why indeed does the mother hold such power? It goes without saying that the mother is the one who, from birth onwards gives one what one wants unconditionally. Thus, because the sun nourishes by giving of its own virtue to all things, the myths of most ethnicities treat it as a woman – indeed for us as well, this is why Amaterasu-ōmikami is worshipped and revered as a woman. The final words of Goethe's *Faust* are "woman, eternal, beckons us on." We Japanese were practicing this from the very beginning – it signifies in particular the mother within the household/family.[101]

This eternal woman, this woman as pure nature (land, environment), this woman, indeed, mother, who opens herself, opens her body in silence, is finally fixed as the woman or mother who gives herself unconditionally. It is precisely this rhetoric of the gift which establishes the "nation." Amaterasu-ōmikami, who guarantees the legitimacy of the Emperor, is not born from a woman. Again, even while this eternal, pure woman/mother as nature or unconditional gift is "revered" – sanctified, made obedient, ordered – at the same time, she is erased and excluded as impurity and death.

Why is there the phenomenon of rape as revenge? How is she impossibly conquered, and thus violently institutionalized, despite the fact that man cannot "possess" the woman (nature) as territory? Irigaray speaks to all of these questions:

As mother, woman remains on the side of (re)productive nature and because of this, man can never fully transcend his relation to the "natural." His social existence, his economic structures and his sexuality are always tied to the work of nature: these structures thus always remain at the level of the earliest appropriation, that of the constitution of nature as landed property, and of the earliest labor, which is agricultural. But this relationship to productive nature, an insurmountable one, has to be denied so that relations among men may prevail. This means that mothers, reproductive instruments marked with the name of the father and enclosed in his house, must be private property, excluded from exchange . . . As both natural value and use value, mothers cannot circulate in the form of commodities without threatening the very existence of the social order. Their products are legal tender in that order, moreover, only if they are marked with the name of the father, only if they are recognized within his law: that is, only insofar as they are appropriated by him.[102]

However, what should be added to this is the problem that these mothers themselves, who are marked with the name of the father and enclosed in his house, for whom exchange is prohibited, whether symbolic or actual, become the targets of violence/rape. This is the problem of war, the problem of the transgression of boundaries. Nation – shame/rape (国 - 辱). The etymology of this "shame/rape" originally stems from the "shaming," in other words, killing of someone who shirked their duty during the plowing season in the rice-fields, a symbol of their domina-tion, making someone "indebted." It is the most pointed symbol of the rhetoric surrounding the female body, in other words, of the violator–violated relation, of the original appropriation.

Thus Amaterasu-ōmikami is an impossible woman, the "virgin mother." Like Vesta's virginity, the violation of the mother of this "un-represented" virgin who must be protected cannot be forgiven, with the exception of one man. Directly seeing her, imagining her is unforgivable. She "guards a hearth fire, located at the physical center of the domus, signifying the sacredness and permanence of home and state" and thus she must remain unseen.[103] This inviolable virginity and un-representability are one and the same thing.[104] Thus Amaterasu-ōmikami's body is "the ground of the culture's system of differences," while her "hymen is also the ground of contention."[105] While she is a "simple exchange-value" in the sense of being a virgin, she is simultaneously a use-value in the sense that she is a mother (or wife) for whom exchange is forbidden.[106] The woman who emerges from Amaterasu-ōmikami as "imperial ancestor" is made into a "woman," and as a mother is linked to eternity by seeking maternal power in her unconditional gift. This rhetorical chain must be divinely protected, and yet at the same time, precisely because of this, is exhibited as the object of possession and violation. Thus Amaterasu-ōmikami who is revered both as this virgin goddess (pure exchange-value) and also as the imperial grandmother (prohibition of exchange), can be understood at the same time as a "holy prostitute," who unconditionally opens her body. This is the whole of the unilateral "giving" as gift.

Amaterasu-ōmikami thus becomes all women/completely woman (*subete no josei, josei no subete*), or woman in capital letters. As all women (completely woman), she secures the rhetorical body which guarantees the legitimacy of the Emperor's reign. This symbol of the woman as "ancient mother." Here the woman – virgin, mother, prostitute – functions as a metaphor for the man's "place of departure to which there can be no return." Even if Kihira tries to fantasize the "beginning of the end in . . . expressing the dialectic in the standpoint of pure 'becoming'," its precondition is that the male does not return to this site. Through the unilateral giving – gift – in this particular sexuality, this "becoming" does not have an end, and indeed its lack of an end is driven by "man's claustrophobia within the maternal body," driven by a fear of being woman, being feminized.[107] Thus in the process of this rhetorical chain, Amaterasu-ōmikami descends from Takamagahara into the actual, present household/family and becomes the mother who is present precisely in her lack. Actual physical women are demanded to contract throughout their bodies the total female-ness/female-sexuality embodied by Amaterasu-ōmikami.

Yet, here the "woman" is simultaneously revered and represented (or un-represented) as "deserted." Indeed it is precisely because of this that "she," if peeked at while she is goddess (light), will be reterritorialized as a blind enclosed space or site of invagination. This reterritorialization is accomplished through the undeclared national language of ancient times (*kan'nagara*). Thus the "bonding of men" in the form of the state "requires the silencing of women" – it points to an "unstated male dread."[108] But this reterritorialization operates only as the other side of the same coin – its deterritorialization, the transgression of the boundaries of the internal or external other. In this deterritorialization, the national language (*kokugo*) becomes "Japanese" (*Nihongo*), and captures the national language of the other. Its watchword is invasion = rape, or family/household = care. This itself is the desire of the nation-as-state.

Thus while the bonding between men finds its excuse in the symbol of the ancient mother, it conceals its body into something, a "harmony" which is "feminine in name only," or nature. In this process, the arrangement (or systematization) of male and female is "secured beneath a spirituality that is nominally female and which serves a normative heterosexuality."[109] This deserted female or mother – at times corresponding to Heidegger's "thrownness," or Irigaray's "déréliction." This deserting woman, Amaterasu-ōmikami, this "woman" as nature is coerced by man into giving the gift – free prostitution, a vehicle for the rhetoric of the "free ride" – and is thus placed in the "original state of lack."[110]

In a different context, Kihira tries to corner this "eternal woman" into "chastity."[111] Of course in his logic too, the image of Amaterasu-ōmikami operates abundantly. The "yin" of "yin-yang," the "unseen" of the "seen and unseen" – Kihira argues that "here, in particular in our nation, the position of the lady within the household/family can be seen" in these unequal or unsymmetrical binaries distributed to the woman. Thus he states in yet another context, "women should truly open themselves . . . and become devoted to nature . . . thus will they actually, in reality be for the first time active participants in giving to themselves eternal constancy in good morals and manners, in the sense of Goethe's 'eternal woman'."[112]

Let us re-cap. The "woman," saying nothing, is positioned to open her body and unconditionally gives that which is desired as gift, "caring" for the one who desires. To this extent, in fact, *only* to this extent is she a "good angel," "a home that can be loved infinitely."[113] This caring home, family or house, "like fire and water, will permit me . . . to recall flashes of daydreams that illuminate the synthesis of immemorial and recollected. In this remote region, memory and imagination remain associated, each one working for their mutual deepening."[114] But in Gaston Bachelard, the permitting "I" is nothing other than the male who exists under a coercive heterosexuality. What is precisely "uncanny" about this "fire," "flame," or "central hearth" which images the woman, is that it is only through this image (the radiance of the daydream), that the male synthesizes memory and imagination.

The body of this woman is its actuality as "eternal now." But this same woman is excluded from this actuality. At the same moment when she is inscribed in the origin she is erased from that origin. Kihira, who understood "Japan" as a "nation ruled by "becoming", theorizes this "eternal constancy," or woman as follows:

> "To become something" (*ni naru*) contains "to exist somewhere" (*ni aru*) and thus "to be" (*aru*) is merely one level of "to become" (*naru*). As a result, Japanese people are not attached to "being," but are diligent in their efforts to ceaselessly "become," they are satisfied with the answer, without asking such questions as "what is the way?," that they ought not be stationary, limited to "being."[115]

Thus, the "woman" is the "Japanese 'eternal now'" (*eien no ima*) – or more accurately, the "eternity of the present" (*ima no eien*) which dominates the "ancient substratum" of historical consciousness with the "drive to go onwards."[116] While this "eternal constancy," "as eternal as heaven and earth," is revered (sanctified, obeyed, ordered) as the beginning or origin,[117] the woman's genitals are burned, and in impurity and degradation, she is born from the man himself, and finally deserted – thus is she the medium or vehicle for this becoming. As vehicle, she is utilized as a "birth canal" for this system of irresponsibility. Although "appropriate to the national conditions of each era," Amaterasu-ōmikami manifested as essence, while converged onto this rhetoric of the "deserted woman," is made to eternally apply pressure for the "unification" of production and reproduction, the "endless, creative evolution of the sublation of that which has become and that which has not yet become."[118] Thus she is both dispossessed of time and yet must present an impossible time as gift.[119] Irigaray discusses the woman, bound to the man as state, as follows:

> The mother is seen as the earth substance which must be cultivated and inseminated so that it may bear fruit. The father is the one who gives form to the child, who uses earth to create him. The father is in the image of God the creator. The mother is occasionally deified because she is capable of bringing a divine son into the world. She is revered as the mother of a son of God, but she does not have, or no longer has, any divinity deriving from her sex, apart from her maternal status. This means that there is no longer any woman God.[120]

Who are the "father" and "son" Irigaray speaks of here? We should already know full well.

The national polity and the unbroken lineage of the imperial throne

The term "national polity" itself[121] can be given at least four general meanings as follows. (1) It can indicate the "inward-facing state," the affairs of the nation, the nation's emergence, and current situation, as in the "direction of the national polity" from the *Book of Han*. At the same time, it can indicate the "outward-facing state," in other words, the appearance of the state, also testified to in the *Book of Han*: "damaging the national polity" or "concealing the national polity." (2) The "body" of the nation, or the closest advisors to the sovereign. (3) The conditions of existence of sovereign right. (4) the form and force of the national territory, represented by "national matters" (*kunigata*) as in texts such as *Izumo no kuni no miyatsuko no kamuyogoto*.

In the first example, the term "affairs or designe" (*gara*) in "national affairs" can have the etymological meanings "basis," "materials," "force," "power," "influence," and thus the national polity is the authority of the nation, its formation and conditions.[122] Consequently, the first and third examples hold largely the same meaning in indicating the conditions of authority or the legitimacy of rule. Further, this national polity as "national affairs" points to the "basis" of the nation, its raw materials, and therefore, as is indicated in the second example of the body of the nation or its components, its advisors – strapping or "well-padded" (*nikuzuki*) and physically armed – are intimately linked to the previously armed body of the nation. As can be seen in the first example of phrases like "damaging the national polity" or "concealing the national polity," these are responses to the transgression, invasion of the national body, its impurity or "shame/rape." This is, as seen in the fourth definition, given in the connotation of the body as territory, the corporeal map of the national polity, the geographical, geopolitical representation of the state. Thus the national polity was an entity which had to be protected by the legitimacy of armed, territorial domination, instituted as a physical body.

Hachijō Takatake gives a clear reading of these interpretations. Hachijō translated the German term *Staatsform* of constitutional law into "national polity" (國体 *kokutai*), and makes the criticism that "the meaning of this term *kokutai* and the previous commonly used concept of *kokutai* have been intermingled, and has come to replace both the original meaning of the term, and the conceptual content of *Staatsform*." For Hachijō, the national polity is the "substance of the state, and only through the existence of this national polity can the state for the first time exist *as a state*."[123] Thus a nation might exist, but without a national polity/body, it cannot be a "national household, family" (國 - 家), that is, it cannot be a state.

Consequently, the national polity in the *Cardinal Principles* is the body of the nation. But this body is not the "outward expression of form." It is "an absolute which must be both actual and eternal, mortal and immortal, physical and spiritual, earthly and heavenly. This unique absolute is the body of the nation."[124] This body has lost its substance, its flesh – it is a "body without organs." What is being spoken of here is the (female) body which guarantees the "eternal now," or the "eternity of the present" as *Urstaat*. Kihira directly refers to this as "the most fundamental cardinal principle of the national polity/body, from which everything has its genesis, and in which everything will end – the unmovable Imperial Throne."[125]

Based on this "immobility of the mother," the nation can embody its own certainty as the nation-state. This is because she is connected to a "physical territory," where "family memory is stored." There, "archaic values . . . continued to flourish," and thus the "space of the mother" endlessly manifests as "utopia."[126] But this longing for the immobility of the mother is a bondage of the woman in the eternal now, stabilizing the female body into a chair (throne) for one of the "two bodies of the king,"[127] the "unmovable" position of the Emperor (imperial throne). She is the "seat" (座) in this "treasured seat" (玉 - 座) or "throne" – she must be, however, a chair, never the "treasure" itself. It is the female body which ensures the point of divergence between the two bodies of the king, the "actual physical body" of the reigning Emperor and the "metaphorically constructed, socially determined body" of the Imperial Throne, which sustains their intimate relation, and which functions as their critical threshold.[128] On the sexual union of the two bodies of this "treasure" and this "seat," Kihira states as follows:

> The function of the harmony of reproduction and nourishment is life . . . Thus our national polity is most effectively clarified when it is compared with such living cellular structures. In other words, what is created in this great harmony, this singular spirit of the entire people which is centered on the wild spirit of Amaterasu-ōmikami, who is the nucleus of the sun, and her successor the Emperor, is the state called Japan. Thus as the protoplasm of the state, it is the subjects of the Empire who produce the field of nourishment, while it is the Emperor who is the subject of eternal vitality as the concrete existence of "that which is Japanese."[129]

The nation in the "national language" was nature as land, as environment. Here "reproduction and nourishment" or the "great harmony" correspond to this determination. For Kihira, the national polity first and foremost grows depending on the "unity" or "nourishment" of the subject as protoplasm. But in this further unification of reproduction, who is united with whom? This is the cooperative "eating together," the symbolic sexual union of Amaterasu-ōmikami (nature) and the Emperor. The woman who experiences her body as the actual phase of Amaterasu-ōmikami is raped every day by the Emperor, this "subject of eternally constant vitality as concrete existence." But even as this woman is kidnapped and taken away to the actual phase of eternal constancy (the eternal now), she is absent. The female body is represented as the shadow of non-representation, and can no longer be seen.

Further, Amaterasu-ōmikami is the "wild spirit (*aratama*) . . . like the center of the sun." Her clitoris is imprinted and substituted by the center of the sun. But Amaterasu-ōmikami as wild spirit is not a mere opportunist. Here the woman must appear as the destroying god of war, as the penis. In the total-war system, even rhetorically, the distinction between the home-front and the front-line was already meaningless.

> War is the collision of the furthest edges of cultures, the so-called birthing pains towards a new creation. It is like the invocation of the "wild spirit" in relation to the unsanctified [Like the opposition between Takehayasu Susano-o and Amaterasu-ōmikami].[130]

> The [unsanctified/inobedient] impure remnants, were, as the ancients did, purified in ritual until they reached a pure and clear spirit.[131]

In this Nazi-esque theory of culture, the fact that the "ascension of Susano-o-no-mikoto" – and indeed the conquests of most of the male gods in the *Kojiki* – was recollected is not put into doubt. In the *Kojiki*, Susano-o-no-mikoto "forthwith went up to Heaven" to confront Amaterasu-ōmikami, whereupon, alarmed at this, she thinks, "the reason of the ascent hither of my elder brother is surely no good intent. It is only that he wishes to wrest my land from me," and "unbinding her hair, twisted it into bunches . . . and stood valiantly like a mighty man, waiting."[132] Here we see the narration of her cross-dressing, disguising herself as a man.

This signifies an attack on the impurity of the unsanctified, inobedient, unorganized remnants, a giving of form to the "noble and clear" spirit of the covenant of war, in other words, it is the "wild spirit" (*aratama*), the "phallus as constitutively veiled."[133] Here the cross-dressed Amaterasu-ōmikami, as this wild spirit, seeks to simultaneously occupy the center and the boundary-edge, the "home front" and the "front line." But according to Kihira, this is still a form of "harmony." Which is to say that the "spirit of harmony and the wild spirit are unified" in the form of the "Yamato spirit," and the four spirits of fortune, uncanniness, wildness, and harmony, are "after all, made to become simply 'one'."[134] The desire for this "one" of Empire, makes manifest the "entire earth under one roof" (*hakkō ichiu*) – it is nothing but the desire for the endless production of the "one" from the "many."[135]

> As long as authority is maintained, the boundaries of the scope of its rule are unclear, and thus its surroundings, that is the "eight directions" (八方) all around it . . . are its national boundaries ("eight wastelands," 八荒). "Wasteland" (荒) and "expanse" (絋) are both pronounced "kō," and between "expanse" (絋) and "rope" (綱), there is "net" (網) for example, which forms such words as "basis" or "mooring." Among these, "綱" is particularly utilized in an abstract sense, as in words like "plan" and "essentials." When the phrase "八絋" is used instead of "八荒," it gives the sense of an organized nation. Thus the phrase "hakkō ichiu" (八絋一宇, "all the world under one roof") was formed. Most likely this "roof" indicates "house, family" (家) . . . at the same time because it signifies the cosmos (宇宙), it indicates the extent of the heavens, and thus "all under heaven," thereby meaning the unity of the household or family and heaven.[136]

Consequently Amaterasu-ōmikami purifies and exorcises the celebrated/mourned/ordered impure "boundaries (eight wastelands)" (八荒) transforming them into the "whole world (eight expanses)" (八紘), subjugates them, and becomes the "wild spirit" (荒魂 *aratama*) manifesting the "one" of imperial organization. Here a version of Amaterasu-ōmikami for the home front, who vainly consents herself to the entire exterior is not necessary. What is necessary here is an armed Amaterasu-ōmikami, dressed as a man, as a wild spirit. It is not only that this Amaterasu-ōmikami embodies the nation of the "national language" (*kokugo*), which "rules and firms up" (*shurikosei*) the "inward-facing state," she also embodies the Emperor-system state – regulated by the rational distribution of resources – of the total-war system, accomplished through the purification and exorcism visited on the exterior by the "Japanese language" (*Nihongo*). Clearly, the fact that a certain sexuality is the necessary mediator for the simultaneous execution of this bilateral drive of Empire, its ecto- and endo-colonization, or its reterritorialization and deterritorialization, continually draws nearer to the cross-dressing of such a symbol.[137]

Thus the rhetoric of the female body is freely, flexibly exploited and utilized. However, precisely because this is the case, "woman" absolutely cannot be represented. Yamada Yoshio explains this mechanism as follows. In his text, he quite frankly sets out the "cardinal principles/real motivations" for the compilation of the *Cardinal Principles of the National Polity*. Here it is stated that during the moment of crisis, theories of the national polity must be narrated (must deceive, 語る/ 騙る), must be re-interpreted, imagined, and re-remembered. But what is most interesting here is the form which is given to the national polity:

> Our national polity is a self-evident thing to we Japanese subjects, something which at this point does not require explanation . . . In a time of tranquility for the state, and no complaints within the national polity, no discussions or historical facts are spreading around. Just as in the perfectly healthy body of a human being, it is as if you forget everything related to your body when you have no ailments . . . When problems with the national polity emerged, the Japanese subjects thought about it, and thought that things related to it needed to be explained . . . This is precisely the same thing as the fact that in ancient times nobody observed the sun – yet as soon as there was a solar eclipse, people became able to observe it for the first time. Our national polity, like the sunlight, has brilliant spiritual power and exceptional prosperity, something which, if directly touched even for an instant, would result in something so dramatic as to make one unable to live out one's years, as in the blinding that would result from looking at the sun.[138]

Here, the national polity as nature-body cannot ordinarily be directly seen. The one who directly sees the national polity will be blinded, one would be "incapable of living out one's years." It shines brilliantly like the sun, which cannot be directly seen by human eyes. It refuses to be seen, and to the extent that this slippage in the directionality of the gaze – who is seeing whom – is thus produced, the national polity which tempts this excess of the gaze was the "vagina" (*mihoto*) of the goddess of the sun, Amaterasu-ōmikami. In order to be seen, the gaze is refused, and through this refusal a mechanism for the management of this excess of visuality must be devised. The only entity which can reflect and play this role is the cross-dressing Emperor unified with (occupying) the "vagina" (*mihoto*); as Uesugi Shinkichi argued, "the Emperor reflects anyone like a colorless and transparent mirror."[139] Like the mirror of Perseus, who attacked the Gorgon, the Emperor becomes the mirror (sacred treasure) itself. Thus, in this crisis of the "solar eclipse," the female body is at last an entity that can be "observed" as "shadow" and "gap," in other words, as the "outside" which has been "tamed by man." The woman can reflect herself only through the mirror of the man (the symbolic order or Emperor), even scorning herself for her own indirectly invisible existence.[140]

Jessica Benjamin and Anson Rabinach argue that "two basic types of bodies exemplify the corporal metaphysics at the heart of fascist perception. On the one side there is the soft, fluid, and ultimately liquid female body which is a quintessentially negative 'other' lurking inside the male body." They continue, "On the other there is the hard, organized, phallic body devoid of all internal viscera which finds its apotheosis in the machine." "This body-machine," which "is the acknowledged 'utopia' of the fascist warrior," is aroused, erect, in relation to its own "woman within."[141] The rhetoric surrounding the female body is thus a device for the gift of the woman's "internal viscera" into the interior of the male body-machine. Here we can see the disclosure of the erection and ejaculation of the executioner, in whom is intertwined this simultaneous fear and attachment towards the Emperor, who usurps the female body and disguises himself with the feminine. Thus Maruo's dreaming executioner, this "political boy" (*seiji shōnen*) orgasms with desire for the cross-dressed Emperor who manifests within him, but his ejaculation is merely an implosion.

In the 1930s, *The Cardinal Principles of the National Polity* was, as in the beginning, a retrospective rendering of the myths of the *Kojiki* and *Nihon shoki* as free from any obstacles, a repetition of the "ruling and firming up" (*shurikosei*) of the legitimacy of the Emperor's reign and its unbroken lineage, "as eternal as heaven and earth." The mechanism which functions here is the rhetoric of the female body. This rhetoric not only declares and enacts in principle the origin of the state in the beginning through the ideal of the national polity or the self-consciousness of the state, but moreover is an essential device for the ceaseless, repetitive imagining and effective maintenance of the bordering of the state, a mechanism which still continues to operate. At the same time, the female body, this national polity or self-consciousness of the state signifies a repeated failure to stabilize this corporeal bordering, an apparatus of the crisis which each time, secures the revision of interpretation. "We" failed to destroy this mechanism in 1945.

It is said that "unlike territory, stories cannot be so easily stolen"[142] – the compilers of the *Cardinal Principles* repeat the rhetoric (politics) of the female body as mediation, and hereafter it will continue to repeat. Thus, the nation-as-state (homosociality) is a memory-apparatus. The woman's body is an encoded hard-drive. Its logic is binary. Thus the national polity/body does not signify "nationality" – it is rather the sign of the national corpus, the national corpse.

Notes

1. Luce Irigaray (1977) *Ce sexe qui n'en est pas un,* Paris: Minuit, p. 88. English translation as *This Sex Which is Not One,* translated by Catherine Porter, Ithaca: Cornell University Press, 1985.
2. Slavoj Žižek (2002) "Afterword: Lenin's choice," to *Revolution at the Gates: Selected Writings of Lenin from 1917,* edited by Slavoj Žižek, London: Verso, p. 255. Žižek quotes this from Eric Santner, "Miracles happen: Benjamin, Rosenzweig, and the limits of the Enlightenment" (unpublished paper, 2001).
3. "Planet of the Jap" (Nihonjin no wakusei) is contained in Maruo Suehiro's (1986) *Paranoia Sutā,* Kawade Shobō Shinsha, pp. 117–44.
4. Mary J. Shapiro (1986) *Gateway to Liberty: The Story of the Statue of Liberty and Ellis Island,* New York: Vintage.
5. Marvin Trachtenberg (1986) *The Statue of Liberty,* New York: Penguin, p. 196.
6. Lauren Gail Berlant (1991) *The Anatomy of National Fantasy: Hawthorne, Utopia, and Everyday Life,* Chicago: University of Chicago Press, p. 27.
7. Irigaray, *Ce sexe qui n'en est pas un,* pp. 181,186.
8. Jeffner Allen (1986) *Lesbian Philosophy: Explorations,* Palo Alto: Institute of Lesbian Studies, p. 40.
9. Kihira Tadayoshi (1938) *Waga kokutai ni okeru wa* (Kokutai no hongi kaisetsu sōsho), Tokyo: Kyōgakukyoku, p. 22.
10. Jean Franco (1996) "Beyond ethnocentrism: gender, power, and the Third-World intelligentsia," in Patrick Williams and Laura Chrisman (eds) *Colonial Discourse and Post-Colonial Theory: A Reader,* New York: Columbia University Press, p. 364.
11. Eve Kosovsky Sedgwick (1985) *Between Men: English Literature and Male Homosocial Desire,* New York: Columbia University Press, p. 7.
12. Patricia K. Joplin (1991) "The voice of the shuttle is ours," in Lynne A. Higgins and Brenda R. Silver (eds) *Rape and Representation,* New York: Columbia University Press, pp. 45–6, 57.
13. Irigaray, *Ce sexe qui n'en est pas un,* pp. 181,186.
14. Allen, *Lesbian Philosophy,* 41.
15. Jacques Lacan (1977) *The Four Fundamental Concepts of Psychoanalysis,* translated by Alan Sheridan, London: Tavistock, pp. 106–8.
16. Maurice Merleau-Ponty (1968) *The Visible and the Invisible,* trans. Alphonso Lingis, Evanston: Northwestern University Press.
17. Elizabeth Grosz (1994) *Volatile Bodies: Toward a Corporeal Feminism,* Bloomington: Indiana University Press, p. 101.
18. Hélène Cixous and Catherine Clément (1986) *The Newly Born Woman,* translated by Betsy Wing, Minneapolis: University of Minnesota Press, p. 69.
19. Joplin, "The voice of the shuttle is ours," 57, 52.
20. Klaus Theweleit (1987) *Male Fantasies,* Vol. 1: *Women, Floods, Bodies, History,* translated by Stephen Conway *et al.,* Minneapolis: University of Minnesota Press, p. 202.
21. Higgins and Silver (1991) "Introduction: rereading rape" in *Rape and Representation,* pp. 2–3.
22. Anne McClintock (1995) *Imperial Leather: Race, Gender, and Sexuality in the Colonial Contest,* London and New York: Routledge, p. 27.
23. All subsequent references to the *Kojiki* are in English to the Basil Hall Chamberlain translation, and in Japanese, to the Iwanami Bunko version. My reading of the *Kojiki* has been stimulated by that of Kōnoshi Takamitsu. See his Kojiki *no sekaikan,* Tokyo: Yoshikawa Bunkan, 1986, and Kojiki – *tennō no sekai no monogatari,* Tokyo: NHK, 1995.
24. See Jacques Derrida, *Psyché, invention de l'autre,* Paris: Galilée, 1987 and *Le problème de la genese dans la philosophie de Hursserl,* Paris: PUF, 1990. Also see

Rodolphe Gasché (1994) *Inventions of Difference: On Jacques Derrida*, Cambridge: Harvard University Press, pp. 8–10.

25. Morishige Satoshi (1976) "Tenchi kaibyaku shinwa no kōzō," in *Tenchi kaibyaku to kuni umi shinwa no kōzō*, Tokyo: Yūseidō, p. 27.
26. Jawaharlal Nehru (1967) *Towards Freedom*, Boston: Beacon Press, p. 272.
27. Cixous and Clément (1986) *The Newly Born Woman*, pp. 63–5.
28. Edward Said (1995) "Secular interpretation, the geographical element, and the methodology of Imperialism," in Gyan Prakash (ed.) *After Colonialism: Imperial Histories and Postcolonial Displacements*, Princeton: Princeton University Press, p. 29.
29. Sara Suleri (1992) *The Rhetoric of English India*, Chicago: University of Chicago Press, pp. 15–16.
30. David Spurr (1994) *The Rhetoric of Empire: Colonial Discourse in Journalism, Travel Writing, and Imperial Administration*, Durham: Duke University Press, p. 171; and Theweleit (1987) *Male Fantasies*, Vol. 1, p. 279.
31. McClintock (1988) *Imperial Leather*, 4.
32. Deniz Kandiyoti (1994) "Identity and its discontents: women and the nation," in Williams and Chrisman (eds) *Colonial Discourse and Post-Colonial Theory*, p. 377.
33. If, as Girard has stated, "the common hearth was in fact the locus of ritual sacrifice, it is all the more important that in myth Procne turns back to the hearth to cook her own child." See Joplin (1991) "The voice of the shuttle is ours," in Higgins and Silver (eds) *Rape and Representation*, 64.
34. George L. Mosse (1985) *Nationalism and Sexuality: Respectability and Abnormal Sexuality in Modern Europe*, Madison: University of Wisconsin Press, p. 18; Berlant (1991) *The Anatomy of National Fantasy*, p. 27.
35. Ileana Rodríguez (1994), *House/Garden/Nation: Space, Gender and Ethnicity in Post-Colonial Latin American Literatures by Women*, translated by Robert Carr, Durham: Duke University Press, p. 140.
36. See Gayle Rubin (1975) "The traffic in women: notes on the 'political economy' of sex," in Rayna Reiter (ed.) *Toward an Anthropology of Women*, New York: Monthly Review Press.
37. Rajagopalan Radhakrishnan (1992) "Nationalism, gender, and the narrative of identity," in Andrew Parker *et al.* (eds) *Nationalisms and Sexualities*, New York and London: Routledge, p. 84.
38. Ibid., p. 85.
39. Sedgwick (1990) *Between Men* and *Epistemology of the Closet*, Berkeley: University of California Press.
40. Parker *et al.* (1992) *Nationalisms and Sexualities*, p. 1.
41. Kandiyoti, "Identity and its discontents: women and the nation," p. 377.
42. Annette Kolodny (1975) *The Lay of the Land: Metaphor as Experience and History in American Life and Letters*, Chapel Hill: University of North Carolina Press.
43. McClintock (1988) *Imperial Leather*, p. 28.
44. Rodríguez (1994) *House/Garden/Nation*, p. 5.
45. Theweleit (1987) *Male Fantasies*, Vol. 1, pp. 298–9.
46. McClintock (1988) *Imperial Leather*, p. 47.
47. Berlant (1991) *The Anatomy of National Fantasy*, p. 20.
48. See Gayatri Spivak (1992) "French feminism revisited: ethics and politics," in Judith Butler and Joan W. Scott (eds) *Feminists Theorize the Political*, New York: Routledge.
49. I have taken this conception of ecto-colonization from the endo-colonization theorized in Paul Virilio's (1976) *L'insécurité du territoire*, Paris: Stock; and *Pure War* (with Sylvère Lotringer) New York: Semiotext(e), 1983, as well as Kenneth Dean and Brian Massumi's (1992) *First and Last Emperors,* New York: Autonomedia.
50. On this point, I found Nina Cornyetz's (1997) "Nakagami Kenji no shintai: yogoreta chi, kikei, seiki kison" in *Gengo bunka* 14(3): 181–9, highly suggestive. I would like to thank Nina here.

51. Rodríguez (1994) *House/Garden/Nation*, p. 43.
52. On the use of the term "invagination" in feminist critique, see Grosz (p. 220) and Anzieu (p. 10).
53. See Theresa Hak-Kyung Cha (1982) *Dictee*, Berkeley: Third Woman Press, pp. 46–7.
54. Marjorie Garber (1992) *Vested Interests: Cross-Dressing and Cultural Anxiety*, New York: Harper Collins, p. 390.
55. Elleke Boehmer (1991) "Stories of women and mothers: gender and nationalism in the early fiction of Flora Nwapa," in Susheila Nasta (ed.) *Motherlands: Black Women's Writing from Africa, the Caribbean, and South Asia*, London: The Women's Press, p. 6.
56. Teresa De Lauretis (1987) *Technologies of Gender: Essays on Theory, Film, and Fiction*, Bloomington: Indiana University Press, p. 33.
57. Cixous and Clément (1986) *The Newly Born Woman*, pp. 67–8.
58. Doris Sommer (1991) *Foundational Fictions: The National Romances of Latin America*, Berkeley: University of California Press, pp. 257–8.
59. Kenneth Dean and Brian Massumi (1992) *First and Last Emperors: The Absolute State and the Body of the Despot*, New York: Autonomedia, p. 83.
60. Sommer, (1991) *Foundational Fictions*, p. 107.
61. Dean and Massumi, (1992) *First and Last Emperors*, p. 163.
62. Spurr (1994) *The Rhetoric of Empire*, p. 11.
63. McClintock (1988) *Imperial Leather*, p. 353; Michele Barrett, *Women's Oppression Today: Problems in Marxist Feminist Analysis*, London: Verso, p. xi.
64. Paul Virilio (1984) *War and Cinema: The Logistics of Perception*, translated by Patrick Camiller, London: Verso, p. 42.
65. Rodríguez (1994) *House/Garden/Nation*, p. 86.
66. Rosi Braidotti (1991) *Patterns of Dissonance: A Study of Women in Contemporary Philosophy*, translated by Elizabeth Guild, New York: Routledge, p. 17.
67. Karl Marx (1963) *The Eighteenth Brumaire of Louis Bonaparte*, New York: International Publishers, p. 108.
68. Berlant (1991) *The Anatomy of National Fantasy*, pp. 19–20.
69. See Dean and Massumi (1992) *First and Last Emperors*.
70. The often-cited Kihira Tadayoshi (employee of the Institute for National Spiritual Culture) clearly specifies that he "oversaw the compilation of the *Cardinal Principles of the National Polity*" (Kihiro, Tadayoshi (1938) *Waga kokutai ni okeru wa* (Kokatai no hongi kaisetsu sōsho) Tokyo Kyōgakuyoku, p. 29), and it is doubtless that the majority of those who authored the series of commentaries related to the *Cardinal Principles*, the sources I utilize here, also directly participated in the writing of the *Cardinal Principles* themselves. In relation to Foucault's sense of style, I would like to insert here a temporary diversion into economic history. The moment when the idea of the national polity was particularly promulgated in modern Japan was precisely the period in which its discontinuity and disconnection was being exposed. Every time that a (re)interpretation of the idea of the national polity approached, it was rearranged into a continuity through a characteristic discursive response ("ruling and firming up," or *shurikosei*). The first disconnection corresponds to the confirmation of the state-ideal of the formation of the nation-state in the transition in Japanese capitalism between the period of primitive accumulation to the advent of the liberal stage. This can be seen in the establishment in 1889 of the Greater Japanese Empire, and the promulgation in the following year of the "Imperial Rescript on Education." At the same time, 1890 was the year of the first crisis experienced by Japanese capitalism. The second was the period of restructuring during the interwar years – the political approval and stipulation of the identification between the national polity and the Emperor-system (*tennōsei*, a supposedly left-wing term) in the process of the enactment of the Maintenance of Public Order Act of 1900 – the time of the reaffirmation of the state-ideal in accordance with the establishment of a "mass democratic" society in the imperialist stage. The third corresponds to the total war

system (*sōryokusen taisei*) – the political problematization of Minobe Tatsukichi's lapsed "Emperor organ theory," the problem of the clarification of the national polity, and the publication of Cardinal Principles – and responds to the affirmation of the state-ideal corresponding to contemporary capitalism. These three – if we include the attempts to protect the national polity stubbornly adhered to in the "Imperial Rescript on the Termination of War," then it would be four – epochal moments conform to the various stages of Japanese capitalism, and to their discursive/non-discursive restructuring. The common point running through these epochal moments was already given in the first disconnection mentioned. In the basic grammar of the state various styles are given. This basic grammar can be understood as follows. The constitution of the Greater Japanese Empire stipulated the legitimacy of the Emperor in an institutional sense, but the Imperial Rescript on Education was nothing more than a civilizing movement for the formation of support for this institutionalization. However, much more interesting than this Rescript itself is Inoue Tetsujirō's "On the Imperial Rescript" (*Chokugo engi*), in the "Preface" of which he expresses his feelings as follows: "When I see the present situation of my mother nation with eyes that have become used to the high civilization of Europe, I cannot but acknowledge the great difference between them and us, and I am deeply hurt. When I look at the situation of the world powers, it is clear that not only the Western nations, but also those countries established and settled by Europeans, are prospering. Eastern nations are the only ones that can compete in progress with the West . . . In the East of today, only China and Japan remain independent and are able to compete for their national interests with the Western powers. However, China's eyes are fixed firmly on the past, and show few signs of a progressive spirit. Only Japan is making progress day and night, and will produce a glorious culture in the future depending on how this progress proceeds. However, Japan is a small nation and surrounded by rapacious enemies on all sides . . . if they ever see a weakness in us, we will have nothing to depend on but our 40 million compatriots." (Inoue (1990) *Chokugo engi*, in Yamazumi Masami (ed.) *Kyōiku no taikei* (Tokyo: Iwanami Shoten). English translation of Inoue by David Askew in Oguma Eiji (2002) *Genealogy of Japanese Self-Images* (Trans-Pacific Press, p. 34, translation modified)). The sentiment being expressed here is the possibility of locating the "East" in relation to the "West," and an exaltation of the possibility of Japan within the "East." This exaltation of these two possibilities constituted two sides of the same coin: the fear of being castrated (colonized) or violated. While corresponding to the crisis seen in the subject (*shukan*) – crisis is always a subjectively interpreted crisis – the constant haunting fear behind the ideal of the nation-state of Japan, and indeed behind the declarations of the ideals of most nation-states is variously expressed, variously narrated. Even in the symbolic Emperor-system which reached its completion in the postwar, this fear functions, although its stylistic expressions have changed. Maruo Suehiro's bizarrely imaged icons have their roots in precisely this anxiety and fear of castration.

71. Itō (1982) *Kazoku kokkaron no jinruigaku*, Tokyo: Minerva Shobō.
72. Kawashima Takeyoshi (1963) *Ideorogī toshite no kazoku seido*, Tokyo: Iwanami Shoten, pp. 53–66.
73. In the knot of nationalism and sexuality, we can posit the existence of five broad fields: (1) the biological reproduction of the members of the national assemblage; (2) the reproduction of the national boundaries mediated by the limitations imposed on sexual, or matrimonial relations; (3) the production and active transmission of national culture; (4) the symbolic signifiers of national difference; (5) active participation in national struggle. See Nira Yuval-Davis and Floya Anthias (ed.) *Woman-Nation-State,* London: Macmillan (1989), p. 7. Of the fields above, I will here attempt to address (2) and (4).
74. Kihira, *Waga kokutai ni okeru wa*, p. 22.
75. Muraoka Tsunetsugu (1962) *Kokuminsei no kenkyū*, Nihon shisōshi kenkyū V, Tokyo: Sōbunsha.

76. Kihira Tadayoshi (1941) *Waga kuni ni okeru ie to kuni* (Kokutai no hongi kaisetsu sōsho) Tokyo: Kyōgakukyoku, p. 6.
77. Ibid., pp. 1–2.
78. Ibid., pp. 5–6.
79. See Nagahara Yutaka (1989) *Tennōsei kokka to nōmin*, Tokyo: Nihon keizai hyōronsha.
80. Kakei Katsuhiko (1913) *Kokka no kenkyū,* Tokyo: Shimizu Shoten, pp. 17–19.
81. Maruyama Masao (1992) "Rekishi no 'kosō'," in *Chūsei to hangyaku: tenkeiki Nihon no seishinteki ichi*, Tokyo: Chikuma Shobō, p. 334.
82. Kōno Seizō (1938) *Waga kokutai to shintō* (Kokutai no hongi kaisetsu sōsho) Tokyo: Kyōgakukyoku, pp. 2–3.
83. Ibid., pp. 2–3.
84. Ibid., p. 20.
85. Ibid., p. 29.
86. Kihira (1938) *Waga kokutai ni okeru wa*, p. 30.
87. Monbushō, *Kokutai no hongi* (Monbushō, 1937), p. 9; *Kokutai No Hongi: Cardinal Principles of the National Entity of Japan*, translated by John Owen Gauntlett, Cambridge: Harvard University Press, 1949, p. 60. Translation modified.
88. Naganuma Kenkai (1939) *Kokushi jō yori mitaru kokutai to kokumin seishin, Kyōgaku sōsho tokushū*, 13: 2, 4.
89. Kihira (1938) *Waga kokutai ni okeru wa*, pp. 33–4.
90. Kakei (1913) *Kokka no kenkyū*, p. 19.
91. Theweleit (1987) *Male Fantasies*, Vol. 1, p. 299.
92. Gayatri Spivak (1999) "Can the subaltern speak?" in Williams and Chrisman (eds) *Colonial Discourse and Post-Colonial Theory*, p. 103.
93. Kihira (1938) *Waga kokutai ni okeru wa*, pp. 22–4. Also see Sakuta Sōichi (1940) *Wa ga kokutai to keizai* (Kokutai no hongi kaisetsu sōsho) Tokyo: Kyōgakukyoku.
94. Kihira (1941) *Waga kuni ni okeru ie to kuni*, pp. 38–40.
95. Kihira (1938) *Waga kokutai ni okeru wa*, p. 46.
96. Ibid., pp. 46–7.
97. Ibid., pp. 28–9.
98. See *Kojiki* (1883) *Records of Ancient Matters*, translated by Basil Hall Chamberlain in *Transactions of the Asiatic Society of Japan*, Vol. 10 (Suppl), Yokohama: R. Meiklejohn & Co., pp. 18–23.
99. *Kojiki*, pp. 29–30. Translation modified.
100. Luce Irigaray (1991) "Women-mothers, the silent substratum of the social order," in Margaret Whitford (ed.) *The Irigaray Reader*, Oxford: Basil Blackwell, p. 48.
101. Kihira (1941) *Waga kuni ni okeru ie to kuni*, p. 57.
102. Irigaray (1977) *Ce sexe qui n'en est pas un*, pp. 180, 185.
103. Coppélia Kahn (1991) "Lucrece: the sexual politics of subjectivity" in Higgins and Silver (eds) *Rape and Representation*, pp. 146–7.
104. Jean-Joseph Goux (February 1983) "Vesta, or the place of being," *Representations* 1: 91–107.
105. Joplin, "The voice of the shuttle is ours," in Higgins and Silver (eds) *Rape and Representation*, pp. 43–4.
106. Irigaray (1977) *Ce sexe qui n'en est pas un*, pp. 180–1/185–6.
107. Kelly Oliver (1995) *Womanizing Nietzsche: Philosophy's Relation to the "Feminine,"* New York: Routledge, p. 9. As can be frequently seen in Maruo Suehiro's work, the traffic between the interior of the womb and society suggests that he is trying to conceal precisely this fear.
108. Joplin, "The voice of the shuttle is ours," in Higgins and Silver (eds) *Rape and Representation*, p. 42.
109. Jonathan Goldberg (1992) "Bradford's 'ancient members' and 'a case of buggery. . . amidst them,'" in Parker *et al.* (eds) *Nationalisms and Sexualities*, New York: Routledge.

110. Luce Irigaray (1993) *An Ethics of Sexual Difference*, translated by Carolyn Burke and Gillian C. Gill, Ithaca: Cornell University Press.
111. Kihira (1938) *Waga kokutai ni okeru wa*, pp. 64, 66.
112. Kihira (1940) *Waga kuni ni okeru ie to kuni*, pp. 58–9.
113. Theweleit (1987) *Male Fantasies*, Vol. 1, p. 104. See also Mosse (1985) *Nationalism and Sexuality*, p. 17.
114. Gaston Bachelard (1964) *The Poetics of Space*, translated by John Stilgoe, Boston: Beacon Press, p. 5.
115. Kihira (1938) *Waga kuni ni okeru ie to kuni*, p. 10.
116. Maruyama (1992) "Rekishi no 'kosō'," pp. 342–3.
117. Parker *et al.* (1992) *Nationalisms and Sexualities*, p. 6.
118. Kihira (1938) *Waga kokutai ni okeru wa*, pp. 49, 35.
119. Jacques Derrida (1991) *Donner le temps, 1: La fausse monnaie*, Paris: Galilée.
120. Luce Irigaray (1992) *Elemental Passions*, trans. Joanne Collie and Judith Still, New York and London: Routledge, pp. 1–2.
121. On the various theories of the "national polity" (kokutai), see Nagao (1982), in addition to Suzuki (1986, 1993).
122. See Morohashi's *Dai kanwa jiten*.
123. Hachijō Takatake (1941) *Kokutai to kokka keitairon* in *Nihon shogaku kenkyū* 12: 3.
124. Hachijō (1941) *Kokutai to kokka keitairon*, pp. 22, 36.
125. Kihira (1941) *Waga kuni ni okeru ie to kuni*, p. 23.
126. Franco (1996) "Beyond ethnocentrism: gender, power, and the third-world intelligentsia," in Williams and Chrisman (ed.) *Colonial Discourse and Post-Colonial Theory*, pp. 365–6.
127. Ernst Kantorowicz (1957) *The King's Two Bodies: A Study in Medieval Political Theology*, New Jersey: Princeton University Press.
128. Mary Douglas (1982) *Natural Symbols: Explorations in Cosmology*, New York: Pantheon, p. 70. In discussing Origuchi Shinobu and Kantorowicz, Fujitani classifies the "invisible/visible Emperor" or the "Emperor" and the "Imperial Throne," and remarks on the ambiguous gender of the "visible Emperor." He only briefly touches on this in relation to the comparison of Tokyo and Kyoto, but it is a point which hits the mark. See Fujitani, Takashi (1994) *Tennō no pājento*, Tokyo: NHK, pp. 93–4, 133–4, 166–7. For a similar view, see Taki Kōji (1988) *Tennō no shōzō*, Tokyo: Iwanami Shinsho, pp. 96, 195.
129. Kihira (1938) *Waga kokutai ni okeru wa*, p. 53.
130. Ibid., pp. 85–6. [Addition in brackets mine.]
131. Ibid., p. 48. [Addition in brackets mine.]
132. Kojiki (1883) translated by Chamberlain, pp. 45–6.
133. Garber (1992) *Vested Interests*, p. 390.
134. Kihira (1938) *Waga kokutai ni okeru wa*, p. 44.
135. Dean and Massumi (1992) *First and Last Emperors*, 153ff.
136. Kihira (1941) *Waga kuni ni okeru ie to kuni*, pp. 5–6.
137. Garber (1992) *Vested Interests*, p. 390.
138. Yamada Yoshio (1939) *Chōkoku no seishin* (Kokutai no hongi kaisetsu sōsho) Tokyo: Kyōgakukyoku, pp. 3–5.
139. Quoted in Nagao Ryūichi (1982) *Nihon kokka shisōshi kenkyū*, Tokyo: Sōbunsha.
140. As it is said in the chapter on the Yata-no-kagami in the Iwayato caves, despite the fact that Amaterasu-ōmikami peered into the mirror, she was an entity incapable of recognizing herself. Thus as Fujitani explains in relation to the six great Imperial tours of the early Meiji period, while the Emperor was assumed to be a "surveying ruler," his "invisibility" in fact emerged at precisely the same time as his "unprecedent visibility as a public object of power." Thus he argues, the image of the Emperor was "transcendental yet immanent, divine yet personal, female yet male, invisible yet visible" (Fujitani (1994) *Tennō no pājento*, pp. 166–7). This is an incisive analysis. On

the other hand, Taki, who presented a pioneering analysis from a similar viewpoint, discusses the meaning of the Emperor's increasing invisibility, and points out that the long-awaited imperial tours of the first decade of the Meiji era ceased to occur by the second decade, but doesn't pay attention to the significance of this fact. We might say that the problem is shared with his confusion over Foucault's understanding of "panopticism." For Foucault, panopticism does not indicate the aspect in which power has an unobstructed, total gaze; rather, panopticism is a mechanism in which the center is formed as a void through the gazes of ordinary people, a mechanism of the formation of the center from the side of the seeing, the desire to be seen by this void center.

141. Benjamin and Rabinach (1989) "Introduction," in Klaus Theweleit, *Male Fantasies*, Vol. 2: *Psychoanalyzing the White Terror*, Minneapolis: University of Minnesota Press, p. xix.
142. Suleri (1992) *The Rhetoric of English India*, p. 7.

4 Introduction

Ayelet Zohar: Pelluses/Phani . . .

About the phallus Jacques Lacan wrote, "it is the signifier that is destined to designate meaning effects as a whole, insofar as the signifier conditions them by its presence as signifier."[1] Ayelet Zohar challenges Freud and Lacan's privileging of the phallus as the unitary, and unifying, signifier. Aligning herself first with Judith Butler and Kaja Silverman, and other feminists, Zohar decries the relation to the penis that is, she argues, intrinsic to how Freud and Lacan conceptualized the phallus, or sign of lack. Second, Zohar mobilizes Gilles Deleuze and Félix Guattari's notion of "the body without organs" to rethink the pre-Oedipal, or pre-discursive, pre-Mirror Stage "fragmented subject" as an unhierarchized multiplicity, in her own application of their "schizoanalysis." Finally, she theorizes a set of Japanese contemporary artworks and performance pieces – Shigeko Kubota's "Vagina Painting," Morimura Yasumasa's "Black Marilyn," and Takashi Murakami's "My Lonesome Cowboy" – in relation to their "pluralizations" of the penis and/or phallus, and deconstruction of the binarism of penis as "1" and vagina as "0."

Note

1. Jacques Lacan (2006) *Écrits: The First Complete Edition in English*, Bruce Fink (trans.) New York: W. W. Norton and Company, p. 579.

4 Pelluses/phani

The multiplication, displacement and appropriations of the phallus

Ayelet Zohar

> The full body-without-organs is populated by multiplicities.
>
> Gilles Deleuze and Félix Guattari, *A Thousand Plateaus*

The concept of the phallus as "the privileged signifier" is one of the central ideas of psychoanalysis, first introduced by Sigmund Freud in his discussion of childhood development and the dream, and later considered by Jacques Lacan as the origin of the signifying system and culture.[1] Throughout their writings, Freud and Lacan discussed numerous qualities of the phallus as the prominent part-object (Freud), or the primary and only signifier marked by the absence (desire) it signifies (Lacan), while both indicate the phallus as the signifier of "Onement," as compared to the absolute or *the-name-of the-father*.[2]

Lacan's idea of the phallus was challenged by numerous writers, including prominent feminist, gender, queer and sexual studies writers such as Parveen Adams, Kaja Silverman and Judith Butler, whose texts offer varying concepts undermining the place of the phallus, which constitutes the primary stratum of this text.[3] However, these works are all locked within the greater discourse of Western disciplines and, consequently, their critique does not extend beyond this immediate territory. On the other hand, critics such as Gayatri Chakravorty Spivak or Homi K. Bhabha recognized early on the shortcomings of psychoanalysis as a tool for examining non-Western cultures, and therefore proposed more culturally specific concepts within the framework of a particular analysis.[4]

In the context of these discussions, my text offers a new angle, inspired by a selection of images taken from contemporary Japanese art, through which I hope to throw fresh light on the concepts of psychoanalysis. My thesis follows the trajectory outlined by Spivak and Bhabha, by demonstrating that in a specific cultural context (such as contemporary Japanese art), and despite their seeming resemblance, objects, images and concepts may contain very different ideas. Moreover, the works discussed in this text are not exclusively Japanese, and reveal varying levels of engagement with Western culture – ranging from the fact that the artist resided and performed the work discussed in New York (Kubota), to the omnipresence of Hollywood cinema and its involvement with different cultural paradigms (Morimura), and finally, the ironic portrayal of the quintessential

American phallic image of the cowboy (Murakami). The insights contributed to the discussion therefore stem from a complex understanding of the simultaneous separation from, and participation with, Western culture.

My discussion of the phallus has two aims: first, the text deconstructs the apparent dichotomy of the phallus and the penis, as described by Freud and Lacan,[5] and introduces the concept of the pellus/phanis as an alternative terminology to indicate the embodied and multiplied desire of a defused ego structure. I am using this double term, pellus/phanis, to reinforce a more comprehensive perception of psycho-analysis, which refutes the dichotomy of the tangible and conceptual. Second, this text links the concept of the pellus/phanis to ideas of *becoming* and *multiplicity*, in contrast to the uniqueness of the phallus as the sole signifier, which in Lacan's terminology relates to his understanding of the phallus in relation to *the-name-of-the-father*.[6]

My interrogation of these issues points to a possible alternative sexual discourse, one that offers altered, collapsed, syncretic and merged signifying systems in parallel with Freud and Lacan's discourse of presence/absence. My critique is intended not just to negate Lacan's discussion of the phallus, or Freud's considerations of the *phallic stage* or *penis envy*, but to contribute a new angle to this discourse, in order to expand our understanding of sexuality and the construction of the *self* in different cultural contexts.[7] These two objectives will be achieved through an examination of contemporary works of art, which are taken from a potentially large selection in Japanese visual culture; each endows pelluses/phani with a different possible status, and offers a new set of concepts that may shed light on broader cultural thinking.

The phallus in psychoanalytic discourse: Freud and Lacan

The first use of the term *phallus* in Freud's psychoanalytical theory arose in his discussion of the development of the young child. Freud coined the term *phallic stage*[8] to identify:

> a stage of libidinal development of both sexes, [that] occupies a central position in that it is correlated with the castration complex and its acme that governs the setting up and the resolution of the Oedipal complex. The choice offered the subject at this stage is simply that between having the phallus or being castrated.[9]

He therefore established a binary opposition between having and losing, in the extreme sense of being harmed. In mathematical terms, I would say that the opposition created by Freud is between $(+1)$ and (-1), rather than the binary system of (1) and (0), better expressed in Lacan's system as phallus and lack/desire, a perfect match for (0). Castration, as expressed in Freud's text, is not just "not having," but "actively deducting," which I refer to as (-1). Later in his writings, Freud adds the idea that, in relation to female sexuality, the wish to have the father's phallus is transformed into the wish to have a child, collapsing the distinction between the penis, phallus and baby into a psychoanalytic overlap.[10]

In his discussion of the relationship of both sexes to the penis, Freud sees the woman as suffering from *penis envy*, and, according to *the-law-of-the-father*, castration should be the punishment for this incestuous desire.[11] The relation of the subject to the phallus is set up in a similar manner, regardless of the anatomical difference between the sexes. Therefore, according to Freud, the girl fears castration by the mother who holds the phallus, in a phase which he termed the *phallic mother*.[12] The meaning of castration is manifested fully only after the discovery of the mother's castrated state, and feminine sexual maturity is achieved when the feminine phallus (the clitoris) is replaced with the notion of the vagina as the site of genital penetration and potential desire.

The choice offered by Freud significantly differs from the anatomical realities of the penis and vagina as a pair of two separate entities presumably in binary opposition to each other, referring to the possibility of having or actively losing the singular object of significance, an organ that exists as if detached from the body. The idea of the primacy of the phallus for both sexes arises from Freud's notion that a little girl is unaware of the presence of the vagina. Freud was therefore the first to assign the phallus its singular role in a binary system of having or losing, rather than allowing for a variety of sexualities and sexual organs. The phallus is the one and nothing but the one, which gives it enormous potential power in psychoanalytic and religious discourses. The phallus *must* be one, and its "Onement" defines itself in relation to absence in its proximity. The phallus is elucidated by its function: in the Freudian sense the phallus is not a fantasy, and neither is the organ (penis or clitoris); therefore, "it is not incidental that Freud took his reference for it from the simulacrum which it represented for the ancients."[13] In his discussion of the symbolic value of the dream system Freud notes that the phallus is one of the most common and universal objects of symbolization.[14] However, what interests me here is the presence of the phallus as a detachable and transformable object, therefore becoming *a part-object*,[15] with an autonomy attributed to it that sometimes goes as far as endowing it with personification.[16]

The Lacanian version of the *Oedipal complex* is formed in a dialectic conflict, whose major alternatives are *to be* or *not to be* the phallus, or *to have* or *not to have* it.[16] According to Lacan, the symbolic order refers to the allegorical meaning of fecundity, authority and potency; therefore, the phallus tends to be the meaning, the signification, or what is symbolized in its own right. Since the phallus in Lacanian thought is the origin of the signifying system, it emerges as a clear shape of "Onement" from the sea of chaotic nothingness, of unclear, indefinable shapes. In Lacanian theory, then, the phallus is described in parallel terms to Genesis, the beginning of all things as prescribed in the Bible, when the spirit of God, the origin of all, was floating over chaos, attributing to it qualities that place it in parallel to *the-name-of-the-father*, and becoming the origin of meaning and signification. *The-name-of-the-father* brings forward the link with language: man speaks through man and for man it speaks. Man becomes the material of language, since he is constituted by language.

From this point on, the phallus, under its symbolic status, can take part in "symbolic equations" and alternate between various states (penis-faeces-child-gift). Commonly, these objects are all products of the body, but exist separately to be circulated from one person to another. The problem for Lacan (as well as for Freud) was centered on the issue of giving the phallus an explanation that avoids reducing it to the biological difference between sexes, yet provides a differentiated account of its effects for varying genders. Lacan traced his conception of the phallus through the difficulty of the sexual relationship, especially for the woman whose relation to the phallic term is described essentially in terms of *masquerade*, or signified desire.

Freud and Lacan, therefore, established an economy of the phallus, based on ideas of having, being, lack, envy and desire. Given that the phallus is the signifier of desire, and desire is always indirect, veiled, even masqueraded, it results in the perception that the woman *is* the phallus, and the man *has* the phallus.

Phanises, multiplicity, le corps morcelé and the body-without-organs

The image of *"the body in pieces"* (*le corps morcelé*) appears in Lacan's Seminar II, where he discusses the meaning of the *mirror stage*:

> . . . the body in pieces finds its unity in the image of the Other, which is its own anticipated image – a dual situation which is a polar, but non-symmetrical relation, is sketched out . . . The subject is no one. It is decomposed, in pieces. And it is jammed, sucked in by the image, the deceiving and realised image, of the other, or equally by its own specular image. That is where it finds its unity.[18]

There are several instances where Lacan explains that the *mirror stage* is the moment enabling the unification of *the body in pieces* into a continuous, unified being:[19]

> The mirror stage is a drama whose internal pressure pushes precipitously from insufficiency to anticipation – and, for the subject caught up in the lure of spatial identification, turns out fantasies that proceed from a fragmented image of the body to what I will call an "orthopedic" form of its totality . . . that will mark his entire mental development with its rigid structure. Thus, shattering of the *Innenwelt* to *Umwelt* circle gives rise to an inexhaustible squaring of the ego's audits.[20]

Lacan suggests a view of the ego as an orthopedic aid, an external apparatus that supports the I, a device born from the shattering of the distinction between in and out, identity and reality, the self and the world. The discussion of the phallus in Lacan should, therefore, be seen in the light of his views of *the body in pieces*. Butler has already indicated that the phallus should be compared to the *mirror* –

the object within which the *imago* of the unified self is established, and in charge of a unifying concept that overrides fragmentation and multiplicity.[21]

On the other hand, Linda Nochlin has referred to *the body in pieces* while articulating the fragment as a metaphor for modernity,[22] best embodied in techniques such as collage and assemblage that create the unified image as a conglomeration of fragments attached together.[23] This account permits the possibility of appraisal of the Lacanian *mirror stage* and the *imago* fashioned in it, as an assemblage of pieces attached together to create an enforced unity. Lacan's idea of the I perfectly corresponds to this description of modernity as a collage – an assembly of pieces constituting the unified self within the context of modern life. As a result, I use the ideas of re-fragmentation and shattering of the *imago*, and the discontinuity of the imagined unified self, as part of my argument of non-Western views of the image of the self, the body, sexuality and the phallus.

Gilles Deleuze and Félix Guattari (1988) have already identified Freud's tendency to erase any signs of multiplicity and, instead, place singular models,[24] escaping the possibility of a multiplied rhizomatic structure for the sake of the singular, phallic root.[25] The transfer into horizontal structures of relationship is also offered by Juliet Mitchell in her study of sexual fantasies/ relationships between siblings (rather than the Freudian assumption of vertical cross-generational fantasies between parents and children).[26] However, Deleuze and Guattari's suggestion exceeds this view of horizontality, to place it in the context of multiplicities, which is the route my text follows in attempting to deconstruct the singularity of the phallus. Moreover, a close reading of the Lacanian text identifies his argument of multiplicity – that of the body and the *imago*, a concept well articulated through his discussion of *le corps morcelé*. Lacan (like Deleuze and Guattari's argument against Freud) does not recognize the potential encompassed within *the body in pieces*, and his project is targeted at identifying a unifying agent (the *mirror*) that will keep all pieces attached together to create the subject as a unified self.[27]

Yet, a return to the multiplicity of the fragments, and their existence on a horizontal/ rhizomatic plane, may create an alternative discourse of the self, in contrast to Freud and Lacan's description of the process of consolidation of selfhood through separation and individuation. In Deleuze and Guattari's discourse, the metaphor of schizoanalysis is employed for identifying new formats of personal existence beyond the process of consolidation and individuation described in traditional psychoanalysis.[28] I offer a reading that sees the Lacanian concept of the *body in pieces* as similar to Deleuze and Guattari's concept of the *body-without-organs*,[29] in itself an equivalent of the multiplicity of the *penus* instead of the singularity of the phallus or penis. Butler clearly perceives this identification when she draws a parallel between Lacan's discussion of the *mirror* [30] and the phallus, pointing at how Lacan attempts to arrive at an amalgamating principle – forming continuity between the I and the phallus.[31] Butler proceeds from this point to consider the fiction of the phallus within lesbian discourse; I propose to continue my investigation in the Deleuzian context, paying attention to the moment before signification, the moment when the *body-in-pieces* and the *body-without-organs* take their respective places *en route* to multiplicity – first, that of the phallus, which may result in the multiplicity of gender and the self.[32] This method also highlights the presence of *the sex which is not one* – the female sexual organs are a multiple structure of various elements, each with a separate name and function.[33] This multiplicity of the female sexual organs versus the uniformity of the phallus is the key to an alternative structure with new possibilities for gender and personal formations.

Pellus/phanis: penis or phallus?

> The law requires conformity to its own notion of "nature" and gains its legitimacy through the binary and asymmetrical naturalization of bodies in which the Phallus, though clearly not identical with the penis, nevertheless deploys the penis as its naturalized instrument and sign.[34]

Psychoanalytic language distinguishes clearly between the phallus and the penis: while penis refers to the physical male organ in its anatomical reality, the phallus underlines a symbolic function based on an inter-subjective relationship.[35] A close reading of Lacan and Freud reveals that the assumption of separateness between the two contains significant slippage: the distinction between the penis and phallus is on the basis of "being veiled" and "being exposed," as well as in relation to its organic state – the phallus is always and only erected (and veiled), while the penis occupies the place of the deflated.[36] This concept has been challenged by different scholars, who argue that the earlier suggested division is highly questionable.

Silverman, quite early in her text, insists on the veiling of the phallus and the exposure of the penis as the most important distinction between the two, a separation that enables (according to Lacan) the differentiation between the Imaginary and Symbolic attributions of the phallus:[37]

> The erect penis seems to represent both, in the one case as that which no fully constituted subject can any longer "be," and which is consequently "veiled" or lacking, and in the other as that which only the male subject can have.[38]

Silverman, however, identifies another crucial difference between the penis and the phallus – the phallus is not just veiled, but also erected, while the penis must be prone, which is absent from the *mirror*.[39] Silverman clearly notes that "there is a good deal of slippage in Lacan . . . between the phallus and the penis, but [also] between the phallus and the Symbolic capacity, and the phallus and the Imaginary capacity."[40]

Adams adds another level of complexity to the issue. If Lacan identifies the phallus with lack, then the penis (or the breast or womb) will be the signifier of "phallic satisfaction."[41] However, this constitution may deprive the woman of the possibility of her own desire, and therefore one should consider the phallus as *the signifier of the veil* itself, "the signifier of lack and the covering of lack par excellence."[42] In the course of her text Adams shows brilliantly how the constitution of motherhood as the opposite of castration is, in fact, the affirmation of this thought through its establishment of lack and "having." In my view, remaining with the ambiguity of the object and the veil will serve to collapse the dichotomy between penis and phallus in relation to Lacanian discourse.[43]

Butler presents the collapse of the penis and the phallus from a different point of view: by asking about the nature of "veiling" in relation to the phallus, she also questions the nature of "exposure" (within the discourse of the lesbian phallus).[44] Butler's text, therefore, immediately arrives at an argument that undermines the relationship between the Imaginary and the Symbolic, matter and language. The phallus, already collapsed into the penis, to become what I coin the *penus*, functions as a "phantom organ" or "imaginary effect"[45] rather than as Lacan's "privileged signifier."[46]

My reading of the above critiques by Silverman, Adams and Butler, as well as my understanding of Deleuze and Guattari's critique of Freud and Lacan, led to the introduction of a twofold expression that performs this unleashed doubleness: the pellus and the phanis. These two differ from each other in priority: the pellus refers to the tangible and anatomically detailed organ that precedes desire and its conceptual positioning, while phanis refers to the symbolic signifier in language and shape that may resemble in proportion or sound the penis, but not actual or anatomical depictions of the male sexual organ, a position where concept precedes form. Both terms are multiple signifiers, directed at reconciling the previously used double terminology of penis/phallus, male/female, man/woman, be/have, lack/desire, veiled/exposed, by introducing an amalgamated term that takes the discussion into a *third space* of multiplied signifiers and objects – whether in language, flesh, wood, metal or otherwise. The collapse of the dichotomy between the penis and the phallus, the Imaginary and the Symbolic, becomes the epitomization, even the materialization, of the imagined and signified phallus.

My reading, however, adds a new level of engagement with the concept of the pellus/phanis, a reading informed by the field of contemporary art, and considers a new angle to the preceding critical discussion. This text is therefore an attempt to enlighten the issue from a different cultural perspective (Japan) and its visual products, while proposing an alternative discourse that questions a most important concept in psychoanalytic thought.

First and foremost, my text challenges the concept of uniqueness and singularity of the phallus and its link to lack within a binary structure. The end result of this endeavour is not just directed at confronting psychoanalytic thought from a different cultural position, but extends the argument of multiplicity and multi-focality to the discourse of gender identity as a means to understand the construction of gender and sexuality as an economy of diversity rather than as a stranded binary duality. To this end, I have previously argued for the multiplicity of genders, in itself a well manifested phenomenon in Japanese culture.[47]

Last, I accentuate here my hope that this text does not present Japanese cultural products, or "Japan" as a place, as a unique performance of exceptional discourses of sexuality, gender or the self, as I show these to be performed through the signification and manifestation of the pellus/phanis. Quite the opposite: my aspiration is that the readings suggested will serve as a cultural critique and a point of departure to considering gender and sexuality in varying cultures, places or historical circumstances. My aim is to prove the need for an expansion and widening of psychoanalytical tools to include a larger variety of formations and symptoms, psychic structures and points of view, relevant to different cultural climates and times, which avoid the superimposed universalist cultural discourse as performed by Freud and Lacan. My understanding of the pellus/phanis, together with the view of gender multiplicity, is intended to create a more relaxed, diverse and inclusive reading of the human body, gender, sex and the construction of the self.

The works

For my discussion of the multiplicity of the pellus/phanis, this text examines the works of three contemporary Japanese artists, whose work regards special attention to the pellus/phanis either as an abstract shape or as an actual organ. The works I refer to include Shigeko Kubota's *Vagina Painting* (1965), Morimura Yasumasa's *Black Marilyn* (1996) and Murakami Takashi's *My Lonesome Cowboy* (1998). These works show varying degrees of engagement with the penis/phallus, adopting a critical and parodic stand towards the primary values attached to the phallus: its uniqueness, centrality and, above all, its singularity. Through my reading, I challenge this spectacle of singularity, resulting in a destabilization of sexuality and gender as signifying categories.

Shigeko Kubota's *Vagina Painting* (1965): penis envy, the phallic mother[48] and the autonomy of the vagina

Shigeko Kubota's *Vagina Painting* (Figure 4.1) was a performance that took place during the Perpetual Fluxus Festival at the Cinematèque, 4th St, New York, on 4 July, 1965. During the show, Kubota danced and moved along the stage with a piece of cloth soaked with ink dangling from her vagina, creating an abstract action-painting image on the stage floor.

I refer to this work as the opening shot in my analysis of Japanese works of art that challenge the concept of the phallus, because it starts with an ambivalence, produced as a performance of doubleness and multiplicity, which collapses the image of the phallus with that of the vagina. Kubota's work can be examined according to several Freudian concepts such as *penis envy* and the *phallic mother*, but I believe my analysis will foreground their problematic stance, ending with the deconstruction of the phallus by transforming it into a *feminine phallus*, or a *gendered prosthesis*, by a woman who *has* and not *is*, performing Butler's argument of the phallus as a phantom limb.[49] The painting itself, which in this case is the "child" of the vagina and the pretender phallus, works on a different level of representation: the painting mimics and mocks the masculine *action painting*, becoming a moment of *jouissance*. The painting is the *jouissance* of the orgasmic,

Figure 4.1 Shigeko Kubota performing her 'Vagina Painting.' Taken July 4, 1965 during
'Perpetual Fluxus Festival.' (Photograph by George Maciunas, courtesy of
The Gilbert and Lila Silverman Fluxus Collection.)

of the released libido, which has now transformed from sexual energy into dance,
a movement and painting produced by the *vagina-transformed-into-a-phallus*.

Penis envy, the phallic mother/woman and the feminine phallus

Penis envy is a Freudian term that manifests itself in a girl's desire to acquire a
penis, later converted into the desire to have a child and the wish to enjoy the penis
in coitus. However, Freud himself already showed that *penis envy* (the desire for
a child) is not exclusive to the girl. *Penis envy* can be the female aspect of the
masculine *castration complex*: what he is afraid to lose, she desperately wants to
gain. By emphasizing that "the feminine situation is only established, however, if
the wish for the penis is replaced by one for a baby, since the baby equals the phallus
on an ancient symbolic level,"[50] Freud clearly indicates that *penis envy* does not
disappear but just changes format. In the Lacanian context if the phallus is the
one, then the vagina is none. The phallus is the Symbolic order, and the vagina is
absence – a cavity, nonexistent. Kubota's *Vagina Painting*, however, is a rare
attempt to play with the phallus and reconstruct it. Kubota's work alters the
"absent," "non present," "empty" vagina into a positive presence by adorning it
with a powerful creative tool of personal expression through her performance of
painting. The phallus of creativity and personal power is now part of the vagina,
which is the organ that performs the painting – a phallus-like vagina.

The image of a *phallic woman* (not just a mother) is born here, and performed in three different forms: first, she is the subject of her own work, as she occupies the center of the stage and all eyes are directed towards her; second, Kubota is an active woman who undertakes the performance/action that in this case can be specifically compared to Jackson Pollock's action painting – a style conventionally attributed to the masculine discourse of abstract painting and high-modernity, a style encouraged and developed by a group of dominant male artists and critics such as Jackson Pollock and Clement Greenberg.[51] Third, she has the phallus – an elongated object attached to her genitalia, able to move, create, draw, articulate, signify. The piece of cloth comes to life through the multi-layered possibilities that rest on the phallus as *primary signifier*, yet once it is performed by a female agent, it loses its primacy and original status. Kubota's work, then, challenges the psychoanalytic understanding of the phallus as one and the vagina as none, the Imaginary penis and the Symbolic phallus, and the vagina as void (the Real?).

Kubota's *Vagina Painting* is a rare attempt to appropriate the phallus and reconstruct it as hers, while deconstructing its meaning: the castrated woman has reconstructed a (parody of the) phallus, in order to deconstruct its significance; thereafter, she is left with a *masquerade*. The muscles of the vagina hold the masqueraded, masked and pretended phallus, which is, after all, just a piece of cloth dipped in ink . . . This is the moment of melancholia in the Freudian sense: the moment of realization of absence and the presence of the mere masquerade.[52] However, the painting itself (which in this case is the "child" of the vagina and a fabricated phallus) works on a different level: the work embodies a double parody and transgression of the conventional discourse of gender identity, as it simultaneously mimics and mocks the masculine action painting, yet becomes, in itself, a moment of *jouissance* – the *jouissance* of the unruliness of the orgasmic, of the released libido, which is now transformed from sexual energy into dance, a movement, a painting, performed by the vagina-transformed-into-a-phallus. The *phallic woman* is the woman who possesses the phallus (as an imaginary male organ, which is actually a penis – another failure on Freud/Lacan's behalf to separate the two), also equivalent to the active mother who possesses the phallus. This image is, importantly, part of the discourse of fetishism, where the fetishist uses the fetish as a substitute for the maternal phallus whose absence he disavows.

Shigeko Kubota, the only female artist among the three projects I discuss here, becomes the *phallic woman*. Freud does not offer the consideration of a *phallic woman*, only that of a *phallic mother*, clearly clinging to the point of view of the child facing his or her omnipotent mother. However, more recent psychoanalytic discussions have included the term *phallic girls*, especially in a Japanese context;[53] I consider this work as a representation of a *phallic woman*, as a strategy of emptying the phallus from the heavyweight meaning and significance it currently carries. The *phallic woman* is not activated or motivated by *penis envy*, nor by her phallic desire to become a mother (to have a son as a substitute for the phallus); rather, she is a parody, a transgressive critique of the phallus as a concept, because the woman, as everyone can clearly see, can have the phallus, not just be one! The phallus in this case has a double meaning – on one hand it is a *part-object*, as commonly used in the 1950s and 1960s;[54] on the other hand through the allusion to the female body and the abstraction of the (phallic) object, its link to creativity, Kubota cuts through the symbolic *part-object* to engage in a new level of criticism of the Lacanian conception of the phallus as the first and foremost signifier.

If Kubota *has* a phallus in masquerade, then Morimura *is* a masqueraded phallus. Lacan makes a clear distinction that man *has* the phallus – on one hand the symbol, the authority, the language – while woman *is* the phallus; because she arouses desire, she *is* desire. In a complex manner, Shigeko Kubota, acting under what Freud named *penis envy*, is actually having the penis, and Morimura Yasumasa, the man, is *being* the phallus, a *feminine phallus*, all perfectly masquerading in a womanly manner to arouse the desire of the viewer.[55]

Morimura Yasumasa: womanliness as masquerade: the fetish, the penis and the phallus

> In order to be the phallus, that is to say, the signifier of the desire of the Other, the woman will reject an essential part of her femininity, notably all its attributes through masquerade . . . we should not forget that the organ actually invested with this signifying function takes on the value of a fetish.[56]

Morimura Yasumasa's *Black Marilyn* (Figure 4.2) is an image taken from the series entitled "Beauty unto Sickness" (1996), in which Morimura creates a self-portrait as quintessential Hollywood movie stars such as Vivienne Leigh, Rita Hayworth, Audrey Hepburn and Jane Fonda. The image of Marilyn Monroe had three versions, *Marilyn in Red, Marilyn in White* and *Marilyn in Black*, which is the image discussed.

In *Black Marilyn* the photograph shows Morimura himself dressed up in a black dress, *une petite robe noir*, which is a negative version of Marilyn Monroe's lifted-up white billowy dress in the famous scene from *The Seven Year Itch*.[57] Surprisingly, as the dress flutters up, what is exposed is not just a pair of beautiful feminine legs and a faint attempt to hold the dress down, but a fully erected long *pinkish plastic penis* (PPP), which hangs over Morimura's genital area. In the previous section I argued that Kubota *had* a (parodic) phallus – a symbolic object reminiscent of a phallus as a signifier of the power of creativity – while here, Morimura is holding another form of parody – a plastic sex toy in the shape of a perfect penis. The question arising here is whether Morimura's PPP is able to transcend into a phallus, as did Kubota's dangling piece of ink-dipped cloth. In other words, what is the actual status of Morimura's PPP?

In his discussion of fetishism, Freud explains that the fetishist perpetuates the *phallic mother* by the simultaneous disavowal and acknowledgement of the fact of feminine castration. This inconsistency constitutes a splitting of the subject into

Figure 4.2 Black Marilyn, © Yasumasa Morimura, courtesy MEM.

two aspects.[58] The phallus, in this case, functions like a *part-object*,[59] where its inconsistency constitutes a splitting in two of the subject – as having and not having at the same time. This splitting is a rupture between the disavowal (of external reality) and its recognition, a division between two different forms of ego defence, in which disavowal is specifically directed at the denial of perception related to external reality.[60] The fetishist element in Morimura's *Black Marilyn* is performed in a double way, since the picture presents the double identity of a hidden phallus and an exposed PPP. Fetishism here manifests itself as a relationship between the exposed and the hidden, the obscure and the obvious, the parodying and the hidden actuality. Nevertheless, in an unexpected move, he chooses to rupture and parody the perfect masquerade, by bringing the absent penis back into the patina of performed "reality," and embodying it, an absence that enabled him to become a woman. By fully presenting the phallic object within the image, Morimura undermines the idea of singularity and gender specificity to create a moment of multiplicity. Hence, the question of the status of the PPP becomes more specific: it is actually only an image of a penis; therefore it must become a phallus.

Another way to look at Morimura's work derives from the intercessions of Morimura's images in a broader context, where he is immersed in multiple masquerades. Since masquerade is identified in Lacanian discourse with lack, Morimura embodies the multiple presences of the phallus through his manifold masquerades, by the exposure and presentation of the PPP, and through the absence of his own penis from the picture. According to Lacan and Joan Riviere,[61] Morimura is the quintessential woman as he performs a perfect masquerade, beyond his specifically sexualized body. As an object of absence, Morimura plays on the multitude of possibilities of womanly masquerade, and his own image therefore becomes the phallus. What is so tantalizing here is the moment of convergence: as a male performer (and creator blended in one), whose own sexual organ is veiled, Morimura *is* the perfect masqueraded woman (and therefore the phallus).

Never a dull moment. After the viewer finally accepts that Morimura is actually a perfect woman (in the Lacanian sense), he becomes a Lacanian act and refuses to be classified, anchored, known, or resolved. Morimura chooses to stay an enigma, a mystery, and to refuse any possibility of letting the viewer think that he or she may have solved the riddle and reached the core of his essence. I would say, then, that Morimura is the phallus, while at the same time undermining the place and meaning of the phallus as the object of desire and that of the woman. He plays with the given signifiers to insert instability into agreed assumptions, therefore posing the question: What is a woman? and What is a man? This is the *jouissance* of Morimura – the moment of shattered expectations and impossible doubling that resists any pinning down of the phallus as a singular normative signifier. The phallus loses its singularity, uniqueness and omnipotence, becoming transformed and multiplied.

While considering the veiled phallus of the masqueraded man, Morimura successfully produces a double phallus, a multitude of what is imagined to be "the one and only one," the singular phallus. He draws his secret weapon and shuffles the cards in an unexpected way: out of the ultimate masquerade appears the phallic organ – not a real penis but a plastic image of the penis, which must position itself as the phallus/signifier, the object of the viewer's desire.

Murakami Takashi's **My Lonesome Cowboy** *(1998): dissemination, simulacrum and the phallus*

> Sperm, water, ink, paint, perfumed dye: the pharmakon always penetrates like a liquid; it is absorbed, drunk, introduced into the inside, which it first marks with the hardness of the type, soon to invade it and inundate it with its medicine, its brew, its drink, its potion, its poison.[62]

Murakami Takashi's *My Lonesome Cowboy* (1998) (Figure 4.3) is one of three statues titled *Hiropon*. The three sculptures in this group are presented as oversized, sexualized, manga-like images of a boy, girl and waitress, endowed with exaggerated sexual features, as is commonly the case with *hentai manga* (pornographic comics). *My Lonesome Cowboy* features a boy with a cheeky look, legs spread to keep his balance, a large penis and a semen stream held up to form the shape of a lasso. It is an image that carries a significant phallic character, as well as a visual format that works against the phallic lineage it belongs to, as Murakami, early in his career, had already targeted his heroes and set out to place himself in the pantheon of phallic American figures.

The title of the work alludes to two seminal art works featuring important heroes of American popular culture: Elvis Presley performing the song *(I am a) Lonesome Cowboy* in his feature film, *Loving You* (1957). Elvis stands alone on a dark stage, his legs spread out to emphasize his famous thighs and pelvis, performing an exemplary love-song, creating the image of a heartbroken, love-seeking lonesome cowboy, guaranteed to melt every feminine heart. Elvis, one of the fathers of Americana and a quintessential symbol of American masculinity, becomes merged with the mythological cowboy. A parody of this image was created by another phallic father of Americana – Andy Warhol, who, in his *Elvis* of 1963, directed his "lasso" at Elvis, hoping to catch this icon and recruit him to the Warhol enterprise. However, a significant element places Warhol apart from these figures: as a sophisticated critique of American life, Warhol's work parodies its idol. Murakami, who is often compared to Warhol,[63] was careful in selecting his images and titles, clearly targeting Warhol as his *phallic father*, a model figure to be followed, similar to the way a small child follows in his father's footsteps, as described by the *Oedipus complex*. However, Murakami's image contains an undercurrent, which links it to other cultural concepts, namely, the idea of dissemination, which is concerned with deconstructing that very definition of the phallic model.

My Lonesome Cowboy and *Hiropon* are both decorated with curious garlands. A closer look reveals that the girl's milk is flowing from her breast, while the boy's erect penis disseminates a lasso-like circle of white semen. The equation of sperm and milk is an old one: both are products of the sexual organs, and became signifiers of fertility and omnipotence. A high sperm count in semen is considered to be the signifier of the well-nurtured male, while breast milk has its place as elemental food, as precious as gold. While one hand holds the penis, the semen garland is adorned by the other hand of the happy-looking cowboy. The hands-on

Figure 4.3 Takashi Murakami (Japanese, 1962). *My Lonesome Cowboy*, 1998. Oil, acrylic, fiberglass, and iron. 254 × 117 × 91.5 cm. (Courtesy of Blum & Poe, Los Angeles. © 1998 Takashi Murakami/Kaikai Kiki Co., Ltd. All Rights Reserved.)

approach of Murakami, and the absence of a partner in the image (the *lonesome* cowboy), therefore alludes to masturbation. It should be noted here that within the history of pornographic images in Japan (aka *shunga*, spring pictures), according to Timon Screech, their explicit use for masturbation purposes was always a major cause in their production.[64] The semen rises up as if it was a lasso, ready to be thrown forward to catch a wild, uninhibited stallion, to become a new addition to the cowboy's herd of already-controlled wild horses, or make it submissive to the cowboy's ego. Freud had early on described the idea thus:

> ... in its relation to the id, the ego is like a man on horseback, who has to hold in check the superior strength of the horse[65]

This description of the *ego* and the *id*, as a rider and his horse, suggests a new understanding of the cowboy image. The *ego*, driven by its ambitions and deeds, controls the untamed drives of sexuality (described as a horse), to turn them into a useful libido within the context of structured social life. However, in Murakami's sculpture, the whip/lasso-like semen of the lonesome cowboy has another layer of presence: the semen acts as a material extension of the penis to create an enormous, out-of-proportion organ, an imaginary phallus that embodies desire and potency. *My Lonesome Cowboy* is a very sleek and smooth sculpture, with an iron skeleton, fibreglass flesh and acrylic and oil-paint skin, which creates the image of a glossy, silken body. The hyper-real quality of the body works against Lacan's notion of the veiled phallus, but highlights the qualities of the simulacrum, as presented by Deleuze and Guattari, as well as Jean Baudrillard. The hyper-tangible penis, extended by its lasso-semen, becomes a simulacrum of a penis, as defined by Baudrillard – a signified-less signifier. In contrast to representation, which marks a known/specific signified, the simulacrum creates its own signified.[66] Hence, the simulacrum of the *penis-turned-phallus* and the *lonesome cowboy vis-à-vis* his forefathers (Presley and Warhol) is yet another example of the pellus/phanis. In this instance, deconstruction is activated by the imaginary relationship of the pellus and its simulacrum. The act that was geared to create an extreme exaggeration of a hyper life-like penis turns into a process of layering that behaves in a manner similar to that of the veil, to become a simulacrum: the smooth plastic phanis is so far from the reality of the penis, yet too tangible for the imaginary existence of the phallus so that it can only become a simulacrum.

The final part of my interpretation is achieved by means of Derrida's concept of dissemination,[67] as one of the phallic terms of postmodern thought. Despite its structure, dissemination is not the "opposite" of "insemination": the sperm swarms, and the primal insemination is through germination or grafting.[68] The term makes use of the root "semen" to signify a complex proliferation of a decentred deconstruction. Together with Leo Bersani's *self-shattering*, the two terms perform a spectacular appearance of the male orgasm as an explosion, a spectacle that in Murakami's work is taken to its extremes, to the point of losing reference to the "imaginary" penis – the simulacrum mentioned above representing the convergence of the penis and the phallus into the pellus. Derrida's *dissemination* works in accordance with our understanding of the continuity between body and language, between the phallus and *the-name-of-the-father*, and against the phallogocentrism of Western thought, by introducing an alternative mode of decentralization, one that deconstructs the logos and the phallus to disseminate them, and introduces the body as the core of the decentred system (rather than God as a miraculous, veiled, absent center). The multiplication encompassed by the concept of dissemination is what marks, for me, the collapse of the penis/phallus, and the birth of the pellus and phanus.

Conclusion

The conclusions drawn from reading the multiplicity and ubiquity of pelluses/phani in the works presented here may be that the amalgamated concept of the phallus as the primary signifier of culture is to be questioned.[69] The duplication, replacement, mimicry, appropriation and dissemination of phani and pelluses is a serious issue, especially in the context of post-Japanese culture, a term that refers to the multi-focal manner of representation presented here, and the inseparable presence of the American aspect within Japanese culture, which conglomerated the multiplied origins/pelluses that allude to the unconscious in these works. Moreover, these works are not just a mere representation of hybrid issues, but were all produced by Western-style media – Morimura's image production uses photography and digital technology as well as its conventions of dress and place. Kubota's work was produced in New York while she was living there, and uses the medium of performance art/action painting typical of the era. Murakami's work, with its sleek surfaces and manga inspiration, proposes a new language of sculpture and three-dimensionality in relation to the "super flat" concept Murakami promotes.

   Instead of using models of synthesis, I prefer to employ procedures of dissemination and multiplicity, presented here as the multiplied pelluses/phani. My conclusion is that what psychoanalytic discourse disguises is the call for all cultures to be united under a single dominant (narcissistic, one should add) discourse of the phallus, God and Western culture. By exposing the phallus to its own multiplication and deconstruction, multiple signifiers and discourses are admitted, allowing the possibility of multiple layers, multiple phalli, more than one dominant concept, more than one desire, more than one presence, more than one sexuality/libido, more than two genders, and a multiplicity of pelluses/phani as a mosaic picture. By accepting the idea of "more than one," we open the door to an abundance of possibilities and not just the binary system of oppositions of phallus and lack, as Freud and Lacan have defined their concept. The binary structure of Freud and Lacan results in the exclusion of women, what they called "perverts," psychotics and non-Western cultures. The only image defined positively by Freud and Lacan was that of the mature, heterosexual, Western, bourgeois man – therefore, it is about time to expand this discourse to as many variations as possible. In cultural studies there is still much work to be done in introducing multiplied models of the self, in a manner that debates and expands the norms and ideals of Western culture, as expressed by the concept of the phallus in Freud and Lacan. The works presented in this text (among others) are examples of post-Japanese culture that represent multiplicity, hybridity, and the possibility of more than one phallus.

Notes

1. Jacques Lacan (1982) "The meaning of the phallus," in Juliet Mitchell and Jacqueline Rose (eds and trans.) *Feminine Sexuality: Jacques Lacan and the école freudienne*, London: MacMillan Press, pp. 74–85. A previous translation of the text by Alan Sheridan, entitled "The signification of the phallus," was printed in Lacan's *Écrits: A Selection*, London: Routledge, 1977, pp. 281–91. In this text, I primarily relate to Mitchell and Rose's translation.

2. The shift in reading the phallus from a *fetish*, then *part-object*, and finally into a *primary signifier*, is the main change between Freud, Klein and Lacan. This change also marks the modes of representation of the phallus in various art practices, and the shift in relation to it. See Mignon Nixon (Spring 2000) "Posing the phallus," *October* 92: 98–127, 100.

3. Parveen Adams (Spring 1992) "Waiving the phallus"; Kaja Silverman, "The Lacanian phallus"; Judith Butler, "The lesbian phallus and the morphological imaginary," in *The Phallus Issue, Differences: A Journal of Feminist Cultural Studies* 4(1): 76–83, 84–115, 133–71.

4. Not quite parallel, but an enriching text in that it directly opens the gap and the debate between different cultural points of view on a specific issue, is Spivak's "Can the subaltern speak?", in which Spivak tackles the issue of sacredness of life in the West versus Indian conceptions of love and loyalty within the family, as reflected through the *suttee* practice in Indian culture. She analyzes the *suttee* religious and traditional context *vis-à-vis* its critique, prevention and abolition, all promoted by Western/British authorities. Gayatri Chakravorty Spivak (1988), "Can the subaltern speak?", in Cary Nelson and Lawrence Grossberg (eds) *Marxism and The Interpretation of Culture*, Urbana: University of Illinois Press, pp. 271–313; in a similar manner, Homi K. Bhabha reports how the value of the Bible, Shakespeare, or the English text in general, deteriorated to its paper worth, when fish was wrapped with book leaves in the market place, since Western ideas of the sacredness of God, the word and the text could not compete with local feelings regarding the presence of gods (see: Homi K. Bhabha (1994) "Sly cavity," and "Signs taken for wonders: questions of ambivalence and authority under the tree outside Delhi, May 1817," in *The Location of Culture*, London: Routledge, pp. 93–101, 102–22.

5. This aspect has already been extensively discussed by Silverman and Butler, both showing the many places Freud and Lacan fail to clearly distinguish between the penis and the phallus, mixing and merging the two. See Adams (1992), p.78; Butler (1992), pp.137–9; Silverman (1992), pp. 84–5, 89, and more.

6. Lacan links the phallus and the *name-of-the-father*, overlapping desire and language as the primary signifiers within his theory – as the first form and the origin of the signifying system. The question of the *name-of-the-father* and its relationship to the desire of the mother appears in several places. See Jacques Lacan (1977) "On a question preliminary to the possible treatment of psychosis," in *Écrits: A Selection*, London: Routledge, pp. 179–225, esp. 200.

7. The current text does not engage with the issue of gender multiplicity, but is written in accordance with this idea, and expands on how I see this factor construction reflected in Japanese culture. In a previous text, I have argued for a new structure of gender identity, one that identifies a plethora of genders and sexualities (actual and imagined), counting as many as twelve different possibilities. See Ayelet Zohar (2005) "The seven genders of Japan," in *PostGender: Gender, Sexuality and Performativity in Contemporary Japanese Art*, ex. cat., Haifa, Israel: Tikotin Museum of Japanese Art, pp. 43–157.

8. Jean Laplanche and Jean-Bertrand Pontalis (1988) *The Language of Psychoanalysis*,

Donald Nicholson-Smith (trans.), London: Karnac Books, p. 309 (originally published in French as *Vocabulaire de la Psychoanalyse*, Presses Universitaires de France, 1967).

9. Ibid., p. 312.
10. Adams counters this idea through her reading of Kress-Rosen, justifiably arguing that understanding the born baby as the performance of the phallus is a reinforcement of Freud's notion of the primacy of the phallus. Adams (1992), p. 79.
11. Adams (1992), p. 76.
12. Freud mentions the *phallic mother* in his discussion of the process the girl goes through in discovering her femininity. Sigmund Freud (1953) "Lecture XXXIII. Femininity," *The Standard Edition of the Complete Psychological Works of Sigmund Freud,* Vol 22, London: Hogarth Press, pp. 112–35, esp. 126 and 130.
13. Lacan (1982) *Meaning of the Phallus*, p. 79.
14. Sigmund Freud (1953) "The interpretation of dreams" [1900–1], in James Strachey (ed. and trans.), *The Standard Edition of the Complete Psychological Works of Sigmund Freud*, Vol. 5, London: Hogarth Press, pp. 362–3.
15. The phallus as *part object* is also a reference to an art object. For an elaboration on the understanding of the art object as *part-object* in the context of Melanie Klein's theory and modernist art, see Nixon, p. 101, n. 2.
16. An inclination well indicated by the English expressions of Dick and Willie. Freud, "The Interpretation of Dreams," p. 366.
17. Silverman (1992) pp. 98–9.
18. Jacques Lacan (1988) *The Seminar of Jacques Lacan, Book II – The Ego in Freud's Theory and in the Techniques of Psychoanalysis 1954–5*, J.A. Miller (ed) Cambridge: Cambridge University Press, p. 54.
19. See Silverman, pp. 94–5, 166.
20. Jacques Lacan (1977) "The mirror stage as formative of the function of the I as revealed in psychoanalytic experience," in Alan Sheridan (trans.) *Écrits: A Selection*, London: Routledge, p. 6.
21. Butler (1992) p. 147.
22. Linda Nochlin (1994) *The Body in Pieces: The Fragment as a metaphor of Modernity*, London: Thames and Hudson.
23. Ibid., p. 53.
24. The *father*, the penis, castration . . . etc.
25. Deleuze and Guattari (1988) pp. 30–1.
26. Juliet Mitchell (2003) *Siblings: Sex and Violence*, Cambridge: Polity Press.
27. The traditional Lacanian view sees the *mirror stage* as the moment when the subject emerges as an effect of the recognition of the self as such, and it is in psychosis that this fragmentation persists. For Deleuze and Guattari, the possibility to defer the unifying process and use the fragmented *body-in-pieces* works within the grounds of the schizophrenic metaphor, in contrast to the view that sees psychoses as the negation of the (unifying) mirror.
28. For further discussion of the concepts of *schizoanalysis* (Deleuze and Guattari), *self-shattering* (Leo Bersani) and *multivocality* (Michael Bakhtin) as alternative discourses of multiplicity that work against the concept of individuation and conglomeration of the self, see: Ayelet Zohar (2007) *Strategies of Camouflage: Invisibility, Schizoanalysis and Multifocality in Contemporary Visual Art*, PhD Thesis, University of London, Ch. 2, pp. 35, 43–7.
29. The *body-without-organs* (BwO) is a term Gilles Deleuze introduced in his book *The Logic of Sense* (1969), later developed with Felix Guattari in *Anti-Oedipus* (1972). The basic value of the BwO is its existence outside the medicalized view of the body and beyond its definition in various disciplines, such as psychology, sports, the beauty industry etc. The BwO is a conglomerate of sensations and unmediated experiences

that stand parallel to the body in pieces, a presence that exists before signification, socialization and the birth of the I as an over-viewing ego. In *A Thousand Plateaus* Deleuze and Guattari explain the relationship between *schizoanalysis* and the BwO: it is *schizoanalysis* that enables the BwO to see its own desire (p. 155) and dismantle the sense of subjectivity we are locked in (p. 188). *Schizoanalysis*, therefore, goes beyond the signifying system to make a rhizome (p. 251), or, in relation to the Lacanian discourse, *schizoanalysis* is a process that reverses the effect of the mirror, to let *the body in pieces* return and keep its place.

30. Lacan (1977) "The mirror stage," pp. 1–7.
31. Butler (1992) pp. 153–9.
32. Further discussion of the many faces of multiplicity within the discussion of the phallus, gender and the self appears in some of my PhD research; "The multiplicity of the phallus: becoming and repetition," and "Introduction: *Anti-Oedipus*, *Ajase* complex and postgender," both in Ayelet Zohar (ed.) *PostGender*.
33. Luce Irigaray (1977) *This Sex Which is Not One*, Catherine Porter and Carolyn Burke (trans.), Cornell University Press, 1985 (originally published in French as *Ce sexe qui n'en est pas un*, 1977), pp. 30–1.
34. Judith Butler (1990) *Gender Trouble: Feminism and the Subversion of Identity*, London: Routledge, p. 135.
35. Laplanche and Pontalis (1988) pp. 312–14.
36. Silverman (1992) pp. 84–7.
37. Ibid., pp. 91–2.
38. Silverman (1992) pp. 84–115, 97.
39. Ibid., p. 93.
40. Ibid., p. 92.
41. Adams (1992) p. 77.
42. Ibid.
43. See Adams's attack on Deutsch and Kress-Rosen where she points to the weak link in their articulation of the phallus in relation to castration. Adams (1992), pp. 78–9.
44. Butler (1992) p. 159.
45. Ibid., p. 151.
46. Lacan (1982) "The meaning of the phallus," p. 82.
47. See note 7.
48. Laplanche and Pontalis (1988) p. 311.
49. Butler (1992) pp. 158–61.
50. Sigmund Freud (1953) "Instincts and their vicissitudes," in James Strachey (ed. and trans.) *The Standard Edition of the Complete Psychological Works of Sigmund Freud*, Vol. 22, London, pp. 109–40, 128.
51. On the masculine nature of Abstract Expressionism and the New York School of the 1950s, see Izumi Nakajima (2006) "Yayoi Kusama between abstraction and pathology," in Griselda Pollock (ed.) *Psychoanalysis and the Image: Transdisciplinary Perspectives*, Oxford: Blackwell, pp. 127–58. In this text, Nakajima analyzes Kusama's presence as a young Japanese woman in a world perceived to be of masculine nature. Many of the elements discussed in the text, including the considerations of Japan's defeat in the war, the surrender of the emperor and the loss of collective identification with a father figure, replaced by the need to look to the USA as a masculine model of success, may also be relevant to the discussion of Kubota's personal circumstances as a young woman artist in New York during the late 1950s–early 1960s. See also: Midori Yoshimoto (2005) *Into Performance: Japanese Women Artists in New York*, New Brunswick, NJ: Rutgers University Press.
52. Judith Butler (1990) *Gender Trouble: Feminism and the Subversion of Identity*, London: Routledge, pp. 46–54

53. See, for example: Saito Tamaki (2009) "Sexuality of Otaku: Moe, phallic girls and Yaoi in light of psychoanalysis," in Ayelet Zohar (ed.) *PostGender.*
54. Nixon (2000) p. 100.
55. Butler (1990) p. 56.
56. Jacques Lacan (1982) "The meaning of the phallus," in Juliet Mitchell and Jacqueline Rose (eds. and trans.) *Feminine Sexuality: Jacques Lacan and the École Freudienne,* London: MacMillan, pp. 74–85, p. 84.
57. *The Seven Year Itch* (1955), dir. Billy Wilder, USA.
58. I elaborate on this element in my analysis of Takano Ryudai's "Tender Penis" series (2001), in "The multiplicity of the phallus: becoming and repetition," in Ayelet Zohar (ed.) *PostGender.* In this text, I also consider the work of Kusama Yayoi, Sugimoto Hiroshi, and Nagashima Yurie, as well as some classical images of the phallus in Japanese culture.
59. *Part-object* is a Kleinian term that relates to the object towards which the instinct is directed, without implying that the person as a whole is a *love-object.* The main *part-objects* known are breast, faeces, penis or their symbolic equivalent. Even a person can be identified with a part-object – like the baby born to a woman. Freud introduced the distinction between the instinctual aim, the instinctual object, and the instinctual source in his essay "*Three essays on the theory of sexuality* (1905)," *The Standard Edition of the Complete Psychological Work of Sigmund Freud*, Vol 7, London: Hogarth Press, 1953, pp. 197–206; Laplanche and Pontalis, pp. 301–2.
60. ". . . the fetishist has not the courage to assert that he actually saw a penis. He takes hold of something else instead – a part of the body or some other object – and assigns it the role of the penis which he cannot do without." Sigmund Freud (1953) "The psychical apparatus and the external world" (Ch. 8), "An outline of psychoanalysis, Part 3," *The Standard Edition of the Complete Psychological Work of Sigmund Freud*, Vol 23, London: Hogarth Press, pp. 195–204, esp. p. 203.
61. Joan Riviere was the one to suggest that femininity is a process of masquerade in her article, "Womanliness as a masquerade" (1929) in V. Burgin, J. Donald and C. Kaplan (eds) *Formations of Fantasy*, London: Methuen 1986, pp. 35–44 (originally published in *The International Journal of Psychoanalysis* (IJPA), Vol. 10, 1929).
62. Jacques Derrida (1981) *Dissemination,* Barbara Johnson (trans.) London: Athlone Press, p. 150.
63. Murakami Takashi is often billed as the next Andy Warhol. Like the American pop art icon, he fuses high and low art, pulling imagery from consumer culture to produce visually arresting, highly original work. He is vigorously, ingeniously self-promotional. In the past few years Murakami has swept across the USA and Europe, receiving fawning media attention and exhibiting at big-name museums. The charismatic artist even lives and works in what he calls a factory. How much more Warholian can you get? Jeff Howe (2003) "The two faces of Takashi Murakami," *Wired* 11(11) (Nov. 2003). Online. Available at: http://www.wired.com/wired/archive/11.11/artist.html (Accessed 12 June 2008).
64. Timon Screech (1999) *Sex and the Floating World: Erotic Images in Japan 1700–1820,* London: Reaktion, pp. 13–16.
65. Sigmund Freud (1961) "The Ego and the Id," in *The Standard Edition of the Complete Psychological Works of Sigmund Freud,* ed. James Strachey, London: The Hogarth Press, vol. 19. pp. 1–66, p. 25.
66. Jean Baudrillard (1994) "The precession of simulacra," in Shiela Faria Glaser (trans.) *Simulacra and Simulation*, University of Michigan Press, pp. 1–42 (originally published in French, 1981); Brian Massumi (1987) "Realer than Real: the Simulacrum According to Deleuze and Guattari," originally published in *Copyright* no. 1. Online. Available at: http://www.anu.edu.au/HRC/first_and_last/works/realer.htm (Accessed 24 May 2008].

67. Jacques Derrida (1981) *Dissemination*, Barbara Johnson (trans.), London: Athlone Press, (originally published in French, Editions du Soleil, 1972).

68. Ibid., p. 334.

69. Works by different artists that consider the problem of the penus/phallis are discussed in my other texts, as mentioned above. In particular, I am interested in the link between the deconstructed/multiplied and its presence in Japanese myth and art forms.

5   Introduction

Nina Cornyetz: Penisular cartography

In the late 1970s, things were starting to improve for the outcaste (*burakumin*) community of Shingū, Wakayama where the writer Nakagami Kenji grew up. As a result of years of protest and activism the squalid alleyways that had been their home for generations were being razed by the government and replaced with clean, modern apartment buildings, complete with running water and sewers. As Nina Cornyetz argues, however, Nakagami felt very strongly that it was not enough simply to cover over the traces of discrimination. He wanted to find a way of "recording into history an unwritten, unacknowledged part of Japan's history." And yet he was all too aware of the complicity between history writing and the structures of discrimination to engage in a simple project of what James Clifford calls "salvage ethnography." Nakagami's solution to this dilemma, Cornyetz argues, was the enigmatic and genre-defying text, *Kishū: ki no kuni, ne no kuni monogatari*.

While *Kishū* has "no plot and no consistent characters," the province of Kii itself emerges from its pages as a densely overdetermined "topos" in the Japanese imaginary. We hear of Nakagami's hometown of Shingū as the site of what might be called the primal scene of Japanese imperialism – where Jimmu, Japan's first Emperor, first came ashore to subdue the local tribes and found the Imperial line. "Rowdy wrestling matches" and other commonplace events are juxtaposed with scenes from medieval Buddhist tales and premodern ghost stories. Like William Faulkner's Yoknapatawpha County, Nakagami's Kishū is a topos steeped in historical trauma. As such it is also a space in which the past still lives in the present and the linear time of modern history and ethnography is rejected in favor of a temporality that Cornyetz describes, following Michel de Certeau, as at once literary and psychoanalytic. It is not only time, but space as well that Nakagami re-imagines. By reading the peninsula of Kishū as the "private parts" of Japan, as the embodiment of the "actuality of sex," he makes it the Lacanian "real" to the Nation's symbolic. A "real" that his readers repress at their own peril.

5 Penisular cartography
Topology in Nakagami Kenji's Kishū

Nina Cornyetz[1]

Nakagami Kenji's *Kishū: Ki no kuni, ne no kuni monogatari* (Ki Province: the tale of the land of trees and the land of roots) is the record of a "story gathering" expedition made by the writer Nakagami in 1977 to the various towns and villages of the Kii peninsula, particularly those designated as *hisabetsu buraku*, or the quarters of those discriminated against.[2] The narrative was published in 25 installments in the popular *Asahi Journal* weekly newsmagazine from July 1977–January 1978.[3]

My copy of *Kishū* is from the *Nakagami Kenji zenshū*, where it occupies a place within the final two-volume selection of non-fiction, Vols 14 and 15.[4] In the chronological table that accompanies the complete works, *Kishū* is classified as "*dokumento*" or "document" and also as "reportage" (*ruporutājyu*). The installments, now chapter headings, consist of the names of the places he visits – the city of Shingū, the town of Koza, or the village of Hiki. These 23 chapters are framed by an opening preface called, appropriately, "Preface," and a conclusion entitled, "Final installment: The nation of darkness." In the tradition of a travelogue, Nakagami himself is the narrator, hence the overt, identified mediator between the stories he hears and landscapes and people he encounters, more in the style of contemporary ethnography in which the anthropologist identifies and confronts her position directly, rather than earlier attempts at putatively purely "objective" reportage.[5] The chapters in-between the preface and final installment are filled with embedded narrations by or descriptively about the local residents of Ki Province, including many who are elderly and illiterate. These narrations may include their life stories – thus resembling oral histories – and amusing or moving local anecdotes, regional songs, or histories of their localities, and so forth. Nakagami's musings on and associations to these embedded narratives are interspersed throughout. Many – although certainly not all – of these stories remind Nakagami of a host of uncanny tales of archaic and premodern Japan, and which thus constitute a disavowed (repressed yet familiar) cultural past that returns to trouble contemporary national myth.[6] For example, upon completing his description of the rowdy comraderie between three young men in the town of Asso, who tell him tall tales of wrestling matches and sports competitions, Nakagami comments, "Somehow it made me think of passages in Ueda Akinari's 'Hankai' " (p. 547).[7]

In many respects, *Kishū* is thus clearly referential to what is now regarded as the "first" text of Japanese ethnography, the *Tōno Monogatari* by Yanagita Kunio, a text that Mishima Yukio also, interestingly, regarded as a "literary classic."[8] As Marilyn Ivy points out, Yanagita sought out "concealed" tales of "ancestors, of the monstrous, of the unseen, of death," in other words, tales that were "uncanny" in the psychoanalytic sense, and moreover, "Yanagita purports to be directly transmitting tales he has heard from the voice of another, who in many cases is describing his own experience or that of someone he knows or has heard of. The preface tells the tale, usurping as prefaces often do, the authority of the narrative remainder."[9] Nakagami-as-*Kishū* narrator states, "What I want to know is what people don't talk about loudly, things people are closed-mouthed about to outsiders" (p. 481). Unlike the original text by Yanagita, which was written in literary Japanese and eschewed any attempt to replicate the colloquialisms and dialects of his informants and his informants' informants, Nakagami tries to "faithfully" render patterns of speech into writing. This is one clue, of many, that Nakagami's project fundamentally differs from that of Yanagita.

Nakagami was then an up-and-coming young writer, recently awarded the prestigious Akutagawa literary prize.[10] Where, one might wonder, did this ethnographic or historiographic impulse on Nakagami's part originate? As already noted, *Kishū* was written in the late 1970s. It followed the first two books in Nakagami's celebrated Akiyuki triology – *Misaki* and *Karekinada*, and short fiction gathered in *Keshō*, in which the *hisabetsu buraku* appears only in metaphoric or coded form – as the *roji*, or alleys, in which his protagonists live or originate. In *Kishū*, however, the *buraku* is designated directly and literally *as such*, from the preface through the conclusion.[11] This shift, from an encoded treatment of the issue of discrimination or *sabetsu*, to an overt exploration of the biographies, anecdotes, poverty etc. of *burakumin* themselves was, as Anne McKnight has argued and cogently theorized, likely in part a reaction to the Sayama trial of 1963. At 24 years old, Ishiyama Kazuo, a *burakumin*, was convicted of (many say framed) and sentenced to death for the rape and murder of a schoolgirl in rural Saitama Prefecture. McKnight points out that, "The events of the trial – in particular, the suppression of evidence from investigation, and the act of written confession to the police by the nearly illiterate defendant . . . provoked Nakagami to take a new interest in how symbols work in narrative operations of the public sphere."[12] McKnight elaborates that

> the trial which associated *buraku* residents with a pre-disposition to criminality based on their dwelling in the *buraku* ultimately provokes Nakagami to re-examine how geography and identity have been coupled in the meta-narrative of *kokubungaku* – the story that national literature tells about its own conditions of production. By using *monogatari* as an organizing principle to re-orient setpiece scenes of the narrative operations of *kokubungaku*, the public sphere of written culture, Nakagami fashioned a way to talk about a class of people who contribute to the making of a national archive of literature, yet were not granted the status of historical subjects within it – residents of the modern *buraku*.[13]

At the time when *Kishū* was published, Nakagami had not yet publicly announced that he was born a member of the *burakumin* class himself – although as Margherita Long puts it:

> even if he was not technically "out" when he began submitting travel essays to *Asahi Journal* in 1977, readers of that weekly would recognize him from a series of published conversations with writers Noma Hiroshi and Yasuoka Shōtarō analyzing the "Sayama Trial," in which an outcast youth had been framed for murder and sentenced to death. Given also that the Kii Peninsula is known for its outcast communities and that Nakagami was famous as an autobiographical Kii writer, the "open secret" of his status probably functioned itself as a test of the degree to which readers were willing to acknowledge the persistence of Japan's underclass.[14]

To which I would add, readers in Kansai, or the southern parts of Japan's main island, would have been more likely to recognize these markers of outcaste status than those in Kantō, or the northern half, where there had been historically far fewer outcaste hamlets. The persistent discrimination of *burakumin* was something politely *not spoken of* outside of circles of those who "already knew." This was, however, also a time of government attempts to address here and there the concerns of *burakumin* political activists who were demanding a change in conditions and attitudes.[15] Partly in response to these demands, in the 1970s officials razed major parts of the Shingū *roji* where Nakagami had been born; Nakagami's trip around the villages of Ki Province postdated this destruction of his birthplace hamlet.[16] On the very same site, in place of the *buraku* shantytown the government built a hamlet of new concrete housing units with running water and sewers.[17] However, as Nakagami pointed out, these concrete barrack-like housing projects still stood out from the other, mostly single-family houses in adjacent areas. The geographic and material, visible mark of "difference" hence survived *in a new form* the process of putatively effacing the geographic and visual marker of discrimination – the ghetto itself.[18]

Nakagami was ambivalent about the destruction of the *buraku*. While he explores this ambivalence fictionally in *Chi no hate, shijō no toki*, he also traveled about the area surreptitiously filming the area that was earmarked for development and renovation, in an attempt, it seems, to counter its forthcoming potential invisibility.[19] *Kishū* thus follows his earlier filmic "documentation" of the hamlet, in some measure of resistance against the politics of "disappearing" the history of discrimination. While Nakagami surely wanted amelioration of living conditions for *burakumin*, he also appeared to feel strongly that the "erasure" of the history of discrimination was not the solution to the problem of discrimination.[20] I feel it appropriate to regard *Kishū* as a part of the process of confronting, rather than denying, Japan's legacy in relation to oppression. By including among the stories he collected those of elderly residents who had lived through times of overt discrimination, he was in some manner recording into history an unwritten, unacknowledged part of Japan's history.

McKnight has argued convincingly that at least one of Nakagami's intentions in *Kishū* was to postulate the term "*monogatari*" as an alternative narrative of Japanese history. As quoted above, while *kokubungaku* represented the "official" history of Japan, *monogatari,* with its links to folktales and oral narrative, was for Nakagami "the term that allows him to talk about different modes of linguistic sovereignty through seizing the means of signification in the public sphere."[21] *Kishū* thus problematizes the official story of Japan's origins, in which Nakagami's imagined community of ancient ancestors are erased in favor of a history of imperial lineage only. As Long put it, according to Japanese mythology, as depicted in the *Kojiki:*

> Japan's first Emperor, Jimmu, comes ashore to found the imperial line at Shingū, [Nakagami's] own hometown. With the help of Susano-o, brother of the sun goddess, Jimmu conquers Nakagami's people and transforms their obscure Komoriku ("hidden country") into the Yamato no kuni of endless national mythology. Nakagami also reminds his readers that the *Kojiki* was pieced together from oral poems by Hieda no Arei and written down by Ono Yasumaro, thus beginning the written record of an imperial genealogy unbroken, supposedly, for ten thousand generations. Returning to Shingū in 1977, Nakagami wants to understand the process by which the mode of storytelling established by the *Kojiki* in the eighth century made it impossible for other modes, and other stories, to exist. How does it happen that the underclass in Wakayama Prefecture is traditionally illiterate? Why, when Kii people trace their genealogies, do they speak not of their own families, but of the centuries of wandering nobles and political refugees who fled to the wilds of Kishū after falling from grace in the capital? For Nakagami, the Kii Peninsula is a place full of "outsiders with confirmed identities" and "local people whose origins are nevertheless obscure" (96). Calling his homeland "a country that has been sunk in the darkness of continual defeat since the time of Jimmu" (12), his aim in *Kishū* is to trace the inverse of the lineage created by Jimmu, a lineage his inquiries will reveal to be not invisible, but . . . "gleaming."[22]

Such a dichotomy of histories, or perhaps better recognized as rather than a set of two, a plurality of histories, is of course not unique to Japan. In his discussion of the origins of Judaism in *Moses and Monotheism,* Freud notes a similar relation between dominant and popular "histories."

> A difference began to develop between the written version and the oral report – that is, the tradition – of the same subject-matter. What has been deleted or altered in the written version might quite well have been preserved uninjured in the tradition. Tradition was the complement and at the same time the contradiction of the written history. It was less subject to distorting influences . . . Its trustworthiness, however, was impaired by being vaguer and more fluid than the written text, being exposed to many changes and distortions as it was passed on from one generation to the next by word of mouth. Such a tradition may have different outcomes. The most likely event would be for it to be vanquished by the written version, ousted by it, until it grows more and more shadowy and at last is forgotten. *Another fate might be that the tradition ends itself by becoming a written version.*[23]

In *Moses and Monotheism*, Freud proposes just such a counter-narrative to the "official" history of Judaism, which, he postulates, is a history that like all histories, has resulted in part from *unconscious* psychic processes including repression, condensation and projection. In Freud's version two historical personages, the first of whom was an Egyptian prince, were merged into the official figure of a single Moses, and Jewish monotheism was a revival of an earlier, short-lived Egyptian precursor. Moreover, Freud argues that the first of the two Moseses, the Egyptian, was murdered by his followers, and a collective, unconscious guilt eventually led to the resurrection of the religion later under the leadership of the second. The official story has "repressed" the facts of Judaism's origins (and Moses's Egyptian heritage), much like the processes Nakagami highlights when rethinking *kokubungaku* through *monogatari*. Finally, the latter part of Freud's observation that the act of writing down the oral "ends the tradition," cannot have totally escaped Nakagami's awareness. Nakagami must surely also have recognized the oxymoron at the core of such a project as "writing the oral."

Theorists more recent than Freud, such as Roland Barthes, have postulated that the act of writing itself irrevocably severs "voice" from origin, in a sense "killing" the author of any vocalization, as well as of the writing itself:

> Writing is the destruction of every voice, of every point of origin. Writing is that neutral, composite, oblique space where our subject slips away, the negative where all identity is lost, starting with the very identity of the body writing.

> As soon as a fact is *narrated* no longer with a view to acting directly on reality . . . the voice loses its origin, the author enters in to his own death, writing begins. [24]

Because the *meaning* of writing is always produced by the *reader* regardless of the intentions of the one writing, and because writing is predicated on the *absence* of the author, hence, origin, any attempt to represent a fixed reality in writing is constitutively doomed to failure. Many post-structuralist theorists have written extensively on this point; I do not think it necessary to rehash their arguments in any detail here. Suffice to note, as Long has focused on in her "Nakagami and the denial of lineage," Nakagami too spent considerable energy pondering the "fixing" of signification achieved by writing, and attempting to bring a measure of oral indeterminacy to his act of writing in *Kishū*. Long explains how Nakagami would

> string homophonic kanji across the Kii spectrum from sacred to profane and argue that they are metaphorically interchangeable. For instance, he merges the "ki" of "Ki Province" [ki no kuni]—meaning "tree" and evoking the area's dangerous, rapacious logging industry—with the safe ethereality of the "ki" character meaning "spirit." From here, he uses the "ki" of "Kii Peninsula" [kii hantō] – meaning "historical annals" – to connect the dark of the "ki" for "ogre" with the light of the "ki" for "rejoice." The connections are established intermittently across many essays, as anecdotal evidence permits. Whenever

another kanji is added to the list, Nakagami offers the new collection in a line of text that our eyes see as different characters but our inner voice pronounces as the same sound, "ki, ki, ki, ki, ki, ki, ki, ki."[25]

Because so many of the *burakumin* that Nakagami encounters in *Kishū* are illiterate, this sort of homophonic play imagines the possibilities of an unfettered and polysemic explosion of semantic freedom "killed" off by the affixing of one Chinese character to the sound with the acquisition of writing. Yet to reiterate, in the *writing down* of the oral narratives he elicits from the locals in his trip around the province, Nakagami is replicating this very same "killing off" of a semantic ambiguity, at the same time as he resists this fixing by listing alternatives in the manner just described.

Further complicating the issue, and in contradiction to how one might interpret ("read") Nakagami's exploration of the multiplicity of phonetic signification possible in Japanese, Jacques Derrida has argued that written texts put signification into play by the very nature of their textuality. Rather than "fixing" meaning, for writing to signify as such, he argues, it must be iterable, but not only can the intra- *and* extratextual context of any reading change the interpretation of that writing, any written statement can, in the final analysis, be put into quotations, giving it entirely unintentioned and limitless frameworks for signification.[26] And in fact I hope to show how Nakagami's "putting into quotation" of the Ki Province oral tales did indeed frame those narrations in unforeseen and innovative significatory frameworks indebted less to a historical or ethnographic mission and more to Nakagami's literary project of *rewriting Ki as a "topos,"* which one might also read as his "symptom," or *jouissance* in a psychoanalytic sense. And, I hope to argue that Nakagami's *ultimate disinterest* in rendering a "facsimile" of reality in *Kishū* is also what protects the text from falling prey to an ethical pitfall that James Clifford finds in much "salvage ethnography":

Ethnography's disappearing object is . . . in significant degrees, a rhetorical construct legitimating a representation practice: "salvage" ethnography in its widest sense. The other is lost, in disintegrating time and space, but saved in the text. The rationale for focusing one's attention on vanishing lore, for rescuing in writing the knowledge of old people, may be strong . . . I do not wish to deny specific cases of disappearing customs and languages, or to challenge the value of recording such phenomena. I do, however, question the assumption that with rapid change something essential ("culture"), a coherent differential identity, vanishes. And I question, too, the mode of scientific and moral authority associated with salvage, or redemptive, ethnography . . . The recorder and interpreter of fragile custom is custodian of an essence, unimpeachable witness to an authenticity.[27]

Although certainly from a superficial, or literal perspective, *Kishū* might be regarded as engaged, precisely, in such a "salvage ethnography," a more careful reading reveals instead that the "culture" Nakagami records is lifted from its conventions of signification, and forced to resignify in ways that in the end confront the Real, or the limit of signification itself, and are linked to *jouissance*. Nakagami's attempt to preserve Shingū "oral" folklore hence can be read as an ironic, or reflexive, yet "hidden," doubled dealing with literary "ends," or chasing the dying with death, rather than representation.

The rest of this chapter will trace how the mode of narration that Nakagami employed in *Kishū* functions to challenge the very notion of capturing a "truth" or "facts" in writing, the manner in which we imagine writing to "represent" both voice and reality, and in the process deconstructs the imagined parameters between history, ethnography, and literature, at a time before the problematic of ethnography as "constructed truths," or "ethnographic fictions," became a key issue in anthropological writings. *Kishū* blurs the lines between fiction, history, and ethnography in a way still innovative, even radical, in 1978.[28] By insisting that the past inhabits the present in Kii, Nakagami's narrative rejects the linear, temporal teleologies of history and ethnography, evoking instead a literary, hence also psychoanalytic, model of time, as I will argue below. In addition, *Kishū* calls up the haunts of Japanese literature and mythology in order to explore a topos indebted to a topological structure *cut up* into a set of binarisms, or discourses of discrimination, precisely through the agent of narration, but paradoxically also challenged by a different mobilization of that agent of narration. And finally, *Kishū* points towards the place where language as signification itself *fails,* or the limit to signification itself, which is also the Real. I hope to make these last three statements clear in the articulation of my argument that follows.

Simultaneity and narration

At around the same time as Nakagami appeared to be probing the (lack of) distinction between ethnography, history, and literature, debates – which continue to this day – had recently begun in academic circles over the very same problematic.[29] The old supposition, that one could distinguish between history and literature because the former was about "facts" and the latter about "made-up things" was no longer convincing. Roland Barthes pointed out that it was 'not mere coincidence that realism in the novel and objectivity in historiography [history and writing] (both nineteenth century) develop simultaneously – they share a "dependency on a specifically narrative mode of discourse, the principal purpose of which was to substitute surreptitiously a conceptual content (a signified) for a referent that it pretended merely to describe."[30]

Unlike premodern archives, annals or chronicles, modern history, of course, is narrative history. Narration gives "deep" meaning to the events it narrates, and organizes the representations of materiality into coherent "stories" with causes and effects, linearity, relation between parts, description and explanations, and usually, closure or a kind of teleology. In other words, modern history does not just cite events, it *explains* them, arranging its material in service to larger significations or interpretations. As Hayden White put it:

Precisely insofar as the historical narrative endows sets of real events with the kinds of meaning found otherwise only in myth and literature, we are justified in regarding it as a product of *allegoresis*. Therefore, rather than regard every historical narrative as mythic or ideological in nature, we should regard it as allegorical, that is, as saying one thing and meaning another . . . the narrative figurates the body of events that serves as its primary referent and transforms these events into intimations of patterns of meaning that any literal representation of them as facts could never produce.[31]

More generally, Paul Ricoeur points out that literature and history share the same "ultimate referent" which is the "human experience of time" or "structures of temporality," which might be called the "within-time-ness" of human beings.[32] For Michel de Certeau, who takes this debate even further:

Literature is the theoretic discourse of the historical process. It creates the non-topos where the effective operations of a society attain a formalization. Far from envisioning literature as the expression of a referential, it would be necessary to recognize here the analogue of that which for a long time mathematics has been for the exact sciences: a "logical" discourse of history, the "fiction" which allows it to be thought.[33]

Similarly the old convention of distinguishing between ethnography and literature on the basis of insisting that one told tales about "real" things and people, while the other "invented" them no longer sufficed either. For Clifford, not only is there "nothing universal or natural about the fictional processes of biography and auto-biography. . . Living does not easily organize itself into a continuous narrative."[34] Moreover:

ethnographic texts cannot avoid expressive tropes, figures, and allegories that select and impose meaning as they translate it. In this view, more Nietzschean than realist or hermeneutic, all constructed truths are made possible by powerful "lies" of exclusion and rhetoric. Even the best ethnographic texts – serious, true fictions – are systems, or economies, of truth. Power and history work through them, in ways their authors cannot fully control.[35]

As if in recognition of the arguments above, Nakagami's *Kishū* indeed involves a complex layering of the history, ethnography and literature to write a *topos* that simultaneously "assaults" the generic conventions of all three.

I feel as though Kii peninsula, the province of Ki, is a singular country (unto itself). Certainly it is a country that has been enveloped in a dark haze of defeat that has continued ever since (the time of) Jimmu. Kumano/Komoriku appear to also overlay this country enveloped into dark haze. Making the rounds of the towns and regions of this dark country, and, for example, writing the place name which is Shingū, or writing the stories as if to call up (awaken) the regional ghosts (haunts), is after all the method of the *Kojiki* and *Nihon shoki*. (p. 482)

The *Kojiki* and the *Nihon shoki* are of course the collections of legends, mythology, folklore and royal genealogies that comprised the earliest written so-called histories of Japan, which needless to say, are no longer seriously regarded as historical in the modern sense. Likewise, Jimmu is the legendary founder and first emperor of the Yamato ancestors of the Japanese ruling aristocracy. Jimmu, legend has it, was a direct descendent of the Sun Goddess, Amaterasu Omikami. Traveling through Kishū, Nakagami proclaims:

> I, like Jimmu, subjugate Shingū and Kii Tenma and Koza, (by) writing (them) as place names. At the same time, one could conversely say that, by narrating and writing like Hieda no Arei, I am simply narrating and writing in alliance with (*ni shitagatte*) Jimmu, who I cannot see, and Susano-o who I cannot see. (p. 482)[36]

The name, of course, is the framing device that makes possible the inhabitation by the subject of that which is thus framed, bringing into "being" all the "histories" and narratives (discourses) that coalesce around the subject, and hence consolidating that subject as such; and as such also subjugating the subject to the Symbolic, now cut off from an imagined totality. Above Nakagami directly and concretely links his act of marking, or writing place names of the region with the awakening of the ghosts of Japanese legends. What *Kishū* does, first and foremost, is hail the sites with names, and then descriptions, and then associations to antecedent legends, tales, literatures. This "awakening" means also that the mythologies of the past *inhabit* the present.

This structure which, as Freud points out, is *materially impossible*, because in space objects *replace* one another over time, is however an apt description of psychic temporality. In the mind the primitive is preserved alongside transformed versions of that past. "In mental life nothing which has once been formed can perish," instead, everything is preserved *in the unconscious* and given the right circumstances can once more be made conscious.[37] This temporality, a type of simultaneity or coexistence of past and present, that Nakagami discovers in Ki Province is thus psychoanalytic and *antithetical* to the conventions of temporality which operate in history, historiography, and ethnography. De Certeau points out that psychoanalysis and historiography have:

> two different ways of distributing the *space of memory*. They conceive of the relation between the past and present differently. Psychoanalysis recognizes the past *in* the present; historiography places them one *beside* the other. Psychoanalysis treats the relation as one of imbrication (one in the place of the other), of repetition (one reproduces the other in another form), of the equivocal and of the *quiproquo* (What "takes the place" of what? Everywhere, there are games of masking, reversal, and ambiguity). Historiography

conceives the relation as one of succession (one after the other), correlation (greater or lesser proximities), cause and effect (one follows from the other), and disjunction (either one or the other, but not both at the same time).[38]

In a chapter called "The Freudian novel," de Certeau argues that historiography tries to "suppress the void, fill it up," while psychoanalysis recognizes that "the 'writing of history' is produced from events of which nothing remains: it 'takes their place.'" Historically, writing is excluded from that which it discusses and nevertheless it is a 'cannibalistic discourse.' It 'takes the place' of the history lost to it."[39] Conversely, poetics and literature, argues de Certeau, share with psychoanalysis an acknowledgement of a "loss of knowledge," confronting void, or nothingness, rather than disavowing it.[40] ("Jimmu, who I cannot see, and Susano-o who I cannot see.") Freud went so far as to claim that while science could lend nothing to the understanding of the hysteric, detailed descriptions of mental processes found in literature could help one gain insights into the disorder. This is a "displacement toward the poetic or novelistic genre. Psychoanalytic conversion is a conversion to literature."[41] Moreover, literature and psychoanalysis share an emphasis on affect, or as de Certeau defines it, "the return of the passions" and the prevailing "logic of the other."[42]

Hence, one can argue, because of its temporality – a psychoanalytic one in which the past inhabits the present, and writing simultaneously covers over a limit to comprehension as it takes its place, *Kishū* can not exactly be classified as ethnography or history. But the question remains, is it literature?

The return of the repressed

Kishū is clearly in many respects quite distinct from the two so-called fictional genres that critics claim Nakagami most commonly employed – *monogatari*, or tales that are referentially saturated with motifs, images, and themes from the ancient and premodern Japanese canon of legends, folklore, and gothic tales, and *shishōsetsu*, or realistic, personal, confessional fiction. Of course, one of the things that makes Nakagami's fiction most interesting is the way in which his *monogatari* infiltrate his *shōsetsu*, and the other way around, with repeating unsettlements of genre with genre – as I and many others have discussed elsewhere.[43] But *Kishū* appears, at least at first glance, to be something else. Although it has what one might call a "theme," there is no plot, there are no consistent characters other than the province of Ki itself, its folklore and landscapes, and Nakagami himself is the primary narrator. Nakagami encounters folks, talks to them, reflects on what they have said, moves on to the next village. Nothing particularly "novelistic" develops, begins or ends. Instead, in the Preface Nakagami articulates what might be called a "problematic" about the core of Japanese culture in relation to *sabetsu*, or discrimination that he, in a sense, "proves" in the body of the narrative, and reiterates in the conclusion.

According to Watanabe Naomi, Nakagami:

searches out and encounters in the *hisabetsu buraku* of each Kishū location, one after the other, numerous (examples of) the circular flow of the "purity" and "filth" of "Japanese nature," and keeps on speaking heatedly about what this means . . . What is pointedly disclosed is the explosion of an asymmetrical difference that comes unexpectedly busting up and pressing against "beautiful because it is ugly" – [which is] the folkloric oppositional structure that he keeps on discovering moment by moment on this trip – and that is nothing other than the intensity of trying to think in a way that reacts to this very fissure.[44]

Nakagami himself writes, "Discrimination (*sabetsu*), discriminated-against, as words, these exist as such, but one cannot clearly grasp where discrimination begins and where discriminated-against ends. This is also a sort of mysteriousness" (*Kishū*, p. 486). Watanabe singles out an episode in *Kishū* as a model example of this circularity of filth and purity that Nakagami explores throughout the text. In this episode, Nakagami has come to Asso, and upon a young man working in a factory that produces violin strings from horse hair. The following is from that passage:

> The youth was sitting cross legged in the shadows of the farthest interior of the workshop, where he could not be seen from the outside, plucking hairs from a horsetail, which had been hacked off whole, flesh and all. The horsetail was almost as long as a man is tall. A lone radio sat on a dias. The youth was swiftly plucking and ordering the tail hairs surrounded by the stench of rotting flesh. Of course the fleshy tail had been salted but there were still several horseflies on the hair. It was shocking. If I try and put that "shock" into words, it's something akin to awe. (p. 545)

Nakagami discovers that at the core, or origin of the most exquisite, acculturated strains of violin music (a pinnacle of a symbol for cultural refinement) lurks a stinky, rotten horsetail which has not only been literally "hacked" off from the horse, but hacked off from representation, forgotten, disavowed as the origin of that artistic pinnacle in the violin string. De Certeau has discussed this sort of relation between abjected origin and order psychoanalytically as the "return of the repressed":

> any autonomous order is founded upon what it eliminates; it produces a "residue" condemned to be forgotten. But what was excluded re-infiltrates the place of its origin – now the present's "clean" [*propre*] place. It resurfaces, it troubles, it turns the present's feeling of being "at home" into an illusion, it lurks – this "wild," this "ob-scene," this "filth," this "resistance" of "superstition" – within the walls of the residence, and behind the back of the owner (the *ego*), or over its objections, it inscribes there the law of the other.[45]

In applying this notion of abjection to social structures rather than individuals, one could liken the ego to national myth which must abject the pollution of violence, savagery, and death at the foundation of all culture in order to imagine itself as its own ideal. Or in the case of Japan, the abjection of what Nakagami calls *monogatari* from the official discourses of *kokubungaku*. However, as already noted, what I would like to focus on here is less the ethnographic and political intention of Nakagami's intervention in theorizing discrimination, and more on the *mode of narration* with which he pursues this project.

In fact, Nakagami characterizes *Kishū* as a "fact gathering" that has an ambivalent relation to all writing, including fiction writing: "I had thought that by means of a reporting, or rather documentation that recorded the facts (*jijitsu*) I (would) violate (*kuiyaburi*) the novel, while yet fortifying (*hokyō*) the novel" (p. 482). I will return to this relation of factual documentation to a violation/fortification of fiction a bit later. First, I want to take up his contention at the beginning of the statement, that he intends to document a "truth," or something like "the facts" of Kishū. From the same page of the preface we find a very interesting comment. "I will reiterate that this is neither a simple sightseeing trip, nor a descriptive topography of the region. Rather, it resembles American novelist William Faulkner's mapping of Yoknapatawpha in Jefferson County, Mississippi, his method of possessing and writing it" (p. 482).

Faulkner was, of course, born in Mississippi. Nakagami hails from Ki Province, Shingū City. However, Yoknapatawpha was a fictional town invented by Faulkner in *Absalom, Absalom!* What is Nakagami saying here, then? His method is to follow Faulkner's "possession (*shoyū*)" and "writing (*shirusu*)" in a mapping of a *fictional* town. This comment seems to contradict his other statement, that he is "fact gathering." As already suggested above, what Nakagami is doing in *Kishū* cannot really be called either ethnography or oral history in spite of his claims to "documentation." Rather, he is clearly interested here in mapping out what simply must be called a "topos" – or an imaginary realm composed of existing mythologies and folklore, that for him overlays both the more mundane, "real" histories of the region *and* the material contours of the land, or nature, as landscape itself. This is a topos that he *owns* (*shoyū*), or has "proprietorship" over. This in turn links this text of so-called non-fiction to his fictional ones.[46] Of course in *Absalom, Absalom!* Faulkner offered readers a *fictional* text of deferred narrations that circle round and round the historically "true" secret – of the (il)logic of the Civil War-era south, although personalized in a fictional form in the return of the son "tainted" with black blood, Bon. My point – that Nakagami is mapping a topos, not a topography, is not, I believe, mitigated by the fact that unlike Faulkner's fictional town in a "real" county and state, the towns and villages and people that Nakagami visits are "real." I say this in part because what Nakagami "discovers" in his travels through the province are strange "facts" – since it is the haunts – ghosts and legends of the *past* called up by the discourses in the present, that are the "truth" of this topos. Hearing the various life stories and anecdotes of the residents of Kii, Nakagami repeatedly finds assonances between them and oral folklore, the scripted canon of tales from the *Kojiki, Nihon shoki, Nihon ryōiki*, or the premodern versions by Ueda Akinari and others.

If it were not already clear enough that Nakagami is dispensing with the sort of realism, or charting of the "mundane" world of native customs and belief systems that are the stuff of conventional ethnographies or travelogues, he goes on to state that:

The story in the *Nihon ryōiki*, of the man who went into the middle of the mountains, wrapped a rope around his ankle and dangled himself off the edge of the cliff reciting the Lotus Sutra is reality. If to travel about Kumano in Kishū is to enter into the world of the *Ryōiki*, then it is also possible to stare straight at the red tongue that would not rot in the skeleton who kept the Lotus Sutra in his heart. (p. 486)

On the one hand, Nakagami claims he is recording "facts." And, this recording of "real things" (ethnography and history) will somehow both fortify and violate the novel (or fiction). On the other hand, he claims to be following Faulkner's mapping of a fictional town, Yoknapatawpha, but is describing real places. And finally, the haunts – ghosts and legends of the *past* called up by the discourses in the present are the "truth" of this topos. The *Ryōiki*, of course, is a collection of Buddhist miracle tales, not the stuff of modern narrative history. I assume that Nakagami was neither psychotic nor on LSD at this time. So, his assertion that the tale of the devout reciter of the Lotus Sutra is "reality" must be taken somehow *un-literally*. That is, the reality of Kishū is precisely not what we generally take for reality, but its reality lies on another plane, so to speak, an *elsewhere*, where the measure of significance – what he is after by designating it reality, is *something else*. And in fact, this something else is, in *Kishū*, as Watanabe and McKnight have also pointed out, first and foremost a *structure* of *sabetsu,* or discrimination.[47] Nakagami writes, "What is the structure of *sabetsu*? . . . for Japan, if *sabetsu* is what has given birth to Japanese-style nature, then the structure of Japanese literature, and the structure of Japanese culture are also at the same time the structure of *sabetsu*" (pp. 486–7).

Not just literature and culture, but nature as well is marked in this statement by the modifier Japanese, suggesting an affinity of social construct in a "style" of nature, or nature-as-discourse or symbolization born of *sabetsu*. I think that here one must grasp this concept of *sabetsu* at its most fundamental, or as that of signification itself – that to be or mean anything, there must be an opposing, differentiating term, or web of terms, that it is not or does not mean. At the same time, as the word *sabetsu* itself signifies, these terms are rendered into binarisms by being hierarchized. And we should remember that it is also a specific term to describe Japanese discrimination.

To backtrack a bit, Kishū 's "reality" turns out to be a Buddhist miracle tale of a *faithful tongue* that would not rot in an ancient skeleton. To reiterate, I am reading this "reality" as a topos. This topos is also a *narration*, or discourse, of some things unfathomable before which our reason fails. The very bodily organ *that narrates* is what will not rot, because of its faith in the power of recitation, or iteration. A tale of a modern inhabitant of Kishū awakens the ancient miracle tale, which Nakagami calls the "current reality" of Kii. As such, it seems to me that in addition to discovering *sabetsu* as the founding structure of Japanese culture, Nakagami also points us toward what is behind this "reality," or way of signifying and comprehending, to the point where our comprehension *falters*. This is of course what can be called the "Real," in the Lacanian sense, because the Real is always the limit to description, to comprehension itself. Pointing himself towards an apprehension of the Real, Nakagami nonetheless finds himself always in the realm of discourse, which is also to say *sabetsu* or distinction.

Topos: penisular cartography

A topos does not exist, materially, anywhere – it cannot be "mapped" in time or space. One might also make use of the Lacanian notion of topology, or his example of the Möbius strip, as a model of the structure of being that is marked by transformations in shape at the same time as its intrinsic properties are retained. In mathematics, the Möbius strip is a topological *structure* that cannot be explained within Euclidean geometry – a structure that cannot be *oriented*. It is a single continuous strip that when folded and joined at its edges (sutured), *appears* to have two oppositional components, however, if one traces the length of the strip one returns over time to the point of origin, having always been *on the same side of the strip* although it appears to have an inside and outside.[48]

Like the Möbius strip *sabetsu* is the structure at the core of how Japanese culture has imagined and symbolized its "reality." The circular binarism of purity and pollution that, as Watanabe points out, Nakagami discovers everywhere throughout his journey through Kii, are like the sides of the mobius strip. They appear to be two distinct entities, but are no more than opposing modalities of a single, shared structure. Thus inside/outside, conscious/unconscious, love/hate, etc. are not binarisms proper, but continuities. As Tim Dean puts it, "it is not so much a question of "blurring the boundaries" between inner and outer as it is of revealing how the outside – an alien territory – inhabits the subject's most intimate inwardness."[49] Which reminds me of Nakagami's discovery in *Kishū* of things "beautiful because they are ugly," [50]or how pollution lies at the core of pure aesthetics in Japanese culture.

When the Möbius strip is cut down the center it remains one continuous strip, however, it now has two different sides or surfaces. Elsewhere Lacan identifies a cut as being the process that produces the subject as such, and the *objet a*, or object of desire, which *falls away* from the subject.[51] Hence, it is the function of a *cut* in the structure that produces subjectivity. And the "agent" of this cut is, of course, language (or the Symbolic).[52] Later Lacan had recourse to the model of the Borromean knot to perhaps better describe this structure – in which the three interlinked rings (which when cut become three separate rings), representing the realms of the Real, Symbolic, and Imaginary, are interlaced and "connected" to one another by the *sinthome*, or the individual's symptom – his or her particular configuration of unconscious *jouissance*.[53]

Nakagami appears to endow narration itself with the function of a *cut* in the structure that produces *sabetsu*, a cut which delineates oppositions (subject/object, purity/pollution), and also severs us from the Real, yet strives, always imperfectly, to fill in the void of the Real (in the Lacanian sense) with symbolization or representation. In this sense, the narrative of *Kishū* is constitutively self-consciously fictional in the sense that all narration is a mis-representation of "reality," or as

Derrida might put it, a breach in communication, a dis-semination.[54] Language fails as communication, because it *must*. Yet, it is "not nothing."[55]

Probing the limits of an ethnographic discourse with oral histories, folklore, and literature proper, in *Kishū* narration *cuts* out (demarcates) their differences, and yet also sutures over this cut. This "fact gathering" as Nakagami says, "violates and fortifies" the novel (p. 482). Polluting the purity of the ethnographic text with oral histories and a poetics (or literature), Nakagami discovers that each of these distinct narrations ends up narrating *the same reality or facts* – of a topos of a circular logic of *sabetsu* as structure, and which all fail to capture reality as they bump up against the limit of signification itself. This limit of signification is plural. In *Kishū* the narration self-reflexively addresses a failure within narration's insistent *presence.* Simplistically, noting the inadequacy of words' constative function as description, "You can match up words with the hard core one encounters at the heart of the words 'miraculous,' as well as with the knot of the circular flow between the saint [the holy] and the humble man [the base] in Japanese nature. But, they don't satisfactorily transmit the import of that shock" (p. 545). Or, "Mountains piled on top of mountains. The mountains thick with trees washed in sun[light] were too vast to simply be called *fūkei* (scenery or landscape). Words don't measure up" (p. 556).

Or, somewhat more complexly:

> I am a novelist. I am a person endowed with the capacity to connect pretty much anything I see directly to my novels, but in an instant, I saw that there are stories that can be narrated, and dramas that can be performed dramatically, but also there are things completely beyond the realm of (literally: completely boil over) narratives and dramas. That's exactly it. In short, it is the relationship between the novel and the novelist. (pp. 545–6)

This relationship between the novel and novelist resembles somehow the "faith" of the red tongue that would not rot, but it is also the structure of *sabetsu*. One chooses a word instead of another, one organizes a huge web of incommunicable apperception (sounds, smells, affects) into a communication that *must* fail to communicate that reality, but this narration is all there is, hence, it *insists* itself in the place of that which we would, if we could, see, interpret or communicate. Sections of *Kishū* "degenerate" into long strings of mostly *katakana*, a web of sound (pp. 594–7). Hasumi Shigehiko calls this a "style of stuttering," that reveals language's "otherness" and inherent "confusion" as communication.[56] In multiple ways throughout *Kishū* Nakagami explores the insufficiency of language to capture the whole of reality. Language fails itself in writing-as-representation of "the facts."

After introducing the readers to his first local informant in the figure of San Bāsan (Grandma San), Nakagami notes:

> Grandma San was the departure point of Shingū, which I had chosen as the departure point for my trip. The biography that Grandma San narrated had a flavor like that of a solid, trustworthily written realistic novel. And then, from

Grandma San's narration I was able to deduce the peninsular condition of a peninsula being a peninsula. Shall I put it like this – it is the concept of "*kanata*" (elsewhere). (p. 484)

Narration has a sense, or flavor (*aji*) that imparts realism to the biography (facts), "like a trustworthy novel" – somewhat of an oxymoron itself. San Bāsan's biography, an oral narration, is putatively true, or indebted to its being referential to "reality" (real things). However, Nakagami has shifted the discussion suddenly, from a story about an individual living in a particular community (the stuff of ethnography) to a focus on a *place* which is important both *as material that cannot be narrated* and *as a topos constructed of nothing but narration* – an "elsewhere.*" And, not only does her narration sound like a novel – a fictional construct – to Nakagami, this novel-like narration also holds a clue to analyzing the condition of the so to speak ontology of a peninsula, which has something to do with a "beyond-ness" or an unreachable, uniterable alterity, that of "elsewhere." In fact, readers of *Kishū* have already met the peninsula as "limit point" to comprehension just four lines into the preface:

While traveling Kishū on the Kii Peninsula, I thought about the meaning of the peninsula. Korea, Asia, Spain, somehow they have something in common. Also Africa, Latin America. Let's try calling it the condition of (being) peninsulas. It is like **being** the lower crotch of the continent, the shameful part (*chibu*) of continental land and plains. I tried grasping it as the shameful part, the genitals, of the peninsula, no, rather, as the nature that cannot be subjugated, as a metaphor for sex. No, rather, while traveling the Kii peninsula, I thought, the peninsula is not a metaphor for sex, it is the reality of sex, its actuality. For example, Shingū, the very first location I arrived at. Because I, the man who was traveling the peninsula, had been born, and grew up there until the age of 18, I had written novels using as my setting the land I remembered as Shingū, but, I had not thought of it as the nature that cannot be subjugated, the land of sex. Kumano River is a woman's genitals, it is like **being** a vagina. (p. 481)

The material landscape is, as the "thrust of nature," (or "inch of nature")[57] the very limit point of comprehension or signification – the peninsula as (the Real) penis or vagina, which designate the peninsula as not-it, as *kanata* (elsewhere). As de Certeau argues, "The project of historiography is the inverse of the poetic one. It consists of furnishing discourse with referentiality, to make it function as 'expressive,' to legitimize it by means of the 'real'. . . The law of historiography functions to obscure nothingness, to suppress the void, to fill the gap."[58] Conversely, the "history" of Kii is one of a "void," the land that *is* sex itself, that will not be subjugated or named. This is indeed the psychoanalytic concept of sex as the limit to reason.

In his most radical moments, Freud argued that in fact, the unconscious, and indeed the psyche itself, were *not sexed*. This is the meaning of his assertion that human beings are constitutionally bisexual and polymorphously perverse.

Man is an animal organism with (like others) an unmistakably bisexual disposition. The individual corresponds to a fusion of two symmetrical halves, of which, according to some investigators, one is purely male and the other female. It is equally possible that each half was originally hermaphrodite. Sex is a biological fact which, although it is of extraordinary importance in mental life, is hard to grasp psychologically. We are accustomed to say that every human being displays both male and female instinctual impulses, needs and attributes, but though anatomy, it is true, can point out the characteristic of maleness and femaleness, psychology cannot.[59]

"Bisexual" means without sexual difference, composed of both active and passive dispositions (which he argued were too frequently misrecognized as masculine and feminine) and polymorphously perverse describes the function of desire that is neither anchored to any object nor to any body-part, but free-floating and all encompassing.[60] Lacan inherited this radicality, noting that however, with the acquisition of language and entry into the Symbolic, the subject that is the effect of that "castration" must identify as male or female, illustrated by the two restroom doors, "Ladies" and "Gents" – one must pick one or the other.[61] Sexual difference, for Lacan, is a matter of the Real, and therefore to say one is sexed is to confront the *limit* of knowledge, and *not* to affix signification to that sexed positioning.

Sex is the stumbling block of sense. This is not to say that sex is prediscursive; we have no intention of denying that human sexuality is a production of signification, but we intend, rather, to refine this position by arguing that sex is produced by the internal limit, the failure of signification. It is only there where discursive practices falter – and not at all where they succeed in producing meaning – that sex comes to be.

To say that the subject is sexed is to say that it is no longer possible to have any knowledge of him or her. Sex serves no other function than to limit reason, to remove the subject from the real of possible experience or pure understanding. This is the meaning, when all is said and done, of Lacan's notorious assertion that "there is no sexual relation": sex, in opposing itself to sense, is also, by definition, opposed to relation, to communication.[62]

The truth of Ki Province, as "penisula" whose essence is sex itself, then, is that limit to reason, relation and communication. The structure, *sabetsu*, or discrimination, that symbolizes through the cut of narration in the topology of being – and that makes partners of histories, mythologies, and literatures – is the very core of Japanese being. *Kishū,* Nakagami's non-fictional ethnography is neither simply nonfiction nor ethnography, but an ethnography tainted by the rupture of history into the present, and of literature into reality. It is the description of a topos in which "reality" is a *structure* of discrimination, or *sabetsu,* the cut from the Real made by language, that hence makes consciousness and representation possible, and in which narration functions as a constitutively impossible attempt to represent what is at the limit of representation. And in fact, *Kishū* fails as ethnography, fails as oral history, and fails even as literature, because, in part, as Hasumi Shigehiko put it, the text "takes the stuttering to extreme," and in the process "degenerates into nonsense." Clearly, Nakagami's *ultimate disinterest* in rendering a "facsimile" of reality in *Kishū* suggests that the text is indebted less to a historical or ethnographic mission and more to Nakagami's literary project of *rewriting Kii as a topos*, which one might also read as his *sinthome* (symptom), or *jouissance* in a psychoanalytic sense. Hence, perhaps it succeeds as an expression of Nakagami's *sinthome* – the *jouissance* by which he knit together his perception of reality.

Notes

1. An earlier and much shorter version of this essay was presented at the Association for Japanese Literary Studies, Princeton University, Princeton NJ, November 2007, as Nina Cornyetz (2008) "Chasing the tails of tales: Nakagami Kenji and the end of folklore," *Proceedings of the Association for Japanese Literary Studies* Vol. 9, 2008, pp. 246–31.
2. The outcaste class has its origins in the Edo-period class system. It was only in the 1990s, after he died at the age of 46, that Japanese critics began to address the issue of his outcaste status in their commentaries, and to link the metaphoric troping of the *roji* to actual discrimination suffered by the outcastes. Because the word *roji* by itself simply means "alley," and not necessarily those of the outcaste quarters, the connection was not overt. For information on the outcaste in modern Japan see Hirota Masaki (1990) *Sabetsu no shosō, Nihon kindai shisō* 2, Tokyo: Iwanami shoten; in English see Mikiso Hane (1982) *Peasants, Rebels and Outcastes: The Underside of Modern Japan*, New York: Pantheon Books; George De Vos and H. Wagatsuma (eds) (1967) *Japan's Invisible Race*, Berkeley and Los Angeles: University of California Press; and James Valentine (1990) "On the borderlines: the significance of marginality in Japanese Society," in Eyal Ben-Ari, Brian Moeran, and James Valentine (eds) *Unwrapping Japan*, Manchester: Manchester University Press, pp. 36–57.
3. "Nenpyō," in Karatani Kōjin *et al.*, (eds) *Nakagami Kenji zenshū* 15, Tokyo: Shūeisha, 1996, p. 751. *Zenshū* herafter abbreviated as *NKZ*.
4. Nakagami Kenji, *Kishū: Ki no kuni, ne no kuni monogatari*, in *NKZ* 14, 479–679. Further pagination follows citations parenthetically within text.
5. See, for example, Clifford Geertz (1973) "Thick description," in his *The Interpretation of Cultures: Selected Essays*, New York: Basic Books, pp. 3–30; E. Valentine Daniel and Jeffrey M. Peck (eds) (1996) "Culture/contexture: an introduction," in *Culture/Contexture: Explorations in Anthropology and Literary Studies,* Berkeley: University of California Press, pp. 1–33; James Clifford (1986) "Introduction: partial truths," in James Clifford and George E. Marcus (eds) *Writing Culture: the Poetics and Politics of Ethnography,* Berkeley: University of California Press, pp. 1–26.
6. Sigmund Freud (1959) "The uncanny," in *Collected Papers* 4, New York: Basic Books, pp. 368–407.
7. "Hankai" is the tale of the adventures of a rambunctious, and frankly brutal young man who kills his parents and brother but in the end finds his way to a Buddhist path. Available in translation: Ueda Akinari (1970) "Hankai. A translation from *Harusame Monogatari*," Anthony Chambers (trans.) *Monumenta Nipponica* 25(3/4): 371–406.
8. As cited in Marilyn Ivy (1995) *Discourses of the Vanishing: Modernity, Phantasm, Japan*, Chicago: University of Chicago Press, p. 66.
9. Ibid., pp. 80, 81, 84–7.

Penisular cartography

10. Awarded Nakagami in 1976, for "Misaki" (The Cape). Available in translation in Nakagami Kenji (1999) *The Cape and Other Stories from the Japanese Ghetto*, Eve Zimmerman (trans.) Berkeley: Stone Bridge Press.
11. Nakagami also apparently addressed the issue of the *buraku* in a series of published conversations with Noma Hiroshi and Yasuoka Shōtarō on the Sayama Trial, cited in Anne Mcknight (2001) "Ethnographies of modernity: Nakagami Kenji's counter-history of modern literature (1968–1983)," PhD Dissertation, University of California, Berkeley, 83 n. 52; 105–6.
12. Ibid., p. 8.
13. Ibid., p. 3.
14. Margherita Long (2006) "Nakagami and the denial of lineage: on maternity, abjection, and the Japanese outcast class," *Differences* 17(2): 30 n. 8.
15. Emily A. Su-lan Reber, *"Buraku Mondai* in Japan: historical and modern perspectives and directions for the future," *Harvard Human Rights Journal* 12 (Spring 1999): 297–360. Online. Available at: http://www.law.harvard.edu/students/orgs/hrj/iss12/reber.shtml (Accessed 1 June 2008).
16. Eve Zimmerman (1999) "Preface," in Nakagami, *The Cape and Other Stories,* p. 10.
17. Film footage can be seen in "Nakagami: Blind Spot Invisible Shame," Part One of the series *Writers on the Border,* Stephen Javor, director. Produced by LA Sept, Tip TV, MV Films and Floating Island.
18. Personal conversation with Nakagami Kenji in August 1996, Shingū City, Japan.
19. This footage has been incorporated into the film "Roji e: Nakagami Kenji no nokoshita firumu," Aoyama Shinji, director, Slow Learner, 2000; Distributed by Kinokuniya Company.
20. Personal conversation with Nakagami in August 1996, in Shingū City, Japan.
21. McKnight, p. 4.
22. Long, pp. 6–7.
23. Sigmund Freud (1939) *Moses and Monotheism*, New York: Vintage, pp. 85–6. My emphasis.
24. Roland Barthes (1977) "Death of the author," in *Image, Music, Text*, Stephen Heath (trans.) New York: Hill and Wang, p. 142.
25. Long, p. 8.
26. Jacques Derrida (1988) "Signature event context," in *Limited Inc.*, Evanston, IL: Northwestern University Press, pp. 1–24.
27. James Clifford (1986) "On ethnographic allegory," in Clifford and Marcus (eds) *Writing Culture*, pp. 112–13.
28. Clifford, "Introduction: partial truths," p. 6. See also McKnight.
29. In fact, Nakagami's earlier narrative, "Nihongo ni tsuite" "dramatizes the social effects of dispossession produced by the production of narrative between ethnographer and ethnographic object" (McKnight, p. 63). See McKnight for more. She argues that in this way Nakagami "shows how the production of 'meaning' in a realistic, ethnographic text is a dialectical process . . . meaning is in a constant state of changing co-production" (McKnight, p. 61).
30. As quoted in Hayden White (1987) *The Content of the Form: Narrative Discourse and Historical Representation*, Baltimore: Johns Hopkins University Press, p. 37. Addition in brackets mine.
31. Ibid., p. 45.
32. Paul Ricour (1985) *Time and Narrative* 2, Kathleen McLaughlin and David Pellauer (trans.) Chicago: University of Chicago Press.
33. Michel de Certeau (1986) *Heterologies: Discourse on the Other*, Brian Massumi (trans.) Minneapolis: University of Minnesota Press, p. 18.
34. Clifford, "On ethnographic allegory," p. 106.
35. Clifford, "Introduction: partial truths," pp. 6–7.

36. Long notes that the names themselves are already "imprinted" with the politics of subjugation (p. 7).
37. Sigmund Freud (1961) *Civilization and its Discontents*, James Strachey (trans.) New York and London: W. W. Norton and Co., pp. 16–17.
38. de Certeau, p. 4.
39. Ibid., pp. 28–9.
40. Ibid., 30.
41. Ibid., 19.
42. Ibid., pp. 17–34.
43. I do not particularly like these classifications, particularly the rubric "*shishōsetsu*," since although many of Nakagami's texts are deeply *referential* to his life, none of them pretend to transparently translate his life into text.
44. Watanabe Naomi (1995) "Nakagami Kenji zenshū kakukan no yomidokoro," *Subaru* 17(7): 46.
45. de Certeau, p. 4.
46. I have argued previously that Nakagami's *setsuwa*-inspired tales are topoi in which material landscape is subordinated to legend, in much that same way that here I argue the landscape of *Kishū* is subordinated to legend. See my *Dangerous Women, Deadly Words: Phallic Fantasy and Modernity in Three Japanese Writers*, Stanford: Stanford University Press, 1999.
47. McKnight; Watanabe, 46.
48. See Ellie Raglan and Dragan Milovanovic, (eds) (2004) *Lacan: Topologically Speaking*, New York: Other Press.
49. Tim Dean (2000) *Beyond Sexuality*, Chicago: University of Chicago Press, p. 53.
50. Watanabe, 46.
51. Jacques Lacan (2006) *Écrits: The First Complete Edition in English*, Bruce Fink (trans.) New York: W. W. Norton and Co., pp. 486–7 n. 14.
52. Ibid.; see also Dean, p. 59. I borrow the use of the word "agent" here from Dean.
53. See Milovanovic, "Borromean knots, *Le Sinthome*, and sense production in law," in Raglan and Milovanovic (eds) *Lacan: Topologially Speaking*, pp. 368–79.
54. Derrida, "Signature event context," in *Limited, Inc.* pp. 1–24.
55. Jacques Derrida (1986) *Memoires: for Paul de Man*, Cecile Lindsay, Jonathan Culler and Eduardo Cadava (trans.) New York: Columbia University Press, p. 64.
56. Long, p. 9.
57. Freud, *Civilizations and its Discontents*, p. 44.
58. de Certeau, p. 31.
59. Freud, *Civilization and Its Discontents*, pp. 61–2, n. 7.
60. Ibid. See also "Three contributions to the theory of sex," in Sigmund Freud (1938) *The Basic Writings of Sigmund Freud*, A. A. Brill (trans.) New York: The Modern Library, Random House, pp. 552–603.
61. Jacques Lacan, "The instance of the letter in the unconscious," in *Écrits*, pp. 416–17.
62. Joan Copjec (1994) *Read My Desire: Lacan Against the Historicists,* Cambridge, MA: MIT Press, pp. 204, 207.

6   Introduction

Margherita Long: Two ways to play *fort-da* . . .

The notion that separation from the mother is necessary to the formation of a viable, non-psychotic subjectivity has long been one of the most powerful and contested theories in psychoanalytic thought. For Sigmund Freud the resolution of the Oedipus Complex for the male child meant renouncing his incestuous love for his mother under the threat of castration by the father. For Jacques Lacan, the entry into the Symbolic could only be achieved by papering over, or even "murdering" the mother and the "Real" she embodied with language. As Margherita Long argues in her essay which follows, "the magnitude of the problem this presents for feminism is obvious." As long as we believe that the sacrifice of the mother – what Luce Irigaray calls her "dereliction" – is necessary in order for the civilized subject to emerge the result will be ". . . an appropriation of the maternal origin by a 'humanity' that then refuses to speak of the maternal in any language besides that of anxiety, phobia, and disgust."

But what other ways might there be of imagining our relation to the mother? And how might those different imaginings affect our relations to others in general? In Tanizaki Jun'ichirō's *Yoshinokuzu* (*Arrrowroot*, 1931) Long uncovers a dialogue between the story's two narrators about two very different ways of relating to the mother. One narrator, Tsumura, weaves a tale of maternal obsession full of "entrapment," "fusion," "depth, danger, and regression" that echoes not only Freud and Lacan's reading of the famous *fort-da* game, but also Kristeva's association of abjection with the maternal. The story's primary narrator, who remains nameless, focuses instead on the "luminous surfaces" of the Yoshino landscape where he and Tsumura are traveling. While it is he who brings us Tsumura's story of mother-obsession, he places it alongside his own account of an unsuccessful attempt to write a historical novel from materials gathered on the trip. His failure to write the novel is not caused by any lack of materials, but from an overabundance. And this sense of plenty is ultimately what distinguishes his narrative from Tsumura's. While Tsumura is driven by an incurable sense of loss and the desire to remedy it, the first narrator is surprisingly content. By reading these two narrators together but also separately, rather than conflating them as most other critics have done, Long shows how Tanizaki's text offers a delicately balanced portrayal of "two ways of playing *fort-da*." And the result is somehow more than the sum of its parts.

Long's reading of *Arrowroot* has interesting parallels to Nina Cornyetz's reading in this volume of Nakagami Kenji's *Kishū*, another text that treats the area around

Yoshino. What Cornyetz describes as Nakagami's attempt to rewrite the Kii peninsula (where Yoshino is located) as "topos" without resorting to "salvage ethnography" or recapitulating its erasure in nationalist historiography has strong parallels to Long's reading of the way Tanizaki's narrator "clothes" Yoshino in what Irigaray calls "words that do not erase the body but speak the body." Of course Cornyetz is ultimately more Lacanian in her insistence on Nakagami's topos of Kii as a manifestation of the Real and thus a "limit to reason, language, and communication," while Long rejects Lacan entirely in order to explore a different, less all-or-nothing relation to the maternal home. But it is clear that both authors, like Nakagami and Tanizaki themselves, are invested in exploring alternative ways of writing that complicate, enrich, or even derail straight narratives of national and individual subjectivity. In this, their methods might both be described not just as psychoanalytic, but as productively perverse.

6 Two ways to play *fort-da*

In Yoshino with Tanizaki and Freud

Margherita Long

Arrowroot of Yoshino (Yoshinokuzu, 1931) is usually classed with other stories written by canonical author Tanizaki Jun'ichirō (1886–1965) in celebration of mother love, or *haha-koi*. The protagonist Tsumura has always yearned for his mother, who died when he was young. When he is in his early thirties he finds a cache of secret letters to his mother from her own mother in Yoshino. They reveal that she had been sold into prostitution before his father redeemed and married her in Osaka. Tsumura uses the return address to trace his mother's family to a tiny village deep in the mountains south of the city, where he promptly falls in love with his mother's grand-niece. "With a little polishing," he tells his friend, "she might be just like my mother!"[1]

Recent criticism in Japan, however, has taken issue with the text's classification as an ode to *haha-koi*, proposing that the mother is not loved so much as abjected. Pursuing a series of tantalizingly brief remarks made by Nakagami Kenji in the 1970s, both Komori Yōichi and Watanabe Naomi have argued that *Arrowroot* is surprisingly intimate with the codes of Japanese discrimination, so that Tsumura's mother's origins may have been kept secret because her family belongs to Japan's *hisabetsu buraku* underclass.[2] Analyzing Tsumura's decision to bring his friend to Yoshino to meet his prospective bride, Komori argues that "Tsumura's trip is an occasion for him to begin resisting the discrimination [sabetsu] that has been made to circulate like a stain in his blood, and for him to make it clear to his friend that this is what he is doing."[3] Emphasizing the erotics rather than the injustice of abjection, Watanabe writes that, for Tsumura, "the more defiled the 'mother,' the more powerful her seduction."[4]

In this essay, I want to propose that while Komori and Watanabe are right, the mother's abjection is only half the story here. Reading psychoanalytically, we see, on the one hand, that Tsumura offers a textbook citation of Freud's famous fort-da game, and that this goes hand in hand with regarding "mother" as an alluring abyss on the far side of language. On the other, we also see that the novel's second protagonist, Tsumura's friend, offers an entirely different approach to the problem of maternal origin. It is this friend who narrates most of the story, and whose failed attempt to find materials for a novel about imperial history in Yoshino seems to provide a foil for Tsumura's successful attempt to find a wife. But the real contrast is in these two men's differing approaches to the problem of maternal abjection.

In some of the most exquisite language in modern Japanese literature, the narrator stages an encounter with the maternal "home" that replaces his friend's insistence on depth, danger and regression with a new poetry of surfaces, safety, and emergence. It is a second way to play *fort-da*, and it is a textbook citation, I argue, not of Freud's game, but of Luce Irigaray's re-reading of that game. According to Irigaray, it is only by learning this second way to play *fort-da* that we address the problem of abjection at its foundations.

Tsumura's *fort-da* game

What is Tsumura's idea of mother-love, and how do we know that *Arrowroot* does not endorse it? The strongest clue is the way the text isolates his voice. The narrator moves aside to let Tsumura speak in the first person only in the fourth of six chapters, and only for the duration of his account of the "michi no onna" (not-yet-known woman) with whom he associates both his beloved mother and his future wife. Analyzing this section, we realize that what Tsumura most wants from his trips to Yoshino is a chance to re-enact the lyrics to a set of songs that he memorized when he was a very young child, just after his mother died. Reciting the originals to his friend on a rock in the bed of the Yoshino River, he is drawn into a trance from which he emerges much later, after night has fallen. It is fitting that the physicality of his mother's home place should fade during this period of recitation. For the first thing we notice about Tsumura's songs is that they make of "mother love" a kind of substitution game, in which words take the place of the mother's physical body.

One song is remarkably explicit, from a game he remembers being played at his family's prosperous pawn shop in the merchant district of Osaka. Sitting in a circle, a group of shop apprentices and maids would sing and pass a small object, like a bean, from hand to hand. The one who is "it" would sit in the middle and, when the song ended, guess whose hand the bean is in. The lyrics are fascinating for the way they use an extra katakana "u" to draw out their "u" and "o" sounds. The text separates the lyrics into these lines, which I number here for convenience:

1. 麦摘ウんで picking barley (mugi tsu-u-nde)
2. 蓬摘ウんで picking absinthe (yomogi tsu-u-nde)
3. お手にお豆がこウこのつ there are nine beans [here] in our hands (ote ni omame ga ko-u-konotsu)
4. 九ウつの、豆の数より but more than nine, the number of beans (kokono-u-tsu no, mame no kazu yori)
5. 親の所在が恋しゅうて it's the parents' whereabouts you yearn to know (oya no shozai ga koishūte)
6. 恋いしイくば if you're yearning (koishiikuba)
7. 訪ね来てみよ try coming to visit (tazune kite mi yo)
8. 信田のもウりの うウらみ葛の葉 Shinoda Forest's loathsome arrowroot leaves (shinoda no mo-u-ri no u-u-rami Kuzu no ha).[5]

Tsumura explains that the game is popular in Osaka on account of its proximity to Shinoda Forest. Famous from bunraku and kabuki retellings of the "Kuzunoha" or "Arrowrootleaf" folktale, Shinoda Forest is the place to which the fox-mother retreats at the end of that story. She has married a man to thank him for saving her from hunters, and given birth to a son. But when the son is still young, her secret is discovered, and she must flee to her original home. On the shoji she leaves the poem that the bean-game lyrics cite in lines six and seven: "If you are yearning, try coming to visit, in Izumi."[6]

According to Tsumura, people outside Osaka don't play this bean game, or, if they do, they don't play it as elaborately, or with the same investment. But if we are familiar with a game Freud calls *fort-da*, the rules of Tsumura's game are uncannily familiar. Freud introduces *fort-da* in the second chapter of his 1920 essay "*Beyond the pleasure principle*," where he recounts the story of a boy of one and a half, his grandson Ernst, who is remarkable for never crying when his mother leaves him. Freud surmises that the boy has overcome his distress by means of a singing exercise he invented himself. Taking hold of a small toy, Ernst has a habit of throwing it away from him and "giving vent to a loud, long-drawn-out o-o-o-o, accompanied by an expression of interest and satisfaction."[7] His mother and grandfather imagine that "o-o-o-o" corresponds to the German word "fort," meaning "gone" or "far," and remark that "the only use he makes with any of his toys is to play 'gone' with them." One day, Freud observes his grandson throwing a wooden spool with a piece of string tied around it. Tossing it "over the edge of his curtained cot," he repeatedly pulls it out again and "hails its reappearance with a joyful '*da*' ['there']."[8] Freud's famous interpretation of this game of disappearance and return is that Ernst has figured out how to master his mother's absence by staging it himself, repeatedly. Although it is painful—the game appears in "*Beyond the pleasure principle*" as part of a discussion of why people compulsively repeat traumatic memories and events—nevertheless it represents "a great cultural achievement."[9] In Freud's view it is inevitable that the boy give up his mother's physical intimacy in the process of becoming a proper subject. At least with *fort-da* he receives compensation in the form of a game that provides the illusion of mastery.

In the Osaka bean game as well, compensation is clearly at stake, even if mastery remains elusive. Tsumura says the game was touching when played by adolescent apprentices in his parents' shop whose mothers were far away in the countryside. But clearly it was even more meaningful to him, his mother's death when he was four having provided a powerful incentive to stage her return. That he can still cite the lyrics from memory decades later suggests the depth of his investment in this fantasy of "da!" And indeed, sitting in the riverbed in Yoshino, he is about to reel in a wifely version of his mother, as if she had simply been waiting at the end of a string all this time. A second game he recalls, involving a string, a bride, and the lyrics, "Let's catch her! The fox of Shinoda Forest!" makes this clear.[10] At the same time, Tanizaki's *fort-da* is more complicated than Freud's, as if to criticize Tsumura's logic even in the process of explaining it.

In Ernst's game, the drawn-out "o-o-o-o" corresponds to a hand motion that he repeats "untiringly," compensating for the absence of his wooden spool/mother by piling up endless acts of throwing, and endless vowel sounds. In the bean game, the drawn-out "oo" of the extra katakana "u" also combines repetitive hand motions (passing the bean) with images of plenty, and with additional repeated vowels. The "u" of "picking" – *tsu-**u**-n-de* – doubles up in the first two lines, as does the sound of what is picked: *mugi* [barley] and *yomogi* [absinthe]. In the third line, the pun on "*kokonotsu*" also suggests immediacy and amassing. There are nine fruits of one's labor [kokonotsu], right here [koko] in one's hand. But the idea of plenty is compromised not only when there turns out to be only one bean, despite promises of nine, but also when the players themselves admit that they could not care less about the bean, because what they really yearn to know is the whereabouts of the parent! What we have is a highly melancholic exercise in which the only way to master distress over the mother's absence is to repeat that absence untiringly in an act of "compensation" that substitutes representation for the real thing.

Tanizaki's version of *fort-da* is remarkably self-reflexive on this score, even to the point of casting the repeated "u" in the role of marker for the mother who is missing. For if the mother is the bean that passes from hand to hand, she also seems to be this "u" that jumps from line to line in the form of a vowel (in Japanese "vowel" is literally "mother sound" [bo-on]) that sometimes changes its position even within a single word. In line three, for instance, it appears as the second syllable of "ko-u-ko-no-tsu." But in line four it becomes the fourth syllable: "ko-ko-no-u-tsu." Is this a game of hide and seek? The movement of the "u" mimics the movement of the fleeing fox, disappearing quite literally into the middle of the forest, the *mo-"u"-ri*, in the closing line:

8. 信田のもウりの うウらみ葛の葉 Shinoda Fo-o-rest's lo-o-oathesome arrowroot leaves (shinoda no mo-u-ri no u-u-rami kuzu noha)

The line uses the classical pun combining resentment [urami] with "seeing the back of" [ura wo miru]. As the fox-mother slips between the arrowroot leaves and exposes their undersides, she actually *becomes* this vowel, this "u," sinking into their interior: "*u-'u'-rami kuzunoha*." No wonder the leaves are loathsome! They are the language into which the mother has vanished!

Lacan on *fort-da*: the murder of the mother-thing

At least while he is singing the lyrics of the bean-game song, however, Tsumura does not seem to regard the leaves as loathsome. His desire moves not vertically, back through language to some anterior origin, but rather laterally, intertextually, from foxes in the arrowroot play, through other bunraku allusions, and finally to foxes in another play by Takeda Izumo, *Yoshitsune and the Thousand Cherry Trees*. Strangely, he is not in the least put off by the image there of a fox-son responding eagerly when his lover beats a drum stretched with the hides of his dead parents. In his simple acceptance that the mother is always already dead, and in his willingness nevertheless to pursue her through a dense web of language, Tsumura's approach to *fort-da* might be said to be classically Lacanian. For it was Lacan who, in the 1950s, reinterpreted Ernst's game as a matter not of compensation and mastery but of language and desire. And it was Lacan who, in the process, showed how the acquisition of language is one of the most important issues in feminist theory.

In Lacan's reading, it is important that Ernst is at a stage, at one and a half years old, when he "make[s] use of a number of sounds which express a meaning intelligible to those around him," but can only "say a few comprehensible words."[11] He is on the verge of acquiring language with which to communicate abstractly, without his body, but still making meaning with gestures that make sense only to those in close physical proximity. The most important person in this category is his mother, from whose body he issued, and with whom, on account of activities like bathing, caring, and breast-feeding, he continues to maintain a special symbiosis. Freud had already theorized that the subject comes into existence when he renounces this relationship with his mother in an act of primary repression that creates both the unconscious and the superego. This is another reason why he calls Ernst's instinctual renunciation a "great cultural achievement." But Lacan went further, insisting that the great cultural achievement corresponds much more specifically to Ernst's ability to use the words "*fort*" and "*da*." He writes:

> These are the games . . . which Freud, in a flash of genius, revealed to us so that we might recognize in them that the moment in which desire becomes human is also that in which the child is born into language.
>
> We can now grasp in this the fact that in this moment the subject is not simply mastering his privation by assuming it, but that here he is raising his desire to a second power. For his action destroys the object that it causes to appear and disappear in the anticipating *provocation* of its absence and its presence . . . The child begins to become engaged in the system of the concrete discourse of the environment, by reproducing more or less approximately in his *Fort!* and in his *Da!* the vocables that he receives from it.[12]

Lacan means roughly the same thing by "desire becoming human" and "desire raised to a second power." If we call "first-order desire" what Ernst feels for his mother before he starts having to endure her absence, then "desire raised to a second power" is what he feels after having to accept that his original love object will always be missing. He gives her up in exchange for the privilege of "engag[ing] in the concrete discourse of [his] environment." In this sense, "desire raised to a second power" is simply another name for "human desire" as defined by psychoanalysis. Only humans desire what is re-presented as opposed to what is *pre*sented. Only humans, in other words, live lives of desire based in lack and founded in loss. Lacan uses unsparingly violent language to describe what this means for the lost object, the mother herself. He concludes, "Thus the symbol manifests itself first of all as the murder of the thing, and this death constitutes in the subject the eternalization of his desire."[13]

The magnitude of the problem this presents for feminists is obvious. The mother is dead – murdered by "the symbol" – and the result is hailed as the becoming-

"human" of desire. Irigaray has described it as the zero-hour of sexual indifference. The mother's sexual specificity is erased by this second "birth," this birth-into-language that will forever after insist that *it* is primary, that *it* marks the beginning of all meaning and all culture, since any recourse to its outside, now renamed "the Real," would mean psychosis. It is an appropriation of the maternal origin by a "humanity" that then refuses to speak of the maternal in any language besides that of anxiety, phobia, and disgust. "[T]he exclusivity of [the father's] law refuses all representation to that first body, that first home, that first love," Irigaray writes. "These are sacrificed and provide matter for an empire of language that so privileges the male sex as to confuse it with the human race."[14]

Kristeva and Tsumura on abjection: reading "Cry of the Fox"

For a solution to this problem, those of us trained in feminist theory in North America are often taught to look to Julia Kristeva. Her work from the 1970s seems to offer a loophole to Lacan's axiomatic reading of *fort-da*, theorizing a "semiotic" dimension in language that maintains the subject's primary relationship with "archaic, instinctual, maternal territory."[15] Yet it is important to note that Kristeva's theory of the semiotic is closely linked to her theory of abjection. Associated with the sensation that the borders of one's "clean and proper body" are uncomfortably tenuous, abjection in its strict psychoanalytic sense denotes a breakdown in the object relations by which the subject constitutes itself. Rather than *sub*-ject (me) and *ob*-ject (you/it/him/her), there is only an *ab*-ject indeterminacy, "a threat that draws me toward the place where meaning collapses."[16] According to Kristeva, we remain vulnerable to this threat to the same degree that we remain open to the semiotic, since both are vestiges of our pre-Oedipal relationship with our originary "object," our mother. Her body is the "natural mansion" in which we once lived, and in relation to which, even after separated, we feel "the constant risk of falling back under the sway of a power as securing as it is stifling."[17] Thus the problem with the semiotic comes into focus. The maternal in Kristeva is attractive only to the extent that it is also threatening and suffocating, and we still lack any non-phobic language to describe it.

Tsumura provides an astonishingly vivid example of this by means of another song he recites in the riverbed, "Cry of the Fox" [Konkai]. The song belongs to the *jiuta* tradition of shamisen singing that developed in the Kamigata region during the Tokugawa Period, and Tsumura memorized it as a child when his sisters and paternal grandmother were having their music lessons. Though its lyrics are extremely obscure, Tsumura says this obscurity is typical of all *jiuta*, their grammar often so "garbled" [mecha kucha] and their "incoherent places" [tsujitsuma no awanai tokoro] so numerous that one wonders whether the meaning has been made deliberately incomprehensible.[18] Given that the entire genre is thus more or less "rhythmic, unfettered [and] irreducible to intelligible translation," Kristeva might easily classify every *jiuta* as semiotic.[19]

Semiotic articulation is modeled on communication between mother and infant, so it is inherently indeterminate and guttural, like the sounds and rhythms of the oral and anal muscles with which the child first expresses itself. We have seen how Lacan maintains that the subject comes into being only by breaking with this mode of articulation. Kristeva's famous move was to insist that the break is never clean, and that the continued rupture into language of "the workings of the drives . . . and . . . the archaisms of the semiotic body" is proof that the semiotic is inherent in the symbolic, the support for all signification.[20] She implies that this is advantageous for the mother, whose status as the rightful origin of every speaking subject is now acknowledged, especially by the poets who speak most consistently in a semiotic register. "Language as symbolic function," Kristeva writes, "constitutes itself at the cost of repressing instinctual drive and continuous relation to the mother. [. . . But] the unsettled and questionable subject of poetic language (for whom the word is never uniquely sign) maintains itself at the cost of reactivating this repressed, maternal element."[21]

We could hardly ask for a better example of the dubious benefits of reactivating Kristeva's "repressed maternal element" than "Cry of the Fox." In both its rhythms and what we can discern of its storyline, surely no other song could evoke so well how it feels to straddle the border between the law-abiding order of language and what is imagined as its wild, animal anterior. The song takes us back and forth over this border several times as the same son we know from the "Kuzunoha" folktale is tempted much more explicitly than in the bean-song to return "home" to the fox-mother's forest. Tsumura sings:

いたわしや母上は、oh how sad! Mother,
花の姿に引き替えて who was pretty as a flower is changed
しほるる露の床の内 lying withered* in her bed of tears
智慧の鏡も掻き曇る、the mirror of her mind* clouded over,
法師にまみえ給いつつ we have her seen by a healing priest
母も招けばうしろみ返りて when I call her* she flees, looking backward
さらばと云わぬ without saying goodbye
ばかりにて、her silence audible,*
泣くより外の and there is nothing to do
事ぞなき, but cry,
野越え山越え crossing fields and crossing mountains
里打ち過ぎて in and out of villages
来るは誰故ぞ For whom do you come?
さま故 For you
誰故来るは for whom do you come
来るは誰故ぞ様故 for whom? For you!
君は帰るか Are you going home?
恨めしやなうやれ So unbearable! I shall take my leave*
我が住む森に帰らん Let's go home to the forest where I live
我が思う思う心のうらは no one knows* the inside of my longing heart.
白菊岩隠れ蔦がくれ、White chrysanthemum, hidden in crags and ivy
篠の細道掻き分け行けば、scratching down a narrow bamboo path[22]

Around the line "there is nothing to do but cry," the speaker shifts from the son, in a realm of health and reason, to the mother, in a realm of increasing obscurity and desperation. As listeners, we move with the song across this line from the human to the animal, aware of the mother dashing back across it to make her entreaty that the son join her on the other side. The first time it happens so suddenly that the son is bewildered. "For whom do you come?" he asks. "For you! For you!" she insists. The second time her invitation is clearer: "Let's go home to the forest where I live!" But again he resists, more wary of her madness than attracted.

As the song ends, the fox mother retreats into narrowing lanes, deepening moisture, and increasingly frenetic, misunderstood longing. But it is significant that she is never completely lost. In "Cry of the Fox," as in Kristeva's theory of the semiotic, it is not that the laws of psychoanalysis are breached. At a certain moment in his growing up, the child still has to give up the mother to a state of nature. To follow her would mean psychosis for him, or death. Yet, in the song, because fear of nearby humans prevents the mother from stopping in her old home place, she must keep running. And as a result, her retreat feels endless here, a leave-taking never fully accomplished. As she continues to dash and scratch through a parallel register, her sadness is ready to erupt again each time Tsumura assumes now partly his voice, and now partly hers, to sing "Cry of the Fox." The final lines read:

虫のこえごえ面白や pleasant insect voices cry
降りそむる、and the rain* begins to fall
やれ降りそむる、now* the rain* begins to fall
けさだにも even this morning
けさだにも even this morning
所は跡もなかりけり no trace remains in my home* place
西は田の畦あぶないさ、on the western paddy ridge, people* and danger
谷峰しどろに peaks and valleys drenched with rain*
越え行け、as I run and run
あの山越えてこの山越えて、crossing this mountain, crossing that
こがれこがるるうき思ひ loving, longing, oh so sad[23]

"Oh so sad," indeed! The song does a brilliant job of illustrating how Kristeva's semiotic loophole to Lacan's reading of *fort-da* turns out to enforce it by negative example, and according to exactly the same logic. The peril represented by the allure of the abject fox-mother is tragically clear when, with "the mirror of her mind clouded over" and "the inside of [her] longing heart" unfathomable, she tempts her son into this chaos, this schizophrenic mixture of contentment ("pleasant insect voices!") and deep, deep gloom.

But how does it happen that Tsumura and Kristeva end up saying roughly the same thing about the semiotic and the abject? I think it is because they have roughly the same understanding of what produces them: the unspoken rules of *fort-da*. According to these rules, modern subjectivity is founded in the dereliction of a maternal origin whose role as such is acknowledged only phobically and indirectly, in the language of defilement. As Irigaray points out, "How are any other feelings possible, when we are asked to move back toward something that has always been negated, denied, sacrificed for the construction of an exclusively male symbolic world?"[24] Significantly, the same general formula is used by Komori and Watanabe to explain the existence of Japan's *hisabetsu buraku* outcast class. Both writers show how the Japanese imperial line is founded in the dereliction of a class of people who are deemed over-proximate to nature – a powerful national origin whose role as such is acknowledged only phobically and indirectly, again in the language of defilement. Yet, while it is compelling to use *Arrowroot* to illustrate the derivation of *sabetsu* against Japan's *buraku* underclass, it is perhaps even more compelling to use *Arrowroot* to illustrate the derivation of *sabetsu* against what we might call the maternal underclass. For it is only by focusing on the maternal line, rather than the imperial line, that we see how the narrator's decision not to write a novel about imperial history opens onto his discovery of an altogether new kind of politics, and a much more ethical way to play *fort-da*.

The narrator's new way to play *fort-da*

Let us consider how intensely he engages Yoshino even while he declines to collect the materials he would need for his historical novel. Swishing through carpets of autumn foliage as he walks from village to village on his way to Tsumura's mother's home, he marvels at the beauty that rains down: "[l]eaves fell through the rays of light pouring into the valley from between the mountains, fluttering like flakes of gold until they landed on the surface of the river."[25] The spatial relationship he discovers is one of delicacy and symbiosis, the traveler and his environment equal partners in a dance of open glidings and shiftings. And it is amplified when he ponders the same autumn sunshine on the pristine paper in local shoji screens. "Though the sky was radiantly clear," he observes:

> the rays of reflected light were not so bright as to assault the eye; they sank instead beautifully into the skin. As the sun traced its arc toward the river, the shoji of the houses on the left bank reflected it all the way across to the buildings on the right.[26]

The luminous surfaces that shape the narrator's experience of Yoshino are the opposite of the "narrow bamboo path" into which Tsumura descends every time he sings "Cry of the Fox." Rather than suck light away into madness and gloom, they chart for it a much more versatile passage. As skin, they allow light to sink in. As paper, they bounce light clear across rivers. As fluttering flakes of leafy gold, they reflect light now this way and now that. Collectively, these surfaces mediate the narrator's relation to the place of the mother by replacing entrapment and fusion with a mutually safe, perpetually open relationship of gentleness.

When we analyze the narrator's investment in Yoshino's shimmering membranes, we notice that he is taking his cue from a line in one of the letters that Tsumura's mother received from her mother. Tsumura does not tell his friend about the letter until he is sitting on the rock in the riverbed. So it is significant that

Tanizaki gives the narration back to the narrator just beforehand. Chapter five begins, "Well then, why don't I take up Tsumura's story from this point, continuing it indirectly?"[27] In the language of his alternate sensibility, he tells us that the letter is on paper from the mother's papermaking village, and that it holds in its fibers tiny flecks of the mother's own chapped skin. "This too is paper made by your Mama," it exhorts, "never, never let it leave contact with your body."[28] The narrator imagines the daughter pressing it to her chest, so that she is in the tender embrace of a loving membrane that carries the blood of the woman who bore her. Reconnecting with this mother means not danger or regression, but the caress of a kind of heavenly fluttering, as the thin, strong fibers of the paper move in tandem with the rise and fall of the daughter's chest. It is an exquisite example of what Irigaray calls language that does not substitute for our relationship to the mother's body, but rather "accompanies that bodily experience, clothing it in words that do not erase the body but speak the body."[29] And it is emulated, throughout *Arrowroot*, in the way the narrator relates to the physicality of Yoshino itself.

It is fitting that his alternative way of relating to the story's maternal origin should be modeled on a relation between a mother and her daughter rather than a mother and her son. According to Irigaray, the fact that a daughter is born to someone of the same sex makes it imperative for her to negotiate *fort-da* differently from the boy. The boy becomes a subject by turning the mother into an object. As we have seen, his failure to keep the transaction swift and clean results in an *ab*-ject. But the girl cannot reduce her mother to the status of either object or abject without reducing herself at the same time. This accounts for what Irigaray calls the "all or nothing" aspect of the girl's attempt "to find a subjective identity in relation to her mother."[30] Too often, she says, the result is "nothing":

> The *fort-da*, which Freud describes as marking the child's entry into the world of language and culture, does not work for the girl child, unless she identifies herself as a little boy. Then she loses herself in a male other, and makes her children, and subsequently her husband, into quasi-objects.[31]

But what is Irigaray's other scenario? The "all" scenario? In this case, which she locates characteristically both in a utopian future and in a latent now, the little girl is able to come out of an "exclusive relation with the same as herself" having "discover[ed] the relation with a different other, while remaining herself."[32] It is this ability to recognize subjective difference from within a horizon of would-be sameness that Irigaray posits as the *sine qua non* of ethical relations. A loving relation to a truly different other is only possible if one knows how to be oneself, remain oneself, without having to abject or object an other.

In Tsumura's version of *fort-da*, like his father's before him, the mother is turned into a kind of natural resource that can be reeled back in from Yoshino whenever a man needs the raw material to make a wife. Of course, the reeling is not all fun and games. The string, the puller and the pulled must all pass through an abject liminality of animism and fear. In contrast, the narrator's encounter with Yoshino produces an entirely different version of liminality. In his appreciation for surfaces and skins, leaves and membranes, *Arrowroot*'s narrator might be said to be reacting to Tsumura's rendition of *fort-da* the same way Irigaray reacts to Freud's. Why, Irigaray asks, does Freud take note of the curtained cot into which Ernst throws the wooden spool, only to leave it out of his analysis? How do we know that the spool represents the mother, and not Ernst himself? Couldn't the mother be the bed, and not the spool? Irigaray imagines it more likely that, rather than looking ahead to his accession into language, as Lacan decides, Ernst is looking backward. The *fort-da* game allows him to be a fetus again, "playing at going in and coming out of her with a cord, a placental-veil, a womb-bed."[33] And in Irigaray's imagination, all we need do to change the rules of Ernst's foundational game is reconceive our relation to this veil, this placenta. I think this is exactly what *Arrowroot*'s narrator is doing. Uninterested in the women Tsumura and his father make a game of batting back and forth like wooden spools between Yoshino and Osaka, the narrator focuses, like Irigaray, on a "haven of skin, of membranes, of water [. . .] an amnion and a placenta, a whole world with its layers, its circuits, its vessels, its nourishing pathways . . ."[34]

Placentas and persimmons

The most vivid example comes in the form of some over-ripe persimmons called *jukushi*. Is it going too far to call them placental? Let us set up the argument by introducing one last idea from Irigaray.

In her recent work, she often mentions the placenta. Is it not strange, she asks, that we accept the psychoanalytic definition of "mother" as a place of regression and fusion, when the actual biology of gestation tells another story? As an organ designed to mediate between mother and child – to keep the mother's body from rejecting the foreign body that is the fetus – the placenta has an amazing ability to facilitate simultaneous proximity and distance, symbiosis and independence. Although it is produced from the cellular and genetic material of the embryo, it secretes maternal hormones during the interruption of ovulation that is pregnancy. Like the membranes of Yoshino, in other words, it serves first this side and then the other, morphing alternately into an extension of both without allowing the two to merge. The way the placenta manages the mother's immune reactions is also remarkable. Rather than simply block her body from rejecting the half-paternal antigens in the fetus, the placenta activates immunodepressors only after assessing the exact degree of foreign antigens, and only locally, in the uterus, so that the mother's defenses against infection elsewhere are not compromised. In an interview with Irigaray, biologist Helene Rouche points out that this is far more sophisticated than what happens, for instance, in the case of organ transplants, when there is an extreme and immediate immune rejection, or in the case of cancerous tumors, when the body fails to marshal any immune reaction at all. Rouche explains:

> There has to be a recognition of the other, of the non-self, by the mother, and therefore an initial reaction from her, in order for placental factors to

be produced. The difference between the "self" and other is, so to speak, continuously negotiated.[35]

It is on account of this continuous negotiation that Irigaray calls the relationship enabled by the placenta "almost ethical."[36] Rouche notes how curious it is that psychoanalysis disavows it:

> [In psychoanalysis] it's this fusion, implicitly presented as an extension of the organic fusion during pregnancy, which, it would seem, simply has to be broken in order for the child to be constituted as a subject. The rupture of this fusion by a third term – whether it's called the father, law, Name of the Father, or something else – should facilitate entry into the symbolic and access to language . . . But surely all that's needed is to reiterate and mark, on another level, a differentiation that already exists during pregnancy thanks to the placenta . . .[37]

What would it be like if our subjectivity were founded not on rupture but on a more subtle kind of differentiation that allowed us to maintain our relation to our mothers? The example of the placenta is interesting because it suggests that such a possibility exists, as Rouche points out, already. In the USA, "biologism" has long since become the ultimate insult among feminists, its fate sealed in no small part by Judith Butler's argument in *Gender Trouble* that "the language of biology participates in other kinds of languages and reproduces that cultural sedimentation in objects it purports to discover and neutrally describe."[38] Butler's critique of false neutrality is certainly valid. But the example of the placenta reminds us how much we stand to lose if we reject the language of biology out of hand. It is not that that language is inherently any more or less faithful to its maternal referent. But its perceived status as such does have the advantage of suggesting that a different relation to the mother belongs not to a distant utopian future, but to an undeniable, anatomical now.

Arrowroot's narrator invokes the same sense of immediacy in Chapter three, in his description of a Yoshino delicacy so sensual as to provide the most memorable passage in the novel. About half-way to the mother's home place, Tsumura and the narrator stop at a farmhouse to see what turns out to be some phony historical relics. But the visit is more than redeemed when they are served a sublimely gooey treat. The narrator explains:

> The empty ashtray seemed not for cigarettes, but for holding under one's mouth while eating the runny, over-ripe persimmons. With trepidation I tried placing a piece of this about-to-burst fruit on my palm, just as I was told. It was large and cone-shaped with a pointy tip, and had ripened to a bright, half-translucent red. Like a bag made of rubber, it was swollen and jiggly, but with the sun passing through it became a beautiful orb of coral jade. Persimmons sold in the city never turn such a splendid color, and cave in on themselves long before achieving this kind of softness. According to our host, you can

only make *jukushi* from Minō persimmons with thick skins. They are picked while still hard and stored in a box or basket away from the elements. Left untouched for ten days, the insides melt naturally to a jelly sweet as nectar. The insides of other persimmons run like water, and never achieve the marvelous gooiness of the Mino. To eat them you can pull off the top and scoop out the insides with a spoon, as with a soft-soft boiled egg, but they are more delicious eaten by hand from a bowl, the skin peeled back with dripping hands.[39]

Watanabe argues that these *jukushi* are the very essence of abjection, calling them "sweetly beautiful rot" [kanbi na fushoku] and glossing the whole phrase with the *ateji* "abuje" [abject]. According to Watanabe, Tanizaki went so far as to build abjection into the title of his novel. To read it forward is to read "Yo-SHI-no KU-ZU." To read it backward is to find these foul "Z[J]U-KU-SHI" making themselves integral from the start.[40] But couldn't the same argument be made for placental *jukushi*? That *they* have been integral from the start? Whether or not the persimmons strike us as abject depends on how much we learn from the narrator's alternative encounter with Yoshino. Watanabe misses it; for him, the narrator and Tsumura are essentially the same character.[41] But clearly, the narrator's job is to stage a meeting with the mother in which abjection cannot threaten because the threshold is always mediated: safe, open and mutual. As the persimmons become another example of this threshold, coating the narrator's intestinal tract with a coolness that "flow[s] from his gums to his entrails," it is as if the biology of the place itself is teaching him how to relate to it differently.[42] And the point is that that difference was there already, waiting. The irony of its availability is illustrated nicely in *jukushi*'s status as a local delicacy. On the one hand, they are so fragile and rare as to be inconceivable in society at large. One never finds them in the city! On the other, they are completely natural, even inevitable, given the right circumstances and the right sensibility.

Notes

1. Tanizaki Jun'ichirō (1967) *Yoshinokuzu*, in *Tanizaki Jun'ichirō Zenshū* [Complete Works of Tanizaki Jun'ichirō] 13, Tokyo: Chūō Kōron, p. 48. There is an elegant translation by Anthony Chambers (1991) in *Two Novels: The Secret History of the Lord of Musashi and Arrowroot*, San Francisco: North Point Press. Because word-games and semiotics are important to my argument, I offer my own translations here.
2. Nakagami makes oblique reference to *Arrowroot*'s insight into what he calls "the structure of sabetsu" [sabetsu no kōzō] in at least three texts: a 1977 zadankai with Noma Hiroshi and Yasuoka Shōtaro called "Shimin ni hisomu sabetsu shinri" [the psychology of discrimination latent in civil society], a 1979 essay on Tanizaki from the collection of literary criticism *Monogatari no keifu* [genealogy of monogatari], and the "Yoshino" chapter from a 1979 book of travel reportage called *Kishū: ki no kuni, ne no monogatari* [Kishū: country of trees and deeply rooted narrative]. I discuss all three references at some length in the third chapter of my book, *This Perversion Called Love: Tanizaki, Feminist Theory, Freud*, forthcoming from Stanford University Press.

3. Komori Yōichi (1998) <*Yuragi* > *no nihon bungaku* [The "slippage" of Japanese literature], Tokyo: Nihon hōsō shuppan kyōkai, p. 207.
4. Watanabe Naomi (1992) *Tanizaki Jun'ichirō: gitai no yūwaku* [Tanizaki Jun'ichirō: the sedution of mimicry], Tokyo: Shinchōsha, p. 196.
5. Tanizaki, *Yoshinokuzu*, pp. 29–30.
6. "Koishikuba/tazune kite mi yo/izumi naru." This is the poem as it is written on the shōji by the fox mother in Takeda Izumo's *Ashiya dōman ōuchi kagami* [A courtly mirror of Ashiya Dōman] (p. 26), and as Tsumura recites it when recalling the scene where the fox-mother Kuzu-no-ha takes leave of her son in that play (p. 28). For the scene in Takeda's play, see Act II in *Ashiya dōman ouchi kagami,* Tokyo: Kokuritsu Gekijō, 1990, pp. 21–7.
7. Sigmund Freud (1962) *"Beyond the Pleasure Principle,"* in James Strachey (trans. and ed.) *The Standard Edition of the Complete Psychological Works of Sigmund Freud* 18, London: The Hogarth Press, p. 14.
8. Ibid., p. 15.
9. Ibid.
10. Tanizaki, *Yoshinokuzu*, p. 28.
11. Freud, *"Beyond the Pleasure Principle,"* p. 14.
12. Jacques Lacan, *Ecrits* (trans. Alan. Sheridan), New York: W. W. Norton, 1977, p. 103.
13. Ibid., p. 104.
14. Luce Irigaray (1993) *Sexes and Genealogies* (trans. Gillian Gill), New York: Columbia University Press, p. 14.
15. Julia Kristeva (1980) *Desire in Language: A Semiotic Approach to Literature and Art*, (trans. Thomas Gora, Alice Jardine and Leon S. Roudiez), (ed. Leon S. Roudiez), New York: Columbia University Press, p. 136.
16. Julia Kristeva (1982) *Powers of Horror* (trans. Leon S. Roudiez), New York: Columbia University Press, p. 2.
17. Ibid., p. 13.
18. Tanizaki, *Yoshinokuzu*, p. 27.
19. Julia Kristeva (1984) *Revolution in Poetic Language* (trans. Leon S. Roudiez), New York: Columbia University Press, p. 29.
20. Kristeva, *Desire in Language*, p. 136.
21. Ibid.
22. Tanizaki, *Yoshinokuzu*, p. 27. My translation uses asterisks to mark places where I have supplemented the "garbled" passages using a commentary by Yamato Hōmei rather than try to reproduce in English their nonsense syllables and gaps in syntax. See Yamato, *Sōkyoku kashi kaisetsu: jiuta, sōkyoku* [Interpretation of sōkyoku lyrics: jiuta and koto music]. Online. available at: http:// www2u.biglobe.ne.jp/~houmei/ kasi/0_hyousi.htm (Accessed 22 October 2007).
23. Yamato, *Sōkyoku kashi kaisetsu: jiuta, sōkyoku.*
24. Irigaray (1993) *Sexes and Genealogies*, p. 17.
25. Tanizaki (1967) *Yoshinokuzu*, pp. 15–16.
26. Ibid., p. 12.
27. Ibid., p. 33.
28. Ibid., p. 36.
29. Irigaray (1993) *Sexes and Genealogies*, p. 18.
30. Ibid., p. 196.
31. Ibid., p. 195.
32. Luce Irigaray (2002) *Between East and West: From Singularity to Community* (trans. Stephen Pluhacek), New York: Columbia University Press, p. 130.
33. Irigaray (1993) *Sexes and Genealogies*, p. 31.
34. Ibid., p. 33.
35. Luce Irigaray (1993) *je, tu, nous: Toward a Culture of Difference* (trans. Alison Martin), New York: Routledge, p. 41.

36. Ibid., p. 42.
37. Ibid.
38. Judith Butler (1990) *Gender Trouble*, New York: Routledge, p. 109.
39. Tanizaki, *Yoshinokuzu*, pp. 21–2.
40. Watanabe, *Gitai no yūwaku*, p. 199.
41. Ibid., p. 189.
42. Tanizaki, *Yoshinokuzu*, p. 22.

7 Introduction

Gavin Walker: The double scission of Mishima Yukio . . .

Gavin Walker writes that criticism of Mishima Yukio must "maintain the auto-fictional imaginary signification 'Mishima' . . . as the 'quilting point' of the textual field." Lacan described the quilting point as follows:

> Whether it be a sacred text, a novel, a play, a monologue, or any conversation whatsoever, allow me to represent the function of the signifier by a spatializing device . . . This point around which all concrete analysis of discourse must operate I shall call a quilting point . . . This is the point at which the signified and the signifier are knotted together, between the still floating mass of meanings that are actually circulating . . . Everything radiates out from and is organized around this signifier, similar to these little lines of force that an upholstery button forms on the surface of a material. It's the point of convergence that enables everything that happens in this discourse to be situated retroactively and prospectively.[1]

Pursuing a close reading of sections of *Taiyō to tetsu (Sun and Steel)* that employs a Deleuzian and Derridean critical framework (and later, Lacanian), Walker maps out how Mishima orchestrated his own "autofictional machine," as precisely such a quilting point, consisting of a double bind of concealment and confession in fictional and non-fictional forums. This machine functions to ensure that the critic rely on Mishima's "biological life" as the barometer for interpreting his writings, and that his writings refer back to this signifier "Mishima" in a sort of closed interpretive circle. This primary thesis is complicated by Walker's utilization of the concept of "double scission" which foregrounds the problem of taking textual representation literally. Moreover, this Mishima "machine" requires his death as its enabling condition, which Walker calls "necroperformativity." The machine relies on a specific politics of visuality, in which a *fiction* of "being seen" must be interpreted in relation to what Walker calls the "secret," or the (Derridean/Lacanian) remainder of the "I" in the text as its supplement. Mishima as a subject is stabilized from the viewpoint of the other, or the reader/critic, hence the machine is dedicated to enlisting the reader in the project of making Mishima visible, or producing him as a subject, an "I." This, conversely, by fixing the visible with his "autofictional self-representation," limits the possibilities of reading "Mishima." The supplement constitutes a central referential void that in turn gives rise to a "danger" in which writing claims to be presence and the sign of the thing itself. Mishima relies, holds Walker, in the end, on a forced correlation that is incoherent when he forces a connection between the double supplementarity of this "I" as remainder or supplement (that which remains in the text) with a community bound by shared suffering. Finally, Walker finds resonance between the voided center of Mishima's self-referentiality with the representation of the figure of the emperor – the myth that Mishima dedicated himself to resurrecting through his death by suicide.

Note

1. *The Seminar of Jacques Lacan, Book III: The Psychoses* 1955–1956, J. A. Miller (ed.) New York: W. W. Norton, 1993, pp. 267–8.

7 The double scission of Mishima Yukio

Limits and anxieties in the autofictional machine

Gavin Walker

"I began my literary life concerned with how to conceal myself, rather than how to manifest myself," writes Mishima Yukio in his 1968 work *Taiyō to tetsu* [Sun and Steel].[1] While this text can be considered a work of autofiction, "a practice which uses the device of authorial fictionalization for reasons that are not autobiographical,"[2] it structurally resembles a manifesto.

Taiyō to tetsu was originally serialized in six parts in the review *Hihyō* [Critique] between 1965 and 1968. Released in book form that year by Shinchōsha, Mishima's long-time publisher, the text was translated into English by John Bester in 1970, and has become well known outside of Japan. It has been relied upon as an important conceptual source for numerous putatively biographical productions in English, from Paul Schrader's film *Mishima: A Life In Four Chapters* to John Nathan's widely read *Mishima: A Biography*. The Japanese text consists of a single, undivided essay of approximately 100 pages, appended with an epilogue *F104*, and has been primarily treated as a coherent and revealing "autobiographical" essay.

It is decidedly not, however, written in the autobiographical mode, which purports to report on a set of "historical" circumstances in relation to a stable and graspable "I." In Mishima's terms "a form between confession and criticism" (*kokuhaku to hihyō to no chūkan keitai*) or a "secret criticism" (*himerareta hihyō*) (*TT* 9), *Taiyō to tetsu* is plagued by contradiction at every turn: at every moment, the program of the text finds itself imploding under the strain of its impossibility.

Aspects of Mishima's social-historical engagement as a figure, from his appearances in movies like *Karakkaze yarō* [*Afraid to Die*, 1960], his series of glam/kitsch semi-nude photos with photographer Hosoe Eikō, *Barakei* [*Torture by Roses*], the formation of his private "army," the *Tate no kai*, or "Shield Society," his body-building, his militant cultural nationalist posturing, and finally his ritualized suicide performance on November 25th, 1970, are well-known and recurrently sensationalized. Precisely because of this particular historical visibility, the veracity and coherence of the self-representation of Mishima in his texts has been predominantly treated as given, and the status of this self-representation has largely not been put into question. *Taiyō to tetsu* figures a complex set of aporetic schemas that interact and co-determine each other between the work and figure of Mishima, as well as between the role of critique and its limits in relation to this space. Mishima's self-representation, as it is produced by his texts and jointly by critique, constructs a series of devices that continually elide the approachability of "Mishima," serving to continue a mythic discursive circuit of representation, and setting up dangerous limitations for critique.

Critical anxieties

Roy Starrs, in his *Deadly Dialectics: Sex, Violence and Nihilism in the World of Yukio Mishima*, delivers a summation of the social-historical figure of Mishima as follows:

> Scion of a privileged, upper-bourgeois family, completely lacking a "social conscience", but "playing" at revolution merely to gratify his nihilist/narcissist impulses, or, more sinisterly, resorting to fascism to shore up the declining privileges of his class.[3]

Starrs continues, saying, "it would be difficult to defend him except in the usual rather lame way one defends 'disreputable' writers . . . his politics need not be taken seriously as politics, but only for the 'aesthetic' use he makes of them in his works."[4] This then reproduces the primary circular critical trap with respect to Mishima as a figure/author: out-and-out fascist or ambiguous aesthete. It should be clear that the problem with this distinction is that this is not a coherent opposition: first of all, because any given fascist is likely to be an ambiguous aesthete, but more importantly for my argument, because under the guise of presenting a double "option," this perspective in fact critically seals Mishima's own cycle by ensuring that all critique is made in light of an agreement that Mishima the historical figure and Mishima the autofictional figure are an identical subject-object.

Irmela Hijiya-Kirschnereit, among a small number of other critics, has pointed directly towards this problem: here all textual problems are solved by recourse to biography, and all biographical problems are solved by recourse to the texts, thus allowing the "true" critical reading of Mishima to be that defined by *Mishima himself.*[5] She writes, "In a mode that forms a perfect short circuit, the work is 'explained' by the author's mental disposition, while at the same time his psyche is exemplified in relation to his fiction."[6] This serves to continue the "Mishima-myth" – it stabilizes "Mishima" into Mishima Yukio (1925–1970), as he auto-fictionally operationalized "himself" – as a figure who lived and died in strict accord with his own system. Hijiya-Kirschnereit continues:

> Mishima himself would find, to his complete satisfaction, that the carefully crafted web of opinions and interpretations that weaves together the person and his work and the cleverly contrived Mishima myth he successfully founded while his career as an author and public figure developed and climaxed has been kept beautifully intact.[7]

The above is not merely applicable to Starrs' work, it is what Mishima himself does in *Taiyō to tetsu*: in other words, he creates a theoretical system interspersed with seemingly psycho-auto-biographical anecdotes which the reader has no possible way to verify, forcing him or her to cede to Mishima the position of "hero of the story," and thus acknowledging Mishima from beyond the grave as intertwined with his theoretical work. It is the contention of this essay that this problematic is not external to the Mishima text. This double scission is in fact the chief internal pivot of *Taiyō to tetsu*, figured in the theory of "being seen" (*mirareru*) and the discourse of concealment that re-presents through the critic a stable and coherent Mishima figure/work.

Autofictional limits

Mishima texts his body, being, and death into his work in a way which renders the separation of the social-historical Mishima from its textual representation a difficult and problematic critical endeavor. Watanabe Naomi, in his recent *Kakumo sensai naru ōbō: Nihon "68nen" shōsetsuron* [Such a Refined Violence: Theory of the Japanese "68" Novel], states in the preface:

> Whether it is the figure of a person in a work, the separation-connection of time and space, or grammatical person (*ninshō*) and the management of its focalization, sometimes even in the selection of only one word, one phrase, writing, "freely" betraying a romantic, blind belief in representation, always "has suspicious characteristics".[8]

The one word in *Taiyō to tetsu* that raises an entire field of critical issues in relation to both the work of Mishima and its critique is singular – "I." In the second paragraph of *Taiyō to tetsu*, the reader is alerted to the fundamental foundational pivot of the text (and, indeed of much of Mishima's body of work):

> When I say "I," I do not mean an "I" that relates strictly back to me (*gemmitsu ni watashi ni kizoku suru yō na "watashi"*), nor is it the case that all the words that have left me flow back into my interior – When I say "I," I refer to a remnant (*zanshi*) that neither relates back nor flows back. (*TT* 9)

It is precisely this remnant, this remainder that is operationalized as the coherent "I" of the work as a whole, in keeping with its autofictional program: on the one hand, explanations of Mishima's historical engagement are nearly always explained through recourse to his fictional works, allowing Mishima himself to frame the terms of critique of his own legacy. On the other hand, the chief factor propelling and sustaining the continuing fascination with Mishima is without question the historical fact of his thought and politics. This double bind creates a force that both privileges his thought, and simultaneously serves to obfuscate its actual content. Concretely investigating the trajectories, influences, and set of assumptions guiding Mishima's theoretical interventions can provide significant insight not only into the framework he employs, but also into the enduring phenomenon of the "Mishima myth" (the ensemble of rhetorical and institutional gestures that keep

Mishima "relevant") and its ideological program (the central concept that Mishima the social-historical figure is self-identical with the "I" present in the body of his work).

The systemic rhetoric of self-referentiality in Mishima's critical work (by which I mean his work that proceeds largely under the genre assumption *hyōron*) functions ideologically as a mechanism of concealment, not merely as an autofictional aesthetic tool, but more importantly as an insulation from critique *avant la lettre*. By creating a literary corpus that effects a series of continual rising determinations in relation to an "I" and to a performed series of "non-literary" (but nevertheless textual) political and social interventions, the author can ensure that any non-contextual or aesthetic reading of the work will be employed as a biographical lever, and vice versa.

This effectively maintains an autofictional program long after the author as a living figure has ceased to exist by figuring a textual perpetual motion machine: history is displaced into fiction, and as soon as this movement is nearly complete, fiction is displaced into history, forming a sealed unity. I use "machine" here in the sense employed by Gilles Deleuze and Félix Guattari: "a system of interruptions or breaks" connected to another machine, a "material flow," and containing within it a built-in code, one that is inseparable from its means of transmission.[9] By ensuring that the self-referentiality of the work is rhetorically bound to the social history of the self as public figure, creating a framework with no outside, Mishima instaurates a situation that disables the critic from the outset. One must proceed within the Mishima text in an asymptomatic reading: disruption, reconstitution, collage, and dissolution of the pre-programmed structures present in the text, what Gayatri Spivak has called "reconstellation" or "catachresis."[10] Mishima's autofictionally constructed circle of continuity can only be approached critically by bisecting its assumptions. Slicing across this circular field renders it into two parallel lines of inquiry, mirroring the doubling effect of Mishima's anti-critical operation of foreclosure: I refer to both this critical operation and the anti-critical shield it attacks as the "double scission" of Mishima Yukio.

Jacques Derrida has produced a reading of a parallel critical space.[11] This "double session"/double scission understands itself as taking the aporetic problem of textual representation at its word – the necessity of double expression *and* double explication of what is at stake in reading *Taiyō to tetsu* is a question of what is at stake for critique, what is at stake for a critique of critique. The double scission of Mishima contains within it the double problem of representation: to accede to Mishima's machine is to valorize the identification of the social-historical Mishima with the textual figure "Mishima," but in doing so one must set up an incoherent opposition that obtains only if one assumes that texts are not social-historical themselves, an argument which is of course, false.

Thus, the necessity of acknowledging the doubled effect that Mishima's machine sets up: it both acknowledges the falsity of its own motor-force, and at the same time re-valorizes its existence by co-opting certain critiques into service on its behalf. I argue that the theoretical construction of this machine, and the effect of the duplication of representation and referentiality in critical receptions of Mishima can be readily seen in the text of *Taiyō to tetsu*. The double scission in *Taiyō to tetsu* is present in its discourse of the secret. When Mishima calls the text a "secret criticism" (*himerareta hihyō*), we must read this at and against this word. The secret of *Taiyō to tetsu* is the text's self-revelation of its central machine, simultaneously opened and foreclosed in its explication of self-construction, visuality, and confessional collectivity.

Self-construction: Mishima/Shimada

The concept "Mishima"[12] is constructed out of a rhetorical correspondence between what Shimada Masahiko has called "Mishima Yukio the living person" (*seikatsusha Mishima Yukio*) and "Mishima Yukio as work/text" (*sakuhin toshite no Mishima Yukio*).[13] This is the previously mentioned "I" as remainder in *Taiyō to tetsu*, set up at the outset of the text as irreducible to Mishima the living person, and at the same time, in a direct named relationship to him. Shimada has written a series of important texts on the figure of Mishima that represent some of the most incisive exposition of the internal structure of Mishima's self-referentiality. He has suggested a formula that constructs the concept "Mishima":

> The coupling (*kōsetsu*) of the body of language (written things) with the language of the body (the body of Mishima Yukio as a work or text), the coupling of past and present, the coupling of the "I" as a perceptive being (*ninshikisha*) with the "I" as a performer (*engisha*) or experimental subject (*jikkendai*), the coupling of illusion with reality – it is the locus of the coupling of each of these various contradictory things (*sōhan suru mono*) that is the true form of the works/texts that evoke the multifarious imaginary (*tashutayō na sōzō*) that is Mishima Yukio.[14]

One of the key operators in Shimada's passage above is this duality of the "body of language" (*gengo no nikutai*) and the "language of the body" (*nikutai no gengo*). If we treat the "body of language" as Shimada does, in other words, as a *corpus*, or "written things" (*kakareta mono*) what concerns *Taiyō to tetsu* most is a thinking of its physical corollary, or, the "language of the body." Mishima calls this in *Taiyō to tetsu* "the desire to somehow encounter reality in a domain wherein words take no part" (*Nantoka kotoba no mattaku kan'yo shinai ryōiki de genjitsu ni deaō to iu yokkyū*) (*TT* 12). The anti-critical machine of the text returns frequently to this point, to emphasize by rote the concept that Mishima Yukio as a figure has *already* exceeded representation. Shimada carefully exposes the operational machine of the text by emphasizing the double structures of the work, treating "coupling" (*kōsetsu*) as the motor force of the "Mishima" imaginary. This doubling mirrors the doubling of the textual machine itself, creating and enforcing its own limitations, a point I will return to later.

Shimada writes, "The experiencing of reality in words ends up as the writing of something in words that correspond to reality" (*Genjitsu o kotoba de taiken suru koto wa genjitsu ni miatta kotoba de mono o kaku to iu koto ni ikitsuku*).[15] Mishima's imperative is that we must not mistake the picture for the real, for the picture is always corroded (*fushoku*), arguing that words are not "reality" themselves, they give us a picture of reality. But paradoxically, it is precisely the textuality of *Taiyō to tetsu* that remains the central point of reference in Mishima's sentence above. It is under the condition of its written nature, that, as a program, it can function. Judith Butler incisively forms this problematic paradox as follows:

> To posit by way of language a materiality outside of language is still to posit that materiality and the materiality so posited will retain that positing as its constitutive condition.[16]

When Mishima writes that the goal is to encounter "a space in which words take no part," it is the statement of this goal itself that remains the unsurpassable center. By positing the possibility of such a space, Mishima is of course exposing its impossibility. Why is this contradiction not addressed in *Taiyō to tetsu*? Because the only recourse the reader has, in confronting this contradiction, is to resort for explanation to the life and social engagement of Mishima Yukio the living person. This is how the machine functions in *Taiyō to tetsu*, to present concrete impossibilities, absolute contradictions, and to enlist the reader in "solving" them by positing a referentiality that correlates "Mishima the living person" to "Mishima as text."

The injunctions mentioned by Mishima for physical self-creation confront the reader in the fourth paragraph of the text. Mishima states, "If I suppose my self (*jiga*) as a dwelling (*kaoku*), then my body was something like an orchard enclosing it (*kore o torimaku kajuen no yō na mono*)." He goes on to say, "It occurred to me at a certain point to begin toiling away at the cultivation of my orchard (*sesseto tagayashi hajimeta*)." There is thus a material essence, but one without form, one that requires "cultivation" – in other words, the materiality of the body is not in question, but it must be tamed, disciplined. The orchard, if "neglected while overgrown with weeds" (*yasō no oishigeru mama ni hōchi suru*) (*TT* 10), will be a powerless thing – if not created or formed, it remains a part of existence but not a *participant*.

Taiyō to tetsu, on the level of its abstract machine, is filled with a drive to negotiate "forms between" (*chūkan keitai*) ensembles that are posited as "opposed": language and body, theory and praxis, life and death – and here specifically, natural and manmade. The body is natural material, but the "body as work" (*sakuhin toshite no nikutai*) is a manmade product (*jinkō sambutsu*) – the second body abstracts the materiality of the first in order to remold its contents. This is a movement in consciousness, not in social-historical practice, making the gestures and formative background of the "body as work" fundamentally a condition of its positing. It is physicality that is mentally formed, the exteriorizing of the interior, bearing a resemblance to Michel Foucault's discussion of the inscription of the soul "on the surface of the body."[17] This emphasis on charting a "form between" is a direct index of the problem of the double in *Taiyō to tetsu*.

Mishima explicates this exteriority, the physical rather than lingual perception of concepts, in a number of statements in *Taiyō to tetsu*, declaring: "The exercise of the muscles elucidated very simply what words had made mysterious" (*Kotoba ga shimpika shite ita mono o, kinniku no kōshi wa yasuyasu to kaimei shita*). What follows the above statement is a militant summation of Mishima's entire program in *Taiyō to tetsu* regarding the physical:

> I thought: couldn't one extend a fragment of an idea from the psyche (*seishin*) to the body, so that the entirety of the body was made into armor forged from the metal of that concept (*sono kannen no kinzoku de dekita yoroi*)? (*TT* 19–20)

Throughout *Taiyō to tetsu* there is a continued return to the idea that language itself is a corrupt, inaccurate form of describing or encountering reality. Mishima states:

> Since words are a medium that abstracts (*chūshōka*) reality for transmission to our intellect, and because of this, function by corroding reality, they inevitably connote the danger that words themselves will come to be corroded (*kotoba jitai o mo fushoku shite yuku kiken o naihō shite iru*). (*TT* 11)

What is problematic in Mishima's theorizing of words and reality is that he attributes no materiality to words themselves: they are free-floating and untethered signifiers, ways of describing what there is, but because there can never be such a thing as language or a word that perfectly describes its referent, Mishima regards them as a force of "corrosion" (*fushoku*). Language in *Taiyō to tetsu* exists in a doubled relation – on the one hand, language is always already the mode of positing the set of relations in the text, while on the other, language itself is disavowed as a method of coming to terms with the "forms between" that are the programmatic goal of the work.

In relation to language, these attempts to chart "forms between" are always spectral, they always constitute a doubled trace, which contrary to Mishima's efforts in *Taiyō to tetsu*, cannot attain a stable status. This problem finds its own type of confession when he states that "thus, reality and the body became synonyms to me, the objects of a type of *fetishistic interest* (*isshu no fetisshu na kyōmi no taishō*)" (*TT* 13). This admittance of the internal conceptual fetishism of the text revisits the empty center of the text's machine: by revealing the fetishistic relationship borne by the stated goal of the work, Mishima performs another preemptory confession as a way of repelling critique.

Mishima attempts to suture the fetishized divide between the body and words he has set up by suggesting that, as mentioned earlier, the *process* of words or conceptualization can be applied to the physical. Tomioka Kōichirō calls this rhetoric the "process of how *logos* is incarnated (*nikuka*),"[18] and this "texting" of the body is referred to by Mishima by way of comparison to a "second language":

> Much later, thanks to nothing other than the sun and steel (*hoka naranu taiyō to tetsu no okage de*), I learned the words of the body (*nikutai no kotoba*) as if learning a foreign language. This was my "second language," the formation

of my refinement (*keisei sareta kyōyō*), which I will now discuss. It will likely be a heretofore unseen history of personal refinement (*kyōyō-shi*), and consequently will be extremely difficult to comprehend. (*TT* 16)

Maurice Blanchot warns us against this type of rhetorical physicality: "The word 'body,' its danger, how easily it gives one the illusory impression of being outside of meaning already, free from the contamination of consciousness-unconscious-ness."[19] Mishima's continual reference to a "pure" physicality, a materiality capable of bypassing the corruption of language, is from the outset *a fear of the double*. *Taiyō to tetsu*'s emphasis on the language or words of the body discloses the degree to which the text is always under the condition of language, the degree to which the positing of a "realm in which words take no part" renders itself impossible by function of its own positing as written.

Nina Cornyetz points out Shimada's own reduplication and playful reinscription of this problematic in his own works:

> By conflating Shimada-the-author (as referent) with an author-Shimada (as signifier) who appears in his fiction – and with other characters who are thinly veiled, partial representations of himself – and in his other performative venues, he generates a thick web of variant fictional and putatively nonfictional subjectivities.[20]

Shimada's doubled self-referentiality plays precisely the *opposite* role to that of Mishima: here the double supplementarity of the "I" as remainder is employed as a means of drawing attention to this internal collusion of author and critic, not as a mechanism of critical co-optation.

Roland Barthes famously declared that "To give a text an Author is to impose a limit on the text, to furnish it with a final signified, to close the writing. Once the Author has been found, the text is 'explained' – victory to the critic."[21] Autofiction exists in a space that has already internalized the structural impotence of the author-text matrix via this relation. Its re-energizing gesture has been to require the figure of the critic for its own articulation: because the text has a different set of structural relations to an "I" as author and as self-figuration, any reading of it that treats the relationship between the texted author and the social-historical author as formally stable will set in motion this critical double scission.

The machine at work does not cease its cycle when the "I" of the narrative dies; rather it is only posthumously that the machine can work effectively. Precisely because every written effort has been made to ensure that the textual Mishima, as figured in the texts signed by the name "Mishima Yukio," is in fact the stable and self-identical authorial figure, the death of a historical person connected to this flow is paradoxically the enabling condition for the project. This futural or deferred theatricality, what could be called a kind of "necroperformativity," functions by valorizing the dead Mishima-figure as the authoritative interpreter of his own textual field – the work is performed from beyond the grave. By continuing to posthumously act the part of Mishima, the nexus of the machine remains unassailable. Shimada writes, "It is only through playing the role (*furi o suru koto ni yotte nomi*) of Mishima Yukio that Mishima Yukio comes to exist. The illustration of this tautology is the work called Mishima Yukio (*Mishima Yukio to iu sakuhin*)."[22] The "work called Mishima Yukio" comes into being in *Taiyō to tetsu* through its visuality in the purview of the reader. Mishima sets this movement in motion by "playing the role" of "Mishima," but it is the reader or critic who sustains its structure by solidifying Mishima as the coherent object of Mishima the text, what Mishima calls in *Taiyō to tetsu*, "belonging to the world of the seen."

This reversed mirroring effect enlists the viewer in its codification, ensuring that it produces a carefully guarded space that is both infinitely visible, and at the same time, unapproachable or unassailable in its center. It is this problem of the visual and its correlative relation to concealment that concerns the functioning of the machine of *Taiyō to tetsu* and its discourse of the secret.

Visuality and subjectivation

This problem of Mishima's self-construction is directly related to *Taiyō to tetsu*'s vocabulary of the visual. This relation begins its explication by way of a consideration of the standpoint of the "opponent" (*teki*):

> Both the opponent and I are inhabitants of the same world: when I see the opponent, the opponent is seen; when the opponent sees me, I am seen. Moreover, we face each other with no dependency on any mediation of our power of imagination (*sōzōryoku no baikai*) – we mutually belonged to a world of action and power, namely, the world of the "seen" (*"mirareru" sekai*). (*TT* 42)

He follows this saying, "the idea does not return our gaze, the thing does" (*Idea wa kesshite mikaesu koto ga naku, mono wa mikaesu*), and subsequently, "the opponent is indeed the essence of the 'thing' " (*Teki koso wa "mono" no honshitsu na no de atta*) (*TT* 43). Mishima's correlation of the opponent with the thing is a function of his identification of the thing's nature as a stable object – the fact that the idea "does not return the gaze" (*mikaesu koto ga naku*) demonstrates the mirrored conception of the opponent at work here. Because the opponent functions as a stable "objective" obverse of the self situationally, it is the presence of the opponent as object that brings the self (the body of the self) into subjectivity, into a relation of immediacy.

The thing (here the opponent) responds to the presence of its other (oneself), and in doing so, visually acknowledges one's own presence. Mishima's suggestion however, that ideas are not capable of this act of acknowledgement is inaccurate, precisely because the thing here (the opponent) *is an idea*. The opponent's opposition to the self is what creates the sense of the "returned gaze" according to Mishima, but what he is writing of (the thing-ness of the opponent) is not the opponent itself but the concept of the opponent under its condition of positing. Thus, this positing, in relation to Mishima's conception of the visuality of action, as a problem of language, can be considered roughly analogous to the problem of translation: despite Mishima's insistence on the primacy of "being seen," in fact, this "transferential desire to see oneself from another's position is actually created *after the process* of translation."[23] The translational moment (or the moment of the creation of possibility for positing) is thus the enabling condition of the theory of being seen by the opponent, and the entire structure of visuality in the Mishima text.

It is a reaction to what the opponent represents (the Real staring back at oneself, which is self-regard as subjectivation) – in other words, it is a reaction to the symbolic order of the object, not a reaction to the thing itself. Mishima's insistence here on a stable division between "thing" and "idea" is symptomatic of the fear of the double in *Taiyō to tetsu*, but is problematic not simply because it merely *is* binary, but because within its internal structure, the text itself refutes the stability of this division. The theory of action at work here, in the purview of its radical visuality, recalls Jacques Lacan's conception of praxis as "the broadest term for designating a concerted action by man, whatever it may be, which places him in a position to treat the real by the symbolic."[24]

This treatment of the symbolic structure of action and its seen-ness in *Taiyō to tetsu* has at its core a theorization of the moment of death:

> A man should, under normal circumstances, never allow his own objectification (*kyakutaika*) – he can only be objectified through the supreme action. This is perhaps the moment of death, when, even if not actually seen in reality, one is allowed the fiction of being the "seen" (*"mirareru" gisei*) and the beauty of being the object (*kyakutai toshite no bi*); these things are allowed only at this moment. (*TT* 61)

The doubled nature of being the object is clear from this statement: by being allowed the "fiction of being the seen," reproducing oneself as the object in relation to an opponent, one is seen, but what this means on a second-order level of structure is that one sees oneself from the standpoint of the opponent by proxy, thus making this a project of becoming subject, of subjectivation. This process itself has a doubled movement within the machine of *Taiyō to tetsu*. Because the Mishima-object is validated by its visuality within the opponent's field of vision, this creates the most important condition of subjectivity in the machine: the stabilization of Mishima as the "I"-object from the viewpoint of the reader, critic, or observer.

The content of the machine at work in *Taiyō to tetsu* is dedicated precisely to enlisting the critic to participate in the objectification, the making visible of Mishima. But this relation too has a doubling effect: by insisting on this absolute visuality of his own autofictional self-representation, the machine engages in an act of concealment, a closing down of critical possibilities.

It is this fascination with the object in Mishima's above statement that suggests a further clarification of this theorization of "being seen." Here Mishima specifically states that whether or not one's action is *actually* (*jissai ni*) seen, what matters is the "fiction of being 'seen' " (*"mirareru" gisei*). What is at work here is another level of the conjunction of subject and object – the implication being that in being both the subject and object of an action, one is able to encounter *oneself* as the object, and "see" oneself, concretizing one's presence and thus the "encounter with being and action" (*sonzai to kōi to no deai*).

This point is crucial not only for an understanding of Mishima's consideration of "being seen" at the moment of death (*shi no shunkan*), but also for the theory of the collective that I will examine later. What Mishima here calls the "beauty of being the object" (*kyakutai toshite no bi*) is pivotal in *Taiyō to tetsu* because it is *self-contained*. No others are needed precisely because at the moment of death, one is capable of, from the stance of the acting subject, perceiving oneself to *also* be the acted-upon object: in other words, at this single moment one is capable of perceiving oneself as one assumes that one is perceived by others, and this ensures that one has entered the "world of the seen" (*mirareru ningen no sekai*).

Returning to a thematic image used in a number of his works, Mishima poses the following question in *Taiyō to tetsu* in relation to his conception of the visual and the recurrent problem of language in the text:

> Can the blue sky that all see, the mysterious blue sky uniformly seen by the bearers of the portable shrine (*mikoshi no katsugite tachi ga ichiyō ni miru ano shinpi na aozora*), ever possibly be expressed in language? (*TT* 35)

The answer Mishima gives us is that it cannot be given expression in language – but it is equally important to ask after the constitutive aporia in the formation of the question itself. In positing this conundrum (is language capable of encountering the things it names?), Mishima's text folds back on itself. In articulating the goal of encountering that which is unspeakable (the blue sky) as the center of his project, Mishima manages to internally negate his own rhetoric of "pure" physicality, precisely because the machine, the project, is always under the condition of its written positing. William Haver calls this the "inaugural epistemological gesture by which the aspiration to knowledge, whatever else it may posit, and *in* positing whatever else it may posit, posits its own possibility."[25]

This problem of language returns to the concept of the "fiction of being the seen" in relation to the secret: the remainder (*zanshi*) of the "I" in the text as its representative image, or supplement. This "I" as supplement "is not simply added to the positivity of a presence, it produces no relief, its place is assigned in the structure by the mark of an emptiness."[26] The texted body of Mishima Yukio marks the secret of the machine – it leaves its trace on an empty center, an apparatus with a central referential void. The project of creating the moment when one can attain the "fiction of being the seen" is self-contained; it is not a manifesto. This "fiction of being the seen" is actually already attained in its positing in language: by writing this project into motion in *Taiyō to tetsu* in relation to its supplement, the previously mentioned "I" as remainder (*zanshi*), the written text itself attains this project of being "seen."

The fiction (*gisei*) of this relationship between Mishima's "I" as remainder and the reader of text, however, shows itself to be dangerous in its requirements. Derrida reminds us in the *Grammatology* that "writing is dangerous from the moment that representation there claims to be presence and the sign of the thing itself."[27] The rhetoric of *Taiyō to tetsu* requires at all times that the reader or critic solidify the correlation between Mishima's autofictional representation and the social-historical circumstances particular to Mishima as a once-living figure. As a project, it requires a Mishima as stable presence, and in finding this to be an impossibility, marks the central node of self-referentiality as an empty center, a space without content. The rhetoric of visuality in *Taiyō to tetsu*, its emphasis on the radical nature of being seen (and thus being brought into subjectivation), and thus its doctrine of being as unconcealment, sees its theoretical loose strands tied together in its final exploration of the nature of the confessional project in relation to the collective or group. As has been suggested in the previous sections, the conceptual structure of this notion of the collective contains within its theorization aporias and formulations that negate its coherence.

Confession: singular and collective

The double supplementarity of the "I" as remainder is returned to in the theory of the group (*shūdan*) towards the end of *Taiyō to tetsu*. For Mishima, the confessional particularity of the speaking "I" only finds its coherence in the attachment of this confessional standpoint to the partial universality of the group. Mishima's reliance on this forced correlation is incoherent in combination with his emphasis on the "secret" (*himerareta*) nature of confession, which in turn reinforces the ideological (non)opposition of the particular and the universal.[28]

Language again becomes the object against which a material immediacy is posed when Mishima writes, "There is no question that the collective is a concept that ultimately refuses the intermediary of words – a concept of unspeakable 'shared suffering' (*iu ni iwarenu 'dōku' no gainen*)" (*TT* 97). Having unsuccessfully tried to posit a "pure" materiality outside of language, first in the form of the self-creation of the body, and secondly in a theory of subjectivation through visuality in action, Mishima finally posits this space as approachable only by the group, by a kind of "being-in-common" of the group's members. For the members of a group to form a concept of "shared suffering" (*dōku*) one prerequisite is absolutely essential: the project. *Taiyō to tetsu* is the theorization of a project, the putting-into-motion of a machine, but this project, in its central focus on the self-referential creation of "Mishima" and its discourse of the secret, resists at all moments the possibility of its coherence in relation to anything or anyone else.

Within the idea of the radical physicality of the collective is located the possibility of death: "The sensation of 'bravely surrendering one's body' set the muscles dancing. We were all equally seeking glory and death. It was not only I who sought these things" (*"Karada o teishite iru" to iu kankaku wa, kinniku o odorasete ita. Wareware wa hitoshiku eikō to shi o nozonde ita. Nozonde iru no wa, watashi hitori de wa nakatta*) (*TT* 98). Here again, the glory or possible death of the members of the collective is something that presupposes both the existence of an ideal which binds the members to each other, and it also presupposes that these members have acted or are acting in concert towards its realization. Curiously, the third of these sentences is, strictly speaking, redundant. Why the need to re-emphasize in the clearest terms possible that it "was not only I" seeking glory and death? Because this conception of the collective is correlated with nothing besides Mishima's self-representation within the text of *Taiyō to tetsu*.

The death theorized in this work is the catalyst for the Mishima machine's functioning – the machine is turned on, set in motion, not by Mishima's actual historical death, but by the rhetoric of death as unconcealment, death as confession, and death as discovery of a "being-in-common." Yet at the same time, precisely because this theorization of death as unconcealment is used as the final leverage in setting up the anti-critical machine at work in *Taiyō to tetsu*, the actual function of this concept is its inverse: insulation, hiding, the secret. In this connection, Naoki Sakai incisively writes that for Mishima, "death was primarily a mechanism of insulation. It is no accident that the aggressive resoluteness to his own death and nostalgic yearning for integration into the aestheticized image of a 'people' were united in his literary discourse."[29] In *Taiyō to tetsu*, this problem of death as "integration into the aestheticized image of a 'people' is prefigured by the text's clear construction of a concept of death as integration to an aestheticized notion of the group. *Taiyō to tetsu* itself articulates the abstract correlate of the mechanism pointed out by Sakai.

This insulation sees itself expanded on in the final pages of *Taiyō to tetsu*, as Mishima makes a series of remarks on "belonging" (*zoku suru*) as the center of the concept of the collective as follows:

> I belonged to them, and they belonged to me, forming an unquestionable "us" (*utagai yō no nai "warera"*). To belong – is this not an extreme (*karetsu*) state of being? Our small circle of totality (*chisana zentai no wa*) was a means (*yosuga*) by which to glimpse the vast, vaguely gleaming circle of totality (*ōkina oboroge na kagayaku zentai no wa*). (*TT* 98–9)

From out of the confessional particularity of the texted "I," a texted group is posited, and this group is put into circulation rhetorically in the machine. The group here functions as a way of suggesting that the program of the text is not, in fact, really about an "I" at all, but rather about a "being-in-common." As can be seen throughout this work, however, moments erupt in its writing that allow us glimpses into the machinations of the program, moments that reveal the inner workings of the rhetoric.

The last sentence of the text proper, prior to the epilogue *F104*, is as follows: "Thus the collective was for me a bridge to something (*nani mono ka e no hashi*), a bridge that if crossed, left no means of return" (*TT* 99). This eliminates for us the possibility of taking seriously *Taiyō to tetsu*'s theory of the group, in as much as all of Mishima's prior statements posit the group as an end, a *telos* wherein the attempt to chart "forms between" finds its realization. By clearly demarcating the form of the group as a stepping-stone, a platform for the project or machine to take place through, Mishima also delimits the group as possibility. The group thus does not contain the project, nor is it a necessary form for the project to take. The group as bridge is an insulated conduit for the textual machine, moving it along in a form that conceals and hides within it the problem of the "I" as remainder.

Thus when Mishima writes of the wonderful feeling that comes from declaring, "I'm the same as everyone else" (*TT* 97) it is clear that this is an utterly incoherent statement from the standpoint of the project of *Taiyō to tetsu*, which, if anything at all, is concerned in the first instance with instaurating an absolute distinction between a self-identical textual Mishima and everything else. The text's theory of the group and its relation to the machine operating within it are routed through a return to the conception of confession mentioned at the outset of the work. The type of confession present in *Taiyō to tetsu* is, following Karatani Kōjin, a type of "confession as a system" (*kokuhaku to iu seido*) that functions as an inverted "will to power." Karatani describes this sort of confession thus: "Confession does not necessarily imply remorse. Behind a façade of weakness, the one who confesses seeks to become a subject (*'shutai' taru koto*), to dominate."[30] With respect to Mishima's rhetoric of confession, this domination is not a self-domination, or a domination of social-historical circumstances – it represents an attempt to dominate and control the conditions of reception underlying a given reader's critical grasp of this rhetoric itself.

There is another aporetic moment of rupture in *Taiyō to tetsu* in the question of the truth of the project, a passage that demarcates the impossibly singular nature of the confession within:

> There are truths in this world that cannot be seen without changing one's posture (*shisei o kuzusanakereba mienai shinjitsu*) – it's not as if I don't know this. But this was something that could be left to others (*tanin ni makasete okeba sumu koto*). (*TT* 53)

The subsumption of the "I" of the text within the structure of the group, and its correlative emphasis on the collective nature of the group's actions thus disintegrates under the force of the singular project. Candidly articulating the autofictional limits of this confession, Mishima states, "I refused to acknowledge the conditions of my existence, and imposed on myself the process of another existence" (*Watashi wa jibun no sonzai no jōken o issai mitomezu, betsu no sonzai no tetsuzuki o jibun ni kashita no datta*). This he summarizes by saying that this entailed "changing from a person creating words to a person created by words" (*kotoba ni yotte tsukuru mono kara, kotoba ni yotte tsukurareru mono e ikō suru koto*) (*TT* 71). It is the void center of Mishima's self-referentiality that bears most resemblance to the problem of another figure whose representation is also simultaneously overdetermined and ungraspable: the emperor (*tennō*).

Under the sign of the emperor

In order to not confront the complexity of the Mishima myth, approaches to its formative elements are foreclosed from the outset, creating an empty space, an erasure. This lack at the center of the Mishima-situation accounts not only for the background to his particular set of actions, but also for the situation of his posthumous reception. At all times the complexity of Mishima is routed through a forced synthesis, producing figures and frames that can be digested, critically regurgitated, and put back into circulation: Mishima the fascist, Mishima the uniform fetishist gym bunny, Mishima the defender of "Japanese tradition." But in an oddly coherent correlation, the figure Mishima most resembles in terms of his relation to critique is the representation in literary and cultural productions of the emperor (*tennō*). Precisely because of the matrix of necessity and disavowal that re-presenting the emperor as a figure poses, the object is not immediately identifiable with its naming, but rather expresses the whole situation in which it is located, simultaneously determining and being determined by its conditions and instances, and thus requires a new generic articulation in order to be approachable.

Watanabe Naomi's *Fukei bungakuron josetsu* [Introduction to a Blasphemous Literary Theory] incisively formulates the problematic relationship "emperor/novel" by tracing the absence of the representation of the emperor in modern and contemporary literary productions. Stating that while immense amounts of reflections on the emperor-system (*tennōsei*) have been generated, nevertheless *the figure of the emperor himself* has been assiduously avoided in the novel, something that Watanabe early on in his work calls the "discourse of approach-avoidance" (*sekkin=kaihi no disukūru*), he argues that this simultaneous move-towards and retreat-from, rendering the position of the emperor, or "imperial household" (*kōshitsu*) a void and sealed space, produces the conditions that maintain the emperor's discursive unapproachability.[31] I argue, along gesturally divergent but nevertheless conceptually parallel lines, that the figure of Mishima Yukio plays, with respect to criticism, a similar role. Certain strata of agreement underlie the conceptual structures of most critical receptions of him, articulating a locus of mutual determinations that has maintained and reinforced the Mishima myth. These agreements have at their center a conception of Mishima, that, in strict correlation to Mishima's own machine, finds a unity and equivalence between Mishima the texted figure and Mishima the social-historical persona. Watanabe writes with regard to the matrix emperor-novel:

> From the outset of modern history to the Shōwa defeat, precisely at the moment when the existence of the emperor is coming more and more into view (*tennō no sonzai o shiya ni osamen to suru isshun*), the novel is constantly and inevitably being rendered absolutely impotent.[32]

In precisely the same relation of non-relation, as Mishima has ever-increasingly been finally determined socio-historically, critique of Mishima's work has mostly equivocated in the face of complexity, ceding to Mishima the role of critical overseer, and thus co-opting itself into service on behalf of a machine that renders critique impotent.

This construction of an unassailable, unspeakable empty center to the figure of Mishima constitutes the real danger, because it accedes to the manipulative self-figuration set in motion by Mishima's texts. As mentioned above, this situation closely parallels the problem of the figure of the emperor. Ukai Satoshi politically differentiates between two rightist notions of this figure: that of the valorization of his position as sovereign (*shukensha*), in other words, those who advocate a return of the emperor to the actual governing head of state, and on the other hand, those who locate within the figure of the emperor an empty locus, a gathering power of nihilism. Ukai clearly states that it is this latter tendency that is politically a danger; the former rightist tendency is farcical, "it definitely won't go too well" (*umaku iku hazu ga nai shi*).[33] Unfortunately, in its parallel to the problematic posed by the figure of Mishima, this has gone all too well. Critically overdetermined by the social-historical circumstances of its object of inquiry, Mishima criticism has tended to elide the problematic of the textual figure of Mishima in favor of its more sensational obverse: a "writer who committed *seppuku*" (*seppuku o shita sakka*).[34]

Suga Hidemi's discussion of what he calls "Mishima's victory" (*Mishima no shōri*) is important in examining the machine operating in *Taiyō to tetsu*, stating for example, that "when Mishima died, the visibility of fetishism suffered its final bankruptcy. Mishima's idea of the "emperor as cultural concept" (*bunka gainen toshite no tennō*) affirms the empty fetishistic characteristics of the emperor (system)."[35] Suga argues that Mishima's discourse on the emperor as cultural concept prefigured the emergence of a "J-emperor (system),"[36] much in the same way that there is now J-pop, J-art, the J-novel, and so on. This pop-cultural "J" prefix, connoting the English "Japan," is read as the "empty center" of contemporary cultural life, a kind of "postmodern nationalism," and Suga produces a series of schematic glosses for the "J" concept: Japan, junk, *jouissance*.

This schema articulates the void center of the "J" in junk, the cultural products of a late world capitalism, which could be thought of as a shorthand for the commodity forms (including labor-power) specific to a post-industrial consumer organization of life and their enjoyment, the *jouissance* derived from them as they are routed back into a light, hip nationalism, in a "return to Japan" (*Nihon e no kaiki*) or "J-return" (*J-kaiki*).[37] Suga, echoing Benjamin, argues that Mishima's notion of the "emperor as cultural concept," in locating in the emperor an absent, empty center as the expression of a gathering power of cultural "copies without originals," explicated precisely the Zeitgeist of the post-"68 situation.[38] In extending Suga's discussion of Mishima in relation to the emperor, I want to point out that *Taiyō to tetsu* shows *Mishima himself* to be a copy without an original. In a reduplication of his strangely prescient theory of the emperor, under the force of his own machine, Mishima has ceased to be coherent as a social-historical figure and has become strictly "Mishima as cultural concept" (*bunka gainen toshite no Mishima Yukio*) or a kind of "J-Mishima." It is the constant recirculation of a rhetoric that is internal to the machine set up in Mishima's texts such as *Taiyō to tetsu* that sustains and bolsters the Mishima myth and its attendant tropes.

This creates a situation that enlists the critic in perpetuating the workings of the machine. "The most apparently direct writing, the most directly concrete, personal writing which is supposedly in direct contact with the 'thing itself' this writing is 'on credit': subjected to the authority of a commentary or a re-editing that it is not even capable of reading."[39] *Taiyō to tetsu* pushes its own representational apparatus so far that it doubles on itself: by setting up a machine focused on generating an anti-critical field, the text actually requires precisely this dismantling of its concerns in order to constitute itself: it needs "credit" extended to it by the critic in order to articulate its own demands. In following the program of Mishima's anti-critical machine, criticism must maintain the autofictional imaginary signification "Mishima" (Mishima = "Mishima") as the "quilting point" of the textual field. The remainder of the "I" in the text is the node that "everything radiates out from and is organized around," a locus "that enables everything that happens in this discourse to be situated retroactively and prospectively."[40] This one point, that of a clear and stable self-referentiality, balances and sustains the program of *Taiyō to tetsu*, "quilting" together the net of significations that constitute the ensemble of the work. When the machinations of *Taiyō to tetsu* work themselves through the core relations in the text, posing the body of Mishima's "I" as remainder, its standpoint within the collective, and its correlative theory of action against the corruption of language, the machine buckles under itself by showing "itself to be a fiction," exposing its own project of insulation.

In another of the strange aporetic moments in *Taiyō to tetsu* in which a glimpse of the actual form of the machine or project becomes suddenly visible, Mishima articulates both a limitation and a strategy for the functioning of the machine:

> It is "time" that it is responsible for the frustration and failure of this project (*kono kito no zasetsu to shippai*), but in extremely rare circumstances, "time" confers grace on the project (*goku mare ni "toki" wa onchō o tarete*) and rescues it from the same frustration and failure. (*TT* 78)

Here Mishima identifies the sustaining force of the machine as time – its posthumous self-maintenance and its tendency to co-opt the critic into its workings has allowed the Mishima myth to grow and prosper. But it is also time, its passage and the shifting specter of Mishima within its flows, that creates the conditions for its identification and isolation.

As mentioned at the outset of this paper, Mishima's anti-critical machine both delimits the boundaries of critique, and simultaneously creates the conditions of its own destruction. By putting in motion the workings of a textual machine that operates like a binding agent between Mishima the social-historical figure and Mishima the textual representation as remainder, Mishima, rather than being successful at lasting forever, has in fact withered away completely. There is no longer a coherent Mishima other than "the remainder that neither flows back nor relates back" – Mishima's necroperformative bequeathal has, in its incapability of managing the double, eaten its own referential field away. This attempt to exceed the grasp of critique fails utterly because it requires a predetermined and *singular* Mishima-object, and shuts down under its own doubling. By exploding his own relation to representation, Mishima literally "sentence-d" himself to death, and the Mishima machine comes to a halt. But attempts to turn it back on, to recirculate its program, emerge every time "Mishima" becomes an object of inquiry.

Acknowledgments

I benefited from discussions with Naoki Sakai, Brett de Bary, Christopher Ahn, Pedro Erber, Travis Workman, and in particular Takeshi Kimoto, who gave me extensive editing suggestions on the entire chapter. Nina Cornyetz and J. Keith Vincent have been very supportive of this essay, and their suggestions and comments have helped refine my argument. Needless to say, any remaining errors are mine alone. Translations from all languages other than English are mine unless otherwise indicated.

Notes

1. Mishima Yukio (1968) *Taiyō to tetsu,* Tokyo: Shinchōsha, 80. "Jiko o ika ni arawasu ka, to iu koto yori mo, ika ni kakusu ka, to iu hōhō ni yotte bungaku seikatsu o hajimeta." Hereafter all citations of this text are given in the body of the essay as *TT*.
2. This definition, "une pratique qui utilise le dispositif de la fictionnalisation auctoriale pour des raisons qui ne sont pas autobiographiques," is taken from Vincent Colonna's (1989) dissertation *L'autofiction: Essai sur la fictionnalisation de soi en literature*, École des Hautes Études en Science Sociales, p. 390; cited in Serge Doubrovsky *et al.* (eds) *Autofictions et cie*, Université de Paris X-Nanterre, 1993, p. 212.
3. Roy Starrs (1994) *Deadly Dialectics: Sex, Violence and Nihilism in the World of Yukio Mishima*, Honolulu: University of Hawaii Press, 169.
4. Ibid.
5. This problematic has been identified and exposed in other suggestive directions as well, particularly in the articulation of sexuation in Mishima's texts: see Nina Cornyetz's "Kōi suru yokubō – Mishima Yukio" (Performing desire: Mishima Yukio) in two parts: "Niku o tekusutoka suru, aruiwa, (hi)bunsetsu sareta yokubō" ("Textualizing flesh, or, (in)articulate desire"), in *Yurīka* 11 (November 2000), pp. 118–33 and "Narushishizumu to sadizumu – homofashizumu toshite no Mishima" ("Narcissism and sadism: Mishima as homofascist"), in *Yurīka* 1 (January 2001), pp. 225–45. Nagahara Yutaka's essay in the same issue (November 2000) of *Yurīka*, "Yokan suru kioku" (pp. 218–29) opens another decisively important analytic direction on the question of the operation of identity in Mishima's texts. Also see J. Keith Vincent (1998) "Ōe Kenzaburō to Mishima Yukio no sakuhin ni okeru homofashizumu to sono fuman" ["Homofascism and its discontents in the work of Oe Kenzaburo and Mishima Yukio"] *Hihyō kūkan* 2(16): 129–54.
6. Irmela Hijiya-Kirschnereit (1996) "Review of Roy Starrs" *Deadly Dialectics: Sex, Violence and Nihilism in the World of Yukio Mishima*," in *Journal of Japanese Studies* 22(1): 77–182. See also Starrs' reply and Hijiya-Kirschnereit's response in *Journal of Japanese Studies* 24(1): 213–15. In regard to this issue, see also Masao Miyoshi (1996) *Accomplices of Silence,* Ann Arbor: University of Michigan Press, pp. 41–180.
7. Masao Miyoshi (1996) *Accomplices of Silence,* Ann Arbor: University of Michigan Press, p. 181.
8. Watanabe Naomi (2003) *Kakumo sensai naru ōbō: Nihon "68nen" shōsetsuron*, Tokyo: Kōdansha, p. 15. The quotation within Watanabe's text is from Furui Yoshikichi's (1983) essay "Hyōgen to iu koto" in *Furui Yoshikichi sakuhin*, Vol. 7, Tokyo: Kawade shobō, p. 27.
9. See Gilles Deleuze and Félix Guattari (1983) *Anti-Oedipus*, Minneapolis: University of Minnesota Press, pp. 36–41. For a further development of the concept of "abstract machine" also see Guattari's (1992) *Chaosmosis*, Paul Bains and Julian Pefanis (trans.) Bloomington: Indiana University Press, pp. 33–7.
10. See for instance Gayatri Chakravorty Spivak (1999) *A Critique of Postcolonial Reason*, Cambridge: Harvard University Press, p. 14.

182 *Gavin Walker*

11. Jacques Derrida (1972) "La double séance," in *La dissemination*, Paris: Seuil, pp. 217–346. Translated by Barbara Johnson (1981) as "The double session" in *Dissemination*, Chicago: University of Chicago Press, pp. 173–286.

12. Frequently in Shimada's texts on Mishima, this difference between Mishima and "Mishima" is emphasized by using the *katakana* script to write his name, rather than the standard *kanji* characters.

13. Shimada Masahiko (1987) "Mishima ga yume de watakushi ni kataru koto" in *Katarazu, utae*, Tokyo: Fukutake shoten, pp. 52–4.

14. Ibid., p. 54.

15. Ibid., p. 43.

16. Judith Butler (1993) *Bodies That Matter: On the Discursive Limits of "Sex,"* New York: Routledge, p. 30.

17. Michel Foucault (1975) *Surveiller et punir*, Paris: Gallimard, pp. 37–8.

18. Tomioka Kōichirō (1995) *Kamen no shingaku: Mishima Yukio ron*, Tokyo: Kōsōsha, p. 155.

19. Maurice Blanchot (1986) *The Writing of the Disaster,* Lincoln: University of Nebraska Press, p. 45.

20. Nina Cornyetz (2001) "Amorphous identities, disavowed history: Shimada Masahiko and national subjectivity," in *Positions: East Asia Cultures Critique* 9(3): 587.

21. Roland Barthes (1977) *Image-Music-Text*, New York: Hill and Wang, p. 147.

22. Shimada Masahiko, "Mishima ga yume de watakushi ni kataru koto," p. 40.

23. Naoki Sakai and Jon Solomon (2006) "Addressing the multitude of foreigners, echoing Foucault," in Naoki Sakai and Jon Solomon (eds) *Traces 4: Translation, Biopolitics, Colonial Difference*, Hong Kong: Hong Kong University Press, p. 13.

24. Jacques Lacan (1973) *Le séminaire, livre XI: Les quatre concepts fondamentaux de la psychanalyse*, Paris: Seuil, p. 15. ". . . le terme le plus large pour désigner une action concertée par l'homme, quelle qu'elle soit, qui le met en mesure de traiter le réel par le symbolique."

25. William Haver (1996) *The Body of this Death: Historicity and Sociality in the Time of AIDS,* Stanford: Stanford University Press, p. xviii.

26. Jacques Derrida (1976) *Of Grammatology*, Gayatri Chakravorty Spivak (trans.) Baltimore: Johns Hopkins University Press, p.145.

27. Ibid., p. 144.

28. See here Naoki Sakai's (1989) "Modernity and its critique: The problem of universalism and particularism," in H. D. Harootunian and Masao Miyoshi (eds) *Postmodernism and Japan*, Durham: Duke University Press, pp. 93–122, esp. 98–9.

29. Naoki Sakai (1997) *Translation and Subjectivity: On "Japan" and Cultural Nationalism*, Minneapolis: University of Minnesota Press, p. 211 n40.

30. Karatani Kōjin (1988) *Nihon kindai bungaku no kigen,* Tokyo: Kōdansha, p. 100.

31. Watanabe Naomi (1999) *Fukei bungakuron josetsu*, Tokyo: Ōta shuppan, pp. 9–16, 28–37. Also see the discussion between Watanabe, Karatani Kōjin, Asada Akira, Suga Hidemi, and Nibuya Takashi (2000) "Tennō to bungaku," in *Hihyō kūkan* 2(24): 9–26.

32. Watanabe Naomi, *Fukei bungakuron josetsu*, p. 50.

33. Ukai Satoshi (1997) "Nihirizumu ni tsuite," in *Tsugunai no arukeorojī*, Tokyo: Kawade shobō, pp. 125–6.

34. Fukuda Kazuya (2004) "Kaisetsu" in Mishima Yukio, *Wakaki samurai no tame ni*, Tokyo: Bunshun bunko, p. 270.

35. Suga Hidemi (2003) *Kakumeiteki na, amari ni kakumeiteki na: "1968nen no kakumei" shiron*, Tokyo: Sakuhinsha, p. 61.

36. On this term, Suga cites the name of Asada Akira, presumably in reference to Asada's "J-kaiki no yukue" in *Voice*, March 2000 (in the *Hihyō Kūkan* web archive. Online. Available at: http://www.kojinkaratani.com/criticalspace/old/special/asada/voice0003.html

37. Suga, *Kakumeiteki na, amari ni kakumeiteki na*, 137–9.

38. With this problematic in mind, the political engagements of Mishima (such as the famous debate with the Tokyo University Zenkyōtō) can be effectively re-read. In this respect, I have benefited from Guy Yasko's "Tōdai Zenkyōtō vs. Mishima Yukio: the cultural displacement of politics", in his dissertation *The Japanese Student Movement 1968–70: The Zenkyōtō Uprising* (Cornell University, 1997), pp. 156–210. Pedro Erber's reading of this debate has also been instructive – see his "Tokyo, 1969: Mishima Yukio vs. Todai Zenkyoto" in *Anais do XV encontro nacional de professores universitários de língua, literatura e cultura japonesa* (Universidade Federal do Rio de Janeiro, 2004).
39. Derrida (1992) "Counterfeit money I", in *Given Time: I. Counterfeit money*, peggy Kamuf (trans.) Chicago: University of Chicago Press, p. 100.
40. Jacques Lacan (1993) *Seminar III: The Psychoses*, New York: W. W. Norton, p. 268.

8   Introduction

Dawn Lawson: Navigating the inner sea . . .

As Dawn Lawson points out in the beginning of her essay, we are all too familiar by now with the status of Futabatei Shimei's *Ukigumo* as "Japan's first modern novel" thanks to its use of the modern vernacular and its groundbreaking introduction of psychological interiority. But the novel's canonical status may, paradoxically, have kept us from actually reading it. What, exactly, are the contours of Bunzō's fabled interiority? How does Bunzō feel about losing his job and chasing after a fickle woman of whose love he can never be certain? And how are those feelings represented in the text?

While Bunzō's plight has been read as the *locus classicus* of a certain kind of introverted male subjectivity that would soon be seen proliferating itself all across the landscape of modern Japanese literature, Lawson resists the impulse to place Futabatei's text in the context of any such grand narrative, literary, historical or otherwise. She pauses instead to consider Bunzō on his own terms, through a close reading of affect in *Ukigumo* that traces the waves of shame that buffet its protagonist. This reading of *Ukigumo* takes its cue from the American psychologist Sylvan Tomkins, whose work on the affect system offers an alternative to Sigmund Freud's reliance on the instincts and drives as the primary motivating forces behind human behavior. In Lawson's account Bunzō's subjectivity emerges not through a retreat into interiority but through a series of halting movements outside the self: attempts to connect that, while they are repeatedly shut down by shame, nonetheless establish the borders and feedback loops through which a sense of self will develop.

8 Navigating the inner sea

Utsumi Bunzō's affects in *Ukigumo*

Dawn Lawson

It is interesting to study the psychology of any man, be he wise or foolish. An examination of the mental processes of Utsumi Bunzō will prove this.

M. G. Ryan, *Japan's First Modern Novel*[1]

Futabatei Shimei's *Ukigumo* (Floating Clouds, 1887–1889) has long been called "Japan's first modern novel" by both Japanese and Western literary critics. That phrase, in fact, occupies the prominent position of the main title of its English translation, while the original title and author's name, *Ukigumo* of Futabatei Shimei, are relegated to subtitle status. In the essay accompanying her English translation of the work, Marleigh Grayer Ryan emphasizes the novel's connection to modernity in declarations such as "The portrait of weakness, vacillation, fear, and uncertainty is a vivid representation of modern man's dilemma."[2]

Japanese and Western literary scholars alike have tended to base their assertions about *Ukigumo*'s modernity on two intertwined characteristics of the work: its pioneering use of colloquial Japanese and its depiction of what the epigraph to this chapter calls Utsumi Bunzō's "mental processes." Through the decades, critics have used the latter aspect of the work as a springboard to additional generalizations about its place in the history of Japanese literature, asserting that it established "the value of psychological realism"[3] and exemplified "the first use of psychological analysis"[4] in that context.

Descriptions of *Ukigumo* such as these are not inaccurate. However, as I will show, they may be construed as instances of the phenomenon that Eve Kosofsky Sedgwick calls "strong theory," a concept she borrows from the work of the twentieth-century American psychologist Silvan S. Tomkins. In her essay, "Paranoid Reading and Reparative Reading, *or* You're So Paranoid, You Probably Think This Essay Is about You," Sedgwick suggests that, rather than being treated as one possible approach among others, the application of a "hermeneutic of suspicion" has come to be considered mandatory in American critical theory.[5] In order for a reading to count as "theory" at all, deep meanings must be uncovered, ideologies unveiled, and patterns identified. Textual details are not allowed to speak for themselves, but must be corralled as supporting evidence. Sedgwick cites queer theory's privileging of paranoia as an antihomophobic reading practice to be an example of this imperative. Tomkins' work on affects is useful in her development of a corrective approach to such "strong theorizing" for several reasons. First, he uses the very phenomenon that she is grappling with – paranoia – to exemplify one type of strong affect theory, that of shame-humiliation. Second, affect theory lacks the teleological emphasis of drive theory, giving it obvious potential as an approach that is not aimed to fulfill a predetermined purpose. In addition, Sedgwick demonstrates that Tomkins' distinction between strong and weak affect theories, which are distinguished by the size and topology of the terrain to which they are applied – can be fruitfully extended to the realm of literary criticism.

Although using *Ukigumo* as a poster child for Japanese literature's emergence into modernity is not a manifestation of the same kind of paranoia Sedgwick discusses, it is nevertheless a type of strong theorizing in the literary field. Poor Bunzō, in other words, has been the object of so much strong theorizing about Japanese modernity, language reform, and "interiority" that the complexity and subtlety of Futabatei's depiction of affects has been underappreciated. Therefore, following Sedgwick, I intend to use Tomkins' affect theory to examine the novel without the goal of formulating or reinforcing a strong theory. Rather, I will employ it as a lens to show that what critics describe in general terms as Futabatei's psychological realism consists of a depiction of the experience of the specific, interrelated affects of shame, contempt, and anger, which pervade Bunzō's experiences of the world. Following this close reading, I will provide a minimal amount of historical contextualization by examining the portrayal of shame in a Japanese literary antecedent of the work instead of reiterating *Ukigumo*'s position in the broad context of modern Japanese or world literature. But first, I will establish the necessary background for my argument by providing a detailed outline of Tomkins' theory of affects.

Tomkins' theory of affects

In the introduction to *Shame and Its Sisters: A Silvan Tomkins Reader*, the edition of selections from Tomkins that they published in 1995, Sedgwick and Adam Frank explain that they encountered the work of this twentieth-century American psychologist while researching the topic of shame. Tomkins posited a basic set of affects consisting of, along with shame, interest, joy, surprise, anger, fear, distress, and contempt.[6] Interspersing key quotations from his oeuvre, Sedgwick and Frank show that Tomkins' distinction between affects and drives is an important source of the utility of his work:

> A concomitant of distinguishing in the first place between an affect system and a drive system that it analogically amplifies is that, unlike the drives (e.g., to breathe, to eat), "any affect may have any 'object.' This is the basic source of complexity of human motivation and behavior" (1: 347). Furthermore, in a refusal of the terms of behaviorism, the affect system as a whole "has no single 'output' " (3: 66), and, also unlike the drives, "affective amplification is indifferent to the means-end difference" (3: 67). "It is enjoyable to enjoy.

It is exciting to be excited. It is terrorizing to be terrorized and angering to be angered. Affect is self-validating with or without any further referent" (3: 404). It is these specifications that make affect theory such a useful site for resistance to teleological presumptions of the many sorts historically embedded in the discipline of psychology.[7]

As set forth in his essay "What Are Affects?" each of the eight affects Tomkins postulates is constituted as the first of a word pair, of which the second word represents that affect in its most intense form. Each is also associated with physical manifestations and categorized as positive, negative, or resetting (the latter term means that it momentarily clears the affect system, acting as does a circuit breaker). Thus we have the following:

- Positive
  Interest – Excitement: eyebrows down, track, look, listen
  Enjoyment – Joy: smile, lips widened and out

- Resetting
  Surprise – Startle: eyebrows up, eyes blink

- Negative
  Distress – Anguish: cry, arched eyebrow, mouth down, rhythmic sobbing
  Fear – Terror: eyes frozen open, pale, cold, sweaty, facial trembling, with hair erect
  Shame – Humiliation: eyes down, head down
  Contempt – Disgust: sneer, upper lip up
  Anger – Rage: frown, clenched jaw, red face.[8]

The Japanese word *omoshiroi,* often rendered as "interesting" in English, perfectly illustrates Tomkins' definition of the affect of interest. *Omoshiroi* is written using a two-character compound consisting of the character meaning "face" followed by the character that signifies the color white. The first etymology listed for this word in the *Nihon kokugo daijiten* notes that its original meaning corresponds to that of these characters, i.e., the feeling of one's eyes brightening suddenly because of what is in front of them.[9] The narrator's comment about it being "interesting" to study Bunzō's psychology, quoted at the beginning of this chapter, includes the noun form of this adjective (*omoshiromi*: the grammatical structure used in the original literally means "there is interest in . . .").[10]

With the significant exceptions of shame and contempt, Tomkins accounts for the activation of the affects by means of a principle called density of neural firing, which he illustrates in a graph. The density of neural firing (the y-axis of the graph) over time (the x-axis) varies in the case of each of six affects. Shame and contempt are omitted from the graph because they occur only after one or both of the positive affects, interest and enjoyment, has been activated.

The innate activator of shame is the incomplete reduction of interest or joy. Hence, any barrier to further exploration which partially reduces interest or the smile of enjoyment will activate the lowering of the head and eyes in shame and reduce further exploration or self-exposure powered by excitement or joy.[11]

Tomkins' writing style goes far beyond the dry, scholarly psychological description that his content often demands when he introduces the affect of shame. Donald L. Nathanson, a student of Tomkins who expanded his work significantly, notes that the following eloquent articulation of the role of shame in the human condition is often quoted, and it is easy to see why.

If distress is the affect of suffering, shame is the affect of indignity, of defeat, of transgression, and of alienation. Though terror speaks to life and death and distress makes of the world a vale of tears, yet shame strikes deepest into the heart of man. While terror and distress hurt, they are wounds inflicted from outside which penetrate the smooth surface of the ego; but shame is felt as an inner torment, a sickness of the soul. It does not matter whether the humiliated one has been shamed by derisive laughter or whether he mocks himself. In either event, he feels himself naked, defeated, alienated, lacking in dignity or worth.[12]

The affects of contempt and shame are closely related, sometimes inextricably so, as Tomkins explains:

While the affect of shame-humiliation encompasses shyness, shame, and guilt, it is distinct from the affect of disgust-contempt. In its dynamic aspects, however, shame is often intimately related to and easily confused with contempt, particularly self-contempt; indeed it is sometimes not possible to separate them . . . Both affects are impediments to intimacy and communication, within the self and between the self and others.[13]

Tomkins does, however, make one key distinction between the two in terms of a person's relationship to the object associated with the affect: in the case of shame, one does not renounce the object permanently, whereas one does in the case of contempt. This difference is useful to bear in mind when examining the way Futabatei portrays Bunzō's experience of these two affects. As I will show, contempt predominates when he confronts the loss of his job and the action that may enable him to regain it, while the affect of shame pervades his interactions with Osei and his thoughts about his mother. In fact, Bunzō's insoluble dilemma may be summarized in exactly these terms: his contempt for the bureaucracy causes him to renounce it entirely, but his attachment to Osei and his mother causes him to feel shame about his inability to hold a job in that very structure because of his renunciation of it.

Along with shame and contempt, anger is the affect that Futabatei depicts Bunzō as experiencing most frequently. This is not surprising given the inevitable relationship between the two. Joseph Adamson, who used Tomkins' work on shame along with that of numerous other psychologists to develop a psychoanalytic reading of Herman Melville, has elucidated this connection as follows: "What some shame analysts call humiliated fury or shame-anger, or what Kohut calls narcissistic rage, Tomkins would understand as a shame affect that reaches such a painful point of overload that it triggers anger, an affect distinct from but often accompanying shame."[14]

Affects in the text

Any reader familiar with *Ukigumo* whose attention is drawn to the often-quoted Tomkins paragraph on shame above will readily agree – without needing to examine the text closely – that its terms apply to Utsumi Bunzō with uncanny accuracy. In the wake of his dismissal from his job, he suffers indignity, defeat, transgression, and alienation, which certainly result in inner torment and a sickness of the soul. He is both shamed by derisive laughter and mocks himself, and he feels himself naked, defeated, alienated, and lacking in dignity or worth. But how, specifically, does Futabatei depict Bunzō's experience of shame and related affects? Before examining the two scenes in which they are shown most vividly – his confession to his aunt that he has lost his job and his rejection of a former colleague's offer to help him get it back – I will look at the overall development of Bunzō's character in terms of affect.

The story told in *Ukigumo* is triggered by Bunzō's dismissal from his job as a government bureaucrat. The work opens with a panoramic view of a "swirling mass of men . . . marching first in antlike formation and then scuttling busily off in every direction."[15] Futabatei then zeroes in on two men: the main character, Utsumi Bunzō, and his now-former colleague, Honda Noboru. Their conversation begins with a debate about the dismissal of another man, Yamaguchi, rather than that of Bunzō, which is not immediately revealed. In response to Bunzō's defense of Yamaguchi's good work habits, Noboru is harshly critical of Yamaguchi for questioning their chief's orders, no matter how unreasonable they may have been, instead of simply obeying them. Bunzō responds to this with a contemptuous glance at Noboru and an emphatic closing of his lips, bringing the conversation to an abrupt pause. Noboru initiates its resumption with a needling reference to Bunzō's love for his cousin Osei. Bunzō displays what is described as an uncharacteristic smile as they part, perhaps inspired by thoughts of Osei. However, as he approaches the house of his aunt and cousin, where he is lodging, this positive affective display is interrupted by shame-inflected movements: "Bit by bit the smile left his face and his steps grew slower until he barely crawled along. He went a few more blocks, his head hanging forlornly."[16] The contents of a letter that he receives from his mother upon his arrival at his lodgings and two succeeding chapters of lengthy flashbacks help explain the underlying causes of this display of shame: How will his aunt react to the news of his dismissal, and how will it affect his pursuit of Osei?

In addition to providing the history of Bunzō, Osei, and their family members – and an introduction to the pair's awkward relationship – the narrator reveals several crucial aspects of Bunzō's affective nature in the course of filling in the background to the story.

We learn that Bunzō was a reserved, studious child whose only real interest and joy occurred in relation to his schoolwork and scholastic achievements; even as a young boy, he rarely played with friends. Bunzō's preference for intellectual pursuits plays a role in the depiction of his affects later in the story: when he experiences extreme distress, he attempts to interrupt this negative experience by activating the affect of interest with reading, in Chapter 7, and translation work, in Chapter 10. In both cases he is unsuccessful.

A brief paragraph of description in the second chapter of the work refers to the distress and humiliation Bunzō experiences in relation to his aunt, Omasa. When he is taken in by his uncle's family after the death of his father, all would have gone smoothly if Bunzō had simply been able to get along with his aunt, we are told. It is also emphasized that if his aunt had been as good and kind as his mother, domestic harmony would have been the natural course of events. But his aunt is not his mother, and each time she scolds him and calls him stupid, despite his efforts to please her, Bunzō is reminded of this. He is unable to master this disagreeable situation because he is "constitutionally incapable of currying favor with anyone ... Living with his aunt required a great deal of patience and self-control on his part,"[17] and Bunzō weeps frequently in distress when he is alone. He experiences negative affects even more intensely in scenes of dialogue between him and Omasa; there, patience and self-control evade him, and his humiliation intensifies to the point of anger.

Ukigumo's sole scene of Bunzō at work, also included in the retrospective narration of the second chapter, shows the contempt, self-contempt, shame, and distress that will always suffuse his relationship to the government bureaucracy that is supposed to be his road to filial, financial, and marital success. Bunzō's colleagues strike him as eagle-eyed creatures when, as a temporary employee, he surveys the scene on his first day in the office. The actions of one man appear so ridiculous to Bunzō that he bursts out laughing involuntarily, but his mirth is immediately replaced by the realization that despite many exhausting years of study he himself has become just this type of laughable creature. Bunzō sighs deeply and briefly becomes incapable of any action. But just as he was apparently able to exercise self-control with Omasa at first, in the office Bunzō is able to force himself to return to work, and after four or five days he is no longer distressed by the sight of that fellow worker. At this point in the before-our-story-begins world, therefore, a happy ending appears to be within reach. Bunzō is able to send money to his mother each month, and his relationship with his aunt improves. He is promoted and made a permanent employee, and at times it seems conceivable that he will be permitted to marry Osei. However, Bunzō's communication to his aunt of the news of his layoff disrupts the possibility of a tidy, happy resolution, just as it ruptures Bunzō's affective life.

Waiting for his aunt to come home on the evening of his firing, Bunzō begins imagining how she will react to his news.[18] The inevitably unpleasant face she will make appears before his eyes, and his immediate reaction is to tell himself that he hasn't the slightest reason to be ashamed ("sukoshi mo hazukashii koto wa nai"). He resolves to make the announcement that very evening, until he pictures Osei's seeing his aunt reproach him. He decides to find a time to tell his aunt when Osei isn't there, but his thoughts slow to a sputter when he asks himself why: "inai . . . toki o . . . mi . . . naze." The answer, or question, again boils down to shame, as he asks himself rhetorically why a grown man who has experienced a decline in his circumstances need feel shame. He concludes that his firing won't change Osei's feelings for him, but his aunt remains a problem. Thoughts of the employees who weren't dismissed evoke contempt: he was not inferior to them nor they superior to him in any way, so he must have been fired because of a failure to humiliate himself by currying favor with the chief ("obekkaranakatta"). The chief, therefore, is disrespectful ("shikkei"), and the other workers are the height of abjection ("hiretsu kiwamaru"). Bunzō even tells himself that he feels contemptuous of the salary ("wazuka no gekkyū") that, at least in theory, would have been the solution to his problems. Thinking of the salary leads him to scorn the abjection of the others again, in the same terms as before. Finally he thinks about what he would do if he were offered his job back and loses his train of thought as he vacillates between contempt for the management ("This time I'll be the one to turn them down") and self-contempt ("Idiot! I really am an idiot"). His reverie ends with a return to the vision of his aunt's face with which it began. When he hears his aunt arrive, he is so distraught that he literally cannot stand up at first. Although he ultimately manages to go downstairs to join his aunt and Osei, he cannot break the news that night.

The next morning at breakfast after a restless night, Bunzō's state of mind is clearly no better: he cannot eat as much as usual, and he feels as though his body has actually shrunk. As he enters the room where his aunt is, knowing he must tell her now, his affect is conveyed to the reader by the use of no fewer than five adjectives to describe his face: "aozamete ite," "chikara nasasō," "kanashisō," "urameshisō," and "hazukashisō" (pale, weak, sad, resentful, and ashamed). The narrator is not satisfied with this rich recital, however, as he concludes by deeming the face indescribable ("iya iya nan to mo iiyō ga nai"). Once Bunzō finally manages to blurt out the news, his aunt loses no time in reproaching him. Her arguments show her sharp awareness of both the situation and Bunzō's emotional make-up. First she suggests that his dismissal was prompted by his unwillingness to curry favor with the chief, as she herself had recommended. Learning that Noboru, of course, had not been subject to the same fate simply strengthens her argument. This drives Bunzō to declare that he cannot engage in the humiliating behavior ("sonna hiretsu na koto") that Noboru does, regardless of the consequences.

Attributing this to false pride ("yasegaman"), Omasa now scolds Bunzō for the effect the loss of his job will have on his mother. Just hearing the word "mother" causes Bunzō to wither in humiliation ("shiorekaeru"). Seeing this inflames Omasa all the more, and Bunzō can only hang his head in shame as her tirade about his mother intensifies. The abashed son acknowledges having lost face with regard to his mother – "Jitsu ni ofukuro ni wa menboku gozansen."[19] However, this does nothing to slow the torrent of Omasa's invective, and the facial expression Bunzō displays in response to the ensuing onslaught of words is described as "kowarashii." The character used to write this uncommon word has a wide range of meanings, encompassing fear, awe, and respect, warranting an interpretive note from the editors of the Japanese edition: they equate this facial expression with one that is "kataku kewashii," or stubbornly severe, and suggest that Bunzō wants to assert his dignity and claim that it was not his fault that he was dismissed and that he has not lost face as a man.[20] Now almost speechless, however, he simply reiterates that he has disgraced himself before his mother and stammers that what's done is done. As his aunt continues to rail, now accusing him of ingratitude for all she has done on his behalf, he offers the excuse that he is a poor communicator, but she has the last word.

Retreating to his room, Bunzō sheds tears of humiliation. After he is finally able to wipe them dry, we see an example of the affect amplification Tomkins is referring to when he describes affect as needing no further referent for self-validation.

> Tears of vexation dropped on his knees. He wiped his falling tears away with a handkerchief, but he could not erase the fury that kept swelling up within him. The more he thought about it, the more angry he became, until he was completely lost in resentment and mortification.[21]

Next he decides that Omasa's insults go beyond even the words she uttered because she implied that he is ineffective. The additional shame and resentment that this thought brings about triggers more anger. The narrator notes that Bunzō doesn't even have the wherewithal to stop and consider why his aunt may have implied this; he is so angry that all he can do is resolve to cut his ties with his aunt and move out of her house. A vision of Osei's face in his mind's eye gives him temporary pause, but his aunt's evil countenance replaces it, reigniting his anger and reinstating his resolve.

Some three hours later, just as he has finally finished packing in preparation for moving out, Bunzō reverses his decision once again. He has encountered Osei, who indicates that she has taken Bunzō's part in an argument with her mother about his dismissal. Bunzō is so moved by this that he resolves to suppress his anger and pride and apologize to his aunt, and he also asks Osei to be a good daughter and not quarrel with her mother on his behalf. The apology scene is remarkable because we rarely see Bunzō successfully control his feelings and do what is required to get along with someone he feels has humiliated him unjustifiably. Strikingly, though, the effort it takes him to do this is described as making him feel as though he has died ("shinda ki ni natte"). In several other instances, when he contemplates having to make up his quarrel with Noboru in the event of deciding to ask the chief to rehire him, Bunzō thinks that he would rather die than do so. He has this same thought in the same words twice within a brief space of time in Chapter 11. Writing about shame, Tomkins asks, "How can loss of face be more intolerable than loss of life?"[22] As we will see, the answer to this is clear when it is considered in light of shame's crucial relationship to the self.

Bunzō's most intense display of the affects of shame, contempt, and anger comes in Chapter 9, when Noboru approaches him with an offer to speak to the chief on his behalf in order to help him get his job back.[23] Bunzō has known that this possibility, which he naturally finds humiliating, exists and is likely to be suggested to him, but Noboru's articulation of it in the presence of the entire household, including Osei, greatly increases its affective impact. The scene is unpleasant for Bunzō from the outset. When he enters the sitting room where his aunt, Osei, his nephew Isami, and Noboru are gathered, Noboru and Osei are in mid-conversation and do not stop talking to acknowledge him. As the narrator makes a point of noting, it is never very agreeable for a third party to be ignored in such circumstances. After Bunzō grudgingly agrees to Noboru's request for a word with him – the assertion of both that they have little time to spare for this notwithstanding – the two men exchange glares. In the course of informing Bunzō that the chief may be rehiring and suggesting that Bunzō speak to him or, if that is difficult, offering to speak to him on Bunzō's behalf, Noboru makes a teasing reference to Osei. The shame that this arouses makes it impossible for Bunzō even to stammer out the formulaic expression of gratitude in its entirety. Nor can he hide his annoyance, which shows in the color of his face. Although Noboru sees this, he makes matters worse for Bunzō by describing his unwillingness to take action with the same word that his aunt had used earlier: "yasegaman," or false pride. At this Bunzō's face whitens, and when his aunt jumps into the conversation in support of Noboru's point, he is driven to a barely controllable fury, trembling, clenching his fists, and gritting his teeth. Osei's witnessing of the scene – Bunzō literally thinks to himself, "Osei is looking at my face" – causes him to stop and reflect. He doesn't want to leave the scene looking as if he has lost his dignity; more than anything he would like to find a curse so potent that it would kill Noboru ("ki shi saseru hodo no koto"), which is, significantly, equated with making Noboru's face redden ("ano shattsura o akaramete"; he uses the derogatory "shattsura" to refer to Noboru's face, rather than the neutral "kao" or "tsura").[24] But just as he thinks this, Bunzō again notices Osei staring at *his* face, and panic causes his mind to go blank. He overhears the others explode with laughter just after he leaves the room, which naturally intensifies his humiliation.

As a result of this scene, Bunzō's anger, shame, and contempt are so all-consuming that he walks through the city in a trance until a surprised policeman's glance brings him back to consciousness of his surroundings. Bunzō asks himself why Noboru has the right to humiliate him, to treat him like dirt or like an animal, and to add insult to injury by doing so in front of his aunt and Osei. Thinking about Noboru's assertion that he has the trust of the chief, Bunzō is contemptuous, likening Noboru's relationship to the chief to that of a slave to his master and scorning that trust as not being worth three farthings, or "sanmon." Delightfully, "sanmon" is a reversal of the characters that constitute Bunzō's name, and in his analysis Bunzō finds three ways to characterize Noboru's treatment of him: "keibetsu" (scorn, contempt), "choro" (ridicule, derision), and "bujoku" (insult, contempt). When he recalls that final humiliating burst of laughter, he falls down onto a bench, hanging his head. He jumps up once, trying to gird himself into some kind of action, but soon ends up sitting again, motionless, for an hour's time.

Affects and the face

As seen above, depictions of Bunzō's experiences of the affect of shame are accompanied by vivid descriptions of their attendant physical manifestations. Throughout his work, Tomkins stresses the fact that affects show on the face. He is especially emphatic about this when talking about shame and its role in the making of self.

> In contrast to all other affects, shame is an experience of the self by the self. At that moment when the self feels ashamed, it is felt as a sickness within the self. Shame is the most *reflexive* of affects in that the phenomenological distinction between the subject and object of shame is lost. Why is shame so close to the experienced self? It is because the self lives in the face, and within the face, the self burns brightest in the eyes. Shame turns the attention of the self and others away from other objects to this most visible residence of self, increases its visibility, and thereby generates the torment of self-consciousness.[25]

Men can affect the look of their face by whether or not they allow their facial hair to grow and how, a practice that is referred to at several important points in *Ukigumo*. As mentioned, the work begins with a panorama of a crowd of men exiting a gate in Tokyo. In this passage, the very first feature of these men that Futabatei's narrator describes, before their clothing and shoes, is their facial hair. He does so quite self-consciously, announcing to the reader that that there is great variety among the men and that he intends to begin his account by writing about their beards (*hige*). The description that follows takes the playful form of a *tsukushi*, a premodern rhetorical figure in which one lists all possible variants of a particular category. The next reference to a beard occurs in the scene in Chapter 9 analyzed above. Bunzō experiences a sequence of dream images when he finally falls into a restless sleep the night before he knows he has to tell Omasa about his having been fired. The image of his mother's face grows a black beard as it metamorphoses into the face of the chief responsible for his dismissal. Bunzō's unconscious association between the chief and the beard transcends a mere facial feature the next time the word *hige* is used. After his angry confrontation with Noboru, when he has walked the city streets in a trance ruminating on his feelings of shame and humiliation, Bunzō encounters Yamaguchi, who was fired with him. When the topic of Noboru comes up, Bunzō cannot help resentfully mentioning Noboru's suggestion that he flatter the chief in an attempt to be rehired. In doing so, he uses the expression "ohige no chiri o harau," which literally means "brush the dust out of his beard." (Incidentally, the word for beard, *hige*, is homophonous with a word meaning to humble oneself.) The only other reference to a beard in *Ukigumo* occurs in the very last chapter, when, in the midst of one of his most confused reveries, Bunzō is reminded of the face of the Westerner who taught him physics. The progression of this depiction of beards from something outside to something conjured in the mind mirrors the progression of the overall narrative style of *Ukigumo* from depicting outer appearances to inner thoughts.[26]

Shame before *Ukigumo*

In his essay "The Captured 'I,' Tsubouchi Shōyō and the Doctrine of Success," Kamei Hideo underscores the groundbreaking nature of Futabatei's psychological portrayals by means of a comparison with a contemporary work by Tsubouchi Shōyō.

> But Shōyō, when confronted with the problem of a character's internal psychology that could not be perceived from outside, could only resort to methods that revealed that psychology as if to an external observer, as in this passage from *Newly Polished Mirror of Marriage*: "What are Oyuki's true feelings? Let's take out our magic mirror and reflect her innermost thoughts." The problem here is not so much how a person comes to have a certain interiority, but rather how a person becomes aware of their own interiority. Shōyō shows no interest in the situational circumstances that force a person to such an awareness, and as a result he is forced to resort to feeble pretexts like this. Futabatei was the first to overcome this weakness.[27]

Kamei is, of course, referring to Futabatei's depiction of Bunzō, the only character whose interiority he portrays with depth in *Ukigumo*. Another dimension to this contrast with Shōyō's work becomes apparent when we observe what happens when the narrator of *Ukigumo* is confronted with a character whose interiority is not accessible, as happens repeatedly in the case of Osei.

> Back in her own room, Osei changed her clothes and sank weakly onto the bedding spread on the floor. For some time she sat there, her face expressionless. What was she thinking? Was she groping for an answer to her mother's question?[28]

Five additional unanswered questions are posed here by the narrator, but no magic mirror is sought. Instead the following simple statement is made: "Her thoughts were not reflected in her vacant expression, and so we cannot tell."[29]

Futabatei's vividly accurate depiction of the affect of shame-humiliation in both its physical and psychological manifestations was new to Japanese literature. But the affect itself was not new, of course: literary characters who experience shame were portrayed before Bunzō. One natural place to look for these is in the Edo-period literary genre *ninjōbon*, which have been described as books "celebrating the depths of human emotions – joy, suffering, and intense jealousy, particularly as a consequence of falling in love."[30] *Ukigumo* contains a reference to the name of a character in one of the most celebrated of these works, Tanjirō, of Tamenaga Shunsui's *Shunshoku umegoyomi* (1833, Spring-Color Plum Calendar). The reference occurs in the midst of the scene that takes place when Bunzō returns home after the episode described above, in which he walks around the city consumed by his feelings. In a conversation with Bunzō, Noboru and Osei ridicule him by making remarks that refer to Osei's being in love with Bunzō. Bunzō fails to recognize immediately that they are teasing, but once he does, he is, as always, ashamed, then infuriated, when he realizes that he is being made a fool of. Despite a warning from Osei, Noboru continues teasing Bunzō along the same lines, calling him "the Tanji of the Meiji era, a veritable Don Juan."[31]

Like the narrator of Shōyō's *Newly Polished Mirror of Marriage*, the author of *Shunshoku umegoyomi* also requests help in perceiving the feelings of his characters, although not in the form of a magic mirror. After Tanjirō gets into a characteristic jam, in which one of his lovers, Yonehachi, catches him with another, Ochō, he writes:

> Tanjirō is coming down the stairs with Ochō right behind him. What will they feel when they run into Yonehachi? Even the author doesn't know. At a time like this, an attractive man suffers more than others realize. How should the story continue? If readers have any good ideas, the author begs them to contact him as soon as they can.[32]

Although Tanjirō is described later in the succeeding chapter as being lost in thought, we learn nothing of his inner thoughts or feelings about the overall situation, except that he appreciates Ochō's blossoming beauty.[33] Similarly, the first description of Tanjirō in *Shunshoku umegoyomi* bears a resemblance to the condition in which we frequently find Bunzō: ". . . his face was full of bitterness and anger as he lay alone, thinking."[34] However, in contrast to what happens in *Ukigumo*, here the reader is not privy to the content of those thoughts and the way in which they are formed. In Tanjirō's case, references to shame relate to the poor lodgings in which he lives, and that feeling is imagined by other characters ("Yonehachi could imagine how ashamed he must feel at being suddenly seen like this in such a pitiful place"[35]) or referred to in dialogue rather than shown as being part of his affect system. Whereas the characterization of Bunzō is that of an individual, Tanjirō's is that of a generic type; living in shameful lodgings is part of being an *iro otoko,* a character type who "has neither money nor strength," "operates completely by the power of his attractive charms, and simply waits for others to meet his needs."[36] Thus, any shame associated with Tanjirō is depicted in a formulaic way, rather than as part of the complex characterization of a unique individual.

Shame and the individual

One of Tomkins' key achievements was his recognition of the relationship between shame and the self, and the consequences of this for identity formation and socialization. He observed that the earliest physical expressions of shame (head down, eyes averted) by infants occur between three and seven months, *before* they can have any concept of prohibition. As a result of this finding, many developmental psychologists today "consider shame the affect that most defines the space in which a sense of self will develop."[37] It occurs when there is a break in "the circuit of mirroring expressions between the child's face and the recognized caregiver's face."[38] In her inimitable way, Sedgwick summarizes this process as follows: "Shame floods into being as a moment, a disruptive moment, in a circuit of identity-constituting identificatory communication."[39]

Communication is, of course, what *Ukigumo* is all about; literally, in terms of the text's pioneering use of colloquial Japanese, as well as in terms of its characterization and plot. As Indra Levy, who analyzes these aspects of the work in depth in *Sirens of the Western Shore,* writes:

> The movement of this almost plotless novel can be described as an escalating power struggle between two different linguistic practices – the seamless speech of Omasa and Noboru against the mental text Bunzō patches together from pieces of their words and the ethical code inscribed in his consciousness.[40]

What movement the story has is repeatedly catalyzed by a decision by Bunzō to talk to Osei. Each time he convinces himself that a conversation between the two of them will solve everything, and each of his attempts to talk to her fails. Before one such attempt, the narrator even foreshadows the result: "Poor Bunzō – he was living in a dream world."[41] The last time Bunzō resolves to talk to Osei is at the very end of the novel, so neither success nor failure is narrated. Because of this, literary scholars have long pondered whether *Ukigumo* was actually finished by Futabatei; some feel certain that it was not.[42] Regardless, given the communication difficulties depicted throughout the rest of the novel – inevitable for one as shame-imbued as Bunzō – it is difficult to imagine a believable ending that doesn't involve yet another impasse of the kind we have seen throughout. The last sentence of the work shows Bunzō going upstairs to await Osei's return home so that he can try to talk to her once again. None of the many thoughts and feelings he is depicted as experiencing provides any reason to expect results different from those of the earlier conversations he has attempted with Osei.

Strong theories, weak theories

As mentioned in the beginning of this chapter, in addition to making use of Tomkins' work explicating individual affects, Sedgwick also uses his concept of affect theory and his practice of assessing particular affect theories as weak or strong in themselves by expanding its application to literary theory. Tomkins defines an affect theory as "a simplified and powerful summary of a larger set of affect experiences," either about affect in general, or about a particular affect.[43] His use of the adjectives strong and weak to apply to affect theories needs to be considered cautiously to avoid misunderstanding, however. On the surface, a strong affect theory may sound like a desirable thing. But in what appears at first to be a paradox, an affect theory must be weak to be effective. As the following explanation illustrates, rather than becoming stronger as it avoids or attenuates shame, a humiliation theory becomes stronger as it fails to do so.

> Any theory of wide generality is capable of accounting for a wide spectrum of phenomena which appear to be very remote, one from the other, and from a common source. This is a commonly accepted criterion by which the explanatory power of any scientific theory can be evaluated. To the extent to

which the theory can account only for "near" phenomena, it is a weak theory, little better than a description of the phenomena which it purports to explain. As it orders more and more remote phenomena to a single formulation, its power grows . . . A humiliation theory is strong to the extent to which it enables more and more experiences to be accounted for as instances of humiliating experiences on the one hand, or to the extent to which it enables more and more anticipation of such contingencies before they actually happen.[44]

The following statements by Janet Walker exemplify the positing of a strong theory about the development of modern Japanese literature:

Looking at the phenomenon of the rise of fiction – and even of subject-centered fiction – in the Meiji period, in a comparative context of late-nineteenth and early twentieth-century literatures outside of Western Europe, it is evident that the Japanese development of fiction runs parallel to the development of fiction in literatures as diverse as Turkish, Persian, Arabic, Chinese, Vietnamese, Burmese, and Thai, and the various traditions of the African continent and the Indian sub-continent. The rise of a similar kind of fiction with a new kind of critical subject was enabled by similar factors: industrialization, the development of an urban middle class, the rise of science, the emergence of printing and newspapers, and the rise of the ideal of human rights.[45]

Sedgwick urges the use of Tomkins as a model of the way strong and weak theories can interact productively and suggests that the history of literary criticism can be "viewed as a repertoire of alternative models for allowing strong and weak theory to interdigitate."[46] Although she suggests that the imaginative close reading of New Criticism is an embodiment of Tomkins' weak theory and can be "little better than a description of the phenomena that it purports to explain," at the same time she suggests that there are some theoretical tasks that can only be accomplished through local theories, and that the interrelationship between these and strong theories remains largely unexplored.[47]

As I have demonstrated, an analysis of Futabatei's portrayal of Bunzō in terms of his affective experiences shows that shame – with an intermingling of contempt and anger – predominates. "To the extent that man is a social animal, shame is a shaper of modern life," writes Donald Nathanson. "It may be that shame has built the border between what each of us knows as the outside world and the inner realm we have come to call the unconscious."[48] Shame – which is fundamental to the development of a sense of self, the establishment of identity, and the effectiveness of communication – plays a determining role in the style, characterization, and plot of *Ukigumo*. My close reading here of Futabatei's depiction of Bunzō's experience of shame – a weak theory – in the context of the strong theories of its status as Japan's first modern novel in terms of language and depiction of the inner life is an attempt to instantiate Sedgwick's proposed interdigitation.

Notes

1. M. G. Ryan (1965) *Japan's First Modern Novel: Ukigumo of Futabatei Shimei*, New York: Columbia University Press, p. 321.
2. Ibid., p. 190.
3. Ibid., p. xiii.
4. J. Walker (1979) *The Japanese Novel of the Meiji Period and the Ideal of Individualism*, Princeton: Princeton University Press, p. 36.
5. E. K. Sedgwick (2003) *Touching Feeling: Affect, Pedagogy, Performativity*, Durham: Duke University Press, pp. 123–51.
6. Tomkins' original set of affects classified contempt and disgust together, as two poles of one affect. Later, he renamed disgust "dissmell" and designated it as a separate affect. Following Sedgwick, I use the original set. See *Shame and Its Sisters: A Silvan Tomkins Reader* (eds E.K. Sedgwick and A. Frank), Durham: Duke University Press, 1995, p.135.
7. *Shame and Its Sisters*, p. 7. Numbers in parentheses refer to S. Tomkins, *Affect, Imagery, Consciousness*, New York: Springer, 1962–1992, 4 vols.
8. *Shame and Its Sisters*, p. 74.
9. *Nihon kokugo daijiten*, 2nd edn., Tokyo: Shōgakukan, 2000–2001, Vol. 2, p. 1422.
10. The part of the compound pronounced "omo" here, meaning face, is also pronounced "men"; we will see it pronounced this way later in a compound Bunzō uses to refer to losing face with his mother ("menboku gozansen").
11. *Shame and Its Sisters*, pp. 134–5.
12. Quoted in D.L. Nathanson (1992) *Shame and Pride: Affect, Sex, and the Birth of the Self*, New York: W. W. Norton & Co., p. 146.
13. *Shame and Its Sisters*, p. 134, p. 139.
14. J. Adamson (1997) *Melville, Shame, and the Evil Eye: A Psychoanalytic Reading*, Albany: State University of New York Press, p. 9.
15. Ryan, *Japan's First Modern Novel*, p. 197.
16. Ibid., p. 199.
17. Ibid., p. 206.
18. The scenes described here take place in Chapters 4 and 5. For the Japanese text, see *Futabatei Shimei shū, Nihon kindai bungaku taikei* 4, Tokyo: Kadokawa Shoten, 1971, pp. 63–89; the English translation is in Ryan, *Japan's First Modern Novel*, pp. 226–55.
19. The noun used in the phrase meaning to lose face, "menboku," is written with the character for face followed by the character for eye. The phrase used here, consisting of the noun used with a negative of the copula, comes from an earlier adjective, "omonashi" ("no face"), which meant that one was so ashamed one could not raise one's head; therefore, one had no face. See *Nihon kokugo daijiten*, Vol. 10, p. 1126. As mentioned earlier, the character for face is also used in the word denoting interest.
20. *Futabatei Shimei shū*, p. 79, n.12.
21. Ryan, *Japan's First Modern Novel*, pp. 238–9.
22. *Shame and Its Sisters*, p. 136.
23. See *Futabatei Shimei shū*, pp. 128–40, for the Japanese; and Ryan, *Japan's First Modern Novel*, pp. 282–91, for the English.
24. *Futabatei Shimei shū*, p. 83 n.10.
25. *Shame and Its Sisters*, p. 136.
26. H. Kamei (2002) *Transformations of Sensibility: The Phenomenology of Meiji Literature* (ed. M. Bourdaghs), Ann Arbor: Center for Japanese Studies, University of Michigan, pp. 63–5. The chapter quoted was translated by L. Winston.
27. Kamei, *Transformations of Sensibility*, p. 64.
28. Ryan, *Japan's First Modern Novel*, p. 346.
29. Ibid.
30. Shirane, H (2002) *Early Modern Japanese Literature: An Anthology, 1600–1900*, New York: Columbia University Press, p. 761.

200 *Dawn Lawson*

31. Ryan, *Japan's First Modern Novel*, p. 298.
32. Shirane, *Early Modern Japanese Literature*, p. 785. The translation is by Chris Drake.
33. Shunsui does depict the thought processes of some of the women characters, particularly when they are analyzing how best to get their man. See, for example, the paragraph describing Yonehachi's thoughts; Shirane, *Early Modern Japanese Literature*, p. 788.
34. Shirane, *Early Modern Japanese Literature*, p. 766.
35. Ibid., p. 770.
36. Woodhull, A (1978) "Romantic Edo Fiction: A Study of the Ninjōbon and Complete Translation of *Shunshoku Umegoyomi*," unpublished doctoral dissertation, Stanford University, 1978.
37. Sedgwick, *Touching, Feeling*, p. 98.
38. Ibid., p. 36.
39. Ibid.
40. Levy, I. (2006) *Sirens of the Western Shore: The Westernesque Femme Fatale, Translation, and Vernacular Style in Modern Japanese Literature*, New York: Columbia University Press, p. 73.
41. Ryan, *Japan's First Modern Novel*, p. 328.
42. Ibid., pp. 124–37; Kamei, *Transformations of Sensibility*, pp. 64–5.
43. *Shame and Its Sisters*, p. 165.
44. Quoted in Sedgwick, *Touching, Feeling*, p. 134.
45. J. Walker (1997) "Reflections on the entrance of fiction into the Meiji literary canon," in Hardacre and Kern (eds.) *New Directions in the Study of Meiji Japan*, Leiden and New York: Brill, p. 43.
46. Sedgwick, *Touching, Feeling*, p. 145.
47. Ibid.
48. Nathanson, *Shame and Pride*, p. 149.

Introduction

Irena Hayter: In the flesh . . .

If pre-psychoanalytic case studies like that of Sigmund Freud's teacher Jean-Martin Charcot adhered to a synchronic model of illness in which symptoms were simply listed and categorized, one of Freud's great innovations was to add a temporal or diachronic dimension to the case study. The result was that his case studies read more like novels than the charts and slide shows favored by his predecessors. Freud himself recognized this novelistic quality of his work and, as Michel de Certeau has argued, it made possible a dialectical model of illness that could take into account events and contingencies within a narrative without necessarily integrating them into a single, authoritative account.[1] Crucially, it also made it possible to include interactions with the analyst as part of the case study. The result could be somewhat sprawling and messy, but it brought the Freudian "novel" closer to the metafictional strategies of the modernists than the ostensibly "objective" mode of nineteenth-century realism.

In her reading of Ishikawa Jun's *Fugen*, Irena Hayter shows how an exemplary Japanese modernist used the novel form to grapple with the quintessential pathology of modernity: fascism. For Hayter, following Slavoj Žižek, fascism is defined primarily as a culture-wide desire for immediacy: a vision of the social totality in which nothing would intervene between the desire of the individual and that of the collective. During the 1930s the state-sponsored fantasy of the "*kokutai*" offered such a possibility and ideologues across the political spectrum yearned for a Japan in which "mother, nature, emperor and soil become tautological, bound together by the totalizing energies of fascism." If this fantasy was the symptom of fascism's pathology, the reality was that each of these elements stubbornly resisted incorporation into its smooth totality. Hayter argues that *Fugen*'s evocations of the female body as an unsublimated, horrifying instantiation of the Lacanian "real" worked to derail the fascist attempt to cover over the contradictions of imperialism and capitalism. She argues further that the novel's historical particularity can be seen less in its referential content than in its preoccupation with questions of mediation and immediacy.

Hayter shows how *Fugen* is a novel in which fascism's dream of the full and final adequation of individual subjectivity with the demands of a mobilized collective founders on the stubborn remainder of female bodies in the throes of pain and pleasure. "Subjectivity is denatured [here]," she writes, "but not abandoned for a fascist pre-individuated imaginary." Just as in Freud's own "novels," what we end up with is not the history of discrete individuals or nations, but a text in which, as de Certeau wrote in reference to Freud, "the nation and the individual are equal disguises for a struggle, a dismemberment (*Zerfall*), which always returns to the scene from which it is erased."[2]

Notes

1. Michel de Certeau (1986) "The Freudian novel," in *Heterologies: Discourse on the Other*, Brian Massumi (trans.) Minneapolis: University of Minnesota Press.
2. Ibid., p. 25.

9   In the flesh

The historical unconscious of Ishikawa Jun's *Fugen*

Irena Hayter

> Why would the problem of identification not be, in general, the essential problem of the political?
>
> Philippe Lacoue-Labarthe, *Transcendence Ends in Politics*

> "Presence," "immediacy," "real leadership," "restored unity": back to the ubiquitous maternal other.
>
> Alice Kaplan, *Reproductions of Banality*

Toward a political reading of form

Until "theory" burst upon the scene in the 1980s, literary criticism in Japan was focused mainly on explications of single works, *sakuhinron*, or on discussions of the unified *oeuvre* of a writer (*sakkaron*), with a strong biographical slant. The unity of extratextual author, narrator and protagonist was considered self-evident; the concern with ethics usually meant a preoccupation with content at the expense of form. Given the tenacity of this interpretive paradigm, it is striking that most Ishikawa Jun (1899–1987) commentary revolves around his style and language. The sheer density and the radical allusivity of Ishikawa's language – described by Miryam Sas with the Barthesian term "writerly" – has earned Ishikawa Jun labels such as "difficult," "avant-garde," or "opaque"; his rather cerebral explorations of the epistemology of narrative have made him an isolated figure in postwar Japanese literary circles.[1] This is as much true about Japanese writing on Ishikawa, as about the handful of critical discussions of his work outside Japan. Noguchi Takehiko, William Jefferson Tyler, and Miryam Sas, Ishikawa's most sensitive readers, unanimously situate him in the modernist lineage of Stéphane Mallarmé, Paul Valéry and André Gide. Much of the discourse on Ishikawa as a modernist concerned with formal purity originates in studies of his first longer work, *Fugen (Fugen*, 1936).[2] A text which openly flaunts its fictionality and emphasizes the performativity of writing, *Fugen* is animated by an erudite imagination traversing centuries of Eastern and Western culture. This heightened consciousness of artifice in *Fugen* – and in other early works such as *Kajin* (*The Beauty*, 1935) – is often viewed by critics in the context of Ishikawa Jun's engagement with Gide and his *roman pur*. Noguchi

Takehiko has discussed in depth the influence of Gide, Mallarmé and the symbolist movement for pure poetry, while Chiba Sen'ichi's comparative study of modernism includes a chapter on Ishikawa Jun, Gide and the pure novel.[3] Suzuki Sadami finds in *The Beauty* a self-inscription of narrative similar to Gide's *The Counterfeiters*. Suzuki argues that this work represents "pure reflexivity spontaneously generated by words," an experiment more radical than Gide's: the narrator of *The Beauty* is experiencing and writing simultaneously; it is "a novel about writing *this* novel" (kono *shōsetsu o kaku shōsetsu*).[4]

William Tyler, the critic whose studies remain the definitive English-language resource on Ishikawa Jun, has also written about Ishikawa's desire to be identified as a "pure novel" writer in the manner of the symbolists and Gide.[5] Tyler's essays emphasize Ishikawa's resistance to both the rhetoric of the *shishōsetsu*, or the so-called I-novel, and the lyricism of *mono no aware* (the transient beauty of things, the dominant trope of classical Japanese aesthetics), a gesture which effectively severs Ishikawa's work from the broader Japanese historical and cultural contexts.[6] Instead, he situates Ishikawa within a particular strand of Western (post)modernist writing characterized by playfulness and a preoccupation with textual surfaces. The dust jacket of Tyler's English translation of *Fugen*, for example, tells us that Ishikawa's work is often compared to those postmodernists *par excellence*, Borges and Nabokov. In the introduction Tyler writes about *Fugen* that "none of the pre-war work anticipates better his experimental novels, and in none is the metafictional technique more apparent." The critical essay accompanying the translation again makes the point that by anticipating trends in world literature, in *Fugen* Ishikawa created "an early example of metafiction in Japanese literature."[7]

The only Japanese cultural context in which Ishikawa Jun is usually placed is the aesthetics of the Edo era (1600–1867). The Edoesque device of *mitate* has been elevated into a master signifier not only for *Fugen*, but for Ishikawa's whole *oeuvre*.[8] Probably the central trope of the irreverent aesthetics of Edo, *mitate* can be defined very generally as a technique of allusivity which links figures coming from different cultural texts: a humble Edo maid is treated as the incarnation of a Bodhisattva; a commoner is likened to a warrior from the *Tale of Heike*. The following passage illustrates the logic of *mitate* in *Fugen*:

> The motive for bringing together in my writing (*awasekakō*) the maid of Orléans and the old woman from Poissy is my desire to portray the ever-changing face of woman, marked by winds carrying both flowers and dust. The comparison might be a bit lame, but such treatment is part of my design (*shukō*) to relate (*mitate*) these two to Kanzan and Jittoku. If Kanzan and Jittoku are incarnations (*keshin*) of the Bodhisattvas Monju and Fugen ... (pp. 332–3).[9]

Both William Tyler and Miryam Sas emphasize how Ishikawa Jun's linkings are drawn from radically diverse contexts: medieval European figures are superimposed onto Buddhist iconography in a narrative of 1930s urban Tokyo. According to Tyler, the *mitate* allusions elevate *Fugen* to a more global dimension and create a palimpsestic structure which opens up non-linear possibilities of reading.[10] For Miryam Sas, the juxtapositions of images from different traditions betray a culturally – and politically – subversive stance because such a recombinatory imagination not only reveals the multilayered complexity of cultural, literary and religious images, but also undermines notions of a national or cultural unity or unproblematic authority.[11]

This subversive impulse, however, is profoundly *textual*, and no matter how radical the juxtapositions and linkings are, they remain safely within the realm of representations. It is possible to argue that the *mitate* devices employed in *Fugen* have the effect of displacing history. These are typical modernist strategies: in the dehistoricizing imagination of modernism, historically determined artistic techniques become available synchronously (what Andrew Hewitt, drawing on Peter Bürger, has called "full unfolding"); images and devices torn from their original contexts become fragments ready to be recombined.[12] Originally, *mitate* is a trope suggesting the culture of textual play characteristic of Edo: as Karatani Kōjin writes, Edo was "a world without a point of view (a subject), one indifferent to meaning . . .. Japanese literature was without either interiority or objectivity: it offered a pure play of language."[13] In *Fugen*, the superimposition of Joan of Arc and the medieval poet Christine de Pisan (c. 1364–c. 1430), onto Kanzan and Jittoku, the famous pair of Zen eccentrics, who are in turn incarnations of the Bodhisattvas Monju and Fugen, divorces these figures from their original cultural contexts and erases their historicity. What William Tyler identifies as a resistance to the linear, that is, temporal and historical, movement of narrative, is a spatial strategy of signification in which analogies, parallels and allusions refer us to other texts, in an endless intertextual mirroring which obscures referential reality.[14]

My partial and rather sweeping summary of critical writing on Ishikawa and his *Fugen* inevitably does violence to the subtlety and intelligence of the individual readings. My aim is, however, to highlight how some persistent motifs in this writing – Ishikawa Jun's dense, erudite language, the flaunted artifice of his narratives and his heightened consciousness of form, his recontextualization of Edoesque tropes – have effectively resulted in a fetishization of modernist purity and an elision of historico-political particularity. Metafiction, for example, is a mode explicitly associated with the postmodern moment, with the non-linear dynamic of intertextuality and the eclipse of mimetic representation. The postmodern preoccupation with artifice and the performance of language have the effect of effacing the historical; the depthlessness and the weakening of historicity have been discussed as the most ambivalent features of postmodernism. As for the Gidean *roman pur,* for Walter Benjamin it has taken to an extreme the solipsism inherent in the genre of the novel:

> The attitude of the characters to what is being narrated, the attitude of the author towards them and to his technique – all this must become a component of the novel itself. In short, the *roman pur* is actually pure interiority; it acknowledges no exterior . . .[15]

The pure novel's withdrawal into artifice and the shrinking of referential reality can amplify an experience of atomization and isolation. In Benjamin's own heightened historical moment, the retreat into pure *écriture* makes it possible for the cultural forms of fascism to claim the abandoned territories of orality and intersubjectivity.

Without doubt, Ishikawa's text lends itself to such readings and is fully complicit in this critical preoccupation with formal purity and the effacement of the historical. Apart from the reflexive devices working on the microlevels of language and style, *Fugen* invokes one of the most enduring modernist themes: the work of art as the redemption of a fallen reality. But can a text which was serialized during the months of martial law imposed after the coup d'état attempt on 26 February 1936 really be concerned only with writing?[16] How can we restore the ideologico-political context which both the text and the critical discourse around it seem to bracket? There have been attempts to locate the political in Yukari, the narrator's ethereal love, because of her involvement with a communist activist. But a closer look betrays a rather ambivalent attitude: Yukari's connection to radical politics seems to be a gratuitously inserted detail in an image more given to allusion and allegory. She is consistently depicted as a shadow, vague and shrouded in clouds, locked in a chain of transformations which have more to do with archetype and myth. The narrator's mission to warn Yukari of the police trap exemplifies this ambivalence with its sudden turn towards the grotesque in the description of the ravaged face of Yukari, whom the years have turned from a heavenly apparition into a Buddhist devil, *yasha*. This is closer to caricature than to a realistic description of the life of communists on the run, although some critics have taken the political involvement of Yukari seriously.

To restore to *Fugen* its historical particularity, we may need to look beyond thematic concerns and referential content. Form is never purely form, as Fredric Jameson has taught us; it must always be read as "an unstable and provisional solution to a dilemma which is itself the manifestation of a social and historical contradiction."[17] In Slavoj Žižek's deceptively simple formulation, form articulates the repressed truth of the content.[18] This essay is an attempt at a psychoanalytical reading along these lines. It makes use of psychoanalysis in two ways: first, it considers the relationship between text and history as symptomatic, subject to the psychoanalytical dynamic of displacement, containment and repression. It seeks to bring together formal and political concerns, to outline the strategies through which the formal *enacts* the historical. I argue that on a formal level *Fugen* stages the crisis of representation which marked the 1930s in Japan. Second, I draw upon the insights of psychoanalytic theory to show that in its emphasis on language as radical alienation in the symbolic, Ishikawa's text critiques attempts to transcend the modern through the maternalized epistemologies of presence and resists a fascist libidinal economy of pre-discursive affect.

Fugen's dualities and the Showa crisis of representation

Fugen follows the adventures of the narrator *Watashi* for four days around Tokyo giving the impression of simultaneity, of events unfolding as they are being told.

Some of the characters, like his friend Bunzō, his greedy and calculating landlady Kuzuhara Yasuko, and the Tabes, a pet shop owner and his morphine-addicted wife, are introduced through flashbacks and digressions. *Watashi* is writing a biography of Christine de Pisan, the poet whose last work was a passionate hymn to Joan of Arc, and he is torn between the purity of art and the vulgarity of the world around him. He gets seduced, quite willingly, by Otsuna, a bar hostess involved with his friend Jinsaku. The object of his vague platonic passion, however, is Bunzō's sister Yukari, who is in hiding together with her communist lover. The climax of the narrative is *Watashi*'s decision to warn Yukari that the police know about her plan to meet Bunzō. Yukari does manage to escape, but the narrator's glimpse of her shatters his carefully constructed ideal: from an avatar of heavenly purity and beauty, Yukari has become ugly and grotesque. *Watashi* finds consolation in the arms of Otsuna and goes home to find that Bunzō has killed himself.

As William Tyler has pointed out, this linear movement of plot is supplemented by networks of allusion which make possible a non-linear, intertextual dynamic.[19] In a recognizably modernist strategy, the narrative relies on deeper binary structures which draw on archetype and myth. These dualities are essential to the narrative economy of *Fugen*: Joan of Arc and Christine de Pisan (historical figures); Kanzan and Jittoku, characters from the Zen canon; the Bodhisattvas Monju and Fugen; Yukari and Otsuna, or woman as purified ideality and woman as overwhelming physicality. They have been studied in depth, together with the layers of connotation which have coalesced around them. I am interested not only in the historical contexts they actualize, but also the purely *structural* relationships among them. What unites all these dualistic structures and the various other juxtapositions is that they can be seen as different configurations of *mediation* and *immediacy*. The trope of *mitate*, for example, in which one thing stands for another, and the Buddhist concept of reincarnation, imply a mechanism of mediation. About Joan of Arc it is known that she claimed an individual experience of God's presence, without the mediation of the church; her professed direct communion with God prompted the accusations of heresy which eventually led to her trial and execution. Christine, on the other hand, not only uses the mediation of words to sing about the Orléans maiden, she also mediates between the everyday world and the sublimity of Joan. For *Watashi*, Christine stands for Joan – and for Yukari; he confesses that he set out to write about Christine because he is obsessed with Joan – but then Joan's face in his dreams is always Yukari's face (pp. 415–16). In the configurations of desire Christine and Joan become mediators for Yukari. *Fugen* is an exemplary narrative of mediated desire: when he hears Jinsaku talk about Otsuna, *Watashi* experiences his lust for her as physical pain. Otsuna relates to *Watashi* through her body; the direct physical contact is always emphasized: she reaches across his lap, her body collapsing into his (p. 367); he feels the heat generated by her as she presses her body against him (p. 414). Yukari is always somehow removed, veiled, as if direct contact is never possible: the eyes of *Watashi* get blurred at the thought of her (p. 406); she is "an apparition from an unknown world behind a curtain of mist" (p. 377). The dilemmas of mediation are also clearly embodied in the Bodhisattvas Fugen and Monju: Monju is the possessor of ultimate wisdom (*konponchi*) beyond language and does not need words.[20] As the one who "shatters the gems of Monju's wisdom and scatters them on the earth" (p. 333), Fugen is a mediator; he is emphatically associated with words: "for me," *Watashi* writes, "Fugen *is* words" (Fugen to wa, *Watashi* ni totte *kotoba* de aru" (p. 383, emphasis in original). Jittoku, on the other hand, is in a position similar to that of Christine: he mediates between the mundane and the unworldliness of Kanzan. The narrator *Watashi* explicitly identifies with Jittoku ("the lowly and inferior being that I am, a more appropriate religious training for me would be to emulate Jittoku rather than Kanzan, to wield the broom and sweep the dust rather than howl poetry in the wind" (p. 333)) and implicitly, with Fugen; he is also indirectly *connected* to Christine: like him she was enmeshed in the vulgarity of the world, but rose above it to create her ode to Joan.

The various configurations of immediate proximity and distantiation, of unity and mediation are not only the main mechanism of signification in *Fugen*; it is through them that form becomes resolutely political. The crisis of representation in 1930s Japan was marked by the collapse of mediation and the swell of fascist longings for oneness with the emperor. This crisis was overdetermined by the convergence of economico-political, technological and discursive developments. Some purely material transformations – the intensification of totalizing tendencies within capitalism, the rise of finance capital and its heightened logic of abstraction – affected issues of representation.[21] The technologies of cultural dissemination (film, photography, radio) changed profoundly the texture of experience, engendering anxieties about authenticity and cultural loss. The dominant discursive currents of the so-called cultural revival, *bungei fukkō*, as found in the work of figures as diverse as the Japanese romantic school, the philosophers Kuki Shūzō (1888–1941) and Watsuji Tetsurō (1889–1960), the ethnographers Yanagita Kunio (1875–1962) and Orikuchi Shinobu (1887–1953) and the participants in the infamous symposium on overcoming modernity rejected the Meiji project and the epistemological regime established by it. Although the registers and the figures of this revolt differed with each individual thinker, there emerged a shared mistrust of instrumental reason, subject-object dialectics, and the rationality of ends. These discourses were marked by strategic resurgences of the aesthetic and the protofascist epistemologies of empathy and intuition.[22]

I read the formal structures of *Fugen* through the political and ideological dimensions of this crisis of representation: the waning of faith in capitalism and parliamentary politics. I understand fascism as a response to this crisis and an attempt to solve it in the *ideological* domain without, however, changing the fundamental economic arrangements of private property.[23] For Slavoj Žižek the reflex uniting all fascisms is "capitalism without capitalism": fascism imagines a capitalism liberated from its excesses, from inherent class antagonisms; where alienation and fragmentation will be replaced by organic community.[24] Rather than an analysis of institutions and specificities, what I am interested in are the workings of fascism as an *ideology*. Ideology is used throughout this essay not in the classical Marxist sense of false consciousness, but in Althusserian terms, as *unconsciousness* which is, however, sustained by certain material and discursive practices.[25] Psychoanalytical conceptions offer insights into the libidinal workings of fascist ideology; they go beyond the purely political or economistic approaches which inform the bulk of the studies of fascism. The sophisticated analysis of Gilles Deleuze and Félix Guattari – which draws on Wilhelm Reich's classical theorization of fascism as repressed desire externalized in hypernationalism – is valuable because of their emphasis on the libidinal energies mobilized by fascism; on the "micropolitics of perception, affectation, conversation." For them, fascism is "inseparable from the proliferation of molecular focuses of interaction which skip from point to point before beginning to resonate together."[26]

My analysis will be an attempt to understand how *Fugen* relates to the ideological moment of the 1930s, and specifically to ideology as "a reproduction of desires and *discourse*," as Alice Kaplan has put it.[27] I am interested in the way language, in the discourse of the radical right and in the so-called campaign for clarification of the national polity (*kokutai meicho undō*), was used to bind nationalist affect; in the way its rhetorical micropolitics emphasized the unity of emperor and people.

By the 1930s, the right was presenting political parties as Western-style organizations that thrived on antagonisms alien to the Japanese spirit, obstructed the unification of the public with the emperor and corrupted the sacred bonds between ruler and subject through their political pragmatism.[28] Fascist longings for presence, immediacy and restored community were figured as the desire for oneness between emperor and people. These longings animate the writings of rightist radicals: Asahi Heigo (1890–1921), the early avatar of 1930s terrorism who in 1921 assassinated Yasuda Zenjirō, the head of one of the most prominent *zaibatsu* families, wrote: "We want to be true Japanese (*shinsei taru nihonjin*) at the same time as being human. The true Japanese are emperor's children (*tennō no sekishi*), and have the right to preserve the happiness and glory of their relation to the emperor." Social structures created for profit, Asahi wrote, "create terrible divisions between His Majesty and his people, the two fundamentals of the life of the nation."[29]

Nishida Mitsugu (1901–1937), one of the leaders of the February 26 insurgency, wrote in his diary:

> If you look hard at today's reality, the enlightened ideal of the Meiji restoration, "people's emperor, emperor's people" has been resurrected by a fervent spirit casting its sacred light throughout the universe. Indeed, we have perverted the ideals and forgotten the truth, and an unjust, immoral, ignorant and foolish crowd has divided the people and their most sacred, most beautiful and most beloved emperor.[30]

Onuma Shō (born 1911), a central figure in the Ketsumeidan, or the Blood Brotherhood, who assassinated former finance minister Inoue Junnosuke on 9 February 1932, told of his outrage when a policeman stopped him from getting close to the emperor during one of the imperial pageants. Onuma called the policeman an impurity (*kyōzatsubutsu*), because an artificial hierarchy prevented him from unification (*ittaika*) with the emperor.[31]

This desire erupted with full force in the mass movement for the clarification of the national polity from 1935, a hysterical backlash against the respected constitutional scholar Minobe Tatsukichi (1873–1948) and his theory of the emperor as an organ of the state (*tennō kikansetsu*). It is striking how important a role language and affect played in this campaign. Words like *tennō* (emperor) and *kikan* (organ) were torn from their context of specialized terms in legal discourse and transplanted into the sensationalized language of mass culture. In the media there were complaints that *kikan* was a cold-sounding term ill-suited to the warm emotionality of the nation; that it implied subordinate parts, means, implements.[32] It was probably this perceived instrumentality of the term and its lack of aura, its association with soulless machinery and the inertia of matter, that inflamed radical nationalists. Words like *tennō* and *kokutai* were circulating as pure affect, bound with a nationalist identification. Minobe's rational arguments were pitted against the feelings of the imagined community, and feeling won.

The clarification campaign succeeded in harnessing the mythical performative power of that totemic word, *kokutai*. Variously translated as "the national polity" or "the national political essence," the *kokutai* is a profoundly aesthetic concept which does not signify, it *embodies* the national totality, the unity of emperor and people. Contrary to the perceived cold instrumentality of word *kikan*, *kokutai* stands for auratic, irreducible presence. It is written with the Chinese characters for "country" and "body" and even etymologically retains an organic relationship to the body, before the disjunctions of modern rational thought. The central ideological texts of imperial Japan, the imperial rescripts, work rhetorically to strengthen the affective bonds between emperor and people. The Imperial Rescript for Soldiers and Sailors (*Gunjin chokuyu*, 1882), which in the 1930s and during the war was recited several times a day by conscripts, was cast as a direct charge from the emperor to his – not the state's – soldiers.[33] The text consistently employs parallel syntactical structures ("duty is mightier than a mountain but death is lighter than a feather") and organistic corporeal analogies (the relationship between emperor and people is compared to head and limbs); together with the rhythmical incantatory language, they produce presence and immediacy.[34] Ideology reduces language to what Rey Chow has called "the performative aura of the luminous, self-evident, transparent speech act [which] appears through . . . refrain rather than thought and discourse."[35]

In the 1930s, fascist visions of organic community resonated uncannily with more purified aesthetic discourses which privileged empathy and identification against alienated conceptual thought. Ishikawa Jun's *Fugen* relates to this overdetermined historical moment not so much directly, on a purely referential or thematic level, but through *form*, through the binary tropes and the various configurations of directness and distantiation. Mediation, and the characters who mediate, are important: Joan and Christine for Yukari, Fugen for Monju; the mediated nature of desire is emphasized and isolated for contemplation; the role of language as an ultimate mediator is pushed to the surface. Through its formal structures *Fugen* highlights the crisis of representation which fascist discourse works to disguise; the tensions between mediation and organic unity. As the following sections will hopefully show, language is conceived in *Fugen* as radical alienation in the symbolic, against those (maternalized) epistemologies of immediacy and corporeal presence.

The sublime body of Japanese ideology

For a text striving for self-reflexive purity, *Fugen* remains deeply fascinated with bodies. Bodies, and especially female bodies, are described as excessively physical; dead bodies, or bodies close to death, are unspeakably abject. Apart from the ethereal presence of Yukari, all women are associated with flesh; towards the end, even Yukari is transformed into a grossly physical being. While waiting for Yukari at Shinjuku station, *Watashi* is assaulted by an intensely corporeal and unabashedly erotic vision of her:

> Nothing like the blossoms of a heavenly flower, but a lump of human fat; no less than the weight of the flesh of Yukari whom I had only glimpsed ten years ago. Each time I thought of Yukari, what came in front of my eyes were the contours of her face in the dim light; conveniently, her body was shrouded in vague mist. But the apparition I saw now was transformed into the sultry shining naked body of a sorceress: her head was floating in the air, separate from the body; the gushing blood echoed the laughter of Ganesha; the cloying beauty of the limbs was suffocating: they slipped under my underwear, eating into my skin and scraping inside my body, the pure white arms, melting like sweets, clung around my neck . . . (p. 409)

Yukari's ethereal presence has given way to an almost excessive materiality. At the same time, the image is mediated strongly by Buddhist iconography and myth. The Buddhist overtones get even stronger when *Watashi* describes the real Yukari, shocked by how much ten years have changed her: the features are unchanged, but her skin is yellow and rough, with blotches which give her a callous expression, her eyes burning with greed (*kendon*, a Buddhist term), her lips contorted into a curse (*juso*), blowing murderous ghostly light like a *yasha* (p. 411).

The other women share this repulsive physicality: Kuzuhara Yasuko is introduced by the sound of her footsteps on the stairs; her "glowing ample" figure (*mizumizushiku futotta*) gives the impression that she is around thirty-five when in fact she is over forty; she "has smeared her lustful body smell like mud all over herself" (p. 348). Otsuna, as already noted, is also reduced to eroticized corporeality: while sleeping next to her, *Watashi* feels his body "sticky with the mush that was Otsuna's body, hair, sweat, oil, powder" (p. 417); her powerful smell almost suffocates him (p. 418).

The sight of Okumi on the verge of death evokes morbid fascination; on his way to the house of the Tabes, *Watashi* conjures up Okumi's face, "pale like stagnant sewage water," and the soul urging to escape from the "putrefying flesh" (p. 398). But what he sees is beyond his imagination:

It was hard to believe that the body lying before my eyes was human. "Only flesh and bones" is a hackneyed expression, but Okumi's body really was hollowed like an ear of wheat after the grain has been taken out; the shrunken skin was stretched over each and every crumbling bone, the sockets of her half-opened withered eyes, full of black mucus, looked like netsuke, the joints, from the ribs to the fingers and the toes, protruding stubbornly, horrifyingly scraping the crevices of a body from which the blood had dried up . . . (p. 399)

Although all these excessively fleshy bodies are female, to see this as simple misogyny would be hopelessly naïve. On a certain level, these stubbornly material bodies can be read as strategies of resistance to the emergence of an aestheticized nationalized female body in the 1930s, as theorized by Nina Cornyetz with regards to the aesthetics of Kawabata Yasunari (1899–1972).[36] The female bodies in *Fugen* remain close to nature, stubbornly material and corporeal; there is an emphasis on the abject, on the disgusting decay of the flesh which is effaced from the purified bodies of Kawabata. In other words, the female bodies in *Fugen* can be seen to problematize the proto-fascist aesthetization and objectification of women.

But it is also possible to uncover other, less obvious convergences between the textual and the historical, between *Fugen's* obsession with graphic physicality and the new proximity of the *imperial* body in the 1930s, as well as the emergence of deeply ideological maternal connotations around the emperor. The emphasis on immediacy and presence meant that the *visibility* of the imperial body had always been important; in the words of the Meiji statesman Inoue Kaoru (1835–1915), "the emperor's visiting all parts of Japan . . . offers the opportunity of displaying great imperial rule in the flesh, thus dispelling misgivings' about monarchical government.[37] In the 1920s, there was a conscious attempt to overcome the crisis of imperial ideology through the skilful use of new media – and that attempt was centred on the body of the young Shōwa emperor. The NHK pioneered on-the-scene radio reports at the time of the emperor's accession ceremony in 1928. In anticipation of the enthronement, newspapers acquired the technology for wireless transmission of photographs and began transporting film, photographs and other material by plane.[38] An illusion of immediacy and direct participation was produced through extraordinary technological mediation. Live broadcasting created a sense of simultaneity more important than content. Synchronicity of time and space, affect and performativity bound together the imagined community. Hara Takeshi has argued that it was this new visibility of the imperial body in the 1930s that made possible the desire of the young radicals to be one with the emperor. The emperor was not an abstract image, but corporeal presence – it was this perception that triggered the angry reaction of Onuma Shō discussed above.[39]

The imperial body made visible by technology was a masculine body dressed in a military uniform. Takashi Fujitani has traced in detail the efforts to masculinize the imperial figure during Meiji and make a reclusive and effeminate poet-shaman into a virile modern monarch.[40] In the 1930s, however, official ideology also began to emphasise the maternal, all-embracing and forgiving aspects of the emperor. The emperor was associated with Amaterasu, the Sun Goddess, and not with Jimmu, the mythical progenitor of the imperial line. *Tennō no sekishi*, the emperor's infants, was a phrase which often appeared in the discourse of the radical right, as seen from the writings of Asahi Heigo. *Kokutai no hongi* (Fundamental Principles of Our National Polity, 1937), the preeminent ideological text of the 1930s, emphasizes that the emperor "loves and protects [his subjects] as one would sucklings; "nurtures them."[41] The relationship between the emperor and his subjects was presented as natural and spontaneous; as Kanō Mikiyo has argued, it is the mother, not the father, who is identified with nature and carries the strongest meanings of natural. If the authority of the so-called family state (*kazoku kokka*) rests on its naturalness, then the emperor has to be a mother.[42] In the 1930s, the emphasis of family state ideology shifted away from the father; school textbooks on Japanese language and ethics referred more frequently to the mother.[43]

The 1930s saw a proliferation of discourses on the maternal. While in earlier decades the women's movement focused on equality and social participation, the thirties and the forties were marked by a boom of books devoted to the themes of mother and nation, and the media was flooded by eulogies to motherhood. This beautification of the maternal was inseparable from its institutionalization: sexuality and reproduction were to be officially managed and regulated.[44] The official sanctification of motherhood was supported by pre-discursive unconscious currents yearning for presence against the alienation of modernity. A powerful ideological notion, the maternal could offer a respite from the ravages of modernization; from the cold instrumentality of modern reason, from capitalism's relentless logic of abstraction. Maternalist discourse could easily be appropriated by fascism because, as Yamashita Etsuko has observed, the mother represented transcendence and exteriority.[45] Woman, after all, is the embodiment of affect and emotion; maternal love does not know instrumentality. The 1930s crisis of representation, in other words, was a crisis of the symbolic order marked by the resurgence of maternalized epistemologies which rejected the castration of Western modernity emphasizing instead an archaic preindividuated imaginary. The potent ideological identification of the emperor with the maternal was premised again on the naturalness of the imperial system; it being posited as an exteriority to history and modernity. The poet and anthropologist Takamure Itsue (1894–1964) is exemplary in this respect. In *Bokeisei no kenkyū* (*A Study of Matrilineality*, 1938), Takamure conceived of the mother as a transcendental principle which structures everything. Later, in *Kamigokoro* (*The Spirit of the Gods*, 1944), Takamure equates the spirit of the mother (*hahagokoro*) with the spirit of the gods.[46] It is, of course, the emperor who embodies the spirit of the gods, and this is how the august imperial heart (*ōmigokoro*) is elided with the maternal, in a profoundly ideological rhetorical sliding. As long as the emperor is associated with the maternal, he is beyond rational scrutiny. Mother, nature, emperor and soil become tautological, bound together by the totalizing energies of fascism.

But if in Lacanian terms the maternal can be associated with the imaginary, with the plenitude and immediacy of the full body before its mortification by the symbolic, it can also be the Real, that is, the remainder that can never be symbolized, the abject. The association of the emperor with the maternal, so strong in the 1930s and 1940s, is inscribed with this ambivalence: the emperor is aesthetic presence before the alienation of modernity, but he can also be the Real of modernity, the uncanny remnant after modernization. This is how I understand Harry Harootunian's comment that the emperor masks a fundamental disorder which cannot be symbolized.[47] He is certainly not *only* an almighty patriarch or a transcendental signifier, but, as the radical right put it, both father and mother (*chichi ni shite haha naru mono*). Apart from symbolic overdetermination, the emperor *embodies* what Žižek has called the Nation qua Thing, that pre-symbolic maternal thing at the heart of the symbolic order.[48]

Fugen and its repulsive bodies enact this ambivalence; they show that the eternal pleasure of the imaginary can also be the space of the real and the abject. To quote Žižek at length,

> In fantasy mother is *reduced* to a limited set of symbolic features, but as soon as an object gets too close to the Mother-Thing – an object which is not linked to the maternal Thing only through certain reduced features, but is immediately attached to it – desire is suffocated into incestuous claustrophobia. Here we again encounter the paradoxical intermediate role of fantasy – it is a construction enabling us to seek maternal substitutes, but at the same time a screen shielding us from getting too close to the maternal Thing.[49]

The scene in which the narrator meets Yukari stages a similar dynamic. *Watashi's* desire for Yukari is always mediated; she is removed, disembodied, shrouded in clouds. Her closeness, however, proves unbearable: the ravaged skin, the eyes burning with desire (*jouissance?*), the contorted lips. Okumi's body on the verge of death also clearly exceeds the available economy of signification: "I don't have words to tell any more, neither I am allowed to tell" (p. 400). What unites these descriptions is not only their extreme physicality, but also the resort to Buddhist imagery in an attempt to symbolize an unbearable Real: Okumi's half-dead body is compared to a medieval illustration of human suffering, to a shadow picture of Buddhist transformations (p. 399), Yukari to a Buddhist devil, *yasha* (p. 411).

On a certain level, the excessive physicality of *Fugen*'s bodies can be seen to respond to an official maternalist discourse in which the female body was conceived as exclusively reproductive and reduced to biology. But they are also figures of resistance to the reactionary identification of the emperor with the maternal and the mobilization of a prediscursive fascist imaginary. The closeness of the maternal is unspeakably horrifying; imaginary plenitude becomes abject flesh. *Fugen* supplements the fascist longings for immediacy and unity – focused on the technologically mediated presence of the imperial body – with the logic of the Lacanian Real. In other words, Ishikawa's text engages the fundamental political problems of its time, the collapse of mediation and the crisis in representation, through its appropriation of the female body.

Writing against immediacy

As irreducible totality, *kokutai* renders the mediation of language obsolete. The imperial rescripts and the discourse of the radical right do utilize language, but in them language *qua* signification is replaced by language *qua* presence, short-circuiting directly towards affect. Iguchi Tokio has stressed that the archaic language of the imperial rescripts harks back to *norito* and *semmyō* ritual incantations; it transcends history, blurring the distinctions between nature and culture.[50] I would argue that the effect of *Fugen* is *alienation* from this shamanic power of language: language is denatured, materialized, treated as a convention. A number of strategies work to emphasize the *artifice* of writing. There is the narrator's often-quoted polemic with the naïve aesthetics of sincerity (*seijitsu*), a key tenet of Japanese naturalism and the I-novel. Such writing, according to *Watashi*, retains too much of the writer, of his psychology and physicality, and he finds that unbearable:

> If when the pen starts moving, it is caked in the grease of the hand holding it; the blue veins on the writer's face, the sweat on the tip of his nose, or the hunched shoulders – if all this stench adheres to it, how is the flower of sincerity to bloom? If one can see the body and the figure of the writer behind the writing, then the work is a dreadful farce. (p. 340)

Watashi is a typical unreliable narrator who sometimes avoids – or postpones – the narration of inconvenient details, such as his first encounter with Otsuna during the ill-fated night out with Moichi described in Chapter one: he did mean to write about "the woman [he] met in that bar" but somehow his inspiration deserted him (p. 330). Drawing attention to the process of constructing his narrative, the narrator defamiliarizes established conventions. Self-conscious asides are strewn everywhere: after the funeral of Okumi's mother, *Watashi* muses that with some more tweaking, the peaceful image of the urn containing her ashes among the birdcages on the shelf, can become good material for a cheap popular novel (p. 352). In the first paragraph of *Fugen*, the narrator wonders if his acquaintance Tarui Moichi would make a good character for a novel: "But the breezes from the world of narrative," *Watashi* reflects, "are far different from the winds of this mundane world" (p. 323).

Although *Watashi* presents as writing only his work on Christine de Pisan, and refers to his own narrative, i.e. *Fugen*, as spoken, this is a written text, dense and pre-meditated in its techniques. The long sentences and the rather pompous style with its obscure Buddhist terms and the formal Chinese-derived words clearly belong to the realm of writing. But crucially, this conceit of spoken narrative makes possible the juxtaposition of orality and writing with all its ideological implications. Spoken words, *shaberu kotoba*, carry with them the physiology of language: ". . . the quivering of the vocal cords, the rustle of the throat become dregs which clog the folds of the intellect, and make it lose the strength necessary to penetrate the unfortunate heart of the matter" (p. 351). Contrasted to this inescapable physicality of the spoken are the words coming from the pen, "refined words detached from the odour of the flesh" (p. 351). This elevation of the written cannot but strike us as a radical reversal of the fascist cult of the voice. What *Fugen*'s *Watashi* sees as the crushing corporeality of the voice, fascism elevates as authenticity before the abstraction of the written. "Where there is reverence for the voice," Alice Kaplan writes," reverence for presence, nature and immediate communication will often follow."[51] It is actually the technologically amplified voice that fascism reveres; it exploits the paradoxically archaic appeal of new oral media such as the microphone, the phonograph, and most importantly, the radio. *Fugen*, by contrast, rejects the seduction of the raw voice and foregrounds writing instead: the rhetorical convolutions of *Watashi's* style and the sheer visual density of the script highlight the element of mediation inherent in the relationship between signifier and signified. Language is conceived as radical exteriority existing prior to subjective consciousness, removed from affect.

Similar strategies are working to reduce modern interiorized subjectivity to a convention: it is conceived not as organic, but as purely differential. Depth and perspectivalism are denatured; the characters remain modern, but at the same time they are quite puzzling if read in naturalistic terms only, as coherent, psychologically motivated agents of narrative. Like Tarui Moichi, they are put to the test – what would they be like if they were fictional characters? – but such a reflexive gesture has the effect of highlighting the fact that they *are* constructions. This estrangement is achieved through devices of substitution and superimposition and a modernist appropriation of allegory. Yukari's name itself implicitly suggests these operations: "yukari" can mean relation, connection, affinity; the word is used in this meaning at least once in the text (p. 344). Of all the characters, Yukari is the most opaque and ambiguous. The face of Joan which *Watashi* sees in his dreams is actually Yukari's face (p. 353); Joan, the girl from the distant past, is superimposed onto Yukari (p. 415); she is the pure disembodied image contrasted to Otsuna's physicality. But as Yamaguchi Toshio's perceptive reading has made clear, this opposition between Yukari and Otsuna collapses into identity: *Watashi* has a vision of "Yukari's face, shrouded in clouds, and Tsuna's nipples, burning with earthly desires, flashing together" (p. 389); the fantasy of Yukari as a sultry temptress with cloying suffocating flesh, uses exactly the rhetoric and language used to describe Otsuna.[52] The collapse of this carefully constructed opposition makes it impossible for us to consider Yukari and Otsuna as interiorized individuals. Yukari is implicitly associated with Fugen, they are both protean and can change appearance: Fugen can assume any form and be found anywhere; Yukari can be "an unreliable temporary shape" of a returning Bodhisattva or enter the realm of the grotesque and be likened to a Buddhist devil. The characters are interchangeable; difference can turn into identity, substance is emptied out: Joan and Christine can also be elements of a tableau, ciphers of "the ever-changing face of woman" (p. 332). This evacuation of identity makes us uncomfortable; the text refuses us empathetic identification, demanding instead a more detached, intellectualized reading. The modernist conception of subjectivity as pure difference it used to critique certain structures of realist representation; subjectivity is denatured, but not abandoned for a fascist preindividuated imaginary.

It is through these technologies of estrangement – of an organic subjectivity, of the magical performativity of language – that *Fugen* relates to its ideological moment. These are, of course, the exemplary figures of modernist purity which previous Ishikawa Jun commentary has discussed in ahistorical, universalist terms. Modernism is an aesthetic practice which has always disavowed the political, experiencing itself as the transcendence of a fallen reality. But when restored to their original historical context, the tropes of modernist purity in *Fugen* become resolutely political; they isolate for contemplation the libidinal support of ideology and resist a fascist economy of affect.

Notes

1. Miryam Sas (1998) "Chambered Nautilus: the fiction of Ishikawa Jun," *Journal of Japanese Studies* 24(1): 37.
2. There is an English translation by William Jefferson Tyler: Ishikawa Jun, *The Bodhisattva,* New York: Columbia University Press, 1990.
3. Noguchi Takehiko (1969) "Junsui sanbun no tankyū," in *Ishikawa Jun ron,* Tokyo: Chikuma shobō, pp. 54–98; Chiba Sen'ichi, "Ishikawa Jun to A. Jiddo: kongentekina bunmei hihyō to sekai shinpan," in *Modanizumu no hikakubungakuteki kenkyū,* Tokyo: Ōfū, 1998, pp.112–22.
4. Suzuki Sadami (1988) "Fikushon no rasen undō: Ishikawa Jun no shuppatsu o megutte," *Yuriika* 20(8): 200, emphasis in original. In his "Journal of *The Counterfeiters*", Gide argues that the great nineteenth-century realists annexed various heterogenous and indigestible forms; he urges writers to "purge the novel of all elements that do not belong specifically to the novel" (André Gide (1973) "Journal of *The Counterfeiters*," translated from the French and annotated by Justin O'Brien, in *The Counterfeiters* Dorothy Bussy (trans.), New York: Random House, p. 432). *The Counterfeiters* has an anonymous narrator but it also features a character called Edourd writing a novel titled *The Counterfeiters* – which in turn might have a character writing the same novel, and so on, in a mirroring of narratives *ad infinitum*.
5. William Jefferson Tyler (1998) "Introduction," in Ishikawa Jun, *The Legend of Gold and Other Stories*, Honolulu: Hawaii University Press, p. xvii.
6. One of the most potent and at the same time most contested terms in modern Japanese literature, the *shishōsetsu* can be loosely described as a prose narrative predominantly in the third person that claims to represent faithfully the experiences of the author. It strives for sincerity and authenticity, eschewing fiction and the manipulation of narrative material. The epistemology of the *shishōsetsu* originates in ideas of a socially unmediated, organic subjectivity current in the 1910s and 1920s. It is a notoriously protean genre whose very existence has been challenged by recent critical interventions: see, for example, Tomi Suzuki (1996) *Narrating the Self: Fictions of Japanese Modernity*, Stanford: Stanford University Press; and Edward Fowler (1988) *The Rhetoric of Confession*, Berkeley: University of California Press.
7. William Jefferson Tyler (1990) "Introduction," in Ishikawa Jun, *The Bodhisattva,* p. xiii; "The art and act of reflexivity in *The Bodhisattva*," p. 140.
8. See, especially, two essays by Noguchi Takehiko, "Yatsushi" no bigaku' and "Mitate sōseiki no sekai," in his *Ishikawa Jun ron*, pp. 194–221 and 222–71, respectively, Andō Hajime, *Ishikawa Jun ron*, Tokyo: Ōfūsha, 1988, pp. 45–60; and Sas (1998) "Chambered Nautilus," p. 43.
9. All page numbers in the text refer to the text of *Fugen* in *Ishikawa Jun zenshū*, Vol.1, Tokyo: Chikuma shobō, 1989. Tyler's translation is excellent; the reason why I use my own more literal translations is that the language of the original is important to my argument.
10. Tyler, "Introduction," in Ishikawa, *The Legend of Gold*, p. xvi.
11. Sas, "Chambered Nautilus," p. 39.

12. Andrew Hewitt (1993) *Fascist Modernism: Aesthetics, Politics and the Avant-Garde*, Stanford: Stanford University Press, pp. 6–7.

13. Karatani Kōjin (1989) "One spirit, two nineteenth centuries," in Masao Miyoshi and Harry Harootunian (eds) *Postmodernism and Japan*, Durham: Duke University Press, p. 262.

14. Miryam Sas herself detects a certain ambivalence in *Fugen's* focus on the textual – she notes that "such intricacies of playful language may at times threaten . . . to become objects of beauty too rarefied for political effect" ("Chambered Nautilus," p. 39).

15. Walter Benjamin (1999) "The crisis of the novel," in Michael W. Jennings, Howard Eiland and Gary Smith (eds) *Walter Benjamin: Selected Writings*, Vol. 2 Cambridge, MA: Harvard University Press, p. 300.

16. The attempted army coup on February 26, 1936 was the most serious attempt of radical army officers of the *kōdō* (imperial way) faction to overthrow civilian government and bring about a Shōwa restoration. Fourteen hundred soldiers lead by junior officers seized the centre of the capital and shot to death key government figures. The rebels, however, lacked enough support in the army and navy. The insurgency failed; its leaders were dealt with swiftly and mercilessly. The attempted coup marked the end of the radical *kōdō* faction in the army.

17. Fredric Jameson (1979) *Fables of Aggression: Wyndham Lewis, the Modernist as Fascist*, Berkeley: University of California Press, p. 94.

18. Slavoj Žižek (1989) *The Sublime Object of Ideology*, London: Verso, p.188.

19. See note 9.

20. Mitsuta Ikuo (1976) "*Fugen*: naze Fugen na no ka," in Miyoshi Yukio (ed.) *Nihon no kindai shōsetsu*, Vol. 2, Tokyo: Tokyo daigaku shuppankai, p. 185.

21. See Eric Cazdyn (1999) "A short history of visuality in modern Japan: crisis, money, perception," *Japan Forum* 11(1): 95–105.

22. For a general overview, see Tetsuo Najita and Harry Harootunian (1988) "Japanese revolt against the West," in Peter Duus (ed.), *The Cambridge History of Japan*, Vol. 6, Cambridge: Cambridge University Press, pp. 711–74. About separate schools and individual thinkers see Harry Harootunian (2002) *Overcome by Modernity: History, Culture and Community in Interwar Japan*, Princeton: Princeton University Press; Kevin Michael Doak (1994) *Dreams of Difference: The Japan Romantic School and the Crisis of Modernity*, Berkeley and Los Angeles: University of California Press; Alan Tansman (1996) "Bridges to nowhere: Yasuda Yojuro's language of violence and desire," *Harvard Journal of Asiatic Studies* 56(1); Karatani Kōjin (1992) *Kindai Nihon no hihyō I: Shōwa hen*, Tokyo: Fukutake shoten, and "Overcoming modernity," in Richard Calichman (ed.) (2005) *Contemporary Japanese Thought*, New York: Columbia University Press, pp. 101–18; Naoki Sakai (1997) *Translation and Subjectivity: On "Japan" and Cultural Nationalism*, Minneapolis: University of Minnesota Press; Lesley Pincus (1996) *Authenticating Culture in Imperial Japan: Kuki Shuzo and the Rise of National Aesthetics*, Berkeley: University of California Press.

23. Mark Neocleous (1997) *Fascism*, Buckingham: Open University Press, pp. xi-xii.

24. Andrew Herscher (1997) "Everything provokes fascism: an interview with Slavoj Žižek," *Assemblage* 33: 60.

25. "[Ideology] is profoundly *unconscious*, even when it presents itself in a reflected form (as in pre-Marxist "philosophy"). Ideology is indeed a system of representations, but in the majority of cases, these representations have nothing to do with "consciousness". . . Ideology, then, is the expression of relations between men and their "world," that is, the (overdetermined) unity of the real relation and the imaginary relation between them and their real conditions of existence.' (Louis Althusser (1965) *For Marx*, London: New Left Books, p. 234, italics in original.)

26. Giles Deleuze and Félix Guattari (1988) *A Thousand Plateaus: Capitalism and Schizophrenia*, translated by Brian Massumi, London: Athlone Press, pp. 213–14.

27. Alice Yaeger Kaplan (1986) *Reproductions of Banality: Fascism, Literature, and French Intellectual Life*, Minneapolis: University of Minnesota Press, p. 20, emphasis in original.

28. Gordon M. Burger (1988) "Politics and mobilization in Japan 1931–45," in Duus (ed.) *The Cambridge History of Japan,* p. 101.
29. Quoted in Hashikawa Bunzō (1970) "Shōwa ishin no ronri to shinri," in Hashikawa Bunzō and Matsumoto Sannosuke (eds) *Kindai Nihon seiji shisōshi,* Tokyo: Yūhikaku, p. 213.
30. Quoted in Hashikawa Bunzō (1970) "Shōwa ishin no ronri to shinri," in Hashikawa Bunzō and Matsumoto Sannosuke (eds) *Kindai Nihon seiji shisōshi,* Tokyo: Yūhikaku, p. 214.
31. Hara Takashi (2001) *Kashika sareta teikoku.* Tokyo: Misuzu shobō, p. 349.
32. Kakegawa Tomiko (1970) "'Tennō kikansetsu' jiken: Nihon fashizumu no chisei e no kōgeki," in Hashikawa and Matsumoto (eds) *Kindai Nihon seiji shisōshi,* p. 326.
33. Carol Gluck (1985) *Japan's Modern Myths: Ideology in the Late Meiji Period,* Princeton: Princeton University Press, p. 54.
34. The English translation of the rescript can be found in Ryūsaku Tsunoda, Wm. Theodore De Bary and Donald Keene (1964) *Sources of Japanese Tradition,* Vol. 2, New York: Columbia University Press, pp. 198–9.
35. Rey Chow (1998) *Ethics After Idealism: Theory-Culture-Ethnicity-Reading,* Bloomington: Indiana University Press, p. 122.
36. Nina Cornyetz (2007) *The Ethics of Aesthetics in Modern Japanese Literature and Cinema: Polygraphic Desire,* London: Routledge, pp. 46–7, 57.
37. Quoted in Gluck, *Japan's Modern Myths,* p. 75.
38. Takashi Fujitani (1996) *Splendid Monarchy: Power and Pageantry in Modern Japan,* Berkeley: University of California Press, pp. 172–3.
39. Hara, *Kashika sareta teikoku,* p. 349.
40. Fujitani, *Splendid Monarchy,* pp. 236–7.
41. Robert King Hall (ed.) (1949) Kokutai no hongi: *Cardinal Principles of Our National Polity,* translated by John Owen Gauntlett, Cambridge, MA: Harvard University Press, pp. 45, 76.
42. Kanō Mikiyo (1995) "Bosei fashizumu no fūkei," in Kanō Mikiyo (ed.) *Bosei fashizumu: haha naru shizen no yūwaku,* Tokyo: Gakuyō shobō, p. 45.
43. Yoshiko Miyake (1991) "Doubling expectations: motherhood and women's factory work under state management in Japan, 1930–1940," in Gail Lee Bernstein (ed.) *Recreating Japanese Women, 1600–1945,* Berkeley and Los Angeles: University of California Press, p. 270; Kanō, *Bosei fashizumu,* p. 39.
44. The Society of Midwives of Greater Japan (*Dai Nihon sanbakai*) was formed in 1927. Mother's Day (the second Sunday of May) was introduced in 1928. The Mother and Child Protection act was promulgated on 31 March 1937 and became effective on 1 January 1938. In the same year birth control clinics were closed with a police ordinance and the Ministry of Welfare (*Kōseishō*) was created. (Wakakuwa Midori (2000) *Sensō ga tsukuru joseizō,* Tokyo: Chikuma bungei bunko, pp. 69–74.)
45. Yamashita Etsuko (1988) *Takamure Itsue ron: haha no arukeorojii,* Tokyo: Kawade shobō shinsha, p. 168.
46. "... hahagokoro wa ... kamigokoro to dōgi de aru ..." (Takamure Itsue (1979) "Kamigokoro," in Takamure Itsue ronshū henshū iinkai (ed.) *Takamure Itsue ronshū,* Tokyo: Takamure Itsue ronshū shuppan iinkai, p. 254.
47. Harootunian, Harry (2001) "Review article: Hirohito redux," *Critical Asian Studies* 33(4): 610.
48. Slavoj Žižek (1993) *Tarrying with the Negative: Kant, Hegel, and the Critique of Ideology,* Durham: Duke University Press, p. 202.
49. Žižek, *Sublime Object,* pp. 119–20.
50. Iguchi Tokio (1999) "'Joseiteki naru mono' mata wa kyosei (izen): Kobayashi, Yasuda, Dazai," in Hasegawa Kei (ed.) *Tenkō no meian: Showa 10-nen zengo no bungaku,* Tokyo: Impakuto shuppan, p. 105.

51. Kaplan, *Reproductions of Banality,* p. 8. Nazi propaganda was overwhelmingly oral and visual: Goebbels utilized fully the possibilities of radio and film, but denigrated the written word, because the act of reading necessarily meant time for reflection and thought (Jonathan Crary (1989) "Spectacle, attention, counter-memory," *October* 50: 104). For a discussion of the radio propaganda techniques employed by the Nazis and those of the Japanese regime during the war, see Yoshimi Shun'ya, *Koe no shihonshugi: denwa, radio, chikuonki no shakaishi,* Tokyo: Kodansha, pp. 257–60, 264–8. In the Japanese context, Tsuboi Hideto has located a radical rupture between the modernist poetic experiments in the 1920s, which explored the materiality of the printed character on the page, and the spectacular rise of the movement for national poetry, *kokuminshi,* during the war, which eschewed Chinese compounds and loan words and was written specifically for oral recitation, either at specially organized and increasingly popular poetry recitals, or on the radio. (Tsuboi Hideto (1998) *Koe no shukusai: Nihon kindaishi to sensō,* Nagoya: Nagoya University Press, pp. 9, 10.)
52. Yamaguchi Toshio (2000) "Ishikawa Jun *Fugen* ron: sono hassō keishiki ga kano ni shita mono ni tsuite," *Setsurin* 48: 71, 73.

10 Introduction

J. Keith Vincent: Sexuality and narrative in Sōseki's Kokoro . . .

According to the editors of the *Standard Edition*, Sigmund Freud's *Three Essays on the Theory of Sexuality* were "submitted by their author, over the course of more than twenty years, to more modifications and additions than any other of his writings, with the exception of, perhaps, *The Interpretation of Dreams* itself."[1] While in some cases Freud changed or removed passages from earlier editions, most of the time he chose simply to add footnotes reflecting how his thinking had evolved. The result is a text in which the footnotes sometimes threaten to crowd out the main text as we see Freud engage in a twenty-year dialogue with himself over the nature of sexuality. As the titles of the *Three Essays* ("The Sexual Aberrations," "Infantile Sexuality," and "The Transformations of Puberty") suggest, the work as a whole traces a narrative of development from the "polymorphous perversion" of the infant to sexuality's "final, normal shape" in which the genital zone comes to dominate and the opposite sex becomes its exclusive object. But while this normative teleology may appear inevitable and natural once it has already been achieved, it begins, like all narratives, in a state of protean possibility that could lead anywhere. And part of what makes the *Three Essays* such a fascinating text is Freud's exquisite sensitivity to this founding contingency of his own narrative.

J. Keith Vincent's essay uncovers a similarly complex dynamic at work in what is perhaps the most read novel in modern Japanese literature, Natsume Sōseki's *Kokoro*. Much like Freud's text, Vincent argues that *Kokoro* ". . . puts into dialogue two conceptions of sexuality: one that produces the categories of homosexuality and heterosexuality at the opposite ends of a developmental narrative and one that recognizes the performative role of narrative itself in the way sexuality is experienced and understood." In an uncanny parallelism to the Freudian teleology of the oral, anal, and genital psychosexual developmental "steps," *Kokoro*'s first narrator (*Watakushi*) tells the story of his ascent up the ladder to hetero-genital maturity. But at the same time the novel suggests that he is only able to do so by "keeping very tight control over the narrative and pathologizing" his mentor Sensei as fixated at an earlier, homo-anal stage.

Note

1. Freud, Sigmund [1995]. "*Three Essays on the Theory of Sexuality* (1905)," in James Strachey (ed.) *The Complete Psychological Works of Sigmund Freud,* Vol. VII, London: Hogarth Press, pp. 123–245, esp. p. 126.

10 Sexuality and narrative in Sōseki's *Kokoro*

"At last, I was able to read Sensei's letter from beginning to end"

J. Keith Vincent

Early on in Natsume Sōseki's *Kokoro,* Sensei and his young protégé are taking a stroll in Ueno Park talking about love. "Your heart has been made restless by love for quite some time now," Sensei tells the young narrator. Finding nothing in his heart that corresponds to such a feeling, the latter replies:

> "But there is no one whom you might call the object of my love," I said. "I have not hidden anything from you, Sensei."
>
> "You are restless because your love has no object. If you could fall in love with some particular person, you wouldn't be so restless."
>
> "But I am not so restless now."
>
> "Did you not come to me because you felt there was something lacking?"
>
> "Yes. But my going to you was not the same thing as wanting to fall in love."[1]

Several critics in recent years have pointed to this scene as indicative of a historical shift in the dynamic of male–male sexuality in Japan. In these accounts, Sensei (and in many accounts Sōseki himself) is a member of the last generation that still remembers a time when a homosocial continuum stretched unbroken from male bonding to male–male sex. In the intervening generation, however, that continuum has ruptured and the resulting divide is registered here by the young narrator's utter obliviousness to Sensei's meaning. The modern world inhabited by the younger man on this side of that historical divide is thus a world cut off not just from some abstract past but from the possibility of love between men.

The appeal of this notion of a prelapsarian past when modern homophobia had not yet taken hold has given rise to a number of what might be called gay revisionist readings of *Kokoro*. Stephen Dodd gives Sōseki credit for remembering this lost paradise and praises him for being ". . . open to a wider range of erotic possibilities than has generally been acknowledged" (p. 496).[2] Ōhashi Yōichi calls *Kokoro* a "masterpiece of homosexual literature" and sees in the homoerotic relations among men suggested by the novel the possibility of a "rebuilding of communities ravaged by the relentless advance of capitalism."[3] This approach is perhaps most succinctly and delightedly verbalized by Hashimoto Osamu, for whom the opening scene of the novel where the narrator first "cruises" Sensei on the beach, is nothing short of *homo-marudashi* (a phrase we might roughly translate as "queer as a three-dollar bill"). It proves much harder for Saeki Junko to see the beauty in a world from which women are entirely excluded. To Saeki, writing in a similar vein about Sōseki's *Botchan,* this lost homosocial continuum is too saturated with misogyny and patriarchy to be worthy of nostalgia.[4] But however they might evaluate the rupture, most readers of Kokoro have shared the historicist assumption that such a rupture has occurred and that *Kokoro* tells its story. As Reiko Abe-Auestad writes, "Sōseki belongs to the generation of Meiji intellectuals for whom homosocial/sexual relations were not taboo, and yet who were hesitant to acknowledge the sexual component in homosocial relationships openly."[5]

While there is ample historical evidence to suggest that someone of Sensei's age might indeed have remembered a different configuration of male–male sexuality than the one taken for granted by his young protégé, my interest here is not in Sensei (or in Sōseki) as a character who still possesses such a memory, but in the way the novel *Kokoro* in fact works to confound any historicist account of the transition into sexual modernity. *Kokoro*, I will argue, is neither a "gay" novel nor a "straight" one, but a text that puts into dialogue two conceptions of sexuality: one that produces the categories of homosexuality and heterosexuality at the opposite ends of a developmental narrative and one that recognizes the performative role of narrative itself in the way sexuality is experienced and understood. The developmental model is put forward by the novel's first narrator, whom I will refer to as *Watakushi*, or "I" as he is known in the novel, while the second is implied by the text as whole. Like Sigmund Freud's nearly contemporaneous account of sexual development in *Three Essays on Sexuality, Watakushi*'s narrative is "an attempt to rewrite sexuality as history and as story by reinstating structures of organ and object specificity."[6] But, also like the *Three Essays*, Sōseki's novel shows us that what it posited as a natural and inevitable development (from a youthful homosexuality to a "mature" heterosexuality) is in fact the result of an imposed narrative. *Kokoro* shows us how *Watakushi* is able to narrate his own ostensibly "successful" achievement of genital heterosexuality only by drawing a contrast between himself and his mentor Sensei whom he portrays as stuck in the past and arrested in his sexual development.

As this short preview of my own reading has no doubt already begun to suggest, sexuality in *Kokoro* is anything but straightforward and its complexity in this regard has given rise to a wide range of interpretations. Before the gay readings discussed above, *Kokoro* was read first in mostly desexualized homosocial terms and then, partly in reaction to that first reading, in resolutely heteronormative fashion. Which of these two readings one chose depended largely on whether the critic in question considered Sensei or *Watakushi* to be the novel's protagonist. My own reading will step back from both positions to analyze the narrative dynamic *between* Sensei and *Watakushi* and thus to understand what the novel as a whole is saying about sexuality in relation to narrative.

Sensei's homosocial and *Watakushi*'s heterosexual *Kokoro*

For most of the postwar period, few readers of *Kokoro* seem to have cared much about the fate of *Watakushi*. They were much more interested in Sensei. For Etō Jun, the pre-eminent Sōseki scholar of his generation, Sensei was Japan's last great stoic. Perhaps, even, its last real man. "The Emperor Meiji's death and General Nogi's *junshi*,"[7] Etō wrote in 1970:

> ... made [Sensei] realize that the spirit of Meiji had not entirely died within him. Now the shadow of the entire value structure of this great era emerged from his tortured past, smiling at him like the ghost of a loved one. Perhaps the ghost whispered to him: "Come to me." And Sōseki responded, indicating through his novel's protagonist that a part of himself had died with the passing of the Meiji era. Thus Sōseki wrote *Kokoro* to make it clear that he was on the side of the ghost of the traditional, but somehow universal, ethics – the ethics of stoic self-restraint or anti-egoism – even though fully aware that the whole value system of the Meiji era had crumbled long before the Emperor's death, and that a new age was emerging from this chaos – an age in which the unrestrained assertion of the ego would be considered not an act of ugliness but the privilege of younger generations.[8]

Etō's nostalgic reading not only focused primarily on the figure of Sensei but also conflated him with Sōseki himself. For Etō and other conservative critics, the values expressed in Sensei's testament were absolute. For this reason they tended to ignore the mediation of Sensei's story through the younger narrator and focus exclusively on the novel's final section, in which Sensei writes in his own voice. The novel's protagonist was Sensei and his young protégé simply the person who faithfully brought us Sensei's story. "That Sensei is the protagonist," wrote Valdo Viglielmo in no uncertain terms, "is never in question."[9] Miyoshi Yukio, another prominent postwar Sōseki scholar, went so far as to characterize the first narrator as ". . . nothing more than a mouthpiece, a puppet."[10]

By privileging Sensei over *Watakushi* as the novel's protagonist these critics suppressed the possibility of a dynamic interplay between the novel's two narrators and effectively froze *Kokoro* into an atemporal morals textbook. Their critical consensus was reflected and compounded in the popular imagination thanks to the fact that *Kokoro* was not only the most popular text to be excerpted in high school literature textbooks from the late 1950s on,[11] but that the sections chosen were invariably drawn from Sensei's testament alone. As Komori Yōichi wrote in 1985, this "canonical" reading of *Kokoro* made it into:

> ... a text that functions as a mechanism of nationalist ideology centered around patriarchal values of "ethics," "spirituality," and "death." Young readers are forced to kneel before the "ethical" and "spiritual" death of "Sensei" and shrink before the deified author as they contemplate their own ethical and spiritual inadequacies.[12]

In an effort to combat this moralistic and nationalist reading of *Kokoro*, Komori emphasized the first narrator's active role in the framing and narration of Sensei's story. His was the first of a flood of articles that began to shift the focus back to the first narrator in order to read the novel as the story of how the younger man learned from the mistakes of his dead mentor. In Komori's reading, the first narrator's account served to relativize (*saika*) Sensei's testament and cast doubt on the grimly homosocial values it put forth. But the crowning blow of Komori's argument came with his provocative claim that the younger man went on not only to live with Sensei's wife after the latter's death, but also to have children with her (something Sensei himself was never able to do). While the conservative reading of Etō and others ignored the novel's narrative complexity to preserve the disinterested objectivity of its young narrator and make Sensei (and Sōseki) into a national hero, Komori argued that the severing of Sensei's letter from the rest of the novel amounted to a cutting of its "life line" (*seimei no sen*).[13] His narratological approach worked to breathe "life" back into Sōseki's text and rescue it from its own canonization as a masterpiece of homosocial askesis.

Komori's article sparked an intense controversy in Japanese literary circles known as the "*Kokoro* debates." Atsuko Sakaki provides an excellent summary of these debates and argues that they provided the impetus for a new narratological emphasis in Japanese literary studies as a whole.[14] The ins and outs of this debate are fascinatingly complex, but I will spare the reader the details here. For our purposes, what matters is that at some point in the 1980s, many readers of *Kokoro* seem to have become dissatisfied with its lack of closure and decided to supply their own in the form of a classic heterosexual ending. Sakaki mentions the playwright Hata Kōhei's theatrical adaptation of the novel, "*Kokoro* no kodoku to ai," written in 1986 and first staged in 1987, which ends with the marriage of Sensei's wife and *Watakushi*. Sakaki also references an article by Patricia Merivale from 1988 in which the latter speculates on the missing conclusion of the novel to conclude, in Sakaki's summation, that "There is no reason to accept traditional interpretations that have assumed *Watakushi* . . . would never think of his mentor's wife (or widow) in romantic or sexual terms."[15] Miyakawa Takeo cites a manga "parody" of *Kokoro* by Takahashi Rumiko from 1980 set in contemporary Japan in which the "young widow" character marries and has children with a character who combines the characteristics of both *Watakushi* and "K."[16] While the motivations of these readings and adaptations differ, they all point to an anxiety over the lack of closure in what Merivale calls "the usual novelistic sense"[17] and a tendency to remedy this lack with heterosexual union and children. For Sakaki, the fact that Merivale arrived at the same conclusion as Komori even though she was writing on the basis of Edwin McClellan's translation and in complete isolation from Japanese academia suggests "a certain universal plausibility"[18] to Komori's thesis. McClellan's translation itself, as I will argue later, has a markedly homosocial bias and tends to streamline the narrative in ways that actually downplay both the narrative dynamic and the interpersonal rivalry between Sensei and *Watakushi*. That Merivale came up with the idea that *Watakushi* "inherited" Sensei's wife *despite* McClellan's translation would seem to have more to do with the power and seductiveness of the straight marriage plot than its "universal plausibility."

But what concerns us here is why Komori's attack on the (homosocial) consensus among conservative Sōseki scholars came in the form of an imagined heterosexual ending to *Kokoro,* one in which "two people [*Watakushi* and Sensei's widow] enter freely into an alliance in which there is no separation between mind and body." Unlike his morbidly homosocial mentor, Komori argued, the younger narrator managed to enter into a "living relationship of two free individuals"[19] characterized by openness to the other and the liberation of sexual desire from the constraints of family and nation. It is not my intention to dispute the value of such a "living relationship," but rather to ask to what extent such a fantasy is in fact animated through an implicit comparison with the aloof Sensei, resolved as he is to "go on living as if I were dead."[20] Komori's critique of *Kokoro's* homosocial *thematics* (which he identified, as we have seen, with the "patriarchal values of 'ethics,' 'spirituality,' and 'death'") was itself motivated by a deeply heteronormative narrative in which the younger man's achievement of reproductive heterosexuality is held up as a paradigm of successful modernization and maturation. At the same time, Komori's suturing of *Kokoro's* "life line" worked by implicitly homosexualizing Sensei and characterizing him as a man stuck in the homosocial past. The result is a narrative of development from a homosexual/homosocial past associated with Sensei towards a heterosexual future embodied by *Watakushi*. Thus despite his astute formal analysis of the recursive narrative structure of *Kokoro* (an analysis that made it possible for him to read *Watakushi* and not Sensei as the novel's protagonist), Komori did not take into account the fact that Sensei's characterization in the novel is mediated by the retrospective vision of a younger man who is telling the story of his own maturation into heterosexuality. If Sensei seems stuck in a homosocial/homosexual past, this is at least partly an effect of *Watakushi*'s desire to represent *himself* as having moved on. And yet Sōseki's novel breaks off at the end of Sensei's letter without giving *Watakushi* the opportunity to make an explicit statement of how he has learned from Sensei's mistakes. In this way *Kokoro* as a novel in fact resists the heteronormative closure that Komori's reading imposed (and indeed, that *Watakushi* might have intended). My own reading will demonstrate this by paying very close attention to those moments in the novel where *Watakushi*'s strategy to narrate his own maturation at Sensei's expense is both exposed and subtly undermined.

A love without an object

At first glance the conversation between Sensei and *Watakushi* cited above would seem to suggest that it is *Sensei* and not *Watakushi* who subscribes to the developmental model of sexuality. His notion that "The friendship you sought in me is in reality a preparation for the love you will seek in a woman") reads like a novelistic rendering of the teleology of sexual development that Freud proposed in *Three Essays on Sexuality*. In the first essay of that work, entitled "The Sexual Aberrations," the phenomenon of "sexual inversion" provides the initial backward glimpse of the independence of what Freud calls the "sexual aim" from the "sexual object." "Experience of the cases that are considered abnormal [i.e. sexual inversion]," Freud writes:

> . . . has shown us that in them the sexual instinct and the sexual object are merely soldered together – a fact which we have been in danger of overlooking in consequence of the uniformity of the normal picture, where the object appears to form part and parcel of the instinct.[21]

As someone, like Freud himself, who has "experience" with cases that are considered abnormal, Sensei recognizes that the young man's advances toward him may not be without a sexual component. Whether this "experience" comes from his youthful relationship with "K" or simply from the fact that he belongs to a generation that *still remembers* a time when sex between men was within the range of the normal, Sensei is not fooled by the "uniformity of the normal picture, where the object appears to form part and parcel of the instinct." He knows, in other words, that there is nothing inevitable or "natural" about a heterosexuality based on the innate attractions of women for men and vice versa.[22]

At the same time, however, and again like Freud, Sensei places this knowledge within the framework of a developmental narrative according to which the homosexual object will eventually be displaced by a heterosexual one. The young narrator, Sensei claims, has been made restless by *a love without an object*. This is what Freud referred to as the "polymorphous perversion" of the infant. For now, this aimless sexuality has lighted upon another man, but eventually, and inevitably, it will attach itself to a woman. The young *Watakushi*, for his part, finds Sensei's discourse incomprehensible. As we have seen, he claims that his interest in Sensei has nothing to do with "love." Their mutual incomprehension is made perfectly evident in the passage that follows.

> ". . . it was a step in your life toward love. The friendship that you sought in me is in reality a preparation for the love that you will seek in a woman."

> "I think the two things are totally different."

> "No, they are not . . ."[23]

In Sensei's account, *Watakushi* will pass from the stage of "polymorphous perversion," where the sexual aim has no object, toward love for a member of his own sex, and finally on to love for a woman. With this attainment of genital heterosexuality, Sensei concludes his uncannily Freudian narrative of sexual development. And yet what Sensei sees as a process in time, *Watakushi* sees as a set of categories that are distinct in nature and occupy different *spaces*. "I think the two things are totally different."

It is crucial here to remember that this scene, like all of *Watakushi*'s narrative, has been filtered through *Watakushi's* memory and presented to the reader in retrospect. Since *Watakushi* is the narrator here we cannot discount the possibility that he is telling the story in a way that suits him. If that is the case and he still believes that his attraction to Sensei had nothing to do with "love," we might well ask why he goes to the trouble of relating this scene. If, as Ken Ito has argued, it is generally the case in *Watakushi*'s account that "the events narrated have something to do with the narrator's process of maturation,"[24] perhaps he is telling this story because he has either become aware of or become more accepting of an attraction to Sensei of which his younger self remained ignorant or unconscious. The kind of retroactive narrative we have here is typical of what Freud referred to as deferred action or *Nachträglichkeit*, according to which, in the summation of Jean Laplanche and Jean-Bertrand Pontalis,

> . . . experiences, impressions and memory-traces may be revised at a later date to fit in with fresh experiences or with the attainment of a new stage of development. They may in that event be endowed not only with a new meaning but also with psychical effectiveness.[25]

Of course, the possibility of revision at a later date calls into question whether this exchange ever happened at all, or at least whether it happened in the way the narrator recounts it. But regardless of its "historical" accuracy, the contrast between the present of narration and the narrated past sets up an implied path of development in which *Watakushi* grows not only into his own heterosexuality, but also, and not at all paradoxically, into a position from which his *earlier* homosexuality can be recognized and disavowed at the same time. Sensei's Freudian narrative of sexual development is here revealed as the narrator's own. It is by emphasizing his own earlier incomprehension ("I think the two things are totally different") that the narrator demonstrates his retrospective understanding. In this way *Watakushi* claims for himself a heterosexual identity by simultaneously admitting and disavowing the possibility that he may have attained it after passing through a "homosexual" stage. At the same time, while *Watakushi* works hard to tell the story of how he has grown up into a good heterosexual, Sōseki's *Kokoro* goes over his head to let us know that this maturation is a product of motivated narrative rather than a matter of natural development. It show us, in other words, how *Watakushi* asserts or performs his own maturation by projecting "homosexuality" onto his own past and onto Sensei.

This would go a long way towards explaining the homoeroticism evident in the way the narrator describes his relationship with Sensei, beginning with the way he stalks him at the beach when they first meet, as noted by both Hashimoto and Dodd. And it would make sense of the fact that *Watakushi* seems rather proud that his relationship with Sensei was more intimate than the latter's relationship to K. The text begins with a proleptic reference to Sensei's use of the Roman letter "K" to refer to his friend that lets the (re)reader know that the narrator has already read Sensei's letter. "I cannot bring myself to refer to him," he writes at the end of the novel's first paragraph, "with an impersonal [yosoyososhii] Roman letter [yokomoji]."[26] This sentence makes little sense to the first-time reader of *Kokoro* who does not know that Sensei will refer to his friend in his testament with just such an "impersonal Roman letter" ("K"). But to the re-reader it is clearly an effort on *Watakushi*'s part both to differentiate himself from Sensei and to claim a greater degree of intimacy with him. It is almost as if he were jealous of Sensei's relation to "K." And yet in the scene quoted above, *Watakushi* denies outright Sensei's suggestion that there might be an erotic component to their friendship. This contrast could be explained then as the result of a split between the younger, "clueless" *Watakushi* who is being represented in the novel and the older, "wiser" *Watakushi* who is doing the representing.

Kokoro *in English*

This becomes even clearer if we take a closer look at the passages we have been discussing by comparing Sōseki's original with the translation I have been citing by Edwin McClellan. What we find is that while Sōseki's Japanese maintains the sense of a developmental continuum in *Watakushi*'s narrative from homo- to heterosexuality, McClellan's translation works to immobilize that narrative and to downplay both the conflict and the intimacy between the two men. This is not surprising when one considers that during the years between 1914 and 1957 when the translation was made the imaginability of an eroticized male homosocial continuum (already tenuous in 1914) had given way to a strictly policed homosocial divide. McClellan's 1957 translation provides us with a kind of snapshot of that divide as it existed in both Japan and the United States.

Perhaps the most striking omission in McClellan's translation of the conversation between *Watakushi* and Sensei discussed above is of the contrasting terms for the sexes. In McClellan's translation we have, "It's a step in your life on the way to love. The friendship that you sought in *me* is in reality a preparation for the love that you will seek in *a woman*." A more literal translation of Sōseki's sentence would read "It's a staircase on the way to erotic love. You gravitated towards me, a member of your own sex, on your way to embracing the opposite sex." In Sōseki's text it is not simply "me" but "me, a member of your own sex" (*dōsei no watashi*). McClellan's "woman" is Sōseki's *isei*, which translates conventionally as "opposite sex" but can be rendered literally as "different sex," or "heterosex." *Dōsei* and *isei* are sexological neologisms that in this context cannot help but suggest their newly coined relations *dōseiai* (homosexuality) and *iseiai* (heterosexuality). Whereas McClellan's "me" and "a woman" convey a universalized sense of gendered personhood ostensibly defined independently of sexuality (which is to say heteronormatively), Sōseki's *dōsei* and *isei* not only make it difficult to overlook the sexual, but also make room for the Freudian separation of "sexual aim" from "sexual object." In the best Freudian fashion, Sōseki's Japanese places the two categories in a structural relation of opposition that is nonetheless maintained by a temporal (narrative) continuum from sameness into difference.

As we have seen, it is this suggestion of continuity against which *Watakushi* is reacting when he insists that ". . . the two things are totally different." But the Japanese text undermines his certainty by having him echo the very terms that

Sensei has used. McClellan's "totally different" is Sōseki's "mattaku *sei*shitsu wo *koto* ni shiteiru," a rather stiff sentence that contains, *in reverse order,* the characters used to write *opposite sex* (異性). Coming immediately after Sensei's use of the same characters to describe the normative object of male heterosexual desire (McClellan's "woman"), the text thus shows us *Watakushi* insisting on his heterosexuality. Difference, he seems to be saying, lies in the "different sex *(isei)*." But whereas Sōseki's *dōsei* and *isei* reverberate with the possibility of continuity and even reversibility, McClellan's English introduces a qualitative rupture between the male self ("me") and the other ("a woman").

What I have here rendered as "erotic love" (in the sentence "It's a staircase on the way to erotic love"), is the Japanese term *koi.* This term predates the introduction of the Western concept of "love" with its abstract spiritual connotations, and has overwhelmingly sexual overtones.[27] But McClellan subsumes both *daki-au* (embrace) and *koi* (erotic love) under the single English word "love." Thus we have two loves in English where in Japanese we had an erotics *(koi)* and an embrace *(dakiai)* to describe that which *Watakushi* "will seek in a woman." The sensual and erotic connotations of the Japanese terms work to sexualize the unspecified nature of *Watakushi*'s relationship with Sensei, a sexualization that McClellan blocks (in a move that is similar to *Watakushi*'s own) by inserting the word "friendship" ("The friendship that you sought in me . . ."). In Sōseki's Japanese, as we have seen, there is no "friendship," only a movement from one erotic attachment to another.

By thus juxtaposing Sōseki's Japanese with McClellan's English we start to see that by 1957, even the narrative of sexual development that *Watakushi* proposed through Sensei had been frozen into a static homosocial divide. McClellan's rendering, that is, takes the side of the clueless young *Watakushi* as he is represented by his older self. In this historical moment homosexuality and heterosexuality are not points on a continuum but "completely different."

McClellan's choices in 1957 can thus be understood as a result of the immobilization of *Watakushi*'s narrative of sexual development in the years intervening since *Kokoro* was written. If, as I have argued, that narrative produced heterosexuality and homosexuality as the opposite ends of a narrative arc, by the time of McClellan's translation it has succeeded so well that the *narrative* is no longer visible past the rigid homosocial divide it has itself produced. The same immobilization in Japan may explain why the sexual overtones even of the more explicit Japanese text went unnoticed for so long. Most critics skipped straight to the end of the paragraph where the moralizing and melancholic message of the novel is so famously expressed. "You see, loneliness is the price we have to pay for being born in this modern age, so full of freedom, independence, and our own egotistical selves" (p. 30).[28] Sensei and K were *friends. Watakushi* wants Sensei to be his *friend.* But modern society makes people selfish and destroys friendship. *So we should all strive to be nicer to our friends.* But such exclusive emphasis on this sanitized notion of friendship in isolation from Sōseki's careful attention to the intertwining narratives of sexual and national development serves only to stir up nostalgia for a desexualized and homosocial national past. "Sensei's letter,"

McClellan writes, "is ostensibly an attempt to explain his life to his young friend; but it is really not so much of an explanation as an expression of the lonely man's desire to try once and for all to communicate with another human being. Sensei himself knows that it is a vain wish" (p. 55). By erasing the dynamics of gender and sexuality from Sōseki's text and hoisting it up into the airy realms of the existential loneliness of "human beings," McClellan erects a wall between these men that is even higher than the one Sōseki built. Of course this is not to say that a focus on gender and sexuality alone will suffice to redress the homosocial and universalizing readings of *Kokoro* of which McClellan's translation is so typical. One must attend to the social and the sexual at once in order to appreciate Sōseki's particular brilliance.

For Sōseki, the narrativization of sexuality-as-development was inseparable from the narratives of the global Imperial order of which he remained critical throughout his career. We can get a better idea of the nature of this critical edge by attending to the ways in which Sensei's narrative and *Watakushi*'s resistance to it *differs* from Freud's developmental narrative. Despite Freud's efforts to avoid equating the normal with the normative, and despite his recognition of the fact that development is always beset by regressions and repetitions, the narrative thrust of his *Three Essays on the Theory of Sexuality* heads unerringly towards genital heterosexuality. Freud's argument is thus a modernizing one insofar as it postulates a single trajectory of progress and downplays the role of violence and repudiation that fuels that progress.[29] For Sōseki, a Japanese writer who was acutely aware of his position on the global periphery and as a subject of the Japanese Empire, there was no missing the fact that those who have reached the "next stage" have done so by scrambling over the backs of others, only to kick them in the face to keep from being overtaken. They look back with disdain on where they imagine they came from and see those who are "still there" as qualitatively inferior – even as they disingenuously recite the modernizationist mantra that promises everyone the chance to "catch up." If we look once again to McClellan's translation we can see how this violent and hierarchical dynamic of modernization remains palpable in Sōseki's words, only to be muted again in McClellan's English.

"But it was a step in your life toward love" is McClellan's rendering of Sōseki's *koi ni agaru kaidan nan desu*. As we have already seen, a more literal translation of Sōseki's Japanese would read "It's a staircase that goes up to EROTIC love." In McClellan's English the staircase is transformed into a single "step," a step that without the mention of a staircase will be read as a horizontal rather than a vertical one. The verticality of Sōseki's staircase is thus quite literally flattened out as it moves into horizontal English (*yokomoji*). In the process, the hierarchical character of the ascension to sexual normality that is so evident in the Japanese comes to look like a simple matter of lateral progress (*shinpo*). The *violence* inherent in this ascent is made clear a few pages later when Sensei explains why he would rather forego *Watakushi*'s friendship now than face his contempt in the future. In McClellan's translation the sentence reads, "The memory that you once sat at my feet will begin to haunt you and, in bitterness and shame, you will want to degrade me" (p. 30).[30] McClellan's "sat at my feet" suggests a child or a dog in complacent subordination to its father or master. But Sōseki's language is one of sexualized submission followed by violent rebellion. Rendered more literally into English, Sōseki's sentence reads "The memory that you once *knelt in front of someone* [*hito no mae ni hizamazuita*] will make you want to stomp on their head [*sono hito no atama no ue ni ashi wo nosaseyō to suru*]." What was a child/dog in McClellan's translation is here a man on his knees in front of another man – as if to render sexual service. The vivid image of "stomping on someone's head" echoes the verticality of the staircase cited earlier to render explicit the violence involved in "moving on." Here "moving on" is "moving up" over someone else's head. Like his earlier insertion of an anodyne "friendship," McClellan's choice to render this violently concrete metaphor with an abstract verb like "degrade" dulls the force of Sōseki's language. Sōseki's text makes no mention of "haunting," or "bitterness and shame," only unremorseful violence.[31]

Of course, while McClellan's translation may slightly soften the impact of Sensei's dark world view it hardly erases it entirely. But by downplaying the conflict between *Watakushi* and Sensei it does tend to naturalize rather than make available for critique the Oedipal dynamic whereby the younger man purchases his own maturity at Sensei's expense. One famous example of this is McClellan's bizarre omission of the last sentence of the novel's first paragraph quoted earlier, "I cannot bring myself to refer to him with an impersonal Roman letter."[32] As we have seen, the sentence only makes sense if one has already read the novel and knows that Sensei himself refers to his best friend as "K." As a result it does dangle rather awkwardly for the first time reader. But to remove it as McClellan does, presumably in the interest of a smoother, more "natural" narrative sequence has serious consequences for our reading of the text. Not only does it suppress the way the *Kokoro* demands to be read recursively, it also demotes *Watakushi* from an active and interested narrator to a passive observer. The result is not only to downplay *Watakushi*'s ambivalence toward Sensei but also to make the novel into a more straightforward linear narrative.[33] Like McClellan's other choices discussed earlier this can be read as an attempt to domesticate and normalize Sōseki's text. And here too, rather than reading McClellan's choice simply as a mistake or misreading, we might see it as indicative of a way of reading of *Kokoro* that may not be so uncommon among Japanese readers as well. Ishihara Chiaki has in fact argued that many Japanese readers have tended to overlook what he calls "torn seams" (*hokorobi*) like this one in *Kokoro*'s narrative structure that demand a more complex reading.[34]

Surely, the most dramatic "torn seam" in the novel is the way it ends with Sensei's letter and never goes back to the *Watakushi*'s narrative with which it began. One might imagine that if the form of narration had been left entirely up to *Watakushi*, he would have come back to tell us what had happened in the intervening years between Sensei's death and the moment when he sat down to write his story. This would have made it possible to say for certain what *Watakushi* had learned from Sensei's life. If we subscribe to Komori Yōichi's controversial argument, *Watakushi* might have related how he went on to have children with Sensei's wife, thus completing the trajectory of heterosexualization that he outlines in the book's first two sections. But as it is, Sōseki denies *Watakushi* this chance and forces us to go back to the beginning in search of clues (like that Roman letter "K") that might help us guess. If the novel deprives *Watakushi* of the chance to give a final accounting of himself, what is *Kokoro's* last word on *Watakushi*?

Enematic closure

In the last scene before *Watakushi*'s departure for Tokyo he hears his brother's voice calling from their father's sickroom. Preparing himself for the worst, he hurries into the room only to find that the doctor needs help administering a palliative enema. The nurse, exhausted from her labors the night before, has gone to sleep in the room next door and the narrator's older brother stands next to the doctor looking befuddled and unable to help. "My brother," he writes, "who was not used to helping on such occasions, seemed at a loss."[35] As soon as the brother claps eyes on *Watakushi* he orders him to assist the doctor and promptly takes a seat. *Watakushi* then places a sheet of oiled paper underneath his father's behind (*chichi no shiri no shita ni aburagami wo ategattari shita*). The use of the verbal auxiliary of enumeration "tari" here suggests that the narrator did various other things as well to help the doctor administer the enema, but these remain unnamed. McClellan seems to have found this scene distasteful enough to clean it up in his translation. He gives us only "I took his place and helped the doctor."[36] But in both McClellan's and Sōseki's texts the contrast between the narrator's matter-of-fact competence in the matter of the enema and his older brother's flummoxed paralysis constitutes a powerful claim by *Watakushi* that on the eve of his father's death he is well on his way to becoming the mature self who is writing the narrative we are reading. In this scene the father has become an infant, the older brother has become a frightened little boy and the narrator steps up to take care of them both. He is more grown up than they are and his maturity is powerfully figured here as *an ability to deal with shit*. In a subtle echo of this scene just a page later the narrator uses the same verb he used to describe placing the sheet of oil paper under his father's buttocks (*ategau*) to describe the way he presses a piece of paper against the station wall to scribble a note to his family before he leaves for Tokyo.[37] Both instances are clearly efforts at closure that foreshadow the way the narrator will eventually put pen to paper to explain this past.

But *Watakushi*'s assertion of independence and maturity is soon undermined. Sensei's letter has arrived just before the scene with the enema. When he manages to steal away from his father's sickbed to flip through it, his eyes come to rest on that line near its end: "By the time this letter reaches you, I shall probably have left this world – I shall in all likelihood be dead."[38] His head swimming with this devastating sentence, *Watakushi* begins to "turn the pages over backwards, reading a sentence here and there", in the search for some clue as to whether Sensei is still alive. But since neither this letter nor any other can attest to the death of its author, *Watakushi* must piece together what he can by reading the whole letter through. And he is only able to do this once he sits down on the train on his way to Tokyo.

In a desperate desire to act (*omoikitta ikioi de*), I boarded the Tokyo-bound train. The noise of the engine filled my ears as I sat down in a third-class carriage. At last I was able to read Sensei's letter from beginning to end.[39]

And this is the last we hear of *Watakushi*. Coming on the tail end of the scene of the father's enema, the conjunction of movement with stasis, activity, and passivity that comes of *sitting down on a train* is a perfect metaphor for the suspended animation into which Sensei's letter plunges *Watakushi*. For as long as he sits on the train, the letter is his only way of knowing whether Sensei is alive or dead. Every word of it thus becomes a possible answer to this pressing question, even as every moment spent reading it is another moment in which *Watakushi* is powerless to stop his mentor's suicide. When he first receives the letter and glimpses its foreboding end, *Watakushi* literally reads the letter backwards as if to reverse the passage of time. But as soon as he begins to read the letter in its proper order, the twists and turns of the story it tells threaten to become what Freud identified as those of life itself: just so many detours on the "circuitous path to death."[40]

As readers of the novel *Kokoro,* we already know that Sensei is dead when we begin reading his letter. Indeed we have known it from very early on in *Watakushi*'s narrative. But the *Watakushi* on the train over whose shoulder we read remains uncertain. This gives rise to a crucial difference between what motivates the reading of *Watakushi* on the train and what motivated the older *Watakushi* to append Sensei's letter to his own narrative. Trapped on the train and thus deprived of any form of action except, precisely, *reading,* one can well imagine that *Watakushi*-on-the-train would have occupied himself with reading the letter for the duration of his train ride back to Tokyo. In a sense, *Watakushi*'s reading becomes a kind of life support for Sensei. But it is a reading unconcerned with narrative. "All I wanted to know at that moment was that Sensei was still alive. Sensei's past, his dark past that he had promised to tell me about, held no interest for me then."[41] Sensei's "dark past" is of course precisely what *Watakushi*-on-the-train has been interested in up until this point. It is also what the older *Watakushi* has been withholding from the reader throughout the novel's first two sections. But all of that has ceased to matter now that Sensei's threatened suicide looms. For *Watakushi*-on-the-train ("at that moment"), the possibility of death is held in abeyance as he reads and rereads Sensei's letter. Sensei's dark secrets that once so fascinated him are no longer interesting except to the extent that they offer clues as to whether he is alive or dead. And the more powerful the narrative chain of cause and effect from crime to self-punishment, the more likely it is to have eventuated in the ultimate act of expiation. For this reason, we can imagine that *Watakushi* on the train would be motivated to discover not narrative continuity and causality but loose ends and unresolved questions that might offer some hope of a derailment. It is with such a hope in mind that he might have read the letter again and again, skipping back and forth to different passages in a desperate search for something that might make it possible to believe that Sensei had not carried through with his threatened suicide.[42]

For the older *Watakushi*, on the other hand, the knowledge that Sensei is already dead has made every detail of his letter a testament to his death. This is of course why he has given this section the title "Sensei and his Testament (Sensei to isho)." As the ostensible "editor" of the book that is *Kokoro*, the narrator appends Sensei's letter as a kind of extended quotation. Indeed, the entire letter is placed in quotation marks in the Japanese text, although McClellan took it upon himself to remove them in the English translation. The letter is there to explain why Sensei has killed himself and the possible meanings of every detail have been rendered finite by Sensei's death. For the older narrator the question is not *whether* Sensei is dead but *why* he died. While the possibility that he *might* be dead suddenly made the story of his life uninteresting for *Watakushi*-on-the train, the narrator's knowledge that Sensei *is* dead makes his life into a story.[43] Indeed, it provides the fuel that drives the narrative of *Kokoro* itself. But like the reader of a novel who doesn't want it to end, *Watakushi* on the train passes the time by (re)reading Sensei's letter as he hurtles toward Tokyo and the increasingly inevitable reality of Sensei's death. His "desperate desire to act" by boarding the Tokyo-bound train comes smack up against the wish that his journey, and Sensei's life, will be prolonged indefinitely.[44]

The reader of Sōseki's novel, meanwhile, finds herself somewhere in between these two extremes of narrative closure and dilation. If *Watakushi* came back at the end of the novel to wrap things up and tell us what happened in the intervening years between the events he has just described and the present of his narration, *Kokoro* would be a very different (and much less interesting) novel. But he does not come back. The novel ends with the end of Sensei's letter, and the reader who wants to know more can only go back to *Watakushi*'s story to look for the clues left by a narrator who knew, but would not tell, how things would turn out. *Kokoro* is thus a text that not only ends without closure but sends us circling back to its beginning – just as *Watakushi* reads Sensei's letter backwards. The scene when *Watakushi* runs away from his father's exposed anus and jumps onto a train "in a desperate desire to act" is the closest that *Kokoro* gets to closure. The end, we could thus say, is buried in the middle of the novel, on the brink of the deaths of two fathers and suspended between passivity and action.

But precisely to the extent that this scene gestures toward closure, like the anal sphincter itself, it is also one that admits of dilation. Unlike his protagonists, Sōseki was not interested in clean closure. As we have seen, the novel ends with the end of Sensei's letter and we never hear from *Watakushi* again. As a result, despite the Bildungsroman-like tone of first two sections of *Kokoro,* the fact that Sensei's letter is left dangling at the end subverts the closure that would otherwise be necessary to lend a decisive meaning to the novel. This would suggest that what Sōseki is showing us in *Kokoro* is not so much how one man grew up to become a happily partnered heterosexual, but his attempt to narrate that maturation into existence. *Watakushi* tells us that he has completed every stage of Freud's narrative of sexual development. First he has moved beyond the oral and separated himself from his mother. This is made clear in his narrative when he expresses his exasperation at his mother for constantly badgering him about getting Sensei to find a job for him. What McClellan variously translates as a "position" or a "post" is, in Sōseki's uncannily psychoanalytic Japanese, a "kuchi (mouth)."[45] He has passed through the anal stage, as we have seen, by overcoming his aversion to shit. By metaphorically castrating his own father in the scene of the enema, he will achieve genital heterosexuality. And yet however hard *Watakushi* might be working to prove that he has matured into heteronormative adulthood, the text of *Kokoro* makes it clear that he can only do so at Sensei's expense (not to mention that of his mother and father). In other words, he can only *be a (straight) man* by keeping very tight control over the narrative and by pathologizing Sensei. Sensei, as we learn from *Watakushi*'s account, has not only failed to "grow up" into a reproductive heterosexual, he has also failed to progress beyond the anal stage. All of this may in fact be true of Sensei, but it is also true that in *taking the trouble* to portray Sensei in this way *Watakushi* is also able to disavow his own anal regressions and homosexual libido.

What we might call *Watakushi*'s "anality" is clearly evident in the way he structures his narrative. Like the letter Sensei will eventually write to tell *Watakushi* about his past and which forms the last portion of the book, *Watakushi*'s narrative is a retrospective one. But, as Ken Ito has noted, the younger man's narrative is different from Sensei's in its tendency to withhold information from the reader. "Knowing precisely how things turn out," Ito writes, ". . . the initial narrator drops hints about events or revelations that lie in the future . . . Yet, for all that he intimates, the narrator is surprisingly coy about what he reveals."[46] Like a child in the retention phase who, as Freud put it, "retains his faeces . . . for purposes of auto-erotic satisfaction and later as a means of asserting his own will,"[47] *Watakushi* doles out information only as it suits him.

The overall effect of this is that the entire text of *Kokoro*, including even Sensei's letter,[48] comes under the tight control of the first narrator. And yet despite these "anal" characteristics of *Watakushi* himself – characteristics that show up in the tautness of the narrative structure and the almost sadistic scrutiny to which he subjects Sensei – it is Sensei who is portrayed in the novel thematically as being stuck in the anal stage. Sensei is shown to be oscillating between destruction (his virtual murder of K and his own suicide) and possessiveness (his unwillingness to share his past with his wife). *Watakushi*, meanwhile, seems breezily to have moved on to mature adulthood and wishes only to learn from Sensei's experience. Or at least that is what *Watakushi* would like us to think.

It is perhaps for this reason that he takes the trouble to recount the following episode that illustrates, quite literally, how "anal" Sensei is in comparison to himself. In Chapter 32 we read:

> Indeed, Sensei was a very tidy person. His study, for instance, was always in perfect order. Being rather careless myself, Sensei's tidiness often attracted my attention.

> "Sensei is rather fastidious, isn't he?" I once said to his wife. "Perhaps so," she said. "But when it comes to clothes, he certainly is not overcareful." Sensei, who was listening to us, said with a laugh, "To tell the truth, I have a fastidious

mind. That is why I am always worrying. When you think about it, it's a terrible nuisance to have a nature like mine."

What he meant by "a fastidious mind," I did not know. Neither, it seemed, did his wife. Perhaps he meant to say that he was too intensely conscious of right and wrong, or perhaps he meant that his fastidiousness amounted to something like a morbid love of cleanliness.[49]

The rather striking dynamic of this scene, in which *Watakushi* and Sensei's wife team up in their ignorance against the mysteriously fastidious Sensei, works to strengthen the impression of a Sensei closed off from the world and all its (healthy) messiness. The way *Watakushi* shares his bafflement with Okusan suggests a level of intimacy between the two that rivals that between the married couple themselves. At the same time, Okusan's defense of her husband ("When it comes to clothes he certainly is not overcareful") sounds suspiciously like an effort to make him more of a man by casting herself as a willingly overworked wife. The fact that she has another, younger man as an audience makes this even more likely.

It is scenes like this one that lend that "universal plausibility" to the idea that *Watakushi* would go on to marry Sensei's wife. As I noted before, this is a theory that has adherents on both sides of the Pacific. Patricia Merivale argues quite convincingly that *Kokoro* belongs to the genre of the "elegiac romance" in which:

. . . the narrator tends to inherit from the hero, in his capacity as survivor, not only the hero's papers or testament, but also most of the responsibilities (and occasionally some of the pleasures) that go with having to look after the hero's widow.[50]

But due to the truncated quality of *Kokoro's* narrative structure the question of what happened to *Watakushi* and Sensei's wife can only ever be a matter of speculation. By depriving us of a clear ending, Sōseki makes his novel amenable to a whole spectrum of readings, some of which I have surveyed here. Whether one reads it as a "queer as a three-dollar bill," as a national allegory about responsibility and friendship, or about the triumph of a future-oriented heterosexual love over a morbid homosociality, says much more about the critic and his or her historical moment than it does about *Kokoro*.

In a 1994 book on the *Kokoro* debates, Komori wrote (only half seriously, I imagine), "I hope with all my heart (*kokoro*) that this will be the last book to be written about *Kokoro*. But I know my hope is in vain."[51] Vain indeed. It seems as if we will never outgrow *Kokoro*. The attempt to sew the novel's ending back up within *Watakushi*'s discourse and thus to move on to other things is bound to fail. It is this lack of closure, this refusal to suture past with present and even to decide who its own protagonist is, that makes Sōseki's novel such a powerful account of narrative, sexuality, and modern subjectivity.

238   *J. Keith Vincent*

Notes

1. Natsume Sōseki (1957) *Kokoro,* translated by Edwin McLellan, Washington DC: Regnery, p. 26. For the Japanese, see Natsume Sōseki (1995) *Kokoro,* in *Sōseki Zenshū* Vol. 5, Tokyo: Iwanami, p. 36.
2. Stephen Dodd (1998) "The significance of bodies in Sōseki's Kokoro," *Monumenta Nipponica* 53(4): 496.
3. It bears mentioning that Ōhashi also argues that the novel contains the seeds of fascism in its construction of a homosocial community of men centered around the emperor. See Yōichi Ōhashi (1996) "Kuiā fāzāzu no yume, kuiā neishon no yume: *Kokoro* to homosōsharu," *Sōseki kenkyū,* no. 6.
4. Saeki Junko (1996) "Seibo wo kakomu dansei dōmei: *Botchan* ni okeru nanshoku teki yōso." *Sōseki kenkyū,* no. 12: 150–67.
5. Reiko Abe Auestad (1998) *Rereading Sōseki: Three Early Twentieth-Century Japanese Novels, Iaponia Insula, Bd. 7,* Wiesbaden: Harrassowitz, p. 36.
6. Bersani, Leo (1986) *The Freudian Body: Psychoanalysis and Art.* New York: Columbia University, p. 40.
7. *Junshi* refers to the practice of "following one's lord in death."
8. Etō, Jun (1970) "A Japanese Meiji intellectual: an essay on Kokoro," in *Essays on Natsume Sōseki's Works,* Japanese National Commission for Unesco, Tokyo: Japan Society for the Promotion of Science, pp. 49–65, 65.
9. Valdo Viglielmo (1976) *"Kokoro:* A Descent into the Heart of Man," in Kinya Tsuruta and Thomas E. Swann (eds) *Approaches to the Modern Japanese Novel,* Tokyo: Sophia University Press, p. 170.
10. Quoted in Ishihara Chiaki (1997) *Hanten suru Sōseki,* Tokyo: Seidosha, p. 183.
11. Satō Izumi points out that before the Second World War, Sōseki was best known as a stylist. His most popular works at the time were those written in ornate classical styles like *Gubujinsō* (*The Poppy*) and *Nowaki* (*Autumn Wind*), neither of which is read much today. *Kokoro's* canonization (and its inclusion in high school textbooks) began only during the late 1950s and 1960s, when it was perceived as offering a model of the kind of responsible subjectivity or *shutaisei* that modernizationists felt Japan was lacking. See Satō Izumi (2006) *Kokugo kyōkasho no sengoshi,* Tokyo: Keisōshobō. Thanks to Tomi Suzuki for pointing this out to me and giving me this reference.
12. Komori Yōichi (1988) *"Kokoro* ni okeru hanten suru 'shūki'," in *Kōzō toshite no katari,* Tokyo: Shin'yōsha, p. 416.
13. Ibid., p. 420.
14. See Atsuko Sakaki (1999) "The debates on *Kokoro:* a cornerstone," in *Recontextualizing Texts: Narrative Performance in Modern Japanese Fiction,* Cambridge: Harvard University Asia Center. According to Ishihara Chiaki, by 1996 about 450 articles had been written on *Kokoro* since its original publication, but 200 of them were written in the ten years following Komori's article in March of 1985. Iida Yūko *et al.* (1996) *"Kokoro* ronsō ikō," *Sōseki kenkyū,* 6: 156.
15. Patricia Merivale (1988) "Silences: Sōseki Natsume's *Kokoro* and Canadian Elegiac Romance," in Kinya Tsuruta and Theodore Goosen (eds) *Nature and Identity in Canadian and Japanese Literature,* Toronto: University of Toronto and York University Joint Center for Asia Pacific Studies, p. 37.
16. Takeo Miyakawa (1994) "Saiwa sareta *Kokoro,*" in Komori *et al.* (eds) *Sōryoku tōron: Sōseki no Kokoro,* Komori, Tokyo: Shōrin shobō, pp. 179–94.
17. Merivale, "Silences: Sōseki Natsume's *Kokoro* and Canadian Elegiac Romance," p. 37.
18. Sakaki, "The debates on *Kokoro:* a cornerstone," p. 35.
19. Komori, "*Kokoro* ni okeru hanten suru 'shūki'," 437.
20. McClellan, p. 243; Sōseki, p. 294.

21. Freud, Sigmund (1995) *"Three Essays on the Theory of Sexuality* (1905)," James Strachey (ed.) *The Complete Psychological Works of Sigmund Freud*, Vol. VII, pp. 123–245. London: Hogarth Press, p. 148.
22. As Freud wrote in a famous footnote added to the first essay in the 1915 edition, "Thus from the point of view of psycho-analysis the exclusive sexual interest felt by men for women is also a problem that needs elucidating and is not a self-evident fact based on an attraction that is ultimately of a chemical nature" (*Three Essays*, p. 146). It is at moments like these (typically, as here, in his footnotes) that Freud undermines the normative teleology that he is expounding in the main text of the *Three Essays*. But as the text progresses the normative thrust begins to dominate. By the third essay, "The transformations of puberty," in which he describes how infantile sexual life takes its "final, normal shape" (p. 207), we find a section on the "Prevention of inversion." Here Freud claims that the "attraction which the opposing sexual characters exercise upon one another" is the "strongest force working against a permanent inversion of the sexual object." If heterosexuality was "also a problem that needs elucidating" in the earlier footnote, here it has become a force of nature about which, "Nothing can be said within the framework of the present discussion to throw light upon it" (p. 229). I was first alerted to this fascinating contradiction in Freud's work by Leo Bersani's brilliant reading in *The Freudian Body*.
23. McClellan, p. 27; Sōseki, p. 36.
24. Ken K. Ito (1997) "Writing time in Soseki's *Kokoro*," in Dennis Washburn and Alan Tansman (eds) *Studies in Modern Japanese Literature: Essays and Translations in Honor of Edwin McClellan, Michigan Monograph Series in Japanese Studies (MMSJS) Number: 20*, Center for Japanese Studies, University of Michigan, Ann Arbor, MI, p. 7.
25. J. Laplanche and J.-B. Pontalis (1973) *The Language of Psychoanalysis*, Donald Nicholson-Smith (trans.) New York: W. W. Norton and Co., p. 111.
26. Sōseki, *Kokoro*, p. 3.
27. On the meaning of "koi" in premodern Japan and the Meiji-period introduction of the western notion of "love" see Takayuki Yokota-Murakami (1998) *Don Juan East/West: On the Problematics of Comparative Literature*, Albany, NY: State University of New York Press.
28. McClellan, p. 30; Sōseki, p. 41.
29. As I noted earlier, Freud was not at all insensitive to the fact of discrimination against homosexuals and other "perverts," at least in his footnotes. Nor was his teleology of development absolute. But the normalizing thrust of his argument in the *Three Essays* did leave itself open to cooptation by less tolerant readers, as the subsequent history of psychoanalysis demonstrated.
30. McClellan, p. 30; Sōseki, p. 41.
31. Not surprisingly, McClellan's translation was not serviceable for John Bester in his translation of Doi Takeo's discussion of homosexuality in *Kokoro*. The sentence discussed above is rendered much more vividly in Bester's translation as "The memory of having kneeled before someone makes one want to trample him underfoot at a later date." Doi Takeo (1973) *The Anatomy of Dependence*, Tokyo: Kodansha Internation, p. 117. Dodd also found it necessary to retranslate the earlier passage where Sensei uses the term *dōsei no watashi*. In place of McClellan's "me," he has "another man like me." See Dodd, p. 490.
32. Sōseki, p. 3.
33. Ishihara Chiaki has pointed out the ambivalence contained in this crucial sentence. While *Watakushi* insists upon his respect for his mentor by referring to him with the respectful "Sensei" and rejecting a "yosoyososhii" Roman letter, in doing so he is also implicitly criticizing Sensei for his aloofness from K. Thus already in the first paragraph, he is announcing that he has surpassed Sensei. Ishihara Chiaki (2005) Kokoro: *Otona ni narenakatta Sensei*, Tokyo: Misuzu Shobō, p. 106.

34. Ishihara Chiaki (2005) Kokoro: *Otona ni narenakatta Sensei*, Tokyo: Misuzu Shobō, p. 106.
35. McClellan, p. 122; Sōseki, p. 151.
36. McClellan, p. 122.
37. Sōseki, *Kokoro,* p. 153.
38. McClellan, p. 122; Sōseki, p. 151.
39. McClellan, p. 123; Sōseki, p. 153.
40. Sigmund Freud (1995) *"Beyond the Pleasure Principle,"* in James Strachey *et al.* (eds) *The Standard Edition of the Complete Psychological Works of Sigmund Freud*, Vol. 18, London: The Hogarth Press, pp. 1–64, esp. p. 39.
41. McClellan, p. 123; Sōseki, p. 152.
42. This way of reading Sensei's letter would seem to suit the letter itself. As Oshino Takeshi argues, Sensei's letter itself is characterized by its "repetitive and recursive language" (p. 174). He points out that Sensei begins his letter with a digression concerning his uncertainty as to the validity of his mother's last words. Dying of typhoid, the words she spoke "often left no trace in her memory when the fever subsided. That is why I . . . but never mind" (McClellan, p. 130). Oshino cites Sensei's uncertainty as an example of his inability to take anyone's words without subjecting them to repeated analysis. The scene sets the tone for the rest of Sensei's testament which, unable to attest to the death of its own author and indeed prolonging his life by its very length, is characterized by prolixity, repetition and interpretative excess that Oshino contrasts with K's concise suicide note. See Oshino Takeshi (1994) "Isho no shohō: pen to noizu," in Komori Yōichi *et al.* (eds) *Sōryoku tōron: Sōseki no* Kokoro, Tokyo: Shōrinshobō, pp. 166–78.
43. As Komori Yōichi writes, "Only because 'Sensei' is dead and his because his 'letter' has become his 'testament' has *Watakushi* become able to talk of him, pretending to have come to understand 'Sensei'." Quoted in Atsuko Sakaki (1999) "The debates on Kokoro: a cornerstone," in *Recontextualizing Texts: Narrative Performance in Modern Japanese Fiction*, Boston: Harvard University Asia Center, p. 51.
44. The way *Kokoro* superimposes these two ways of reading – one that hurries to the end and one that keeps looping back to the beginning – is strikingly similar to Freud's description of the life and death instincts in his *"Beyond the Pleasure Principle."* "One group of instincts rushes forward so as to reach the final aim of life as swiftly as possible"; Freud writes, "but when a particular stage in advance has been reached, the other group jerks back to a certain point to make a fresh start and so prolong the journey (Freud, *"Beyond the Pleasure Principle,"* p. 41). In his insightful application of Freud's work to our understanding of narrative, Peter Brooks sees this back and forth movement as characteristic of the "highly plotted nineteenth century novel." See Peter Brooks (1984) "Freud's masterplot: a model for narrative," in *Reading for the Plot,* Cambridge: Harvard University Press, pp. 90–112.
45. McClellan, p. 107; Sōseki, p. 134.
46. Ken Ito (1997) "Writing time in Sōseki's *Kokoro,"* in Dennis Washburn and Alan Tansman (eds) *Studies in Modern Japanese Literature: Essays and Translations in Honor of Edwin McClellan*, Ann Arbor: Center for Japanese Studies, University of Michigan, p. 8.
47. Sigmund Freud (1995) "On transformations of instinct as exemplified in anal eroticism" in James Strachey (ed.) *The Standard Edition of the Complete Psychological Works of Sigmund Freud*, Vol. 17, p. 130.
48. It is contained, as I noted earlier, within quotation marks presumably put there by *Watakushi.*
49. McClellan, p. 70; Sōseki, p. 90.
50. Merivale (1988) "Silences: Sōseki Natsume's *Kokoro* and Canadian elegiac romance," p. 129.
51. Komori Yōichi, "Nakagaki," in *Sōryoku tōron: Sōseki no* Kokoro, p. 113.

11 Introduction

Christopher Hill: Exhausted by their battles with the world . . .

Christopher Hill's essay shows how in the late Meiji period, modern civilization itself was increasingly understood in psychological rather than political terms. He charts the almost simultaneous emergence in Japan, the USA, and Western Europe of the diagnostic category of "neurasthenia" (*shinkei suijaku*) as an illness thought to be caused by the stresses and strains of modern life. Encompassing both somatic and mental symptoms, neurasthenia reflected the as yet undifferentiated state of the disciplines of psychology and psychiatry. It also served as a literary trope in many novels of the time, where characters suffering from the disease lodged what Hill calls "utterly compelling and absolutely ineffectual" complaints against the injustice and anomie of modern society. While youth in early Meiji still believed in the possibility of collective political action, the late Meiji "neurasthenic" tended to withdraw into rooms filled with bromides and tinctures or, like Ichirō in Sōseki's *The Wayfarer*, to abandon themselves to philosophic despair.

While such social withdrawal could register as a protest against the evils of civilization and even, in the case of Sōseki at least, as a critique of Japan's semi-colonial subjection to the West, the critique was ultimately ineffective, Hill argues, because the very phenomenon of neurasthenia was internal to the discourse of civilization, constituting a kind of closed circle with no outside. In this sense, Hill's essay provides an interesting contrast with Carl Cassegard's contribution to this volume. While Cassegard traces the reemergence of the possibility of political action and engagement as a kind of recovery from the traumatic defeat of the radical protest movements of the 1960s, Hill shows how the early promise of the Meiji Movement for Freedom and People's Rights gave way to a withdrawal into a pathologized privacy. While the then relatively young field of psychology worked as a depoliticizing force in the Meiji context, in Cassegard's analysis it is Freud's notion of trauma, repetition, and recovery that points the way toward renewed engagement with the world. But if we are left at the end of Hill's essay with a sense of Japan as what art critic Sawaragi Noi would later call a "bad place" of claustrophobic closure, the open-ended narrative forms and generic hybridity employed by Sōseki and Tōson and described by Hill stand as a reminder that all was not lost.

11 Exhausted by their battles with the world

Neurasthenia and civilization critique in early twentieth-century Japan

Christopher Hill

The novelist Natsume Sōseki may be Japan's most famous neurasthenic, but in the early years of the twentieth century he was not alone in complaining of a nervous exhaustion whose origin seemed to be modern civilization itself. *Shinkei suijaku* or "nerve fatigue," as neurasthenia was translated, first appeared as a diagnostic category in Japan in the late 1870s, and by the turn of the century was recognized as a widespread affliction whose symptoms ranged from insomnia and loss of appetite to debilitating fatigue and melancholy. Debates on the causes of this modern malady and its implications for Japan reached well beyond the medical community. As a "disease of civilization" (*bunmei no yamai*), the plague of neurasthenia worried not just patients and their doctors but also a range of commentators reflecting on the changes in the economy, education, and daily life that followed the Meiji Restoration of 1868. From its beginnings in the USA this neurological diagnosis, based on the idea that somatic dysfunction of the nerves produced psychic symptoms such as melancholy, was susceptible to a variety of metaphorical appropriations that turned it into a social condition. In Japan after the Russo–Japanese War (1904–1905) a boom in writing about neurasthenia made *shinkei suijaku* a keyword for social critique as *shakai mondai*, "social problem," had been for the 1890s. The story of the rise and fall of neurasthenia is a medical history – of neurology, psychiatry, and psychology before Freud – but also a cultural history properly told in both international and national terms. An essential part of the period Yamazaki Masakazu called "The Grumpy Era," neurasthenia was an opportunity to question the transformations of the Meiji period and their ideological justification, from the pursuit of European models of civilization to the state's suppression of dissent.[1]

Writers were prominent among those who in posing such questions turned the discourse on neurasthenia toward social critique. Japanese writers had been engaged with new views of mental disturbance as nervous illness since early in the Meiji period. In the preamble of a tale whose title punningly promises a "true scene of nerves," the storyteller San'yūtei Enchō observed that of late "there are no more ghosts, everything is said to be nervous illness [*shinkei byō*]," adding that the enlightened intellectuals who dismiss ghosts and possession by animals have much to learn about human misbehavior.[2] In contrast to Enchō's ambivalence, Tsubouchi Shōyō enthusiastically scattered nervous pathologies across *The Character of*

Today's Students (*Tōsei shosei katagi*, 1885–1886). The novel set out to practice the character description based on "psychological principles" (*shinrigaku no dōri*) that Shōyō advocated in his manifesto *The Essence of the Novel* (*Shōsetsu shinzui*, 1885–1886). Kawamura Kunimitsu points out that the novel reflected not only the popularization of the language of nerves but also its impact on the representation of sensation and perception.[3]

Neurasthenia, in the late nineteenth century the most prominent of nervous disorders, too entered the literary lexicon and shaped the representation of mental life. Nagayoshi, a character in Nagai Kafū's novel *The Flowers of Hell* (*Jigoku no hana*, 1902), suffers bouts of the illness as the consequence of social ostracization and inner torment over the crimes of his youth. (The heroine, a young teacher named Sonoko, develops melancholia [*in'utsushō*] through her involvement with Nagayoshi's family.[4]) After the Russo–Japanese War, novels featuring neurasthenic characters proliferated, particularly in the rising naturalist school, and writers more pointedly connected the condition to the society in which they wrote. The debates between Professor Sneeze and friends in an early work by Sōseki, *I am a Cat* (*Wagahai wa neko de aru*, 1905), are a well known comic example, but more common were tormented figures like Yoshiko, the rebellious girl student in Tayama Katai's "The Quilt" ("Futon," 1907), the suicidal poet Aoki in Shimazaki Tōson's *Spring* (*Haru*, 1908), Yoshio, the bitter protagonist of Iwano Hōmei's *Wandering* (*Hōrō*, 1910), and Ichirō, the truth-seeking academic in Sōseki's *The Wayfarer* (*Kōjin*, 1914), all of whom suffer neurasthenia.[5] That many of these ailing figures were modeled after life, sometimes after the writer himself, suggests an emerging self-image of intellectuals as dysfunctional products of civilization. They take their place in a literary scene that critics and historians have observed turned frequently to images of disease to reflect on the consequences for individuals of the changes in daily life encouraged by the state since 1868. Among other "epochal maladies" like tuberculosis, whose depiction frequently dramatized the confrontation of individuals with social mores, neurasthenia was a particularly rich vehicle because as a nervous affliction with symptoms both somatic and psychological its metaphors entangled physical infirmities with subjective attitudes toward contemporary society.[6] Two important novels of the late Meiji period, Sōseki's *The Wayfarer* and Tōson's *Spring*, show that as writers appropriated neurasthenia as such a means of reflection they transformed the complex etiology of the disease into an aesthetic that unexpectedly expresses an unhappy suspension of judgment on the era.

The view that melancholy was caused by a disorder of the nervous system emerged in European medical discourse in the seventeenth century, and the idea that wealth and civilization were fostering an "English Malady" of nervous ailments in the British elites became fashionable in the eighteenth century.[7] Medical and popular discussion of nervous affliction and its relationship to society increased during the nineteenth century. Two physicians in the USA, George M. Beard and E. H. Van Deusen, proposed "neurasthenia" as a formal diagnosis for nervous disorders in separate journal articles in 1869. Beard's formulation, advanced in numerous publications including the widely read *American Nervousness* (1881), became the basis for the international discourse of neurasthenia. In the view of

Beard, a neurologist writing at a time when the field included aspects of physiology, psychiatry, and anatomy, the diverse symptoms of neurasthenia were caused by a deficiency of "nerve force" that could be traced to physiological changes in the nerves, although the specific pathology was yet unknown. Immediate causes could include business woes, sexual excess, and abuse of tobacco and alcohol, but the fundamental cause was modern civilization itself, distinguished from ancient civilization by five features: steam power, the periodical press, the telegraph, the sciences, and "the mental activity of women." Beard argued that "When civilization, plus these five factors, invades any nation, it must carry nervousness and nervous diseases along with it."[8] Neurasthenia, which Beard described as a consequence of "progress and refinement," thus was closely linked to the liberal ideas of social evolution propounded by Herbert Spencer and other social philosophers of the time. Neurasthenia was an acute and growing problem in the USA precisely because of the advanced state of its civilization.[9] The peril, however, was selective: "Muscle workers" only rarely developed neurasthenia, according to Beard. It was the modern vanguard of "brain workers" – business leaders and members of the liberal professions – that risked contracting the "distinguished malady" of neurasthenia, through overwork and the burden of responsibility.[10] Alongside such an elitism in matters of class one may observe in Beard's focus on professions dominated at the time by men an exclusivity in matters of gender. The typical North American neurasthenic was a man of affairs well able to afford the "rest cures" in plush resorts usually prescribed as treatment.

Beard's diagnosis gained attention abroad in the 1870s and during the following decade, aided by the publication of his *Practical Treatise on Nervous Exhaustion* (1880), was incorporated into the theories of mental disturbance circulating in international medical circles.[11] The iterations of the diagnosis took diverse forms. German physicians and commentators highlighted industrial stress and "democratized" the disease by extending the diagnosis and treatment to members of the working class.[12] In France, in contrast, the emerging disciplines of psychiatry and sociology accepted the idea that modern civilization was the cause of neurasthenia, but linked it to atavistic degeneration as one feature of what Robert Nye calls a "medical model of cultural crisis" that explained the plague of crime, suicide, and moral decay thought to be undermining the country.[13] In Japan, where physicians began to adopt Beard's diagnosis in the late 1870s, neurasthenia was a disease of the civilized elite but the diagnosis contributed to campaigns by neurologists and psychiatrists to discredit popular conceptions of mental derangement, and thus to efforts to civilize the masses. (Beard said in *American Nervousness* that the fine physical constitution of people living in Japan would make them prone to neurasthenia if they developed civilization, and perhaps psychiatrists were out to prove him right.[14])

Across the regions where neurasthenia boomed, the diagnosis seems to have appealed to physicians because it accommodated a wide range of symptoms short of insanity for which they knew no organic cause, at the same time unifying what by the 1880s was an extensive literature on nervous exhaustion.[15] It also played a role in the economics and competition of medical specializations. Promoting the diagnosis allowed neurologists to gain patients who might otherwise be treated by general practitioners, alienists (those specializing in the severely insane), or gynecologists, who wanted charge of female patients, often for surgery.[16] Association with Beard and S. Weir Mitchell, the major proponent of the rest cure and like Beard a prestigious social commentator, meanwhile enhanced neurology's prestige.[17] For their part, patients seemed drawn to neurasthenia because it spared them the label of insanity and was distinct from hysteria, hypochondria, and melancholia, which all carried a stigma.[18] That patients, doctors, and social commentators used neurasthenia to so many different ends in so many different places attests to its *international* existence, as part of what Regenia Gagnier and Martin Delveaux call the "global ecology" – cultural, political, and economic – of the *fin de siècle*.[19]

As a psychosomatic illness in the original sense of the word – involving both mind and body – neurasthenia contributed both to the ongoing medicalization of the body and the disciplinary transformation of madness. Its roles are especially clear in the case of Japan, where nerves were not a part of the Chinese-derived system of medical thought that was dominant until the Meiji period. *Shinkei*, the word now used to refer to this part of the body, was coined in 1774 to translate the Dutch *Zenuw* in a translation via Dutch of Johann Kulmus' *Anatomische Tabellen* (1722). In the early nineteenth century compounds of *shinkei* appeared, including *shinkei suijaku* (later used to translate neurasthenia), but at the time these referred solely to physical conditions. In the 1880s *shinkei* gained connotations of feeling and mind, while a Japanese–English dictionary that is an important source for historical lexicography defined *shinkei byō* as "nervous or mental disease."[20] The establishment of this sense of *shinkei byō* was insured by the confrontation of the emerging field of psychiatry with popular explanations of unusual human behavior as the result of possession by animals, particularly foxes. To discredit such ideas and legitimate their field, pioneering psychiatrists such as Kure Shūzō classified the *belief* that one has been possessed by a fox as a nervous disease, of physiological origin, that was the charge of psychiatry.[21] In such assertions that previous conceptions of mental disturbance were in themselves pathological and had to be overcome one glimpses the support that evolutionary social thought – already present in the idea of neurasthenia as a disease of civilization – lent to the medical disciplines that claimed responsibility for the diagnosis and treatment of nervous disorders.

These disciplines were increasingly at odds, however, and by the turn of the century they were dismantling neurasthenia and reapportioning its symptoms to form the twentieth-century fields of neurology, psychiatry, and psychology. The failure of Beard and his followers to find the physical pathology responsible for neurasthenia was a significant factor in the demise of the diagnosis, but the change was more fundamental. Beard's diagnosis encompassed both body and mind and had a strong social dimension, as seen in his assertions that the modern division of labor contributed to the development of the disease. In the early twentieth century, however, neurology as a discipline gravitated toward research on observable organic pathologies, in the process abandoning social commentary as unscientific.[22]

Psychiatry, meanwhile, established its disciplinary *bona fides* by reorganizing diagnostic categories by cause rather than symptom and stressing quantitative research, two directions promoted by the German psychiatrist Emil Kraepelin beginning in the 1880s, through which neurasthenia ultimately disappeared as a distinct diagnosis. (Kure introduced the revision of diagnoses that began in Germany to Japan in the 1890s.[23]) In many parts of the world, the somatic aspect of the disease lingered in the idea of inherited neuropathic constitutions, which through their association with theories of degeneration offered a scientific basis for stigmatizing the mentally ill and their families.[24] The increasing tendency, however, was to attribute melancholy and malaise to purely psychogenic causes. Freudian psychoanalysis, which came to dominate psychology, notably offered a purely psychogenic conception of mental distress. What most obviously disappeared in such a turn were the material social factors that had been an important part of neurasthenia.[25] In international medical circles the diagnosis was fully obsolete by the 1920s. Treatment of mental distress was divided between psychology and psychiatry, with less debilitating manifestations of what had been considered neurasthenia treated by psychologists as functional neuroses.[26]

Outside of medical circles, specialists' arguments were too arcane to diminish the metaphorical appeal of neurasthenia, letting it enjoy a different career. The affliction could express everything from individual discontent to the crises facing entire nations. (Beard appears to be the only commentator who took pride in a national tendency toward neurasthenia.) The great utility of neurasthenia came from the way its combination of physiological, psychological, and social causes could be juggled to support an enormous variety of opinions on the subject's relationship to changing social and economic conditions, from the daily routines of home, factory, and company office to the chronic competition for subsistence in capitalist economies. Critics who exploited neurasthenia to dissect the pathologies of modernity argued through rapid shifts between individual and social diagnoses, regardless of the positions they took. The feminist Charlotte Perkins Gilman charged in *Women and Economics* (1898) that primitive conditions in the home condemned women in the USA to a life of "nervous strain" and "waste of nervous force," the individual malady impeding overall social progress.[27] (During a miserable first marriage Gilman undertook a rest cure for her own neurasthenia, described in agonizing detail in the 1892 story "The Yellow Wallpaper.") The physician and journalist Max Nordau, in contrast, enlisted neurasthenia to condemn Symbolist poets, Nietzsche, and Wagner, among many others, as agents of moral and social disintegration in his acclaimed book *Degeneration* (*Entartung*, 1892). In Nordau's view technological innovation, industrialization, and urbanization were pitching people into neurasthenia and other nervous disorders at an unprecedented rate. Among artists and writers the result was a wave of "degenerate" art. Admirers transmitted the degeneracy they acquired as readers and spectators to their offspring, in Lamarckian fashion.[28] For Gilman, the epidemic of neurasthenia showed the need for social and economic reforms; for Nordau, moral and artistic vigilance. Their fundamental difference did not concern the nature of the malady but rather the proper response to the much greater forces believed to cause it.

In Japan, the novelty of the idea of nervous illness aided the use of neurasthenia to examine social problems only distantly related to its medical etiology. Initially, at least, terms such as nervous illness (*shinkei byō*) seem to have replaced fox possession (*kitsune tsuki*) and other common designations for mental disturbance without affecting many people's views of the causes.[29] San'yūtei Enchō's comic treatment of nervous illness, mentioned earlier, suggests the skepticism that physicians met as they promoted their theories. The connection of neurasthenia to the liberal theories of social evolution invoked by the Meiji government and civic reformers in their programs of "civilization and enlightenment," however, seems to have given neurasthenia an appeal in the social imagination that other nervous disorders did not enjoy. Neurasthenia made it possible to argue over the consequences of civilization in civilization's own language. Early on the affliction was associated with the vanguard of civilization. An 1890 article in the reformist magazine *Women's Education* (*Jogaku zasshi*) noted the danger neurasthenia posed to students, male and female alike, and warned against excessive study.[30] By the turn of the century writers in mass-circulation magazines such as *The Sun* (*Taiyō*) were warning that the increase in cases threatened the state and economy because of the special role that scholars, bureaucrats, financiers, and others who "labor the spirit" (*seishin o rō suru mono*) play in them.[31] On this basis Kure and prominent figures such as the statesman Ōkuma Shigenobu proposed confining the nervously ill to prevent them from harming society, which by this logic was not sick *per se*.[32] The view that neurasthenia was a disease of the age affecting all touched by the transformations of the period was increasingly common, however. One promoter of therapeutic hypnosis wrote in 1909: "Cerebro-neurasthenia [*nōshinkei suijaku shō*] may be considered the Meiji period's own endemic, intractable malady," the fierce struggle for existence and the complexity of modern learning increasing its incidence so much that "in a manner of speaking one should call it Meiji Disease [*Meiji byō*]." Nervous health is the key to thriving in an age where survival of the fittest is the rule.[33]

Although written to promote a cure, such comments suggest growing unease and indeed weariness with Meiji-era ideologies of success and striving. Neurasthenia took its place alongside concrete economic and social dislocations such as government-induced deflation, the impoverishment of former samurai, and the growth of slums in major cities as a consequence of civilization. The surge in discussion of nervous fatigue in the late Meiji period, one might say, was the result of an endemic "ideology fatigue," with the strains of mobilization during the Russo–Japanese War of 1904–1905 the immediate cause.[34] In Japan such appropriations of neurasthenia to express doubts about the rapid changes in social life since 1868 touched on both the relationship of the individual to new and transformed social institutions, but also the relationship of Japan, as a nation, to the European models of civilization against which Meiji ideology measured it.

Late Meiji writers such as Sōseki and Tōson offer particularly revealing examples of the possibilities and limits of neurasthenia as a vehicle for cultural critique. These writers were not only acutely aware of the changes that had occurred in Japanese society during their lifetimes, but also understood that their own work – written in the *genbun itchi* "vernacular" style and serialized in news-papers – was an aspect of the Meiji transformation. Although in some ways their work differs markedly – Sōseki is known for psychological realism and Tōson for creating several of the most important novels of Japanese naturalism – their appropriations of neurasthenia reveal a tension typical of many writers at this time, between the mandate to pursue the new that had been a part of the literary field since the 1880s and their own doubts about progress. To writers eager to learn of the latest developments in Europe, the "degenerate," neurasthenic literature they encountered through the work of detractors such as Nordau was the product of highly refined civilization *and*, perhaps, a symptom of social catastrophe.[35] Many late Meiji writers thus labored against the suspicion that their ambition to create a literature able to express their attitudes toward the society around them might be the sign of a sickness produced by that same society. Unlike Kure and Ōkuma, writers like Sōseki and Tōson rejected the idea that civilization could be insulated from its byproducts and questioned the clarity with which medical and political authorities distinguished the two. Perhaps because of the same self-doubt, however, their appropriations of neurasthenia tended to neutralize its political implications. Their position is reflected in both the characters and narrative form of *The Wayfarer* and *Spring*.

Sōseki diagnosed himself with neurasthenia in the early 1890s and described the condition in notes for his critical work *Theory of Literature* (*Bungakuron*, 1907) as a consequence of "self-consciousness." As mentioned earlier neurasthenic characters appeared quickly after he began writing fiction.[36] Around 1911 he seems to have embarked on a more intensive examination of the place of neurasthenia in Japanese society, most notably in the essay "The Civilization of Contemporary Japan" ("Gendai Nihon no kaika," 1911) and novels including *To the Spring Equinox and Beyond* (*Higan sugi made*, 1912) and *The Wayfarer*. The essay, which compares late Meiji civilization to the civilization of the "West," establishes many of the arguments on neurasthenia that appear in Sōseki's late work. Although the development of civilization is driven by efforts to diminish labor and increase pleasure, Sōseki says, competition increases with civilization's advance. Paradoxically, the anxiety and strain of civilized societies are no less than in the past and possibly greater.[37] The "special circumstances" of the development of civilization in Japan – the external forces that recently impelled it to take a particular form – further complicated its impact there. Civilization in the West (which Sōseki glosses as "civilization in general") is "intrinsic" (*naihatsu teki*), having developed "like a blossoming flower." As the result of external forces Japan faced in the Meiji period, however – essentially the threat of European imperialism – the civilization of contemporary Japan is "extrinsic" (*gaihatsu teki*) and displays two contrary tendencies.[38] Although many people try to pretend their civilization is intrinsic, it is fundamentally "superficial and shallow" (*hisō uwasuberi*) and leaves those who live such a lie feeling empty, dissatisfied, and anxious. The few who defy superficiality and try to cultivate a truly intrinsic civilization, by retracing the scientific discoveries of Europe from theory to successive theory, for example, develop neurasthenia because of the immense effort required. Because the circumstances of Japanese civilization force it to change merely mechanically, Sōseki says, "we either skim along its surface, or if we resolve not to slide and stand firm, we contract neurasthenia as a consequence."[39] Thus in "The Civilization of Contemporary Japan" neurasthenia is a disease of Japanese civilization's discontents, those cultivated dissenters who resist the dominant pathology of superficiality. Its appearance in Japan, moreover, does not indicate the advanced state of Japanese civilization, as neurasthenia does in North America and Europe (Sōseki predicted Britain would be the first country destroyed by neurasthenia), but rather the impact of semi-colonial domination.[40]

A conflict between the two national maladies of superficiality and nervous exhaustion marks the characters and form of *The Wayfarer*. Sōseki's treatment of neurasthenia in the novel dramatizes the critique of late Meiji society in "The Civilization of Contemporary Japan" and at the same time, curiously, reduces it to an emotional position in a way that suggests the limits of critique within the constraints Sōseki imposes on it. *The Wayfarer* centers on the relationship over roughly a year between the narrator, a recent college graduate, and his elder brother, a university professor prone to self-absorption. Early in the novel the brother asks that the narrator try to seduce his wife, whom he feels he cannot know or love. Refusing, the narrator nonetheless agrees to ask about her feelings toward her husband. She divulges little, but reveals that she muses frequently on the circumstances of her death. The narrator repeatedly postpones telling the brother what he has learned, seeding lasting resentment between them over the brother's strange demand and the narrator's negligence. Increasingly withdrawn, the brother spends more and more time alone in his study and begins to conduct research on telepathy and spiritualism. By this time a number of characters judge him to suffer neurasthenia. At the narrator's request, a university colleague named H takes the brother away on a walking trip. In a long letter to the narrator that forms the final part of the novel, H explains the brother's view of his spiritual struggles. Prior to the letter, important sections of the narrative are devoted to the narrator's observation of his brother's mental state and his speculation that the brother is moving from overwork through neurasthenia toward a state verging on madness, while H's letter imparts his own reflections on the brother's bizarre behavior and anguished state of mind.[41]

Through their actions the narrator and his brother personify the contrary tendencies discussed by Sōseki in "The Civilization of Contemporary Japan." In contrast to the brother's slide into neurasthenia Sōseki lets it be clear that the narrator is propelled by a shallow desire to avoid confrontation or recognition of human suffering, as when he avoids reporting his conversation with the brother's wife.[42] The two brothers' exemplifications of these tendencies, however, are complicated by the fact that they also remark them in each other. An initial indication comes in a comment by the narrator that "My elder brother had sensitive nerves, while I was excitable and impatient."[43] The brother, for his part, observes similarities between the narrator and their father, who had been a politically astute bureaucrat. "Isn't there something oddly frivolous about our father?" he asks the narrator, who responds: "In Japanese society today if you aren't that way you can't get anywhere, so can he help it? In the world there are people horribly more frivolous than father. You may not know that because you lead a highbrow life at school and in your study." The brother, in fact, concurs: "I do know ... There's no getting around the fact that in Japanese society today – and maybe in the West too – it's reached the point that only people good at being shallow [*uwasuberi no ojōzu mono*] can live." He insists that in their father's case, however, the tendency is innate. That the narrator tries to defend him is proof he takes after the father.[44] To the arguments that appear in "The Civilization of Contemporary Japan" the brother adds the suggestion that the plague of superficiality is hastened by the ability of the inherently superficial to thrive in such a world. Considering that the diagnosis is delivered by a man showing signs of debilitating neurasthenia, however, the brother is not a simple mouthpiece for Sōseki in such exchanges with the narrator. Through the brother Sōseki underscores the connection of neurasthenia to resistance to the superficiality of "extrinsic" civilization, yet the very fact of the brother's nervous disturbance casts doubt on the veracity of his objections.

The brother's major defense of himself comes via H's account of their conversations in his letter to the narrator. On one occasion the brother describes his daily life as one of constant anxiety because nothing he does brings him closer to his goals. The anxiety ultimately stems from the advance of science, he says, frightening because its relentless progress gives humans no rest. Although H agrees with this view of science, the brother retorts that his friend's fright is "just fright of the head," whereas he experiences "fright of the heart . . . a fright that lives and beats a pulse." He explains: "It's frightening because I have to experience in my life, alone, the fate that all humanity will arrive at several centuries from now . . . I mean that I experience fright that gathers the anxiety of all mankind into me alone and condenses it to the span of an hour or minute."[45] As Ochi Haruo observes, Sōseki's depiction of the brother's mental state shows an increasing stress in his late works on the psychological impact of civilization on his protagonists.[46] The physical aspect of his suffering is also strong, however: that the brother feels anxiety pulsing in his heart (Sōseki uses the anatomically specific *shinzō*) reflects the somatic character of neurasthenia. Neurasthenia thus comes to represent a spiritual and philosophical response to civilization. The brother explains that he aspires to a pure state of mind (*kokoro*) in which the world and everything in it would vanish, leaving only the self. Such a state, which he refers to as "the absolute" (*zettai*), would transcend not only the contemporary moment (*gendai*) but life and death. The ultimate cause of his unhappiness, he says, is that the more he understands his aspiration in abstract terms the more impossible it seems for him to accomplish it in practice.[47] What the narrator regards as near madness spawned by neurasthenia is in the brother's view exhausted frustration caused by his inability to find a philosophical position unaffected by the social instability and individual anxiety of modernity. Although H professes to being dull-witted in philosophical matters, in the closing passages of his letter he stresses the sincerity of the brother's aspirations, and implicitly the critical stance toward late Meiji society and civilization *per se* that inspires them, while warning of the gravity of the unhappiness that is their consequence.[48]

The Wayfarer ends with H's warning, providing no indication of the narrator's reaction to the letter. Formally, the novel comprises two distinct personal examinations of the brother whose conclusions could not be more different: the narrator becomes only more convinced that the brother's problems are caused by nervous exhaustion, while H regards his peregrinations as a sincerely pursued philosophical project. The two views are reconciled neither in the novel's story, for example in a conversation between H and the narrator, nor in its form, as they might be by a more elaborate framing of H's letter in which the narrator indicates his reaction. The bifurcated form resembles the pairing of the narrator and his brother as characters, and their tendency to comment on each other, but with a significant shift. In a strictly parallel transposition the narrator's first-person observations on his brother would be matched with a similar narrative by the brother about his sibling, but the place of the brother's voice is taken by H's letter about him. The form of the novel casts further doubt on the brother's critique of late Meiji society, which becomes something on which to reflect rather than act. In formal terms *The Wayfarer* calls only for recognition of the sincerely expressed anguish of the neurasthenic – regardless of his views of its causes – while stripping the condition of any specific indications about what is to be done. If for the narrator neurasthenia names the consequences of needless ratiocination, for the brother a philosophical impasse, and for H the sincerity of discontent, for the novel neurasthenia seems to name a self-doubt that becomes more incapacitating as the forces reshaping society appear more unstoppable and impersonal.

Like *The Wayfarer*, Tōson's novel *Spring* pursues a critique of the civilization of the Meiji period by pairing two characters who struggle in a shallow, hostile social environment. *Spring* too has a dual, albeit rather different, narrative structure that supports the novel's examination of responses to Japanese modernity. Tōson, however, enlists neurasthenia and broad notions of nervous illness to criticize the here-and-now without the detour through "civilization in general" found in Sōseki's treatment of late Meiji Japan. The novel begins as a *roman à clef* whose characters are recognizable as the young writers who animated the journal *Literary World* (*Bungakukai*) in the 1890s, including the poet Kitamura Tōkoku and Tōson himself. As he examines the frustrations of his generation, which one observer in the novel calls "the youth of the new age, battling forward," Tōson also takes a sympathetic position in contemporary debates over the generation that came of age after the Russo–Japanese War, which commentators considered individualistic, materialistic, and apathetic to national concerns. In one of the novel's most famous lines the neurasthenic poet Aoki (modeled after Tōkoku) declares that "Japan today is nothing but a tomb for youth." In the novel's "double vision" – to use Miyoshi Yukio's phrase – Aoki's indictment applies to the postwar period as well as the 1890s, and ultimately to the Meiji civilizing project as a whole.[49] Such a critical attitude toward Japanese modernity does not waver but the novel's form gradually shifts from a generational *roman à clef* to what later critics would call an "I-novel" that is focused on the character modeled on Tōson, Kishimoto. As Kishimoto labors to carry on alone the literary battles once waged by the group, the broad social critique of the early part of the novel narrows to a story of personal aesthetic struggles that are a markedly different response to the social changes of the Meiji period.

Spring is structured by a series of reunions of what the narrator refers to as "the group" (*renchū*), opening with Kishimoto's meeting with three friends near Mt. Fuji after an extended journey to Kansai. Early in the novel the gatherings are dominated by literary debates and lamentations over the indifference of society toward the young men's ambitions. At one gathering Aoki shouts of sepulchral Japan, "There's no life! Or originality! Naïve drivel, that's all the poetry you hear!"[50] Another member, Ichikawa, tells Kishimoto that the present age doesn't tolerate the dreams of the young. He wonders if they all were born too early.[51] Over three some years the gatherings' energy wanes as the enthusiasm of some cools and others seek practical ways to support their work. The drift from aesthetic fraternity to nostalgic companionship is punctuated by two events, Aoki's suicide and Kishimoto's departure at the end of the novel for a teaching position in Sendai that will support his poetry. Up to Aoki's suicide the narrative focus moves from character to character, supporting the novel's depiction of "the group" as representative of a generation. Although the longest sections of this first part of the novel focus on Kishimoto and Aoki, the two appear as first among peers. After Aoki's disappearance Kishimoto gradually becomes the novel's sole narrative focus. His increasing distance from members of the group is highlighted by the fact that his meetings with them are staged from his perspective. Although some critics argue that even in the beginning of *Spring* the other characters only serve to reveal Kishimoto's personality and state of mind, the narrowing of the narrative focus in the later part indisputably changes its thematics, from the anguish of a generation to that of an individual.[52]

Tōson's examination of the quandary of youth in the Meiji era pairs Aoki and Kishimoto from an early point. Aoki's wife Misao remarks the similarity of their temperments, each imagines himself in a metaphorical prison, and Aoki first attempts suicide with a dagger (he succeeds with a noose), a method that Kishimoto considers himself.[53] Aoki is described at the beginning of *Spring* as having a "nervous disposition" (*shinkei shitsu*), and the more his aesthetic ambitions are frustrated the more his nerves deteriorate. (The attention *Spring* gives to the decay of Aoki's nerves reflects the role that the degenerate body plays in naturalist mimesis.[54]) Kishimoto remarks that Aoki's recent work reveals "unfathomable anxiety" and may show him on the way to madness.[55] Struggling against intense fatigue and losing the will to write, Aoki meditates ceaselessly on his situation: "It became a habit, and even when there was no need, he thought," the narrator explains. "He thought, he thought, even worn out he still thought. There was hardly a moment when his mind was at rest."[56] The similarity to the brother's descent through neurasthenia into madness in *The Wayfarer* is unmistakable. Like Sōseki, Tōson ties Aoki's decline to larger trends. In an old letter that Misao finds after his death Aoki describes his condition in ways that entwine it with the history of Meiji Japan. According to the letter (drawn from a letter by Tōkoku), the first of many periods of "melancholia" (*kiutsubyō*) came when his teenage ambition for a career in politics was thwarted by the government's suppression of the campaigns for liberal democracy in the 1880s.

His indignation and anger "as a youngster of nervous disposition" sent him to bed for several months. Entering the university he resolved to battle the philosophy of survival of the fittest spreading to Japan from Europe, then to fight through political fiction in the manner of Hugo, only to face continuing despair as a result of his "brain disease" (*nō byō*) and a final fall from the ladder of worldly ambition.[57]

In an unremarked aspect of *Spring*'s compound vision, Aoki's story inserts nervous illness, the vocabulary of social critique in the postwar period, into the often observed passage of intellectuals in the 1890s from politics to a depoliticized literature. Although Aoki possesses a nervous disposition, his illness is precipitated by the collision of his idealism with the Meiji state and compounded by the indifference of society toward the poetry into which he transposes his aspirations. Tōson repeatedly underlines the connection between Aoki's "exhausted" nerves and the fatigue of such "battles with the world."[58] Or rather, Tōson uses nervous illness to indicate a fundamental conflict, greater than one poet's nervous dysfunction, between individuals and the priorities of the Meiji state: order and material progress. This is not an argument on a "neurasthenic Japan" of the sort Sōseki makes in "The civilization of contemporary Japan" and *The Wayfarer*. Rather it is an argument on "neurasthenic youth" who are driven to mental decline by the Meiji state and the society it has created. In *Spring* it is not "civilization" in its universal or national versions but the specific society of the Meiji here-and-now that pushes Aoki into nervous exhaustion and despair so severe that the only respite he sees is death.

Although Aoki's counterpart Kishimoto too contemplates suicide he arrives at an individualistic accommodation with the world. Noted early in the novel to have a "depressive temperament" (*ukkutsu shita seishitsu*), Kishimoto suffers from both uncertainty about his artistic ambitions and the frustrations of love for a former student.[59] He retreats for a time to a monastery in Kamakura and then, after renouncing the girl by sleeping with a prostitute, begins a pilgrimage to nowhere. Arriving at the coast he contemplates the sea, "a cold, meaningless tomb" where he might "bury his hopes, his love, his young life." Thinking it would be "pointless" (*tsumaranai*) to die when there is so much in the world that he does not know, however, he turns away.[60] It is not clear until after Aoki's death that such a commitment to experience, periodically reiterated, ultimately is a commitment to artistic creation. In his dark moments Kishimoto repeats to himself, "create, create," and as the life of the group becomes sterile he shuts himself up in pursuit of a "way" (*michi*) that would be his alone, a means to complete the work that Aoki left unfinished.[61] During this period the obligation to support his mother and the family of his brother, who has been jailed on suspicion of fraud, emerges as the greatest obstacle to Kishimoto's aspirations. He again considers suicide and emerges with a renewed commitment by reasoning that the obligation to "find his own way" is more important than the obligation to his family: "Everyone must find his own way. Not knowing even why one lives as one does, where would be the filial devotion in that?" As he departs for Sendai, where he will teach and write while sending money to Tokyo, he "dreams of a fantasy world not knowing when it would arrive," and thinks to himself, "Even as I am I want to live."[62]

Kishimoto considers himself Aoki's successor, but the denouement of Kishimoto's story shows that their responses to Meiji society differ fundamentally. Where Aoki's art was connected to the common undertaking of political struggle, and in some ways memorialized its failure, Kishimoto's is a personal undertaking. Of the surviving members of the group only he remains true to its artistic aspirations but is little different from the other members in drifting off alone. If Aoki's nervous exhaustion indicates a conflict with a misshapen society, and the difficulty of maintaining a critical view of it, we can say that Kishimoto's struggle is to find a desire to live (a "way") that such a society will condone. In concrete terms, for Kishimoto the question of how to live becomes one of money rather than ideals. Significantly Kishimoto, regardless of his depressive tendencies and the toil of supporting his family, never is described in the novel with the vocabulary of nerves or nervous exhaustion. The figure of the neurasthenic and the critical position neurasthenia indicates is replaced by a merely struggling artist in search of a way to live in rather than change the society around him.

The shift in the form of *Spring* from *roman à clef* to I-novel is often attributed to the appearance of Katai's autobiographical story "The Quilt" while Tōson was working on his novel. The change of genres underscores the difference between Aoki's and Kishimoto's responses to the predicament of a generation, however, and through the narrowing of the narrative focus supports the elaboration of Kishimoto's individualistic solution. It thus seems far from coincidental.[63] The genre shift is curiously similar to the bifurcation of form in *The Wayfarer*, which divides the narrator's view of his brother's slide into neurasthenia from the philosophical defense related by H. The change of genres in *Spring* isolates Aoki's critique in formal as well as temporal terms: Aoki's rejection of the society created by the Meiji state belongs to another form and another time, both seemingly left behind in the advance toward Kishimoto's "mature" commitment to the self at the novel's end. The difficulty Aoki's friends have grasping his motives for suicide (his wife's comment "I don't understand either" expresses a common sentiment) further suggests that for the survivors Aoki's critique may be ineffective if not meaningless, as the brother's critique in *The Wayfarer* is a matter for puzzled reflection rather than action for the narrator and H.[64] Where the brother's objections to Meiji civilization never gain their own narrative voice in *The Wayfarer*, however, Aoki's position is supported by a distinct formal apparatus in *Spring*. The discontinuity of genres both isolates and preserves Aoki's critique because it blocks a reading of Kishimoto's response as a simple overcoming of Aoki's despair. That Kishimoto's response requires a crass selfishness, identified unstintingly in the later scenes of the novel, moreover underlines its limitations when compared to the example offered by Aoki. The ambivalence that the narrative discourse of *Spring* displays toward Kishimoto, and Kishimoto's acknowledgment of his flaws in the novel's last line, suggest an ambivalence toward the desertion of Aoki's uncompromising position. Although the view of Meiji society that *Spring* elaborates through Aoki's demise is more pointed than the critique of "civilization" that *The Wayfarer* pursues through the brother's crisis, an element of self-doubt thus also runs through Tōson's novelistic appropriation of neurasthenia. Both novels seem unwilling to fully embrace or reject the critical view of late Meiji society that emerged from the debates over neurasthenia.

As the examples of *The Wayfarer* and *Spring* suggest, late Meiji appropriations of neurasthenia for social critique often arrive at an impasse whose traces can be found not only in overt arguments but also in aesthetic form. In literature, character pairings and bifurcations of narrative introduce conflicting responses to the Meiji-era reorganization of social, economic, and political life while insuring that they will remain unreconciled, as if the proposition of neurasthenia as a disease of civilization requires a suspension of judgment. The reasons for such a seeming failure of neurasthenia as a vehicle for critique reveal much about the reassessment of the Meiji civilizing project in the years after the Russo–Japanese War. Although neurasthenia disappeared from international medical discourse because the physical pathology of the nerves that Beard considered the cause could never be found, the collapse of the diagnosis among professionals meant little for those who used it in critical examinations of turn-of-the-century societies. Such appropriations of neurasthenia always exploited the medical etiology of the disease selectively. A more decisive factor was the entanglement of the condition, in both its medical and social variants, with liberal theories of social evolution. To argue that neurasthenia was a disease caused by the advance of civilization required recapitulating the underlying premise that societies by nature "advance," incrementally but irreversibly, with only a minor variation on the results. "Neurasthenic critique" thus reiterated the premises of the ideologies of progress, such as the ideology of nation-building that legitimated the transformation of Japan in the Meiji period, that were its target. Because liberal theories of progress were both its foundation and limit, such criticism could not but stop short of imagining a fundamental transformation of social relations in the manner of Marxism or a radical psychiatry.

Few late Meiji writers, however, showed much interest in breaking with liberal notions of progress or destabilizing the ideologies based on them. One thus should ask if the seeming impasse in writers' treatments of neurasthenia might have carried out positive ideological labor. The roles that neurasthenia plays in *The Wayfarer* and *Spring* suggest that the paired characters, bifurcated forms, and affect of self-doubt associated with novelistic treatments of the condition are ways of separating social critique from its application in practice. The complaints that the brother in Sōseki's novel and Aoki in Tōson's lodge against the hostile, shallow societies in which they live are utterly compelling and absolutely ineffectual. Action belongs to other characters, whose segments of the narrative tell stories of accommodation. The novels avoid measuring critique and practice against each other and question whether the two can ever meet. That such a separation of critique and practice becomes part of the novels' forms suggests that as a metaphor for the consequences of progress neurasthenia lent itself easily to aesthetic legitimations of political quietism, in the guise of resignation or a sense of belatedness.[65] Put another way, in the late Meiji period neurasthenia lent itself to the quietist legitimation of a particular aesthetic – an aesthetic of disheartenment and fatigue that was not the disappearance of politics so much as the severing of critical consciousness from worldly action. The conspicuous presence of neurasthenia in many works of the postwar period – with Tōson turning one of the most notable figures in the depoliticization of art, Tōkoku, into a neurasthenic and Sōseki presenting his many neurasthenic characters as epitomes of the dejected intellectual – shows that this disease of civilization played a crucial role in propagating such an aesthetic as the proper response to state-sponsored social dislocation. In the process the protean illness of neurasthenia, a confluence of psychological, somatic, and social forces, became the chronically unhappy consciousness that is such a durable theme of twentieth-century Japanese literature. And yet within this aesthetic the decaying body of the neurasthenic remains, an unbanishable reminder of such a turn from the world, at once a signifier of mourning for futures relinquished and of the possibility that they might be regained.

Notes

1. Yamazaki Masakazu (1986) *Fukigen no jidai*, Tokyo: Kōdansha, pp. 12–35.
2. Quoted in Kawamura Kunimitsu (1990) *Genshi suru kindai kūkan – meishin, byōki, zashiki rō, ariui wa rekishi no kioku*, Tokyo: Seikyūsha, p. 104. The title of the piece, published in shorthand form in 1888, is *Shinkei kasane ga fuchi* (*True Scene of Kasane Marsh*). *Shinkei* is written in characters meaning "true scene" but whose pronunciation homophonically suggests "nerves," as Enchō's preamble attests. The story seems to have originated in a different form, with a different title, in 1859.
3. Kawamura, *Genshi suru kindai kūkan*, pp. 108–9.
4. Nagai Kafū (1993) *Jigoku no hana*, Tokyo: Iwanami Shoten, pp. 28, 104.
5. Natsume Sōseki (1965) *Wagahai wa neko de aru*, Sōseki zenshū 1, Tokyo: Iwanami Shoten, pp. 508–10, 522–3; Tayama Katai (1972) "Futon," *Futon, Ippeisotsu*, Tokyo: Iwanami Shoten, p. 15; Iwano Hōmei (1955) *Hōrō*, in *Hōmei gobusaku*, Tokyo: Shinchōsha, Vol. 2, pp. 53–4; see below for *Haru* and *Kōjin*.
6. On the turn to images of disease, see Iwasa Sōshirō (1986) *Seikimatsu no shizen shugi – Meiji yonjūnendai bungaku kō*, Tokyo: Yūseidō, p. 141. On tuberculosis and dominant morality, see William Johnston (1995) *The Modern Epidemic: A History of Tuberculosis in Japan*, Cambridge, MA: Harvard University Press, pp. 131–2.
7. Roy Porter (2001) "Nervousness, eighteenth and nineteenth century style: from luxury to labour," Marijke Gijswijt-Hofstra and Roy Porter (eds) *Cultures of Neurasthenia from Beard to the First World War*, Amsterdam: Rodopi, pp. 31–3. The phrase "The English Malady" was coined by Scottish physician George Cheyne in 1733.
8. George M. Beard (1869) "Neurasthenia, or nervous exhaustion," *Boston Medical and Surgical Journal* 3(13): 217–18; *American Nervousness: Its Causes and Consequences*, New York: Putnam, 1881, pp. 5, 9–13, 96. Van Deusen (1869) proposed his diagnosis in "Observations on a form of nervous prostration (neurasthenia), culminating in insanity," *American Journal of Insanity* 25: 445–61.
9. Beard, "Neurasthenia," p. 217; *American Nervousness*, pp. vii–viii; F. G. Gosling (1987) *Before Freud: Neurasthenia and the American Medical Community, 1870–1910*, Urbana: University of Illinois Press, pp. 10–11.
10. Beard, *American Nervousness*, 22, pp. 96–8.
11. George M. Beard (1880) *A Practical Treatise on Nervous Exhaustion (Neurasthenia), Its Symptoms, Nature, Sequences, Treatment*, New York: William Wood and Co.
12. Doris Kaufmann (2001), "Neurasthenia in Wilhelmine Germany: culture, sexuality, and the demands of nature," *Cultures of Neurasthenia*, p. 164.
13. Robert Nye (1984) *Crime, Madness and Politics in Modern France: The Medical Concept of National Decline*, Princeton: Princeton University Press, pp. 134–49.

14. Watarai Yoshiichi (2003) *Meiji no seishin isetsu – shinkei byō, shinkei suijaku, kamigakari*, Tokyo: Iwanami, p. 160; Kawamura, *Genshi suru kindai kūkan*, pp. 82–6; Beard, *American Nervousness*, pp. 162–3.
15. Gosling, *Before Freud*, pp. 14–15; Janet Oppenheim (1991) *"Shattered Nerves": Doctors, Patients, and Depression in Victorian England*, New York: Oxford University Press, p. 92.
16. Gosling, *Before Freud*, pp. 17, 19–25.
17. Tom Lutz (2001) "Varieties of medical experience: doctors and patients, psyche and soma in America," *Cultures of Neurasthenia*, p. 58.
18. Gosling, *Before Freud*, pp. 9–10.
19. Regenia Gagnier and Martin Delveaux (2006) "Towards a global ecology of the Fin de Siècle," *Literature Compass* 3(3): 572–87.
20. Arao Yoshihide (1983) "Shinkei," *Kōza Nihongo no goi*, Vol. 10, Tokyo: Meiji Shoin, pp. 236–7. The definition of *shinkei byō* appears in the third edition (1886) of J. C. Hepburn's *Japanese–English Dictionary*. The translation of neurasthenia did not stabilize until the 1890s; alternative translations included *shinkei kyosui* (lit. nervous debility) and *shinkei shishō* (nervous stimulation). Watarai, *Meiji no seishin isetsu*, pp. 159–60.
21. Kawamura, *Genshi suru kindai kūkan*, pp. 82–6, 90–1, 99.
22. Lutz, "Varieties," p. 58.
23. Volker Roelcke (2001), "Electrified nerves, degenerated bodies: medical discourses on neurasthenia in Germany, circa 1880–1914," *Cultures of Neurasthenia*, pp. 187–8; Kin Yoshiharu (1998) "Nihon ni okeru seishin shitsugan gainen oyobi bunrui no jidai hensen," *Rinshū seishin igaku kōza 1*, Tokyo: Nakayama Shoten, pp. 441–2.
24. Roelcke, "Electrified Nerves," p. 184; Kawamura, *Genshi suru kindai kūkan*, p. 89.
25. Kaufmann, "Neurasthenia," pp. 165–6; Roelcke, "Electrified Nerves," p. 188.
26. Lutz, "Varieties," p. 64; Kaufmann, "Neurasthenia," pp. 164–5.
27. Charlotte Perkins Gilman (1966) *Women and Economics: The Economic Factor Between Men and Women and Women as a Factor in Social Evolution*, New York: Harper, pp. 155–6.
28. Max Nordau (1993) *Degeneration*, Lincoln: University of Nebraska Press, pp. 34–44, 556–7. Nordau, a Hungarian Jew, practiced medicine in Paris while writing for German and Austrian publications.
29. Kawamura, *Genshi suru kindai kūkan*, pp. 105, 116.
30. Yabunaka Shun"an (Iwamoto Yoshiharu) (1890), "Danjo seito no shinkei suijaku," *Jogaku zasshi* 204(March 15): 17.
31. XYZ (anon, 1902) "Shinkei suijaku shō – sōkosha, bunshi, kanshi, gakusei shōkun no ichidoku o yō su," *Taiyō* 8(7, June 5): 134.
32. Ōkuma Shigenobu (1906) "Seishin byō ni taisuru zakkan," *Shinkeigaku zasshi* 4(12): 622–3; Kawamura, *Genshi suru kindai kūkan*, p. 89.
33. Morishita Yūdō (1909) *Shinri ōyō nōshinkeisuijaku hitsujisaku*, Tokyo: Hakubunkan, pp. 3, 20.
34. On postwar fatigue, see Yamazaki, *Fukigen no jidai*, pp. 109–10.
35. Kamakura Yoshinobu (2002) examines the complex reception of Nordau's work in "Shizen shugi bungaku to Makkusu Norudau – 'Daraku ron' no yomare kata," *Kokubungaku gengo to bungei* 119: 68–73. Appraisals of Nordau, many by writers who contributed to the rise of a naturalist school, began to appear in Japan in 1901.
36. Natsume Sōseki (1986) "Danpen," in Miyoshi Yukio (ed.) *Sōseki bunmeiron shū*, Tokyo: Iwanami Shoten, p. 311. On Sōseki's self-diagnoses, see Miyamoto Moritarō (1997) "Seishin suijaku to bunmei – Natsume Sōseki to Uiriamu Jeimuzu," *Seiji keizai shigaku* 373(September): 2–6.
37. Natsume Sōseki, "Gendai Nihon no kaika," *Sōseki bunmeiron shū*, pp. 14–17, 21–3. A translation is available as "The civilization of modern-day Japan," Jay Rubin (trans.) in *Kokoro: A Novel and Selected Essays*, Latham, MD: Madison Books, 1992, pp. 257–83.
38. Sōseki, "Gendai Nihon no kaika," pp. 25, 26.
39. Sōseki, "Gendai Nihon no kaika," pp. 33–4, 35, 36.

258   *Christopher Hill*

40. Sōseki, "Danpen," p. 312.
41. Kawamura Kunimitsu (2002) "Sōseki to shinkei suijaku – 'Kōjin' to sono shūhen kara," *Sōseki kenkyū* 15: 86. For examples of the narrator's observations, see Natsume Sōseki (1966) *Kōjin*, in *Sōseki zenshū* 5, Tokyo: Iwanami Shoten, pp. 467, 470. *Kōjin* has been translated as *The Wayfarer* by Beongcheon Yu, Detroit: Wayne State University Press, 1967.
42. For other examples, see Sōseki, *Kōjin*, pp. 578, 585.
43. Sōseki, *Kōjin*, p. 463.
44. Ibid., pp. 583–5.
45. Ibid., pp. 709–11.
46. Ochi Haruo (1985) *Sōseki to bunmei*, Tokyo: Sunagoya Shobō, p. 36.
47. Sōseki, *Kōjin*, pp. 738–9, 742. In the brother's aspiration to transcend contemporary times Sōseki refers to a well-known remark by the critic Takayama Chogyū. See Furukawa Hisashi's notes in *Kōjin*, p. 825, note to p. 739, line 14.
48. Sōseki, *Kōjin*, p. 759.
49. Shimazaki Tōson (2000) *Haru*, Tokyo: Iwanami Shoten, pp. 106, 107; on the novel's historical vision, see Miyoshi Yukio (1993) *Shimazaki Tōson ron*, Tokyo: Chikuma Shobō, pp. 243–4, and Uryū Kiyoshi (1999) "Tōson no shinjidai ishiki to Haru," *Fukuoka kyōiku daigaku kiyō dai-ichi bu bunka hen* 48: 4; Oka Yoshitake (1982) examines the postwar debates on youth in "Generational Conflict after the Russo–Japanese War," *Conflict in Modern Japanese History: The Neglected Tradition*, Tetsuo Najita and Victor Koschmann (eds), Princeton: Princeton University Press, pp. 206–11.
50. Tōson, *Haru*, p. 107.
51. Ibid., pp. 186, 243.
52. On other characters as foils for Kishimoto, see Kōno Kensuke (1990) "'Seishun' to iu tekusuto: Shimazaki Tōson Haru o megutte," *Bungaku ni okeru nijūdai*, Satō Yasumasa (ed.) Tokyo: Kasama Shoin, pp. 126–32.
53. On their temperaments, see Tōson, *Haru*, pp. 61–2, 110; visions of prison, pp. 145, 269; suicide by dagger, pp. 153, 285.
54. Tōson, *Haru*, p. 6. On naturalist mimesis, see my essay "The body in naturalist literature and modern social imaginaries," in *Tradition and Modernity: Comparative Perspectives*, Beijing: Peking University Press, 2007, pp. 348–63.
55. Tōson, *Haru*, pp. 82, 85.
56. Ibid., p. 136–7.
57. Ibid., pp. 208, 209, 210–11.
58. Ibid., pp. 107, 132. That Aoki suffers physically as well as psychologically thus is an important aspect of both his life and art. On this point I differ with Michael Bourdaghs' view that Aoki's struggle is only spiritual, in contrast to the corporeal suffering of Katsuko, Kishimoto's former student, who dies in childbirth. One might say instead that because public indifference contributes to Aoki's nervous ailment his suffering is in the social domain, while Katsuko's is in the domestic sphere that Tōson asserts is her natural place. The same would be true of their respective writings. See Michael Bourdaghs (2003) *The Dawn that Never Comes: Shimazaki Tōson and Japanese Nationalism*, New York: Columbia University Press, pp. 126–9.
59. Tōson, *Haru*, p. 42.
60. Ibid., pp. 100–1.
61. Ibid., pp. 251, 253.
62. Ibid., pp. 285, 299.
63. On the impact of Katai's story, see for example Miyoshi, *Shimazaki Tōson ron*, pp. 166–7.
64. Tōson, *Haru*, p. 213.
65. On the expression of belatedness in late-Meiji narrative form, see Jonathan E. Zwicker (2006) *Practices of the Sentimental Imagination: Melodrama, the Novel, and the Social Imagination in Nineteenth-Century Japan*, Cambridge, MA: Harvard University Asia Center, pp. 201–5.

12 Introduction

Kazushige Shingu:
Freud, Lacan and Japan

"Japan" has been a rich source of material for psychoanalysis. Sigmund Freud mentioned Japan twice in his writings: once in describing the taboos surrounding the emperor (or "Mikado") during the Edo period, and once in a reference to the totemic feasts practiced by the Ainu tribes of Hokkaido. And Jacques Lacan, as we mentioned in the introduction, famously argued that the Japanese were unanalyzable. Kazushige Shingu draws our attention to each of these instances in which "Japan" figured in the imagination of Freud and Lacan. Shingu suggests that underlying both men's understanding of Japan was an interest in the unsettling but productive tension between unity and multiplicity, sovereign subjectivity and the fragmented self. To take one example, the Mikado as Freud described him with the help of Engelbert Kaempfer, may have been sovereign in name, but he was also subject to the most outrageous taboos on his person and relieved of temporal power by the Shoguns who ruled in his place.[1] This model of power and subjectivity, Shingu suggests, has continued relevance in Japan today in what he calls the "muted national debates over the responsibility of the tennō (the Mikado at the time) for the war." But it is also, we might add, a fascinating model for thinking of subjectivity itself as something deeply riven by ambivalence, vulnerable to the incursions of the other, and yet capable of wielding enormous *symbolic* power.

Of course the power of the Symbolic, as Lacan has taught us, comes only at the price of castration. But what if castration itself were to lose its traumatic power? This possibility, it seems, is what made the Japanese immune to analysis according to Lacan. In place of the tyrannical either/or logic of Western phallocentrism, Lacan thought that Japan was blessed (or cursed) with a writing system and an honorifics that somehow made obvious and unremarkable the central premise of psycho-analysis: that something always gets left behind (or cut off) when we try to put our bodies into language. Lacan saw in Sada, the woman in Ōshima Nagisa's *In the Realm of the Senses* who blithely cuts off her dead lover's penis and carries it around Tokyo with her, a feminine jouissance that threatens to negate the symbolic phallus, hence symbolic castration, or the process that produces the subject-as-subject in language through the repudiation of jouissance, the elision behind the signifier, and the production of that piece of the real around which desire accrues, and which falls away from the subject as *objet a*. However provocative this reading of Oshima's film might be, Shingu cautions against extending it into a theory of

Japanese culture in general. He is reluctant to concede the importance of castration and its corollary, the experience of the "unary trait," to a Japanese psychoanalysis. Shingu concludes his essay with a sensitive reading of a dream recounted to him by a Japanese patient that shows that in fact any Japanese who is alienated within Japan can indeed find the unary identification necessary to castrate him (or her) into subjectivity.

Note

1. Freud, Sigmund (1950) *Totem and Taboo*, James Strachey (ed. and trans.) New York: W. W. Norton, pp. 56–7.

12 Freud, Lacan and Japan[1]

Kazushige Shingu

Freud and Lacan on Japan

Sigmund Freud was born when Japan was still in its pre-Meiji isolation from the outside world, and during his younger days, information on Japan remained scarce. It is therefore hard to imagine that he encountered discourses that would have aroused his interest in the island nation. Nonetheless, Freud touches briefly on Japan in *Totem and Taboo*.

In this work, Freud cites Sir James George Frazer's quotation of Engelbert Kaempfer's 1727 description of the Mikado as an example of how outrageous taboos have been imposed on kings. Freud reproduces and comments on Kaempfer's description as follows:

> . . . "The idea", writes Frazer, "that early kingdoms are despotisms in which the people exist only for the sovereign, is wholly inapplicable to the monarchies we are considering. On the contrary, the sovereign in them exists only for the subjects; his life is only valuable so long as he discharges the duties of his position by ordering the course of nature for his people's benefit . . . An account written more than two hundred years ago reports that the Mikado . . . thinks it would be very prejudicial to his dignity and holiness to touch the ground with his feet; for this reason, when he intends to go anywhere, he must be carried thither on men's shoulders. Much less will they suffer that he should expose his sacred person to the open air, and the sun is not thought worthy to shine on his head. There is such a holiness ascribed to all parts of his body that he dares to cut off neither his hair, nor his beard, nor his nails. However, lest he should grow too dirty, they may clean him in the night when he is asleep; because, they say, that which is taken from his body at that time hath been stolen from him and that such a theft doth not prejudice his holiness or dignity. In ancient times he was obliged to sit on the throne for some hours every morning, with the imperial crown on his head, but to sit altogether like a statue, without stirring either hands or feet, head or eyes, nor indeed any part of his body, because, by this means, it was thought that he could preserve peace and tranquillity in his empire; for if, unfortunately, he turned himself on one side or the other, or if he looked a good while towards any part of his dominions,

it was apprehended that war, famine, fire, or some other great misfortune was near at hand to desolate the country."

... Weighed down by the burden of their sacred office, kings became unable to exert their dominance in real affairs and these were left in the hands of inferior but practical persons, who were ready to renounce the honours of kingship. These, then, became the temporal rulers, while spiritual supremacy, deprived of any practical significance, was left to the former taboo kings. It is familiar knowledge how far this hypothesis finds confirmation in the history of old Japan.[2]

This passage brings to mind a patient of mine who, after awakening from a catatonic state, offered the following explanation of the immobile condition she had experienced: "I believed that if I moved my limbs or fingers even slightly, everyone's body would go to pieces. That's why I stayed all stiff and rigid." The patient experienced an extraordinary sense of one-ness with the world as a whole. Likewise, the subjects of the Mikado may have imposed an extraordinary taboo against movement on his person for similar reasons. This sort of taboo is not unique to Japan; Freud also cites a report of a tribe in the South Pacific that loses its candidate for king as a result of a similar, extremely unnatural custom – an episode he interprets as an expression of ambivalence of the son for the father.

During his stay in Japan, Kaempfer's life must have been confined to a small area in Nagasaki city, far from the imperial capital of Kyoto where the Mikado resided, due to the narrow restrictions that the Shoguns (Japan's *de facto* rulers during this period) imposed on foreign visitors. His impressions, then, must have been based on Japanese books (including some authentic ones) as well as the reports of local informants. Considering these circumstances, his detailed description of the taboo on the Mikado may seem especially incredible, but it is not unlikely that the Shoguns made much of the Mikado taboo to ensure their own political dominance. In this regard, the Shoguns of the Edo government were effective Freudian psychologists. I would suggest that such manipulation of social dynamics is a tradition of the Japanese government that persisted even beyond the Second World War, in the muted national debate over the responsibility of the Tennō (the Mikado at the time) for the war.

Another reference by Freud to Japan concerns the Ainu tribe (Aino in the Standard Edition). The taboo on the Mikado and the customs of the Ainu seem quite a well-balanced combination of cultural references, whether intentionally or not, in light of the historical relationship between the Japanese royal court and the Ezo, as the Ainu were derogatorily called.

Freud describes various characteristically "animistic" customs of the Ainu such as the well-known "Bear Feast", a good example of the totem feast. In this custom, all members of the community participate in killing, eating, and grieving over the totem animal. Thereafter, all participate in a fanatical orgy, for having eaten the totem, the members of the community are imbued with sacred life, and identify with each other completely. Freud argues that the totem animal is a substitute for the father, ambivalence towards whom is indicated by the coincidence of grief and fascination at the feast.

In interpreting both the Mikado taboo and the totem bear in terms of ambivalence, Freud may sound exceedingly mono-focused, but Freud's recognition of the remarkable importance of the animism that imbues the life of the Ainu reveals that animism is exactly what is missing in the case of the Mikado taboo; the animistic way of thinking is, so to speak, repressed into the body of the Mikado, and is no longer accessible to his subjects. Freud argues that animism provides the most consistent and comprehensive view of the world. It can be devalued as superstition, but it nonetheless lives on under the surface of modern language, belief, and philosophy.

In fact, animistic arguments are often found in magazines and newspapers, especially in the language of articles on ecological subjects. What such language implicitly values most highly is the emotional experience of union with nature. In such rhetoric, the language system merges into Nature, gaining the power to encompass all other arguments. Animism thus comes to possess the "omnipotence of language", as Freud puts it, providing for the indispensable need to explain the world (that is, to have a *Weltanschauung*).

The Mikado's Japan, after many years of war against the Ainu, faced a deficit of animism for which Buddhism came to compensate. The Buddhism of the time taught that inherent in every tree and every blade of grass resided the Buddha. This teaching may no longer be considered consistent with Buddhism, but faced with the impulse towards animism of the Japanese people, the Buddhism of the time did not hesitate to provide it. Indeed, Japanese Buddhism found its function in doing so, and developed into a tremendously eclectic system encompassing the pre-existing autochthonous religions (a system known as the merger of Buddha and the gods). Under this belief system, the Japanese now lead lives endowed with a religious-imperialistic politics capable of absorbing their ambivalence toward the father, as well as an animistic religious philosophy that is always available.

Yet essential aspects of Buddhism were also conveyed to Japan, and have been preserved in contemporary Japanese Buddhism, and in this regard comments by Lacan are germane. Lacan visited Japan twice, first in the early 1960s and again in the early 1970s. Soon after his first visit, he conducted a seminar on anguish in which he enthusiastically introduced a Japanese Buddha image in the form of a photograph he circulated.[3] The image was said to represent a Nyo-i-rin-Kan-non. "Nyo-i" means "according to the will". Because psychoanalysis deals with desire, this Japanese word must have attracted Lacan's attention. In his seminar, Lacan taught that the central proposition of Buddhism is that desire is illusory. Yet if this is true, the subject who "wants" to teach this truth must himself be elided as an illusion, but just before vanishing can appear as an object of desire for others. It can also be said that if desire desires to be true, it must desire to have its truth as an object. And if this last desire is to be realized, its truth must come in the form of an object that is destined to be an illusion. If this ultimate object of desire vanishes, it is Buddha, but at the last moment before vanishing, it appears as Kan-non.

Castration symbolizes the final vanishing of desire. From beyond castration, something rare returns to appear as an object of desire; thus did Lacan introduce the Buddha image. This explanation is congruent with the everyday beliefs of the Japanese people in regard to Buddha, and may even expand our understanding of our individual relationships with the Buddha. That most Buddha images are made with an ambiguous sexuality must be related to castration.

Are the Japanese unanalyzable?

In preparing for his second visit to Japan, Lacan studied the Japanese language. During the course of his studies, a singular idea seized him: he began to suspect that because of the inherent nature of their language, the Japanese were neither in need of psychoanalysis nor analyzable. In accordance with a way of life balanced between Mikado politics and Buddha-merged-with-the-gods animism, the Japanese language balances between *on yomi* and *kun yomi* (two ways of reading and pronouncing the ideographic characters, or *kanji*, of written Japanese), and this frustrates the process of true repression, or the aphanisis of the subject in relation to language. The subject is born and exists in a state of being pinched between these two ways of reading and pronouncing.[4] This positionality is manifested in the lines (*traits*) of Japanese orthography. Japanese subjects are visible to themselves in the form of their written characters. It is as if the men in black on the bunraku stage oscillate between being visible and invisible.

Divided not only in speech and writing, the Japanese subject is fragmented in the formality system of the Japanese language, in which a variety of modal expressions indicate social situation, and grammar requires different declensions according to these modalities; there are also multiple terms for the first-, second-, and third-person pronouns. Notwithstanding this fragmentation, or more correctly, owing to it, the Japanese subject maintains unity through a principle of constellation: the Japanese see themselves reflected in the social-institutional hierarchy, which they perceive as being as eternal as the celestial bodies. Thus, the Japanese seem to be exempt from the anxiety of aphanisis that arises at certain times in life. For such people, psychoanalysis is neither necessary nor possible.

While it is true that the pious Japanese man praying before the Buddha image depicted by Lacan in his seminar of 1963[5] differs greatly from the Japanese subject satisfied by the illusory unity provided by fragmentation, whom Lacan denounced in *Lituraterre* in 1971,[6] both are true descriptions of the Japanese. If the Japanese are to decide between the two self-images, the decision is up to us, whether we make it with the help of psychoanalysis or not.

To locate a psychoanalysis that is meaningful for the Japanese, let us consider Lacan's comments on the subject more closely. As is well known, Lacan recapitulated his views on psychosis in relation to James Joyce in one of his last seminars.[7] Joyce was born in Ireland, and in due course, Lacan came to address Catholicism. "Catholics" said Lacan, "are unanalyzable". Jacques-Alain Miller responded to this comment by pointing out that Lacan had said the same thing about the Japanese.

In reply, Lacan began to comment on the Japanese film *In the Realm of the Senses* (*L'empire des sens*). This topic may not seem to speak directly either to Miller's point or to ours, but it is not without relevance. Lacan described the intensity of Japanese feminine erotism, which in his view belongs to the order of *fantasme*; by pointing to the turn of plot in the film in which the heroine, Sada, carves off her lover's penis only after she has killed him. If this were an act of castration in a proper sense, she would have done so while he was still alive. To cut it off after death means that for Sada, what is important is the play of the penis, or the on-off phenomenon of the organ (ϕ and -ϕ). (Incidentally, the film was based on a true story; it is well-known in Japan that the real-life Sada was carrying the ϕ with her at the time of her arrest.)

For psychoanalysis to work, symbolic castration must be possible; in other words, the desire for the Other should be introduced by the signifier "ϕ". According to Lacan, this symbolic phallus cannot be negated.[8]

However, given the extreme intensity of Sada's *fantasme*, the signifier "ϕ" is at risk of being negated and rendered back to the play of "ϕ and -ϕ". This is the very risk entailed in Japanese psychoanalysis. This explanation accords with a widely held belief of Japanese popular cultural psychology that Japanese families tend towards a combination of strong maternal and feeble paternal roles. Whether Lacan was attempting in his own terms to express this notion or really wanted to engage in such speculation is not known, but feminine erotism in itself, however intense, cannot render analysis impotent. Hence, let us return to the crucial period when the idea of the unanalyzability of the Japanese occurred to Lacan.

As I have discussed, the Japanese writing system, in particular the Japanese ideographic characters, or kanji, are at the root of Lacan's pessimism about psychoanalysis in Japan. If the Japanese subject really were poised between *on yomi* and *kun yomi*, the aphanisis of the subject would not be possible. Symbolic castration would be blocked, in favour of the *fantasmes* of the Sada type, and the rediscovery of the subject through the *objet a* in the process of psychoanalysis would be longed for in vain.

Mr. Jean-Louis Gault, one of the secretaries of the *Groupe franco-japonais du champ freudien*, explains how Japanese kanji might work in analysis concretely. In Japan, one series of sounds may be written in several possible ways in kanji, because there are so many homonyms in Japanese. Of course, this occurs in French as well: the sound – *dϕ* may be fixed by the letters "*deux*" (two) or "*d'eux*" (of them). It is difficult to find cases of the reverse in French, however, for in French one series of orthographic symbols determines almost univocally one series of sounds. In contrast, Japanese kanji, through *on yomi* and *kun yomi*, can lead to two or even more series of sounds.

The effects of this difference are profound. According to Lacan's argument in *Lituraterre*, writing (*écriture*) is at best a semblance of truth, but it also has a connection with truth. It is when analytic discourse touches the real, especially the corporeal real, and brings about some product in the form of writing, that truth is revealed in the analytic space. Formulae in physics are a good demonstration of the function of writing of representing truth. Psychoanalytic fixation points, it bears noting, are writing that performs this function. In fact, when a fixation point for the subject comes to the fore in analysis, it betrays subjective truth. It is one of the properties of the "instance of the letter", as "reason since Freud", that it manifests the relationship between truth and the fixation point.

However, if a single instance of writing can lead to multiple signifiers, as in writing using Japanese kanji, the relationship between writing and truth is to a great extent relativized. Writing itself falls to the status of a signifier among other signifiers.

In the Japanese writing system, this relativization occurs because of the assignment of phonemes of both Japanese and Chinese linguistic origin to a single character. Writing does not require the subject to confront his own destiny; he is allowed to stop thinking, sustained in a state of balance between Japan and China that might be called interpretation, or rather, auto-interpretation. In other words, the Japanese have access to an "instance of the letter" more systematically and more directly than the analytic "instance of the letter" in the proper sense of the term. This salvages the Japanese subject from the unconscious, satisfying him with a collective myth of the history of Japanese culture. In Lacan's view, the Japanese subject is divided between "reference to writing and the act of speech", and it is natural for such a subject to live as an interpreter between the two.[9] Faced with this condition, psychoanalytic interpretation is invalidated or rendered superfluous even before it is given.

When the system of formality in the Japanese language is also taken into consideration, the Japanese subject emerges as being not only divided but also pulverized. Or as Lacan puts it, the Japanese subject "relies on the constellated sky, rather than on the unary trait, for his primordial identification".[10] The primordial identification, as Freud conceptualized it in *The Ego and the Id*, is the premise for the analysis of the Oedipus complex. Lacan's perspective on the structure of the unconscious of the Japanese subject may make the prospects for psychoanalysis in Japan look pretty dismal. Lacan himself felt a shiver of unease during his visit to Japan, from which he recovered completely only upon returning to France.[11]

Japanese people are all forced, in effect, to live within the haunted or perhaps enchanted world of the Japanese writing system. Therein the Japanese have invented multiple practices for enjoyment, such as *waka* and *haiku*, two well-known examples of arts in which the equivocal relation of the letter to the signifier is utilized to the utmost.

Is psychoanalysis possible in such a cultural context? In the published version of *Lituraterre*, Lacan suggests that the Japanese subject's reliance on the "constellated sky" is only comparatively more important than his reliance on the "unary trait". In his lecture, however, Lacan seems to have said that it was almost out of the question for the Japanese to find the unary trait. His pessimism about psychoanalysis in Japan is thus definite. Yet, I would like to suggest that the potential of the Japanese to rely on the unary trait might be greater than Lacan thought.

Writing and the unary trait in Roland Barthes

The potential that I have in mind is suggested by Roland Barthes's beautiful *L'Empire des Signes* to which Lacan also refers. In this book, Barthes discusses his experiences of various Japanese cultural elements as writing (*écriture*).[12] For instance, Japanese cooking for Barthes is an accumulation of traits or lines. In my view, Barthes finds in Japan, beyond all particular writings, the unary trait in the Japanese eye. Barthes writes:

> The several traits which compose an ideographic character are drawn in a certain order, arbitrary but regular; the line, beginning with a full brush, ends with a brief point, inflected, turned away at the last moment of its direction. It is this same tracing of a pressure which we rediscover in the Japanese eye. As if the anatomist – calligrapher set his full brush on the inner corner of the eye and, turning it slightly, with a single line, as it must be in painting alla prima, opens the face with an elliptical slit which he closes toward the temple with a rapid turn of his hand.[13]

What is the meaning of the "slit" to which Barthes refers? It appears on the faces of the Japanese, foreigners to Barthes, but it is a place from which he can behold himself. What he witnesses in this slit, then, is the slit of signifiers, or the signifier as a primary slit. It comes to him in the form of a line, reminding him of an incision in the skin by an anatomist.

It is all the more necessary when one is in a foreign country to find a place from which to watch oneself. Or rather, it is only upon finding such a place that one can watch oneself. Barthes visited Japan, found himself in the midst of a crowd, and discovered a renowned self-awareness.

This act of Barthes's is consonant with Lacan's argument in his seminar of 1964. The unary trait is something by which man marks himself on the world. Man counts himself as *a* person. Man's self-awareness is none other than the act of counting. "I showed you", says Lacan, "the traces of this first signifier on the primitive bone on which the hunter makes a notch and counts the number of times he gets his target".[14]

Such a primordial experience is just what the unary trait offers to human beings. The subject begins to be aware of its being by situating itself in it. It originates there and dwells there, counting itself from there. It can thus be conscious of itself only because that place is devoid of any characteristic; it is just a line, but a fundamental line in the absence of which any concept of unit or unity would be erased from this world. The constitution of this line allows us to abstract a universal property of oneness from all entities, human or astral, sets or objects. In my view, such a line or slit is what Lacan conceptualized as the unary trait. It might be the eye of God, but even in the absence of God, this trait is a structural necessity for humans, which Barthes rediscovered in a foreign country in the line-like eyes of foreigners.

It was Barthes who situated himself in the unary trait he found while living among the Japanese, but this is what the Japanese subject, as a matter of course, can also experience when he is placed in an estranged position. For any Japanese subject who is alienated in Japan, and situated in "foreignness" in some way or another, it is possible while still living in Japan to experience the unary trait. This is the potential for analysis I have in mind.

A case of anxiety and the *objet a* in Japan

When we are forced into a situation in which we experience "foreignness", we feel anxiety; according to Lacan's reading of Freud, this anxiety is proximity with the *objet a*, and the anxiety that we feel is the signal of the approach of the *objet a*.

Let us consider how anxiety and the *objet a* function in the Japanese subject. Becoming independent from one's family does not necessarily entail any experience of "foreignness", but in the case I shall discuss here, the subject is alienated from the unity of the original family in a somewhat particular way; an estrangement, though apparently maturational, lies behind the case.[15]

One day, a patient burst into the consulting room, literally breathless from running. He was so anxious he could not stay in one place for two minutes at a stretch. It was the first time he had sought psychiatric help, and he had been driven to do so by a dream he had had that morning.

> I was clinging to this dried-up old tree. Underneath was mud. I couldn't get down even if I wanted to. Then I noticed that there were all these corpses floating in the mud. I hung onto the tree even tighter, and then I woke up. I was so freaked out I didn't know what to do with myself. What's going to happen to me? What does my dream mean?

In analysis he remembered something that had happened before he had the dream. His sister, who was married and had been pregnant, had had an abortion. I interpreted immediately. The corpses floating in the mud were the aborted fetus, and that fetus was him.

Some time later, he went home, and yelled at his parents, "The baby Kyo aborted is me!" The analysis transformed his anxiety into this single, true utterance. Of course, his words strike us as utterly meaningless at first, and in all likelihood, either he himself or his parents ultimately interpreted it to mean, "I was never loved, just like the baby she aborted!" But the true essence of psychoanalytic interpretation lies in making contact with the meaninglessness that flashes momentarily in his cry.

When we hear a member of the South American Bororo tribe (made famous by the research of Claude Lévi-Strauss) say, "I am a parrot," we are assailed for an instant by the feeling of a meaningless blank, a feeling of radical unfamiliarity. Originally most people thought that the sort of totemic thinking behind the utterance of the Bororo was pre-logical, but Lévi-Strauss demonstrated that it was in fact a complex and systematic body of thought;[16] and in the essay on aggressivity, Lacan points out that even the utterance "I'm a man" ultimately contains the same logical difficulties as the totemic statement – the basic contradiction of stating that "one" is any "other".[17]

When our patient declared, "I am the aborted child!" he foregrounded this logical difficulty, but at the same time he enabled himself to shoulder the difficulty squarely, and assume it afresh. It is plain to see why he fell into such acute anxiety. He had placed his mirror image in safekeeping inside his pregnant sister's womb, comfortable in the idea that it could thrive there free from harm. (Of course, it was not just since his sister became pregnant that he had situated his mirror image inside her, rather it had occurred long before, when the "deflection to the social" first took place at the mirror stage. She had first taken on his specular self.) Instead, it was destroyed without warning, and the result was the corpses in his dream – the carcasses of countless repeated identifications tried and discarded before he arrived at the self of the specular image. It was to remind himself that the grim denizens of the dream were in fact his own cast-off husks (to acknowledge their *identity* with him) that he announced that he was the aborted child.

The object of his anxiety is these denizens, who are also avatars of the *objet a*. On the other hand, where does he find the unary trait for him? As a matter of fact, he resides *in* it. If it is now possible for him to recognize that he and his sister have been in such a tight relationship, it is because he is looking at himself from the viewpoint of his family, his lineage, his origin. Once his family was where man witnessed his birth as a human being. This familiar place had gradually been obliterated through his sister's marriage. Now he is recuperating this place for him, and is verbalizing his identity.

As we can see from this case illustration, the unified self-image is squirreled away inside the other, unbeknownst to the subject itself. Against this, the thing that constitutes our origin is left isolated, a corpse smashed and scattered and abandoned to the winds. In this case, the specular image the patient had secreted away inside his sister was obliterated by chance events of his sister's making, and his fragmented internal body image was revealed starkly in his dream. When his anxiety drove him to the analyst, he was looking for a place where he could reconfirm that this body image was in fact his own.

We can fairly say that, in the case of such important dreams as this one, the dreamer is almost never the subject themselves. Rather, the way the subject appears *to the other* is inscribed into the dream. The other dreams, and we, are merely "dreamt", as it were. It may sound mystical to say that an other dreams within us, but in fact it is no different from Bertrand Russell's assertion that we should say, "It thinks in me," rather than "I think";[18] a comment he made in the context of a highly rational argument. Because of the fragility that the structure of self-referentiality implants in human thought, this sort of interference from the other (and the Other) is unavoidable. In the dream, we do not so much encounter the other, as become the Other.

From this perspective, the subject appears as the *objet a*, that is, we rediscover ourselves from the viewpoint of this Other. Anxiety is that which indicates the approach of this object. In the case we have considered, this anxiety was interpretative, and the interpretation was effective. The patient's acute anxiety became transformed into his unique utterance. The modern structure of self-referentiality, which is nothing other than totemic identification and identification through mirror image, was brought into the subject's clear view by the interpretation.

Reflecting on this analytic experience, I hesitate to share Lacan's pessimism about the analyzability of the Japanese. It should be noted that my patient was experiencing a degree of "foreignness" due to his own life history, and it was this that made the analysis effective. Discussion of whether analysis itself can engender such "foreignness", a requirement for progress in analysis, lies beyond the scope of this essay. One can only hope that the possibility of analysis is not necessarily obliterated by the duplicity of Japanese writing and the pulverization of the subject. In any case, Lacan's observations will continue to make Japanese analysts attentive to the structure of the subject as determined by language.

Acknowledgment

This chapter was presented as a paper, at Manchester Psychoanalytic Matrix on 3 April 2006, and was originally published in the Summer 2005 edition of *The Letter: Lacanian Perspectives on Psychoanalysis* 34: 48–62 (Dublin: APPI).

Notes

1. The paper was first presented at the 2nd International Conference of the Japanese–Korean Lacanian Psychoanalytic Groups, 5 March, 2005.
2. Engelbert Kaempfer (1727) *The History of Japan*. J. C. Scheuchzer (trans.) (London, 1727). (The English translation was published earlier than the German edition: *Geschichte und Beschreibung von Japan*. [Hrsg, Dohm: C. W., Lemgo, 1777, which was based on another manuscript].) Cited in Sir James George Frazer (1911) *Taboo and the Perils of the Soul* London: Macmillan; Sir James George Frazer (1922) *The Golden Bough*, 3rd edn. London: Macmillan, Part II, and in Sigmund Freud (1953–1974) *Totem and Taboo, SE*. XIII, London: Hogarth Press, pp. 44–7.
3. Jacques Lacan (2004) *Le Séminaire de Jacques Lacan, Livre X, L'angoisse*, 1962–1963, J. A. Miller (ed.) Paris: Éditions du Seuil, pp. 257–64.
4. Jacques Lacan (2001) *Lituraterre, Avis au lecteur japonais, Postface au Séminaire XI*, in Jacques Lacan (2001) *Autres Écrits*, Paris: Éditions du Seuil, pp. 11–20; 497–9; 503–7.
5. Lacan, *Le Séminaire, Livre X*, pp. 262–3.
6. Lacan, *Lituraterre*, p. 19.
7. Jacques Lacan (2005) *Le Séminaire de Jacques Lacan, Livre XXIII, Le Sinthome*, 1975–1976, J. A. Miller (ed.) Paris: Éditions du Seuil, pp. 126–8.
8. Jacques Lacan (1997) *Écrits: A Selection*. Alan Sheridan (trans.), New York, W. W. Norton, p. 320.
9. Lacan, *Autres Écrits*, p. 19; 498.
10. Ibid. p. 19.
11. Ibid., p. 505.
12. Roland Barthes (1970) *Empire of Signs*, R. Howard (trans.), London: Jonathan Cape, p. 36. Original: *L'Empire des Signes*. D'Art Albert Skira, Paris: Flammarion.
13. Ibid., pp. 103–6.
14. Jacques Lacan (1977) *The Four Fundamental Concepts of Psycho-Analysis*, Alan Sheridan (trans.), New York: W. W. Norton, p. 256.
15. This case is taken from my recent publication, Kazushige Shingu (2004) *Being Irrational: Lacan, the Object a, and the Golden Mean*. M. Radich (trans.) Tokyo: Gakuju shoin, pp. 110–12.

16. Claude Lévi-Strauss (1966) *The Savage Mind,* Chicago: University of Chicago Press, p. 42.
17. Lacan, *Écrits: A Selection*, p. 23.
18. Bertrand Russell [1921] (1971) *The Analysis of Mind,* London: George Allen & Unwin, p. 18.

13 Introduction

Jonathan E. Abel:
Packaging desires . . .

In the 1950s, the average Japanese woman had one, or at most two pairs of underwear. By the 1980s, she had dozens. This explosive proliferation of panties was made possible by sophisticated marketing campaigns that made "Japanties" into a cultural phenomenon and a crucial stop on the circuit of male heterosexual desire. Jonathan Abel tells us all about this fascinating social and economic history of underwear while at the same time engaging in a speculative reading of how underwear itself, thanks to its ambiguous status as a tool of censorship, a sign of lack, and a fetish object in its own right, might actually help us to think psychoanalytically. More useful even than Lacan's notion of "suture," "lack" or "split subjectivity," panties, particularly as they appear to work in 1970s *roman poruno* film, might provide the paradigm for a new theory of subjectivity that does not depend on worn-out binaries of presence and absence, public and private, sign and signified. Perhaps most crucially for this volume, Abel suggests that an Area Studies that continues in its obsession with uncovering the authentic "Japan" or the real "Asia" might have something to learn from the underwear fetishist who understands that it is not what the panties hide, but the panties themselves that produce desire and motivate knowledge.

13 Packaging desires

The unmentionables of Japanese film

Jonathan E. Abel

Does the English word "unmentionables" really not mention? Are certain nether regions actually hidden by the Japanese phrase 隠し所 (*kakushi dokoro*, lit. the hidden place)? In practice, these terms do not hide and do not not-mention; rather they are the means by which private parts are publicized. They signify something that has been deemed worthy of hiding or packaging in euphemism. When the collective speakers of the words have decided something ought to be hidden or disguised, language changes to accommodate. When the language signals what ought not to be mentioned, how aware is an individual speaker of the continued hiding performed by the words? When do these euphemisms cease to function as euphemisms for something else? How does filmic language recast these terms of apophasis?

Since at least Freud's interpretation of fetishized lingerie as a substitute in a moment of lack, underwear has rarely been seen as desirable in and of itself, but rather as a desire displaced, a substitute for a lack elsewhere. As highly valued and extremely overpriced commodities, skivvies may also represent Marx's commodity fetish par excellence. The underpants shown again and again in the studio porn of postwar Japan are the result of the interaction of these economic and sexual desires. The place of underpants in postwar Japan, and more specifically in postwar Japanese film, provides the grounds for questioning the degree to which sexual fetishes can ever be said to transcend commodity fetishes and likewise to which market value can ever be said to exist outside of structures of desire and erotics. Rather than explaining them solely within the terms of Freud and Marx, the functions of underpants in Japanese studio porn film may best be understood through Lacanian critical language developed for revealing split subjectivities.

From the underwear boom of the late 1950s through the refinement of panty design in the 1960s and innovations in marketing and distribution in the 1980s with door-to-door sales, to vending machines in downtown Osaka today which sell the purportedly unwashed underpants of high school girls, underwear has played a central, if somewhat cloaked, role in consumer education and desire.[1] But in the classic studio sex films of the 1970s, the fascinating role played by underwear is not as readily apparent. Continually flashed, scratched, cut, and torn, underpants are featured as both a substitute for the object of sexual and commodity desire and as the object of desire itself. As such, the functioning of underpants in the famed

Nikkatsu *roman poruno* films (a series of studio sex films from the 1970s and early 1980s) provides a particularly useful way of thinking about desires split between covering up and presenting through packaging. Stretched across the crotch connecting the public and private, the mainstream and the obscene, *roman poruno* underpants are perfect screens for projecting the vortex drawing in the realms of the imaginary, symbolic, and real.

Peeling off the historical, theoretical, and filmic layers of the production of underpants and their images in Japan reveals their function as neither a lack nor a substitution, but as the desired. Japanese underpants may be a fetish for a covering, packaging, or wrapping, but as such the covering has ceased to cover, the packaging has ceased to package, and the wrapping has ceased to wrap; in short, the panties do NOT need to be stripped away to reveal modes of desire, consumption, aesthetics, and politics—for they are as clear as the flowery patterns and bright colors of the undies consumed across the Japanese nation. Representing moments of filmic signification that can help us articulate new understandings of criticism, the flash of panties in *roman poruno* are spaces of filmic paralepsis that name without naming the status of desire, that bind the subject with the object of heterosexual male desire, and that publicize otherwise private desire. Here, of course, emphasis will be less on the thing itself than on the play of the thing in the shot, the function of panties as they are celebrated and detourned through the spectacle on the screen.[2]

In her 1989 theoretical musing *The Theater Under the Skirt: Why People are Hung Up on Panties*, cultural critic Ueno Chizuko attempts to elaborate the desires behind underwear, making a distinction between the narcissistic desire of women who collect underpants and the fetishistic desire of males who obsess over them. While Ueno divides the reason for women choosing underwear into two categories – sex appeal (to arouse the desire of men) and narcissism (stemming from women's own thoughts on how they appear or feel),[3] she does not consider why what appeals to heterosexual men is appealing. On the basis of her argument and photos included in the book, it would seem that the largely solid color pants of Nikkatsu's roman poruno are entirely out of place. Rather Ueno suggests that it is the diaphanous and crotchless variety alone that holds particular allure for heterosexual men, not the generic and often pattern-less undies of the used panty shops. While Ueno is correct that an entire variety of flashy, gaudy, gauzy, overtly erotic underwear exists for what seems like the sole purpose of arousing viewers, the existence of this variety of garment does not preclude the possibility that the flat appearance of the everyday, generic bundle-packed type of underwear might have a similar effect precisely because they seemingly reject the explicit sexuality of the other variety. In Ueno's account, passage through the material to the real object of desire is necessary for the male consumer of feminine undergarments; women purchase, collect, and otherwise consume the underwear, while men consume the female body through and underneath the mitigating membrane of underwear. However, the often solid, plain, quotidian underpants that appear in *roman poruno* from 1972 to 1984 seem to work against this view, privileging not a desire for the revealing and transparent, nor for the opaque and occluded, but rather for the occlusion and packaging themselves.[4] Scenes that feature underpants in Nikkatsu films of this period take the material as a block and a wrapping, a convenient and highly-valued cover, rather than a passage to the body. What is the history of this desire and consumption of the cover? How did this screen hiding the female crotch become for a brief moment the crux of Japanese porn?

From underhair to underwear and back again: a brief history of pubic desires in modern Japan

> Gossipers gawk outside the apartment building of the town panty thief who has been arrested. His girlfriend who runs a lingerie café (ranjerī kissa) enters his living-room where a note to her is posted: "Thank you, my scanty (skimpy, tight underpants) doll." She gets on her bicycle with presumably his collection of underpants in her basket and bikes all over town throwing panties at the faceless apartment buildings shouting, "stupid, stupid, stupid!" at no one in particular. Finally she dumps the remaining underpants in a river. The underpants-shaped balloon that advertises the lingerie café rises out of the river, the theme music fades up, and the credits role.

This finale to *Scanty Doll: Scent of the Just-worn* (Mizutani 1984) exaggerates the focal position of underpants in Nikkatsu's famed *roman poruno*, but raises perplexing problems for understanding the historically-formed modes of male desires the entire series exposes. Here at the dawn of Adult Video and the new modes of covering that would accompany it, the film posits a nostalgic view of a period not yet entirely passed when underpants could be both a cover and plot device. What could possibly explain a woman throwing underpants at a world that just doesn't understand? How in under a century did Japan go from being a country where women did not generally wear underwear to one where panties could form the fetish of millions, the grist for narrative, and the material of sexploitation? A brief history parallels and provides a stunning, shrouded comparison to the rise and decline of the economic powerhouse that was modern Japan in the twentieth century.

On one hand, we could say that there was always underwear in Japan. If the tales of nobles burdened to the point of immobility by layers upon layers of robes, which themselves were signs of rank, are of any indication, it would seem that undergarments have been at least as important as those garments worn on the surface since at least the Heian period. And yet, on the other hand, the history of Japanese women donning underpants as we know them, modern underpants, covering and protecting the private parts of the pubes, is relatively short. At the turn of the twentieth century, in the general absence of female underpants, pubic hair itself became an object of the male fetish in the Japanese metropolis, where stories of perverts collecting the woolly remainders left behind on department store floors, park benches, train seats, and film theater pews circulated widely.[5] As in the USA, where the Hays film code "forbade males with heavily matted chests"[6] resulting in the necessity of body hair shaving and giving rise to the contemporary fetish for shaved and waxed, pubic hairless bodies, Japanese fetishes surrounding the pubes have changed over time and relate directly to particular imposed restrictions on the consumption of the body through filmic images.

In Meiji and Taishō, women's underpants were a rarity such that in the sanitizing, reforming post-Great Tokyo Earthquake moment of December of 1923, Shitagawa Hekoten published a cartoon beseeching, "Women of Japan, Wear Drawers!"[7] Yet despite this sort of effort to have women wear native loincloths (the boxer-short-like *sarumata*) or the fashionable and expensive Western drawers (*zurōzu*) being imported in small numbers, undergarments that covered the pubes did not become part of mainstream daily women's wear in Japan until the postwar period. Even though Occupation soldiers brought many of the daily novelties of American life to mainstream Japan, such as chocolate and kissing, they failed to bring *pantsu* to the masses. While the rapid democratization and Americanization ushered in with the Occupation saw the rise of "sports, screen, and sex," it did not see women wearing underpants in vast numbers. And in the context of starvation, rebuilding a country, and generally figuring out life outside of wartime mobilization, it is not surprising that the underpants, which were never a part of mainstream daily life before, could seem like a frivolous luxury.

Although in no major sense an origin for the popularization of *shitagi*, the "W. Underwear Exhibition" held at the Osaka Sogō department store in 1955 provides a convenient beginning to the history of the relationship of mainstream Japan to underwear. The exhibition was a major advertising venture that sought to create a market from virtually nothing through the appeal of Western fashion. It made a splash in the newspapers, leading to subsequent underwear exhibitions in a variety of department stores across the country. Bringing historical examples from the West together with the latest contemporary designs, the exhibition normalized and publicized the wearing of underwear and is generally taken as the beginning of the underwear boom (*shitagi būmu*) of the late 1950s. Inspired by the exhibition, panty designer and underpants activist Kamoi Yoko only three years later produced and directed *Underwear Makes the Woman* a film about freedom, feminism, and the power of underpants to effect change. The film continues the work of the exhibition to bring to light what had been enshrouded in secrecy and privacy, celebrating underwear most notably by projecting images of panties tied to balloons, floating through the atmosphere, released for retrieval by Japanese women across the nation.

But publicity stunts alone were not sufficient to bring underwear into daily lives of Japanese. The advent of the washing machine solidified the fate of *shitagi* as the up and coming fashion commodity and sexual fetish. Underpants are labor-intensive commodities requiring frequent cleaning. The relative lack of ability to perform the required cleaning is attested to in a 1956 *senryū* (poetry akin to limerick in its affinity to the ribald) that joked about a typical situation: "as you darn your socks, your underwear lies filthy."[8] But all that changed in the course of a few years; in "1955 most Japanese had still never seen a washing machine" but by 1960 over 6 million households owned one.[9] And this shift in the prevalence of washing machines accounts for the rapid proliferation of underpants described by Inoue Shōichi in his *We Can See Your Panties*: in 1946 even dancers, whose livelihood depended to some degree on possessing, wearing, and flashing their underpants every day, only had one pair; in 1951 some women had as many as two pairs; by the 1960s contemporary statistics estimated around 13 pairs per woman; and by the 1980s fashion magazines were claiming 200 per woman might be adequate.[10] Takeda Naoko notes that by 1976, underwear sales were a 150 billion yen a year industry.[11]

Though a variety of underpants designs were available to interested thrifty women at least in DIY format from mid-Meiji through the 1950s, skimpy and colored underpants were not generally available for mass consumption through ready-to-wear styles until the late 1960s, coinciding with and in large part spurred on by the worldwide miniskirt boom (1968–1973).[12] Kamoi Yōko's role in the shrinking of underpants in Japan was pivotal. Not only were her activities promoting underpants as a commodity and a fetish through public underpants showings with live models a big hit, but her revolutionary puny designs that she labeled "scanties" (appropriating a word from the 1920s in American culture that had long gone out of fashion) began their journey into the mainstream. According to Kamoi, scanties were both *scant* and *scan*dalously scant panties.

In order to understand the refining of the fetish over the 1970s and the return of the pubic hair fetish in the 1990s, it may be necessary not only to reflect upon the sudden skimpification of panties during the miniskirt boom, but also to consider the history of one of the primary, mainstream venues for presenting and publicizing images of underpants to men – Nikkatsu's *roman poruno* film series. The brief history provides some bounds to the project of analyzing underpants in these mainstream softcore films. The lack of underpants in premodern, early modern, and prewar Japan limits the scope of underwear analysis here to films portraying modern and contemporary situations (*gendai geki*), excluding period films (*jidai geki*). During the height of the series, panties reigned in contemporary films as the package or cover of choice, while extra-diegetic blocks on viewing (framing, black boxes, blurring portions, digital mosaics) dominated the period films. This aesthetic changed by the mid-1980s such that extra-diegetic blocks on viewing began to dominate even in films of contemporary stories. Finally, "underhair" (*andāhea*) or "hair nude" (*hea nūdo*) returned in the adult films of the mid-1990s as the aftershocks of the "no panty" (*no-pan*) boom of the 1980s, which, as the term itself suggests, was a new fetish arising directly out of the negation of the past panty fetish.[13]

The flash of panties: the gradual de-briefing of Japanese cinema

As with the changes in the fashion of undergarments enabled by the entrance of one electrical appliance – the washing machine – in the Japanese home in the early part of the 1960s, purchases of another appliance – the television set – led directly to shifts in the focus of capital and frame of lens in some film studios. Between 1971 and 1988, Nikkatsu (one of the big three studios in Japan) maintained its solvency in the face of the threat posed by the cathode ray tube through the production and distribution of roughly 600 films in what the studio dubbed its *roman poruno* series.[14] The term refers not to a coherent genre of film (there are over 60 subgenres within the series according to the Nikkatsu website)[15] so much as mega-category of film in which sex and images of naked female bodies figured predominantly; the films are around 70 minutes in length with a nearly bare body scene every 10–15 minutes. Having witnessed the existence of a potentially lucrative market defined by a growing number of independent "pink films," Nikkatsu's new series was created as a concerted effort to use its studio and distribution powers to garner market share and, thereby, rescue the company from impending bankruptcy.

Early in the history of the series, Nikkatsu suffered some setbacks. Despite having received approval of the Ethics Board (*Eirin*), the day after the debut of their film *Love Hunter* on January 18, 1972, the Tokushima Prefectural Police raided the Kansai office of Nikkatsu, seizing videotapes that were to have been distributed for consumption at love hotels. Two days later, members of the Nikkatsu staff were arrested under accusation of distributing obscenity to minors through the motels and love hotels. Then on January 28, two other films were seized: *Office Lady: Scent of a She-cat* and *High School Girl Geisha*.[16] The *Asahi* newspaper article covering the seizures and arrests explained "There Cannot be 'No Underwear': Police Headquarters Explains Reason for Prosecution of Nikkatsu's Porn."[17] The police would go on to comment that the "frank portrayals of sexual intercourse with men and women not wearing underwear" meant that "the story was created for the purpose of showing acts of sexual intercourse" and, therefore, was obscene (*waisetsu*).[18] The solution for Nikkatsu was clear: frontal shots of female actresses necessitated underpants.[19]

This revealing police stipulation was certainly not the origin for an underpants fetish in Japan, yet the police encouragements fostered the latent fetish. And Nikkatsu's reaction of upping the number of scenes featuring underpants would enhance the burgeoning fetish. In the years directly prior to the overt police statement that offending film scenes would have been acceptable if the women had worn underpants, the underpants frenzy had reached something of a crescendo with the skirt-flipping (*sukāto mekuri*) fad of 1969 and 1970. In that year, a Maruzen gasoline television commercial featured pop star Ogawa Rōza in a famed appropriation of the well-known scene from *The Seven Year Itch* in which Marilyn Monroe thrills over an exhaust grate. In the advertisement, the 23-year-old model and singer rides in a white convertible wearing a short, white A-line skirt, go-go boots, and a white riding helmet with goggles. In a shot considered risqué at the time, she shifts her bare legs and the car into high gear. This is followed by the sportscar speeding by a billboard displaying Ogawa in the same outfit. As the wind rushes by the billboard in the wake of the speedster with Ogawa in the driver's seat, the skirt of the billboard Ogawa flies up revealing her white panties and we hear the tag line "Oh! Intensity!" (*'Oh! Mōretsu!'*). The final image so pushed the envelope of the televisual possibilities that it became an instant hit. The popularity of the billboard image led Columbia records to use it on the cover of Ogawa's record "Tears felled by the wind" (*"Kaze ga otoshita namida"*) released later that year (Figure 13.1).

Figure 13.1 Cover of the record album
"Tears Felled by the Wind"
reproduced from the image
on the Maruzen gasoline
billboard.

Two events that took place within a year of the Maruzen commercial's debut set the stage for both the police comments and for Nikkatsu's response. Perhaps more directly relevant to Nikkatsu's *roman poruno* series than the television advertisement itself, the October 1969 issue of *Adult Films* magazine contained a multi page photo spread (Figure 13.2) and an article directly connecting the advertisement to the film industry. The magazine feature summarized a charity show at the Adult Film Festival where young pink filmstar Aihara Kaori's bra and panty set fetched 1,500 yen at auction. In a direct reference to the Maruzen gasoline ad campaign, the spread is headlined with "Oh! Intensity, Pink Actresses Line-up."[20] This event not only testifies to the growing fetish for panties, but also directly relates the fetish to the filmic experience. What was already the case for several independent pink film ventures (that they consciously appealed to prurient desires through the flash of panties), would become codified with the police seizures at Nikkatsu.

Even prior to the police seizures, the studio was aware of the importance of underpants on screen. Nikkatsu's own live action film version of Nagai Gō's

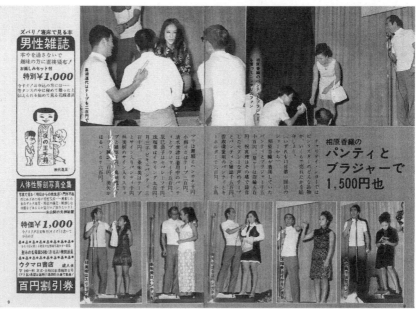

Figure 13.2 Sex Films Magazine October, 1969. "Oh! Intensity, Pink Actresses Line-up: Performance and Charity Show at the Adult Film Festival."

Shameless High, which was released in May of 1970 (before the police call for underwear), gives some idea of what the police would have found palatable. The film is punctuated by moments of flashing undies via skirt flips (*sukāto mekuri*) and various other contrivances. In the first scene, at a high school graduation, the vice principal's *happi* coat is flipped up to reveal his *fundoshi* (traditional t-back loincloth worn by men). Later, a young female teacher's skirt is lifted to reveal her predictably white bloomers, and the teacher in a history class demands that all of his female students remove their school uniform, insisting that bra and panties are the uniform for his class. In the manic chase scene that concludes the film, the one girl whom the audience knows is not wearing underpants beneath her uniform is pursued by a mob of teachers. Told that they should not flip her skirt up because she is panty-less, all admit that this is precisely what they would like to do. Here in this early moment, Nikkatsu's panties are portrayed simply as a covering that covers something else itself highly desirable, a substitute for something else that exists, the signifier of an absent presence.

What underpants had provided Japanese film was "not so much a system of censorship as an alternative to one: a system by which . . . censurable content could be coded and codified so as to avoid censorship."[21] While it is clear in this early example that Nikkatsu was already aware of this possibility prior to the police seizure in 1972, the seizure itself made the code explicit. What Richard Maltby writes of gaps and fissures in Hollywood storytelling is equally apropos to underpants at Nikkatsu during the 1970s and early 1980s. That is, if a cut away from lovers followed by a presumably post-coital cigarette translates to sex for some viewers of *Casablanca*, the flash of panties in Nikkatsu's films was to be equivalent to showing the naked female pubes for some viewers of Japanese porn but deemed completely natural to others – a smooth part of diegesis, not a substitution for something else, but rather just underpants. The equivalence, however, was not to last long as the fetish evolved its function from a substitute for the covered, substituted female genitalia itself into a valued object of desire of itself. Later films taking place in contemporary times are less concerned with using "natural" diegetic covers or packages like underpants and creative framing for the private parts; this new lack of concern is evident in the proliferation of extra-diegetic covers like black boxes and digital "mosaics" covering the dirty bits in post-*roman poruno* Adult Video (AV). But this shift coincides precisely with a growing recognition that the covering alone (and not the revealing) stimulates sexual desire in Japanese porn. What André Bazin argued for pin-ups is only partly true for what would become of *roman poruno*: "The precise balance between the requirements of censorship and the maximum benefits one can derive from them without lapsing into an indecency too provocative for public opinion defines the existence of the pin-up girl, and clearly distinguishes her from the salaciously erotic or pornographic postcard."[22] The presumed salaciousness of the later forms were defined more directly and explicitly by the censorship system than far more subtle modes of conformity to which *roman poruno* adhered.

Overrating underwear: theories of Shitagi

As with many new commodities, for which not only new consumer desires must be stirred, but also thoughts, beliefs, and theories must grow to support and promote daily use, so too with underwear in Japan; attempts to explain the logic, place in society, and role of underwear in modern desires abound. This rich commentary on *shitagi* and *pantsu* in Japan provides one local version from the global fetish for underwear warming the hearts and loins of millions. In Japan, the discourse on the new mass product over the long postwar rise to affluence took on a particularly corporeal aspect. In the 1950s, underwear was viewed as a practical foundation that would make the clothing layered on top of it look correct. In the 1960s, it began to be considered as an indispensible part not only of everyday life, but also as an extension of the body itself. By the 1980s, underpants could be used both for the self and for the other. Underpants occupy a nexus of in-between values in contemporary society. They span the crotch in between us and our clothes, our world, the public. Thinking about the space of the underwear exhibition in a department store, Takeda Naoko writes: "In order to make the transition from 'underwear that is embarrassing' to 'underwear you want to show,' it was necessary to have a place separated from reality that regular people could easily enter."[23] The physical space of the exhibition was both public and individual, such that viewers did not have to feel embarrassed to be seen walking in and that they could experience the underwear displayed alone. The success of the exhibition itself then was predicated on structuring itself like underwear – something betwixt and between – a thing for private consumption and public pleasures, and the personal pleasures of public consumption. Underpants are between our legs. They are in between commodity fetish and sexual fetish. They are private wear that are occasionally made public. This conundrum of underwear's mediation of public and private seems to have annoyed author Yasuoka Shōtarō who wrote the following on the early *shitagi* boom: "it's not underwear, and yet it is not worn on top. I don't know whether it will help, but there is nothing else but to call it a thing to be shown."[24] In Japan, theorists of underwear have been concerned with a range of such issues, but few have discussed the role of this interstitial underwear in the desire of both its wearers and watchers.[25]

The most prevalent common feature of theorizations about underwear made from the 1950s to the 1970s is their view of underwear from the standpoint of the wearer. Writing at the height of the first underwear boom of the mid-1950s, Fujita Yukiko published *Underwear Classroom* (1958), a major argument for the importance of underwear, including a history of underwear, designs for the do-it-yourselfer, and suggestions for when to wear it. In this classic interpretation of underwear, Fujita commented on the usefulness and pleasure of wearing a variety of colors to a readership that had only begun to think about wearing panties, let alone what colors they were. In the book, she emphasized the "the fun of wearing colors."

> Just saying the words "the colors of underwear" I can somehow feel a light ambience. Wearing colorful underwear is fun for everyone regardless of who

they are. Depending on the mood of the moment, or the atmosphere of the place you are going you can choose a color and it's a gas:

White – Of the color called white, one imagines the words pure and innocent. Let's call it the representative color because it gives an elegant and pure feeling. I want to recommend hygienic white for everyday going to school or work.

Pink – This is a junior color. I think the cute color suits teen girls. This is not limited to solid pink . . .

Salmon Pink – Even though it is still pink, salmon pink has a different feeling . . . like a bit of skin. It rather suits we Japanese.

Saxe blue – a light blue that really is quite fashionable for underwear. It has a cold feeling to it, so it's for intellectuals.

Lilac – it has the slight sense of sexiness to it, so I want to recommend it to young housewives.

Black – Black underwear gives off the sense of the word chic. And this I really want to recommend for stylish middle-aged housewives. With only a quick glance at their black slip, these women are somehow taken as the best dressers.[26]

Long before fashion designer Ishizu Kensuke would appropriate the police lingo of TPO (Time, Place, Occasion) for the fashion world in the 1970s,[27] Fujita theorizes appropriateness of color to age and activity. Despite her efforts to normalize colorful underwear, white remained the most popular color by far until the seventies when beige took over, finally to be succeeded by colors only in the 1980s. To some extent, this sort of nuanced reflection on the color of underpants is refracted through the lens of studio porn from Nikkatsu, as in the following example of the theme song to the 1978 hit film *Peach Butt Girl*. In the opening sequence, the young schoolgirl protagonist sleeps with an older man, discovers she may be pregnant, and decides to leave home for the city. As we see her lugging a huge bag onto a train platform the theme song fades up:

pink, pink, pink,
pink, pink, pink,
pink, pink, pink,
without a destination I hit the road
on a clichéd trip
but somewhere along the line
I hoped something in my life would change.
Even without wearing my pink cotton panties,
when I lean back stretching out on my wanderings,

it always comes out,
no matter how much I hide it –
I'm a peach butt girl.
Growing up without knowing a thing
can definitely be embarrassing
tomorrow I will go home,
put on my pink cotton panties.
I think I'm all grown up
on my solitary trip
pink, pink, pink,
pink, pink, pink,
pink, pink, pink,

(Theme song to *Momojiri musume: Pinku hippu gāru*, 1978)

The song itself associates this pivotal moment of becoming adult with the color pink as suggested 20 years earlier in Fujita's conception of the appropriateness of color. And in this way it is clear that Nikkatsu's use is in harmony with Fujita's theory. But as they focus more on the wearer than the visual consumer, neither the notion of underwear portrayed in these suggestions for panty decorum nor the filmic adoption of the rules for wearing of said panties speak to the modes of desire raised for the watcher by underpants over the course of its postwar rise as a commodity and sexual fetish. And yet Nikkatsu's new venue for this aspect of panty-dom (separated by time and audience from Fujita's 1950s advice for young women as potential wearers) reminds that the watcher provides an important subject for analysis.

More relevant to the studio porn films of the 1970s and early 1980s are examples of postwar thinking on underwear that address the place of underwear in society, particularly those with attention to the watcher. Fujita's 1958 *Underwear Classroom* is prefaced with the comment that underwear is the foundation to western dress and modern life. Her assertion that modern western clothes could not possibly look as they were supposed to without modern western underwear worn beneath them was later elaborated in her 1962 article titled "Underwear decides your style".[28] Underwear then is conceived as a building block for public appearance that is just as important as the body being packaged in cloth. Aoki Hideo continued this line of thinking about the corporeality of the undergarment beginning with his 1957 *Cultural History of Underwear* and in his many recycled, updated versions: "There is a saying that underwear is a second skin. That is to say, underwear is something that modern people cannot do without."[29] *Shitagi* activist Kamoi Yōko brought the bodily relation of the garment into the realm of sex in her *Cultural Theory of Underwear*: "Skin is one aspect of sex. And underwear is a thing that is in intimate contact with that skin, so it is natural that people who wear this new underwear desire an alteration of the common understanding of underwear, which means they desire both a new skin and a new mode for sex."[30] Every pair of underwear has the potential to be consumed in at least two actions—the wearing and the viewing.[31] Here Kamoi is claiming the new underwear would remake the wearer and the viewer in the course of courtship and sex. Underwear is then part of the exchange value in the corporeal marketplace of intercourse and, as such, is not only occupying interstitial position between bodies, but also performing a catalytic function promoting their interaction. Yet even Kamoi is vague on exactly how underwear might effect change in sexual interactions, desire, or the world. Mainstream postwar pornography provides the ultimate testing ground for her theories.

Theories of porn

> A long time ago, everyone lived buck naked, but Adam and Eve covered their important parts with fig leaves and the advancement of sex between people began there. If it's covered, everyone wants to see it. Right?
> Bearded Godzilla, Caveman/History Teacher in *Shameless High*, 1970

Assumptions about what pornography can show or can't show tend to underlie various debates on censorship of pornography in the West generally and in the USA specifically and presuppose a metaphysics of presence. Those arguing for controls and the administration of the arts of pornography (Dworkin, MacKinnon) have tended to assume that, because porn can present everything about sex (porn shows everything), it is obscene, oppressive, and worthy of censure. On the other hand, those who argue that porn is at the center of popular culture and, in turn, allows modern society function, tend to see porn as always representing something unseen and unseeable (porn shows nothing – Williams, Žižek). The dichotomy between these positions is precisely the issue at stake in obscenity and yet, there are ways of resolving the binary that stitch together what seems at the outset like mutually opposed notions of visibility.

Since at least the 1970s, a third position has been consistently articulated by Japanese voices commenting on pornography. Commenting on the nature of taboo expression, Ōshima Nagisa wrote in his "Theory of experimental pornographic film," "Isn't 'obscenity' contained in that which is not expressed, not seen, hidden?"[32] To show it renders the thing public and therefore by definition not off scene or obscene but in the main. This view is often repeated in the literature in Japanese that seems to seek a uniqueness to Japanese pornography in the face of the Western intrusion, that reifies contingent historical and cultural differences as natural, proper, and preferable, that justifies what is with normative claims about how what is also is what should be. Here only the obscured supplies the thrill of the obscene, of tempting by suggestion. Of course, the claims of this being a uniquely Japanese phenomenon are as overblown as those that claim minimalism as the unique aesthetic of Japanese Zen Buddhism, but the frequency of the rhetorical claims that not showing is particularly Japanese are worth entertaining less for their supposed cultural specificity than in their power for describing the spectacle of underwear in Japanese film from the 1970s.

In his history of Roman Porno, Matsushima Toshiyuki gives a simple historical version, namely that due to the expanding desires of spectators over time, porn tends towards revealing more and more: "Porn in some way attempts to show certain things as that which should not be shown; from the audience side their desire to see expands more and more as that which can't be seen is shown. And from the producers' side the parts able to be shown expand over time."[33] This view masks a potentially reactionary view, but also has the potential for a progressive one. We might imagine from Matsushima's point that he is positing that a zero point existed long ago when the arts were entirely safe from pornographic representation, then bit by bit artists and pornographers have revealed more to the point where now nearly everything is shown; this may mask a lamentation for older more refined times when porn was artistic and not as crass and bald in its representation. Like the tales of the stripper who never completely stripped, this privileging of a particular moment of the fetish for showing and not showing overlooks the continuities over history, the dynamics of revealing and covering that are predicated on what can and cannot be represented. On the other hand, Matsushima's notion may in fact be referring to a timeless (or at least static since the dawn of modernity) dynamic wherein each new device purporting to reveal is rendered insufficient after enjoying its time as the reigning fetish.

For Ōshima, as for Matsushima and many others, the central feature of porn is this idea that there is always something else present off-screen to be shown. And while this notion belies a fetish for a presence albeit a presence removed from general purview, this recognition also suggests an idea that the process, the masquerade, the performance of covering is the most important thing rather than the idea that the cover might be covering something.

Pornographic desire is dependent on the fantasy of the possibility of mimetic representation, the ability to show something of reality not otherwise shown. For porn to continue to be the commodity fetish it is, pornography must perform for its audience's desire as if showing all is possible here and now in a way it never had been before. How does porn continually do this? Invoke a history in which the previous moment seems almost laughable and quaint in the contemporary period in which nothing seems shocking and anything seems to go.

Linda Williams' powerful reading of American porn's capturing of the involuntary male orgasm – the money shot – as a substitute for the unrepresentable, fakeable female orgasm reveals how the dynamics of porn are never quite what they seem. The power of Williams' reading stems from the readers' presumption that hardcore film shows all (that anything goes), and precisely not that it shows how all can't be shown. Williams' reading effectively reverses this. The representation male ejaculation stands in for the unshowable real of the female orgasm. But what of this concept of substitution in other moments and places in the world history of pornographic film?

Our consideration of a form of pornography that openly embraced a requisite hiding by means of a common device is instructive as to how the performance of showing all continues to function, even as covers themselves are revealed as the all. Pornography can not show all, but is still risqué, showing too much, pushing the envelope, going beyond the point of permissibility or just up to it, defining the point, and exposing it.[34] And in not showing all, historically porn shows all that can be shown.

In this light, it is important to note one of the most common nativist tropes used to differentiate Japanese pornography from western pornography; Japanese pornography is often said to encompass the aesthetics of "chirarism." A compound word composed of an abbreviation of *chirari to miru* (to glimpse or catch sight of) and the English suffix "-ism," *chirarism* was probably coined and certainly circulated widely as a near synonym of eroticism beginning in the early 1950s when the buttocks of a young starlet of swashbuckler films, Asaka Mitsuyo, were flashed during a fight scene.[35] If three and a half seconds were enough for love scenes in Hollywood's golden age, a millisecond flash of undergarments were enough to ignite the desires of audiences at the height of Japan's golden period of filmmaking. Taken to be of a uniquely Japanese flavor, the attraction of the barely perceptible or the slightly hidden in the usage of chirarism is, however, not far from the Greek dramatist's meaning of obscenity (the violence that was not portrayed on stage, but rather off-scene) and still presupposes a presence off-screen or a present absence on screen. What does seem to be a unique manifestation of the dynamics of desire implicit in the terms obscene or chirarism is the term *panchira*, which derives from a combination of panties (*pantsu*) and to glimpse (*chirari to miru*). And while this neologism too may seem a uniquely Japanese phenomenon, panchira gained prominence in Japan in the post-*Seven Year Itch* phase of skirt-flipping.[36] So the notion that *panchira* (the flash of panties) in other fields of cultural production, most notably otaku-related areas of anime and manga, where glimpses of panties abound, is somehow a uniquely Japanese phenomenon is problematic at best and essentialist at worst. Rather we might do better to look at specific examples of *panchira* in Japanese film to arrive at a more comprehensive understanding that *panchira* itself becomes the object under which, outside of which there is nothing.

Underpants in *roman poruno*

More than theories on panties or pornography, Lacanian psychoanalysis is well positioned to help reflect on the function and being of underpants in Nikkatsu's *roman poruno*. And yet there are ways in which Nikkatsu *roman poruno* reveal current psychoanalytical terms to be lacking. Lacanian criticism, with its attention to the relationships amongst the imaginary, the symbolic, and the real, is uniquely situated to uncover the coverings effected in the filmic representations of policed borders of expression, taboo modes of desire, and absent presences onscreen. And while a Lacanian criticism will help open several avenues otherwise blocked in our pursuit of the driving functions behind underpants, in the end the dynamic turns of *shitagi* exceed the limits of Lacanian mapping as we know it. What the *roman poruno* panties illustrate is perhaps the need for a new term for (psychoanalytic film) criticism.

It is odd that Lacan's point, elaborated in his preface to the Japanese translation of *Eçrits*, that the Japanese could not be or do not need to be psychoanalyzed has not been taken up by critics as having particular relevance for the art form most dependant on visual representation – film. In 1972, Lacan, whose career was founded on the revolutionary notion that the psyche is structured like language, claimed that the structure of the Japanese language rendered psychoanalysis unnecessary for the Japanese mind. Lacan, like so many French thinkers of his time (most notably, Barthes, Kojève, and Derrida), was fascinated by a written language using ideographs; in addition, Lacan was fascinated by his misunderstanding of *kanji* (Chinese characters) and their relation to *on* (Chinese) and *kun* (Japanese) phonetic readings. What held importance for Lacan was the notion that two phonetic readings were always possible for the characters. In Lacan's view, the Japanese were fortunate to speak a language that had "taken for its writing (*écriture*) of the language (*langue*) so foreign [a script] that at every moment the distance of the word (*parole*) from thought or the unconscious is tangible."[37] The distance and misfit between thought and the manifestation of expression which Lacan envisioned his mythical Japanese people feeling at every moment of being and utterance provided a convenient, almost one-to-one replication of the split subject as Lacan had been articulating it throughout his career.

To take Lacan's reading of the Japanese psyche at face value and apply it to the language of film and specifically Japanese film results in the argument that film and especially Japanese film needs no interpretation because it reproduces the structure of the unconscious in an open, transparent way; that is, film, as a language where the exposed, developed, and projected celluloid (the writing) is utterly estranged such that the image/sound (word or *parole*) is tangibly separate from thought or the unconscious (of the filmmaker/spectator), should need no interpretation. It is odd then that over the course of the late twentieth century, Lacan, who thought a language based on pictographs with a unique mode of pronunciation would represent something not necessary to disambiguate, has come to hold a uniquely powerful position in cinema studies. For if the language of cinema itself is an exemplar of the mythical language Lacan calls Japanese, that is a language that is both pictographic and comprised of two unnatural modes of pronunciation (call them light and sound, or voice and music, or voice and subtitle), then interpretation of film is, according to the words of the master, unnecessary.

Here Lacan's constructions of Japan and the Japanese language behave like a cover for the fear of the seemingly universal big Other type claim that everyone needs psychoanalysis. So Lacan simply invents a fantasy Japan (very similar to Barthes' invention of Japan in *Empire of Signs*). However, none of this is necessary, because, in the postmodern global moment of the early seventies, to say everyone needs psychoanalysis is more a comment on that particular moment in world history than it is a universal transhistorical claim. And so Lacan's fear of being an old-school Humanist is misplaced or is itself a repressed desire to rewrite the history of nineteenth- and twentieth-century EuroAmerican empire and its relation to modernity and its concomitant psychological crises requiring analytical disambiguation.

But, while Lacan's idea may be thinly veiled bunk, since (among other reasons too numerous to state) analysis is necessary even to make the claim that the subject was already divided and thus not requiring of analysis, it is tempting bunk. For, the inverse of the notion may not necessarily be bunk. That is, we could agree with Lacan that if what he claims for Japanese language were true, his conclusions might also be true; if there were such a thing as a language that was openly divided phonetically and unified graphically (call it cinema), then the psyche of people who conversed in such a language (the spectators/film-makers) would not need to be analyzed; that is revealing the split between, for instance, spectators and filmmakers would have to be self-evident. And conversely if this were not the case, then analysis would be necessary. But there is also a post-humanist, post-historical third position: all languages may now be so foreign to their own speakers that they may be written in a form so distant as to obfuscate thought or the unconscious tangibly enough for all speakers cry out for analysis; in such a post-historical linguistic predicament, to speak is to require analysis. Just as there is no language in which to feel at home, there is no subject that does not need analysis. Japanese filmic language and the experience of Japanese film, in fact, need interpretation precisely because they reproduce the structure of the psyche not as a unified narrative (genre or national film), but because they are so openly rife with fissures. Specifically with *roman poruno* the modes of desires cultivated by the history of underwear necessitate such interpretation. The *roman poruno* series provides the perfect testing ground not only for Lacan's off-hand remark in his preface, but also for essaying the applicability or elasticity of "Western" psychoanalytic terms "outside" of their place of origin at a point in global history when the very term Western had already finished a century of work of remaking the global entity in its image.

The term "suture," derived from an off-hand remark by Lacan and coming to mean "the junction of the imaginary and the symbolic,"[38] is particularly helpful for thinking about the use of terminology derived elsewhere for a local application. And, on the other hand, suture (as elaborated for purposes of bringing the audience into play with the gaps and fissures present in film) lacks the capacity to account for all the effects of underpants.

The opening sequence of the coming of age story *I feel it* (1976) presents at least three moments or places that might be read through standard definitions of the suture in order to explain some of the effects of the seen and the obscene in these Nikkatsu films. However, reading the underpants as suture may also limit the possibilities present for them in the films. The film begins with the phallic symbol par excellence – a gun (Figure 13.3).

Figure 13.3 Starting gun: Jun's story begins with a phallic symbol.

Like Magritte's pipe, it is not a gun as such, but rather a poster of a gun. The camera begins its pan around an apartment that is plastered with images of guns, finally landing on the heroine Jun. Her narration begins, "She said she'd show me, so she brought me here. I was a bit scared, but I was more curious. Oh, me? I'm Jun." The camera pulls back from a close-up on Jun to reveal that she is in a hammock beside a bed with a young man and woman in the throws of intercourse. "These two are Pandie and Walther. She's like a panda, so we call her Pandie; he likes pistols, so we call him Walther. They were my seniors in high school." The camera pulls back to reveal Jun studying the action. "And I guess these two are bit perverted. Oh, the one watching, that's me."

In this scene, Jun's gaze, like that of the little bean man (*mamemon*) who stands off to the side staring at the action in early modern Japanese pornography,[39] can be viewed as a suture that stitches together the subject with the cinematic fiction. Her gaze and voiceover allow viewers their own point of access, publicizing for the audience the private act of coitus. Perhaps to learn something, perhaps out of curiosity, perhaps out of pleasure, like Jun, the audience watches. But the audience can gaze at one thing which Jun herself will not see in her personal point of view – Jun. So the spectator is positioned within the world presented in the frame through Jun's gaze, but Jun's gaze divides the frame against itself. Yet the world within the frame is not divided: for Jun's sightlines within the frame are unobstructed; she is only blind to the spectator outside her frame. Jun is blind to us, but not silent. Her narration breaks the frame in direct address to the audience, retrospectively highlighting her blind spot and reminding the spectator of the always possible gaze of another – the big Other who may always be watching the watcher, enjoying the spectacle of the spectator. Here Jun's perverse situation inverses and doubles the spectator's watching of Jun watching; where she watches Pandie and Walther and talks about the scene, we watch Jun, Pandie, and Walther in silence. By so emphasizing this point of view, the film reaches out into the dark abyss of the theater, acknowledging not so much the power of the gaze as the erotics of witnessing. Watching is portrayed as important as what is being watched. Or rather watching is to be watched.

The meticulous framing of every shot in this opening sequence adheres strictly to the codes of not showing that had been settled between police, Eirin, and producers. A strategically placed chair blocks our view of what Jun is watching. Christian Metz convincingly articulates the necessity of the strategic frame of pornography:

> Cinema with directly erotic subject matter deliberately plays on the edges of the frame and the progressive, if need be incomplete revelations allowed by the camera as it moves, and this is no accident. Censorship is involved here: censorship of films and censorship in Freud's sense . . . the point is to gamble simultaneously on the excitation of desire and its non-fulfilment (which is its opposite and yet favours it), by the infinite variations made possible precisely by the studio's technique on the exact emplacement of the boundary that bars the look, that puts an end to the "seen", that inaugurates the downward (or upward) tilt into the dark, towards the unseen, the guessed-at.[40]

So if occlusion is part of the strip tease Metz describes, the presence of the chair or the use of the camera's gate to cut out as well as set up what cannot be shown, draws the spectator's attention to itself, particularly in this scene predicated on viewing (Figure 13.4). The chair, while blocking the view of the pelvises locked in action, also stitches the subject to the realm of fiction. If Jun is the first suture in the scene, the chair is the second.

The third and final possible suture in the scene is Jun's underpants which are not shown until after the title scrolls down over Jun's face. "You get it, right? This is the most orthodox position [Pandie says of the missionary position]. And next [Pandie climbs astride Walther] see, this is girl-on-top. Ah, I'm in ecstasy, because you're watching Jun." The camera moves in on Jun's face who is finally feeling something from her watching experience. The audience knows this from the contrapuntal sounds of landing planes, which fade up just at the moment Jun's narration tells us "Ah, I think something is happening" ("*A, dō ni ka narisō*"). The sound of the unseen planes outside is a direct appropriation of Takechi Tetsuji's

Figure 13.4 Chair and Jun: Two sutures in shot and reverse shot occluding the gaze and opening the gaze as content.

use of airplane noises from the American base to stunning effect in his *Black Snow* (*Kuro yuki*, 1965). So it is overdetermined that Jun is feeling something at this moment, when the frame freezes, the cheesy 1970s electronic tones of a wah-wah pedal fade up, and the title scrolls down – "I feel it!" (Figure 13.5).

Of course, at this moment, Jun's hand is in her crotch, so it would be odd if she were not feeling anything. But the cutting away from her face and the title to her underpants in the following shot confirms the feeling and stitches the symbolic underpants that stands in for the unshowable to the very real, fantasy world of the fetishist.

And yet, it is precisely because this unremarkable three-second flash of panties can so easily go unnoticed that the suture terminology is not as helpful in working through the issue of underpants as it would seem. Or rather, the suture metaphor can only get us so far in understanding the function of underpants in Nikkatsu films. The underpants might seem entirely natural to a one-time viewer of *roman poruno*, because in the post miniskirt boom of 1968–1973 Japanese women were wearing underpants under their dresses and skirts. Despite the police and the mass media

Figure 13.5 Jun feels it, but is it blocked or shown by her panties?

frenzy over underwear in the years preceding the film, we can easily imagine that all viewers were not necessarily underpants fetishists. As such, there is nothing odd or out of place with the underpants, nothing jarring in the way there is with the framing and the chair. This is after all supposed to be a risqué film with lots of sex in it; one expects to find people in various states of undress. The suture is supposed to be dependent on the spectator/subject's awareness of an absence that "breaks the immediate delight in the image."[41] So the question is whether or not the subject notices anything odd, wrong, unpleasant, or not present in *roman poruno*. In short, the underpants might just be underpants and not covers for something else for some viewers.

As we move from the pistol to the underpants over the course of the scene and throughout the film, what is absent is of less importance than what has come, by default, to replace those absences, the present images of guns, the presence of gazing, the present image of underpants. If the accretion of images of guns and panties in the room signal castration, as Žižek has claimed of the "multiplication of phallus representatives" generally, then what we have in miniature in this scene is the lack of phallus not only in this film about a young Japanese woman's discovery of sexual pleasures, not only in all of *roman poruno*, but also, as Etō Jun and Ueno Chizuko have both suggested in reference to literature,[42] in all of postwar Japan. But this is a ruse, providing a big Other – a grand narrative explanation of the surplus of fetish objects filling in for some lack – where there is none. What Žižek himself would call the big Others do not, of course, exist here. There may only be the surface with nothing underneath. We buy into the existence of a lack and phallus as giant intersubjective fictions created by society in order to mask the fact that vaginas and penises as lacks and phalluses do not exist. And these moments of flashing panties allow the fictional status of the big Other to shine through, giving the films their sublime camp.

In this case, the fact that the spectator need not have been aware of underwear as anything other than underwear signifies not ambiguity, but the range possible for underwear. Like Maltby's reading of a cut that connects two scenes in *Casablanca* as both referring and not referring to an absent sex scene or D. A. Miller's interpretation of the blackouts in *Rope* that refer both to the hidden homosexual anus in Hollywood film and to the violence of cuts and cutting to the smooth flow of the supposedly cut-free film,[43] the panties can always go unnoticed as a diegetic covers, ones that do not necessarily disrupt the denouement of the narrative in the same way for all viewers. Depending on the viewer, underpants can both pass and not pass unnoticed. Therefore, while thinking about underpants as suture at first seems to fit, in the end the concept itself cannot cover the range of use of underpants in these Nikkatsu films. If the "suture closes the cinematic discourse . . ., closes the spectator-subject in that process, ceaselessly, throughout the time of the film," then underpants as suture close, but also tear an opening.[44] Dwelling in the balance between lack and fulfillment, absence and presence, underpants cover over and are revealed again and again. "These veiling and unveiling procedures"[45] continue throughout *roman poruno* and provide a useful starting ground for analysis, because it is only once the seemingly free floating, empty signifiers have been identified that they can begin to be anchored to and filled with meaning. Signification does not end with undecidability; meaning-making begins there.

If suture is predicated on the presence of a noticeable absence in the present moment of viewing, *point de capiton* (the quilting point) or master signifier necessitates a retroactive analysis only possible after signification comes to rest. We only can identify a master signifier once meaning is clear. If heterosexual male desire or pornography are signifiers in a free floating field and may be attached to any number of meanings depending on their context, underpants of *roman poruno* nail down these fields, buttoning or stitching the free floating quilt of signifiers to a specificity otherwise indeterminable. If underpants are a free floating or empty signifier that wavers between covering and revealing, occluding and packaging, erasure and eros, to become erasure as eros, the quilting point that buttons down the quilt of the free floating field of signifiers would depend on specific individual uses of the apparel. Underpants in Nikkatsu films perform at least two functions, the prevalence of which change over the history of the genre – first, they appear as simple covers which may then be fetishized and later they pop-up with increasing frequency as objects within the structure of the narrative driving the narrative themselves. When underpants are figured as consequential objects in the world of narrative, not ones that merely serve the director's purposes as a cover of the potentially offensive and not ones that merely serve the characters' purposes as an item of clothing, but ones that motivate key plot points, the position of heterosexual male desire which otherwise floats adrift in a sea of free signification is moored in place through the anchor provided in panties.

The film *Sailor Uniform: Raising Carnal Desires* (1982) provides a simple example of this. Here the desires of the Humbert Humbert figure of the stalker-teacher who enters the simple life of the single mother and her pubescent daughter are clear from the outset. When he calls on the phone, not identifying himself, and masturbating from the safe distance of his own apartment, the young girl picks up. "Panties, what color are your panties? Maybe white? Maybe pink? Do you get yourself off?" The unsettled girl calls for her mother. The mother picks up, and the teacher continues. This substitution from panties, to girl, to mother works for a while until the teacher begins to date the mother. Sleeping over one night, he waits until the mother is asleep before he ventures to find answers to his earlier line of questioning. First, he goes to the girl's room and lifts her sheets to examine the underwear in which she sleeps—white. Still unsatisfied, he goes to the laundry basket, moving aside a blue pair in favor of a white pair. He sniffs this keepsake until dawn. While this manages to suffice for a time, the teacher eventually kills the mother in order to live with the white-panty-clad teen. The film portrays the murder as a success, the teacher living on with his life's dream. Here, in retrospect, the on-screen panty fetish is revealed to have specific nasty effects, to represent a particular underside of male desire—the oppressive, violent, ubiquitous phallic dominator.

The teacher's protestations that the girl is his life may be an attempt to elevate the love of the teacher for the girl to the point of providing ambivalence. Indeed, her last line of the film delivered in a voiceover as she wanders aimlessly around town speaks to her two fathers: "Daddy, please love me forever." The final ominous scene of the girl wandering about town as aimlessly as she started the film gives the sense that whether the phallic dominator is absent (as the biological father is from the start of the film) or present (as in the case of the teacher at the end), women can do nothing more than to obey their man. Indeed, the teacher gets the last line of the film directly following her "love me forever": "I'll teach you many things from now on . . . And you'll become my perfect Venus." Her request for love can only be met by the promise to mold her to fit his fetishes.

A more complex use of underpants as plot point can be seen in its function as the deus ex machina of *The Redhead* (1979). A truck driver picks up a hitchhiker with the intention of raping her. But the titular redhead is a woman with a dark past who ends up seducing the truckdriver. Panties are the pivotal actor of the final scenes. First purchased as a necessity for replacing a thoroughly consumed other pair ("I can't stay pantyless forever," she says as she goes off to buy the new pair), the new panties are shown to the truckdriver as a fetish item ("These will dazzle you." "Hey, they're small. Your hair will show."). But after washing them back at her apartment, the panties slip from their role as simple object of desire. When the redhead goes to hang them out to dry from her second story window, they accidentally drop on the head of the junkie downstairs, who happens to be hanging out her laundry. Assuming herself to be the butt of some unknown joke, the neighbor flies into a rage. Panties in hand, she runs upstairs and pounds on the door of the redhead's apartment. After getting no response, she tears the panties. Finally she forces the door open, rushes in, beats, and strangles the redhead with the panties until the fight is broken up. When the truckdriver returns later he finds the bloodied panties in the hallway and misreads them as evidence of the redhead's sexual infidelity. He flies into a rage and beats her.

In this quick succession of scenes (Figure 13.6) which use underpants as fetish motivating the desires of the characters in the diegesis and as the extradiegetical material upon which the plot turns, signified is stitched to signifier. Underwear is "the point of convergence that enables everything that happens in this discourse to be situated retroactively and prospectively."[46] The cover here comes both from within the narrated world and from without.

A sublime moment at the opening of *The Core of an Angel: Red Classroom* (1979) illustrates the extradiegetical functioning of underpants as cover. Here when the victim's underpants are removed by the rapers in the film-within-the-film, the framing film cuts to the screening room and the projector covers the crotch projected on the wall (Figure 13.7). The point here is to see the underpants of film not as a cover of the desired vagina (and certainly not a cover of the buttocks, which are everywhere revealed as popping out of, over, and through the underpants), but as a desire. This is not a deferral of meaning or reference, but rather the settling of signification in one place – that is both here and there onscreen. This is yet another way in which underpants function as the master signifier or quilting point, fixing underpants to projection and therefore film, showing, and narrative. But the director's joke here is too explicit or self-conscious to be funny. Cinema itself prevents the adequate representation.

Figure 13.6 Underpants as plot device in *The Redhead* (1979).

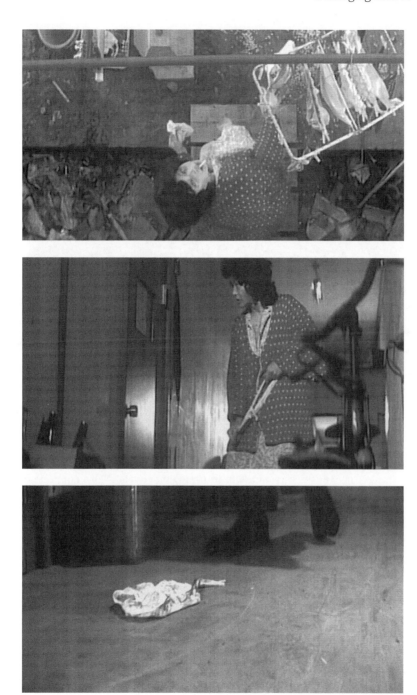

Figure 13.6 Continued

298 Jonathan E. Abel

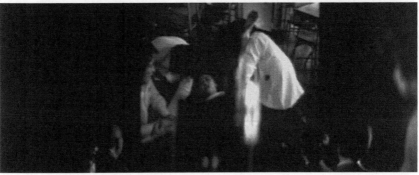

Figure 13.7 The film is revealed to be a film-within-a-film at the very moment the
 underpants vanish and the projector that is projecting the snuff film in the
 screening room replaces it, partially obscuring the screen-within-the-screen.

As a relatively new postwar commodity in Japan, underwear is also connected
to the rapid economic growth leading up to the bubble economy. So it should
not be surprising that during the height of the bubble economy the cover became
overt. With the advent of the home video recorder and the concomitant birth of
Adult Video (AV), the fast-forward button rendered concern for story something
of the past. In the new aesthetics of desire, titillation through reference to
the process of deletion itself became enough. The filmic fetish for underpants
changed from a cover both diegetic and extradiegetic to more and more clearly
extradiegetical covers – from underpants to tape (maebari), black boxes, fuzzy
clouds (bokashi), and digital "mosaics." While of course some of these techniques
had long been employed in period pieces for which underpants would have been
ahistorical and therefore extradiegetical anyway, their rise in contemporary dramas
is locatable to a particular moment in the mid-1980s when the fetish for covering
as covering became the sole and ultimate end. With the bursting of the bubble the
entire ruse itself ended, and the desire to attain the real (however impossible)
reached a crescendo, leaving nude hair itself as the prime fetish of the no-panty

boom, as if the pubic hair was not something that was to stand in for something else.

A third and final term may be of some help as far as underpants in *roman poruno* are concerned, because it does not fit. In the case of *la voix acousmatique*, a voice that cannot be attributed to anything in the narrative reality and so garners as even more power, there is no easy matching to underwear which makes very little sound onscreen or off. Though many other kinds of low-budget porn film are awash in disembodied voices of unnatural, orgiastic moans that always seem to emanate from a body and mouth off of which light cannot bounce to be captured on film, the notion of a disembodied voice is useful for the higher-budget studio *roman poruno* films as well.[47] In the free floating blots on Nikkatsu's period piece films and on the later post-panty Adult Video that we have a visual corollary of this auditory phenomenon. Here the sights do not match the narrative. The blots come from outside reminding us that what we are watching ought not to be seen. How does this inform our understanding of underpants which, as we have seen, served as both a reality effect which mimes the function of underpants, in our world (practical, daily clothing) and as a plot, device used to move and turn narrative?

By rethinking the blacked out portions of films as the videomatic or optomatic sight rather than acousmatic voice, we can see that underpants, even when heavy-handed contrivances for pushing plot, inhabit a different realm of diegesis. The heavy-hand in plotting feels different than the blackening hand that scratches out portions of film. If the black or fuzzy portions come from outside the narrative and remain unsettling and disruptive to the flow, even the heavy-handed use of underpants within the diegesis appears smooth and natural by comparison, almost part of the skin of storytelling. If underpants cover the vagina which is a utopia in film, then they also become the sign or name of that feminine no-place or atopia. But there is another atopia or dystopia in *roman poruno* indicated by underpants – the viewing, powerful man who in a sense is everywhere in the films and is also nowhere in them.

Until now as a study of male heterosexual fetish, this study has ignored the problems in fetish theory that are predicated on Freudian phallocentric logic. The boy sees a lack in his mother and replaces it with a fetish object. A future problem necessary for investigation would be to rethink this notion of lack specifically through the function of men's underwear in film and the extent to which they constitute a fetish for female heterosexual and male homosexual desires. Integral in such a reading would be the expansion of the range of films to include both homosexual porn and heterosexual romantic comedies and soap operas (the melodramatic pornography of the NHK morning drama, etc.). Or cross-dressing males dawning women's underpants as in the case of the comic relief of the scanty boy who serves coffee in the lingerie café along with the girls in the film *Scanty Doll*. I would expect such a study to at least answer the question of whether or not the site of labor (the washing of the family underpants) may also be a site for resistance as Ueno Chizuko has suggested. I would not expect that underpants in these other places and times would necessarily be a cover for anything, including the big nothing called the Other, or the no-place, or phallus. In recent years, the presumption of feminine lack has been rightfully taken to task and by now it seems just as likely that a boy could see potential and promise in the mother or that a young girl confronted with the body of her father might see lack in the progenitor.

So it seems only fitting to end these thoughts on the underpants of women with one last example that should illustrate how male underpants can similarly be a sign of atopia even in mainstream heterosexual porn. The fantastic series of references in *roman poruno* through the signifying underpants to the Other, which itself is of course a fiction, is at the heart of the monetary and psychic success of genre. If the pants of women in the films represent the unrepresentable and therefore non-existent object of male heterosexual desire, the pants of men in the films seem to be in some similar relationship to absent-presences or present-absences, those surrounding heterosexual male relations to sex films. The desire to become the absent spectator is perhaps most evident in the opening credits in one of the more campy films in the series *Invisible Man: Do It!* (1978). The film centers on a man whose sex life is enabled in a number of ways by his drinking of a potion of invisibility, thus providing the seemingly perfect surrogate to the invisible men in the dark theaters watching the film. The opening scene features the nerdy fan watching two sex symbols modeled on the famed "Pink Ladies" duo here called the "Pink Babies" on TV.[48] He dreams about the two young women jumping out the TV screen and into his room. He turns invisible and makes love to them. Shots of women making love to the invisible man, that is, to nothing but air, would seem to allow the presumably male spectator to easily imagine stepping-in for the invisible man on screen, but the animated credit sequence reveals a key that marks the film: male underpants.

When the man vanishes, his underpants are left as a lasting reminder or blot that cannot be erased (Figure 13.8). If female underpants cannot last as a fetish, are a temporary substitute for something (big Other) that will never come (arrive), male underpants are a permanent erasure, a scar, marking what has already taken place – another reactionary, phallocentric claim about the emasculated male in postwar Japanese society. The transparency of men allows the opaque stain of underpants to stand to recall to our mind the fetish that despite its changing appearance and manifestation will not vanish for it covers that which is most feared, that there may be nothing underneath, nothing other than underpants.

Underpants as theory: theory as underpants

By now it should be overwhelmingly clear that I'm taking Nikkatsu's underpants as a new model for a poetics of covering, for the aesthetics of showing, and for the metaphysics of presence in film. When we strip away layers of meaning brought together over the crotch, we are left with underpants that package, that cover, that veil, that are a suture between non-meaning and meaning, that can master signification by tying down meaning to narrative, and that can exceed their own space because they are flashed so nonchalantly that they eventually become normalized. The cover suggests a covering, that something will have been covered (the package a packaging, that something will have been packaged), but as each layer is peeled off, we find only another new layer in its place. Underpants are

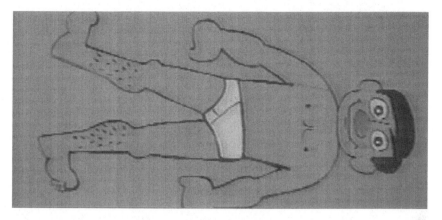

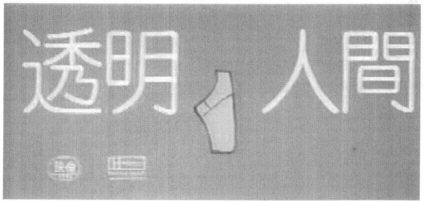

Figure 13.8 Transparent man: opaque skivvies.

euphemisms that are hardly recognizable as euphemisms, because they can be so easily passed over. But the passing-over enables meaning to be made. The euphemism intended to cover over some unnameable, eventually becomes so useful a term that what it covers ceases to matter, cease to be matter. Towards the end of their reign as the cover of choice, underpants took on other uses beyond the cover, enabling narrative closure.

So how might the Japanese word *shitagi* or the neologism Japanties, in homage to *roman poruno* underpants, be mobilized as useful terms for criticism? Where might we engage in *panchira* outside of Japanese films? When are other moments in which we might catch glimpses of the dynamics of Japanties? Here I would like to suggest three examples where the modalities of *shitagi* might be of use. Enumerating this range of places where *shitagi* might be glimpsed should render self-evident the elasticity of the new critical term.

First, the compound name *roman poruno* itself can be read as a kind of *shitagi* purporting to display while covering over in the same steamy breath – *roman* gesturing to the romantic and plot driven subtleties of narrative while *poruno* pointing towards the bald truths of sex. The fact that its function as a name might smoothly cover our notice of its split functionality only reinforces its *pantsu*-like process that names without defining a group of films that have few (if any) unifying traits (other than the historical ones of having been produced and marketed in unison by the same company). When the word is used as a simple proper name rigidly referring to a group of films predefined, its original tantalizing function is lost and it performs solely as surface material to be desired. This smoothing over of the hole covered by the term is inevitable, but not ubiquitous, because all shitagi can be exchanged for more explicit blots. In this regard, we need to remember that *roman poruno* gave way to "AV" in the 1980s.

Second, we might read Lacanian film critique (whether by Cornell, Heath, Metz, Mulvey, Oudart, or Žižek) as *shitagi* covering the big Other, unapproachable, nonexistent Lacan. Their approachable, ubiquitous cultural criticism which performed as sexy lingerie from the 1970s through 1990s sold and seduced spectators into presuming the possibility of arrival at the core/kernels of Lacanian obscurantism without the pain of having to read the original (as if reading the original could ever have been enough).

Third and most significantly, this article itself should have performed like *shitagi*; if not, then how could it have been written or read to this point? Thus far having meticulously avoided disclaimers about the subject matter, meticulously framed the argument such that methodology falls outside its reach, I will engage these here askance in conclusion by way of occlusion and deferral. Justifications, apologies, or histories may seem to provide a cold enough distance to prevent and occlude in-depth, perverse readings. Yet perverse material rife and riven with gaps and fissures seems to call more for this sort of in-depth analysis, not to suture but to attend to the violence of the omissions while recognizing their fecundity. And even after having gone through all the requisite disclaimers, it is far from clear that enough attention will have been paid to cover all the debts owed and abuses perpetrated (to feminist criticism, cultural studies, to history, to film theory, to gender studies, to women portrayed in the films, to humanity refracted through the films). Despite any such disclaimers, the underpants of *roman poruno* provide a useful critical term to describe a difficult phenomenon – the persistent problem of the cover or package, the fantasy or fetish, that smooths over the fact that there is no big Other.

The possible criticisms that this is all just a "montage of attractions"[49] or mere "porn chic"[50] has been clear from the outset and necessitates some sort of antici-patory response if not a disclaimer. To merely capitulate critique in the face of potentially crass and warrantless claims that this is not really feminist or not particularly Marxist would be to give up the pleasure and power of analysis before it even would have begun, to yield at the very moment when analysis should have begun. If the conclusions were to be already apparent from the beginning, analysis would not have been necessary.

So why risk the misunderstanding? That is to say, why choose the fetish object par excellence of the overly exoticized and eroticized Asian culture par excellence represented in the liminal medium par excellence as the object of inquiry? Why do this in this way? There can only be one answer: because this "montage of attractions" presented as "porn chic" and thinly shrouded in the silky finery of Asian/Cultural/Cinema Studies is itself *shitagi* that tantalize by covering over some unnameable big Other, a utopia. Japanties are triply fetishized for English-reading audience: representing not only the fetish for underpants, but the fetish for porn film, the fetish for an exotic foreign, and the fantasy of the big Other. I, as the analyst, am in a sense covering and packaging your view of the unknown, exotic, presumably desired pubis of Japanese film, the analysand.

And the shitagi-like function of this essay gains momentum not only from the recent wave of porn studies, but also from the recent growing interest in Japanese porn from the 1970s here in the USA.[51] If the continued survival of Japanese Studies in the USA rests no longer on US government grants to prevent future wars (Second World War enemies having long since been replaced by Cold War opponents and now terrorist cells), no longer on the continued belief in a threatening economic powerhouse (long since having been replaced by a European Union and now China), but rests on Japan's gross national cool[52] (as recent claims have been made), then nothing could be more relevant, nothing could be cooler than Japanese porn. So if the "soft power"[53] of culture hailed as the new flagship of peace and prosperity is truly as good as its word and not yet another rhetorical *shitagi*, then Japanese porn studies should not only be at the forefront of intellectual concern, but also political movement. Simply put, the move from softcore to soft power is short.

Japanese porn features in a fascinating play of possible culturally relativistic arguments, the polar positions of which can be summed up as follows: While it is argued that Japanese society is so much more restrictive about pornography (you call that porn? where are the pussies, dicks, and cumshots?), it is simultaneously held that Japanese porn reveals more (nuns, underage girls, bondage, rape are mainstream in J-porn! It's so weird). The first statement stigmatizes Japan as a culturally backwards nation that is not up to contemporary standards of freedom of expression, but bases the argument on the American (and therefore presumably global and transhistorical) culturally defined fetishes (split beavers, hard cocks, and messy jizz). The second begs the question why is SM and rape so normalized in Japan? This line of inquiry presuming transhistorical cultural difference rather than historically contingent variances among global markets of fetish occlude the big Other, the unspeakable of the collective myth that our pornographies are somehow less violent than theirs. As such these fantasies may, in fact, be too good to be true, may in fact mask our shared desire and necessity to uphold the veil of otherness qua Other.

As such, this repeats the persistent fetish of Area studies. Like underpants in the Nikkatsu films of the late 1970s that cover naturally within the narrative, Area Studies attempts to cover the myth of Asia with odorless objectivity. Namely, Asian or Japan Studies encourage us to think that what we arrive at is not an Asia or Japan sifted through the tantalizingly diaphanous filter of respective discourses, but rather the opaque real McCoy that is, of course, a big Other that somehow continues to be held to exist outside of the discourse.

But this being-underwear of Asian Studies and the Japanchira of Japan Studies are not so bad. As underpants can be experienced smoothly within the context of the desires plotted in a film, Asian studies can be read smoothly within the context of the desires of knowledge plotted in the pursuit of the fantasy of Asia or Japan. As in the case of the underpants fetishist consuming *roman poruno*, if the audience is aware they are not getting object of desire, as long as they are aware that the rhetoric of an Asia is nothing more than a convenient artifice, critical work can continue.

Finally it should be noted that we have returned to the tautological: if they are elastic in their applicability, Japanties also may reach a tearing point, beyond which they cannot be comfortably stretched. Like suture, *veil, point de capiton, voix acousmatique, shitagi* and the use of theory itself behave as a kind of *shitagi* that at once appears to give something desirable and erase the uneraseable.

Acknowledgment

This article began as the fanciful paper "Die, Žižek, Die: A Prehumous Requiem for the Elvis of Theory" to be presented at Bowling Green State University's Ray B. Browne Pop Culture and Theory Seminar in June of 2007. A more complete version was actually presented at the New England Association of Asian Studies Conference in September of 2008. I thank Sari Kawana for inviting me to present the early version to her students at the University of Massachusetts, Boston in November 2008 and Abe Markus Nornes for his encouragement to present a later version at KinemaClub XI at Harvard in March 2009.

Notes

1. Miyadai Shinji (1994) *Seifuku shōjo-tachi no sentaku*, Tokyo: Kodansha.
2. Guy Debord, "User's guide to détournment" (1956) and "Détournment as negation and prelude" (1959) Ken Knabb (ed.) *Situationist International Anthology*, New York: Bureau of Public Secrets, 2007, 14–21, 67–9. Guy Debord (1998) *Society of the Spectacle*, New York: Verso.
3. Ueno Chizuko (1989) *Sukāto no shita no gekijō: hito wa dōshite panti ni kodawaru no ka*, Tokyo: Kawade Shobō Shinsha, p. 23.
4. The evidence for the male fetish for the everyday and real abounds. Alexander Zahlten has highlighted an aesthetics of "ero-real" as one of the primary driving forces of desire behind pink film. See Alexander Zahlten, "The Role of Genre in Film from Japan: Transformations 1960s–2000s," Dissertation, Department of Film Studies, University of Mainz, 2007. As early as 1955 it is clear that the underwear fetish was part of this urge for the realism of everyday existence. An early panty collector by the name of Ishihara was quoted in several young women's magazines such as *Josei jishin (Girls Alone)* and *Yangu Redei (Young Ladies)* as being able to distinguish the occupation of the women who had worn his soiled panties by the smell. Shimokawa Kōshi (1992) *Dansei no mita Shōwa seisōshi*, Vol. 2., Tokyo: Daisan shokan, p. 194. I thank Zahlten for this reference.
5. See Inoue Shōichi (2002) *Pantsu ga mieru: shūchishin no gendaishi*, Tokyo: Asahi Shinbunsha, pp. 86–93.
6. Jack Vizzard (1970) *See No Evil: Life Inside a Hollywood Censor,* New York: Simon and Schuster, p. 117. For more on pubic hair stylings, see Slavoj Žižek (1997) *The Plague of the Fantasies,* New York: Verso, pp. 5–6.

7. Shitagawa Hekoten (1923) "Nihon zenkoku no fujin yo, sarumata o hake!" *Chūō shinbun,* December 8. Reprinted in Inoe, p. 41.

8. Cited in Inoue, p. 239.

9. Simon Partner (1999) *Assembled in Japan: Electrical Goods and the Making of the Japanese Consumer,* Studies of the East Asian Institute, Berkeley: University of California Press, pp. 142, 162.

10. Inoue, p. 239.

11. Takeda Naoko (1997) *Shitagi o kaeta onna: Kamoi Yoko to sono jidai,* Tokyo: Heibonsha, pp. 315–21.

12. Several books in the NDL digital Meiji collection hold plans for making ones own undergarments or shitagi. For instance the 6th edition of Noguchi Kizaburō's *Instructions for Sewing Western Clothes* contains two chapters, one the construction and design of Men's and Women's underwear. Noguchi Kinzaburō (1901) *Wafuku saihō kudensho tsūshin kyōjo,* Tokyo: Tokyo Saihōkyōjujo. Online. Available at: http://kindai.ndl.go.jp (Accessed June 2005). On the mini-skirt boom, see Inoue, p. 254.

13. The no-pan kissa or no-panty café was featured in *Co-ed: The Hotspot (Joshidaisei: za anaba,* 1981). Also, see Anne Allison (2000) "Pubic veilings and public surveillance: obscenity laws and obscene fantasies in Japan," *Permitted and Prohibited Desires: Mothers, Comics, and Censorship in Japan,* Berkeley: University of California Press.

14. The Japanese Wikipedia entry for *roman poruno* lists over 600 films in the series. Nomura Masaaki cites more conservative estimates basing his figures on the number of films marketed as *roman poruno* rather than on the fact of their sexual content and production by Nikkatsu. Nomura Masaaki (1994) "Otoko to onna no shigarami o sarake dashita Roman poruno Jūshichi nen no ayumi" *Ano shīn o mō ichido: Nikkatsu Romano poruno,* Tokyo: Kindai eigasha, p. 135.

15. Genres, largely based on categorizing the identities of the central female characters of the films, range from Nurse, Rape, Geisha, Female Prisoners, Office Lady, though other subgenres include comedy, bad guys, scandal, animals, sports. Online. Available at: http://www.nikkatsu-roman poruno.com/jyanru/index.html

16. *Ol nikki: meneko no nioi* and *Jokōsei geisha.*

17. " 'Shitagi nashi' ga ikenai: Nikkatsu poruno nado no tekihatsu keishichō ga riyū setsumei," *Asahi shinbun* January 30, 1972, p. 3.

18. 8823blue. "Yami no naka no yōsei." Online. Available at: http://www12.ocn.ne. jp/~nacky/yousei/yousei09.html (Accessed June 2005).

19. It should be noted that while for the viewer of *roman poruno* underwear reigned as the supreme cover, for the producers and actors in the films *maebari* (tape used to literally cover and tape up genitalia during the shooting of sex scenes) were what kept the filming of such scenes in pink film and *roman poruno* legal. So there was a real cover that prevented actual sexual intercourse between actors from occurring just behind a chair, underneath an obstructing blanket, and outside the refracted frames of Japanese sex films as well as a presentation cover or package that presented the covering – underpants. The difference between what the actors experienced under the studio lights and what the spectator viewed on screen gives a sense of at least two kinds of covering: first, there is the actual cover that covers and blocks something (an organ of sexual intercourse) from its function; second, there is the representation of a cover as a means for inciting desire. In this sense we might do well to make a distinction between a block and a packaging, wrapping, or covering. If the block prevents something real from happening, the package, wrap, and cover advertise, taunt, tantalize, and titillate and therefore encourage the happening. And yet all this assumes that there will have been an "it" that will have taken place during a "real" sexual act that would be different from a performed or virtual one. So rather than draw a strict distinction between the block and the cover, I want to suggest that they are different manifestations (doing and showing) of the same dynamics in achievement and representation.

20. "Oh! Mōretsu," *Seinen eiga,* October 1969, 4–9.

21. Richard Maltby (2003) " 'A brief romantic interlude' Dick and Jane go to 3 1/2 seconds of the classical Hollywood cinema," in Slavoj Žižek (ed.) *Jacques Lacan: Critical Evaluations in Cultural Theory*, New York: Routledge, p. 173.
22. André Bazin (2004) "Entomology of the pin-up girl," *What is Cinema?* trans. Hugh Gray, Los Angeles: University of California Press, p. 159.
23. According to Takeda, Kamoi would use a graphic design as her entry point assuring a smooth insertion into a taboo field. Takeda, p. 18.
24. Yasuoka Shōtarō (1976) "Shitagi būmu," *Yasuoka Shōtarō essai zenshū*, Vol. 1, Tokyo: Yomiuri Shinbunsha, p. 135.
25. While it might be tempting to make the Foucaultian claim that panties as they stretch across the gap between the public and private construct a liminal space in order to straddle it, or construct the binary between public and private by spanning it, here I would rather like to argue that the subordinate position of underwear (always already in relation to clothes or overwear (*uwagi*)) itself coincides with and is symptomatic of the same.
26. Fujita Yukiko (1958) *Fujita Yukiko no shitagi kyōshitsu*, Tokyo: Fujita Yukiko Yōsai kenkyūjo, p. 66.
27. See "The TPO of Underwear" ("Shitagi no TPO") in the "Junior Underwear Series" from the August 1978 issue of *Junior Style: Dressmaking Edition* (*Jyunia sutairu: doresu mīkingu no jyunia sutairu*).
28. Fujita Yukiko (1962) "Shitagi ga anata no sutairu o kimemasu," *Katei zenka,* June, pp. 25–32.
29. Aoki Hideo (2000) *Shitagi no bunkashi*, Tokyo: Yuzankaku. See also Aoki Hideo (1957) *Shitagi no bunkashi: oshare wa shitagi kara*, Tokyo: Matsuzawa Shoten; Aoki Hideo (1960) *Oshare wa shitagi kara*, Tokyo: Shinkigensha; Aoki Hideo (1968) *Shitagi erotisumu: sekkusu apīru igaishi,* Tokyo: Banchō shobō; Aoki Hideo (1973) *Shitagi no rekishi*, Fūzoku bunkashi senshō, Tokyo: Yuzankaku Shuppan; Aoki Hideo (2000) *Shitagi no bunkashi,* Tokyo: Yuzankaku.
30. Kamoi's *Shitagi bunkaron* quoted in Aoki Hideo (2000) *Shitagi no bunkashi*, Tokyo: Yuzankaku, p. 217.
31. I write "at least" because it is clear one might add at least buying, selling, soiling, eating, ripping, and cutting to the list.
32. Nagisa Oshima (1993) "Theory of Experimental Pornographic Film," *Cinema, Censorship, and the State: The Writings of Nagisa Oshima*, trans. Dawn Lawson, Boston: MIT Press, p. 261.
33. Matsushima Toshiyuki (2000) *Roman poruno zenshi: meisaku, meiyū, meikantokutachi*, Tokyo: Kōdansha, pp. 154–5.
34. Slavoj Žižek (1991) *Looking Awry: An Introduction to Jacques Lacan Through Popular Culture*, Cambridge, MA: MIT Press, pp. 110–11.
35. Kaneto Shindō makes the claim that chirarism began even earlier with Makino Tomoko. Imamura Shōhei and Kaneto Shindō (1988) "Gendai eiga to sei," in Shōhei Imamura (ed.) *Nihon eiga no tenbō*, Vol. 8, *Kōza Nihon eiga*, Tokyo: Iwanami Shoten, p. 139.
36. See Inoue's discussion of *panchira.* Inoue, pp. 316–74.
37. In my attempt to replay the split Lacan seems to be articulating here, I have chosen to derive my translation from both Japanese and French versions of Lacan's preface. Jacques Lacan (1972) *Ekuri*, (trans.) Miyamoto Tadao, Tokyo: Kōbundō, pp. iv–v. Jacques Lacan (1981) "Préface à l'édition japonaise des *Écrits*," *La lettre mensuelle de l'École de la cause freudienne* 3(October): 3.
38. Stephen Heath (2003) "Notes on suture," in Slavoj Žižek (ed.) *Jacques Lacan: Critical Evaluations in Cultural Theory*, New York: Routledge, p. 30.
39. See Timon Screech (1999) *Sex and the Floating World: Erotic Images in Japan, 1700–1820*, Honolulu: University of Hawai'i Press, 213.
40. Christian Metz (1982) *The Imaginary Signifier: Psychoanalysis and the Cinema*, Bloomington: Indiana University Press, pp. 77–8.
41. Heath, pp. 32–3.

42. See Ueno's postface to and Etō Jun's *Maturity and Loss.* Etō Jun (1993) *Seijuku to sōshitsu,* Tokyo: Kōdansha.
43. See Maltby and also D. A. Miller (1990) "Anal rope," *Representations* 32(Fall): 114–33.
44. Heath, pp. 32–3.
45. Metz, p. 88.
46. Jacques Lacan (1993) "The quilting point," *Seminar of Jacques Lacan, Book III: Psychoses 1955–1956,* Russell Grigg (trans.), New York: W. W. Norton, p. 269.
47. Of course, this has a very real history in the low budget pinku films some of which could not afford synchronized sound equipment, so the sounds were added later.
48. The film may have been inspired by the pink film *Invisible Man: Doctor Eros (Tōmei ningen ero hakase,* 1968), but took its immediate impetus the more mainstream Pink Ladies' hit song "Invisible Person" which had debuted earlier in 1978.
49. "These are lined up in what Eisenstein liked to call 'a montage of attractions'," a kind of theoretical variety show, in which a series of "numbers" succeed each other and hold the audience in rapt fascination. It is a wonderful show; the only drawback is that at the end the reader is perplexed as to the ideas that have been presented, or at least as to the major ones to be retained." Frederic Jameson (2006) "First Impressions: Review of Slavoj Žižek's *The Parallax View," London Review of Books,* September 7.
50. "Porn chic is not feminism, though it is sometimes taken up as such. Porn chic reinforces both the power and predominance of the male gaze over women's bodies . . ." Hannah B. Harvey and Karen Robinson, "Hot bodies on campus: the performance of porn chic," Ann C. Hall and Mardia J. Bishop, *Pop-porn: Pornography in American Culture,* Westport, CN: Praeger, 2007, 72–3.
51. Jasper Sharp (2008) "Pink thrills: Japanese sex movies go global," *Japan Times* December 4.
52. Douglas McGray (2002) "Japan's gross national cool," *Foreign Policy,* June/July, pp. 40–54.
53. Joseph S. Nye (2005) *Soft Power: The Means to Success in World Politics,* New York: Public Affairs.

References

Abe, Auestad, Reiko (1998) *Rereading Sōseki: Three Early Twentieth-Century Japanese Novels, Iaponia insula, Bd. 7*, Wiesbaden: Harrassowitz.

Abe, Susumu (1978) *Harenchi gakuen*. Nikkatsu.

Adams, Parveen (1992) "Waiving the phallus", in Naomi Schor and Elizabeth Weed (eds) *The Phallus Issue, Differences: a Journal of Feminist Cultural Studies* 4(1): 76–83.

Adamson, Joseph (1997) *Melville, Shame, and the Evil Eye: A Psychoanalytic Reading*, Albany: State University of New York Press.

Alexander, Jeffrey C. (2004) "Toward a theory of cultural trauma", in J. C. Alexander *et al.* (eds), *Cultural Trauma and Collective Identity*, Berkeley: University of California Press, pp. 1–30.

Allen, Jeffner (1986) *Lesbian Philosophy: Explorations*, Palo Alto: Institute of Lesbian Studies.

Allison, Anne (2000) "Pubic veilings and public surveillance: obscenity laws and obscene fantasies in Japan", *Permitted and Prohibited Desires: Mothers, Comics, and Censorship in Japan*, Berkeley: University of California Press, pp. 147–88.

Althusser, Louis (1965) *For Marx*, London: New Left Books.

Anderson, Benedict (1983) *Imagined Communities: Reflections on the Origin and Spread of Nationalism*, London: Verso.

Aoki, Hideo (1957) *Shitagi no bunkashi: oshare wa shitagi kara*. Tokyo: Matsuzawa Shoten.

Aoki, Hideo (1968) *Shitagi erotisumu*. Tokyo: Yūzankaku.

Aoki, Hideo (1973) *Shitagi no rekishi*, Fūzoku bunkashi sensho, Tokyo: Yūzankaku Shuppan.

Aoki, Hideo (1991) *Shitagi no ryūkōshi*. Tokyo: Yūzankaku.

Aoki, Hideo (2000) *Shitagi no bunkashi*. Tokyo: Yūzankaku.

Aoyagi, Hiroshi (2003) "Pop idols and gender contestation", in D. Edgington (ed.) *Japan at the Millennium: Joining Past and Future*, Vancouver, Toronto: UBC Press, pp. 144–67.

Aoyama Shinji, director (2000) *Roji e: Nakagami Kenji no nokoshita firumu*, Slow Learner, distributed by Kinokuniya Company.

Arao Yoshihide (1983) "Shinkei", *Kōza Nihongo no goi* 10, Tokyo: Meiji shoin, pp. 236–40.

Asada Akira (2000) "J-kaiki no yukue", in *Voice*, March (in the *Hihyō Kūkan* web archive. Online. Available at: http://www.kojinkaratani.com/criticalspace/old/special/asada/voice0003.html

Asahi Shimbun Tokuha Kishadan (1972) *28 Years in the Guam Jungle: Sergeant Yokoi Home from World War II*, San Francisco: Japan Publications, Inc.

Assmann, Jan (1997) *Moses the Egyptian, The Memory of Egypt in Western Monotheism*, Cambridge: Harvard University Press.

Bachelard, Gaston (1964) *The Poetics of Space*, John Stilgoe (trans.) Boston: Beacon Press.

Barrett, Michele (1988) *Women's Oppression Today: Problems in Marxist Feminist Analysis*, London: Verso.

Barthes, Roland (1970) *L'Empire des Signes,* D'Art Albert Skira, Paris: Flammarion.

Barthes, Roland (1977) *Image-Music-Text*, Stephen Heath (trans.) New York: Hill and Wang.

Barthes, Roland (1982) *Empire of Signs*, R. Howard (trans.) London: Jonathan Cape.

Baudrillard, Jean (1994) "The precession of Simulacra", in Shiela Faria Glaser (trans.) *Simulacra and Simulation*, University of Michigan Press (originally published in French, 1981).

Bazin, André (2004) *What is Cinema?* Hugh Gray (trans.) Los Angeles: University of California Press.

Beard, George M. (1869) "Neurasthenia, or nervous exhaustion", *Boston Medical and Surgical Journal* 3(13): 217–21.

Beard, George M. (1880) *A Practical Treatise on Nervous Exhaustion (Neurasthenia), Its Symptoms, Nature, Sequences, Treatment*, New York: William Wood and Co.

Beard, George M. (1881) *American Nervousness: Its Causes and Consequences*, New York: Putnam.

Befu Harumi (2001) *Hegemony of Homogeneity: An Anthropological Analysis of Nihonjinron*, Melbourne: Trans Pacific Press.

Benjamin, Walter (1969) "The storyteller: reflections on the work of Nikolai Leskov", in Hanna Arendt (ed.) *Illuminations: Walter Benjamin, Essays and Reflections*, New York: Schocken Books, pp. 83–109.

Benjamin, Walter (1999) "The crisis of the novel", in Michael W. Jennings, Howard Eiland and Gary Smith (eds) *Walter Benjamin: Selected Writings,* Vol. 2, Cambridge, MA. Harvard University Press, pp. 299–304.

Berger, James (1999) *After the End: Representations of Post-Apocalypse*, Minneapolis: University of Minnesota Press.

Berlant, Lauren Gail (1991) *The Anatomy of National Fantasy: Hawthorne, Utopia, and Everyday Life*, Chicago: University of Chicago Press.

Bersani, Leo (1986) *The Freudian Body: Psychoanalysis and Art.* New York: Columbia University.

Bhabha, Homi K. (1994) "Signs taken for wonders: questions of ambivalence and authority under the tree outside Delhi, May 1817", in *The Location of Culture*, London: Routledge, pp. 102–22.

Bhabha, Homi K. (1994) "Sly civity", in *The Location of Culture*, London: Routledge, pp. 93–101.

Bhabha, Homi K. (1994) *The Location of Culture,* London: Routledge.

Blanchot, Maurice (1986) *The Writing of the Disaster,* Ann Smock (trans.) Lincoln: University of Nebraska Press.

Blowers, Geoffrey and Serena Yang Hsueh Chi (2001) "Ohtsuki Kenji and the beginnings of lay analysis in Japan", *International Journal of Psycho-Analysis* 82: 27–42.

Borggren, Gunhild (2006) "Ruins of the future: Yanobe Kenji revisits Expo '70," *Performance Paradigm*, Vol. 2, pp. 119–31.

Bourdaghs, Michael (2003) *The Dawn that Never Comes: Shimazaki Tōson and Japanese Nationalism*, New York: Columbia University Press.

Braidotti, Rosi (1991) *Patterns of Dissonance: A Study of Women in Contemporary Philosophy*, Elizabeth Guild (trans.), New York: Routledge.

Brooks, Peter (1984) "Freud's masterplot: a model for narrative", in *Reading for the Plot,* Cambridge: Harvard University Press, pp. 90–112.

Budick, Sanford (2000) *The Western Theory of Tradition: Terms and Paradigms of the Cultural Sublime*, New Haven: Yale University Press.

Burger, Gordon (1988) "Politics and mobilization in Japan 1931–45", in Peter Duus (ed.) *The Cambridge History of Japan*, Vol. 6, Cambridge: Cambridge University Press, pp. 97–153.

Butler, Judith (1990) *Gender Trouble: Feminism and the Subversion of Identity*, London: Routledge.

Butler, Judith (1992) "The lesbian phallus and the morphological imaginary", in Naomi Schor and Elizabeth Weed (eds) *The Phallus Issue, Differences* 4(1): 133–71.

Butler, Judith (1993) *Bodies That Matter: On the Discursive Limits of "Sex"*, London: Routledge.

Butler, Judith and Joan W. Scott (eds) (1992) *Feminists Theorize the Political*, New York: Routledge.

Carr, Edward (1961) *What is History?* New York: Vintage.

Cassegard, Carl (2007) "Exteriority and transcritique: Karatani Kōjin and the impact of the 90s", *Japanese Studies* 27(1): 1–18.

Cassegard, Carl (2007) *Shock and Naturalization in Contemporary Japanese Literature*, Folkestone: Global Oriental.

Cazdyn, Eric (1999) "A short history of visuality in modern Japan: crisis, money, perception", *Japan Forum* 11(1): 95–105.

Cha, Theresa Hak-Kyung (1982) *Dictée*, Berkeley: Third Woman Press.

Chiba Sen"ichi (1998) "Ishikawa Jun to A. Jiddo: kongentekina bunmei hihyō to sekai shinpan", in *Modanizumu no hikakubungakuteki kenkyū*, Tokyo: Ōfū, pp. 112–22.

Chow, Rey (1993) *Writing Diaspora. Tactics of Intervention in Contemporary Cultural Studies*, Bloomington and Indianapolis: Indiana University Press.

Chow, Rey (1998) *Ethics After Idealism: Theory-Culture-Ethnicity-Reading*, Bloomington and Indianapolis: Indiana University Press.

Cixous, Hélène and Catherine Clément (1986) *The Newly Born Woman*, Betsy Wing (trans.) Minneapolis: University of Minnesota Press.

Clifford, James and George E. Marcus (eds) (1986) *Writing Culture: The Poetics and Politics of Ethnography*, Berkeley: University of California Press.

Colonna, Vincent (1989) "L'autofiction: Essai sur la fictionnalisation de soi en literature", PhD Dissertation, École des Hautes Études en Science Sociales.

Copjec, Joan (1994) *Read My Desire: Lacan Against the Historicists*, Cambridge, MA: MIT Press.

Cornyetz, Nina (1997) "Nakagami Kenji no shintai: yogoreta chi, kikei, seiki kison", *Gengo bunka* 14(3): 181–89.

Cornyetz, Nina (1999) *Dangerous Women, Deadly Words: Phallic Fantasy and Modernity in Three Japanese Writers*, Stanford: Stanford University Press.

Cornyetz, Nina (2000) "Kōi suru yokubō – Mishima Yukio" (1): "Niku o tekusutoka suru, aruiwa, (hi)bunsetsu sareta yokubō", *Yuriika* 11: 118–33.

Cornyetz, Nina (2001) "Amorphous Identity, Disavowed History: Shimada Masahiko and National Subjectivity", *Positions* 9(3): 585–609.

Cornyetz, Nina (2001) "Kōi suru yokubō – Mishima Yukio" (2): "Narushishizumu to sadizumu – homofashizumu to shite no Mishima", *Yuriika* 1: 225–45.

Cornyetz, Nina (2007) *The Ethics of Aesthetics in Modern Japanese Literature and Cinema: Polygraphic Desire*, London: Routledge.

Crary, Jonathan (1989) "Spectacle, attention, counter-memory", *October* 50: 96–107.

Culler, Jonathan (1981) *The Pursuit of Signs: Semiotics, Literature, Deconstruction*, Ithaca: Cornell University Press.

Daniel, E. Valentine and Jeffrey M. Peck (eds) (1996) *Culture/Contexture: Explorations in Anthropology and Literary Studies*, Berkeley: University of California Press.

de Certeau, Michel (1986) *Heterologies: Discourse on the Other*, Brian Massumi (trans.) Minneapolis: University of Minnesota Press.

de Lauretis, Teresa (1987) *Technologies of Gender: Essays on Theory, Film, and Fiction*, Bloomington: Indiana University Press.

de Vos, George and H. Wagatsuma (eds) (1967) *Japan's Invisible Race*, Berkeley: University of California Press.

Dean, Kenneth and Brian Massumi (1992) *First and Last Emperors: The Absolute State and the Body of the Despot*, New York: Autonomedia.

Dean, Tim (2000) *Beyond Sexuality*, Chicago: University of Chicago Press.

Debord, Guy (1998) *Society of the Spectacle,* New York: Verso.

Debord, Guy (2007) "User's guide to détournment" (1956) and "Détournment as negation and prelude" (1959) Ken Knabb (ed.) *Situationist International Anthology.* New York: Bureau of Public Secrets, pp. 14–21, 67–9.

Deleuze, Gilles and Félix Guattari (1984) *Anti-Oedipus: Capitalism and Schizophrenia*, Robert Hurley, Mark Seem and Helen R. Lane (trans.) London: Athlone Press (originally published in French, Paris: Les Editions de Minuit, 1972).

Deleuze, Gilles and Félix Guattari (1988) *A Thousand Plateaus: Capitalism and Schizophrenia*, Brian Massumi (trans.) London: Athlone (originally published in French as *Mille Plateaux*, Paris: Les Editions de Minuit, 1980).

Derrida, Jacques (1972) *La dissemination,* Paris: Editions du Seuil.

Derrida, Jacques (1976) *Of Grammatology*, Gayatri Chakravorty Spivak (trans.) Baltimore: Johns Hopkins University Press.

Derrida, Jacques (1981) *Dissemination,* Barbara Johnson (trans.) London: Athlone Press (originally published in French, Editions du Soleil, 1972).

Derrida, Jacques (1986) *Memoires: For Paul de Man*, Cecile Lindsay, Jonathan Culler, and Eduardo Cadava (trans.) New York: Columbia University Press.

Derrida, Jacques (1987) *The Post Card: From Socrates to Freud and Beyond,* Alan Bass (trans.) Chicago: University of Chicago Press.

Derrida, Jacques (1987) *Psyché, Invention de L'autre*, Paris: Galilée.

Derrida, Jacques (1988) "Signature event context", in Jeffrey Mehlman and Samuel Weber (trans.) *Limited Inc.*, Evanston, IL: Northwestern University Press, pp. 1–24.

Derrida, Jacques (1990) *Le Problème de la Genese dans la Philosophie de Hursserl*, Paris: PUF.

Derrida, Jacques (1991) *Donner le temps, 1: La fausse monnaie*, Paris: Galilée.

Derrida, Jacques (1992) *Given Time: I, Counterfeit Money*, Peggy Kamuf (trans.) Chicago: University of Chicago Press.

Derrida, Jacques (1998) *Archive Fever: A Freudian Impression*, Eric Prenowitz (trans.) Chicago: University of Chicago Press.

"Did he really kill them? The Mysterious Past of Yokoi Shōichi" [Hontō ni futari o koroshitanoka: Yokoi Shōichi san no misuterii kako], *Shūkan myōjō*, May 21, 1972, pp. 198–9.

Dodd, Stephen (1998) "The significance of bodies in Soseki's Kokoro", *Monumenta Nipponica* 53(4): 473–98.

Doi, Takeo (1973) *The Anatomy of Dependence*, John Bester (trans.) Tokyo: Kodansha International.

"The 'domestic affairs' of Yokoi and the two comrades with whom he split" [*Yokoi san ga futari no senyū to bekkyo shita "katei no jijō"*] *Shūkan sankei*, February 25, 1972, pp. 20–3.

Doubrovsky, Serge *et al.*, (eds) (1993) *Autofictions et Cie*, Université de Paris: X-Nanterre.

Douglas, Mary (1982) *Natural Symbols: Explorations in Cosmology*, New York: Pantheon.

Dower, John (1999) *Embracing Defeat: Japan in the Wake of World War II*, New York: W. W. Norton.

Egon (2003) "Kinkyū kikō: Hansen undō 'Korosu na' no yobikake" (Urgent contribution: the appeal of Korosuna), Web Dengei, Online. Available at: http://www.indierom.com/dengei/society/korosuna/korosuna.htm (Accessed 28 June 2006).

Egon (2003) "3/21 'Korosu na' demo hōkoku" (A report of Korosuna's demonstration on 21 March), Web Dengei, Online. Available at: http://www.indierom.com/dengei/society/korosuna/korosuna2.htm (Accessed 23 October 2006).

"The Emperor's Last Soldier, Yokoi Shōichi: Five Days in his Homeland", [*Tennō no saigo no heishi, Yokoi san: sokoku no itsukakan*], *Sandei mainichi*, February 20, 1972, pp. 16–25.

Erber, Pedro (2004) "Tokyo 1969: Mishima Yukio vs. Todai Zenkyoto", in *Anais do XV Encontro Nacional de Professores Universitários de Língua, Literatura e Cultura Japonesa*, Rio de Janeiro: Universidade Federal do Rio de Janeiro.

Etō, Jun (1970) "A Japanese Meiji intellectual: an essay on Kokoro". In Japanese National Commission for UNESCO (ed.) *Essays on Natsume Soseki's Works,* Tokyo: Japan Society for the Promotion of Science, pp. 49–65.

Etō, Jun (1993) *Seijuku to sōshitsu: "haha" no hōkai*. Tokyo: Kōdansha.

Eyerman, Ron (2001) *Cultural Trauma: Slavery and the Formation of African American Identity*, Cambridge: Cambridge University Press.

Foucault, Michel (1975) *Surveiller et punir*, Paris: Gallimard.

Franco, Jean (1996) "Beyond ethnocentrism: gender, power, and the third-world intelligentsia", in Patrick Williams and Laura Chrisman (eds) *Colonial Discourse and Post-Colonial Theory: A Reader*, New York: Columbia University Press.

Frazer, Sir James George (1911) *Taboo and the Perils of the Soul*, London: Macmillan.

Frazer, Sir James George (1966) *The Golden Bough*, 3rd edn., London: Macmillan, 1922; New York: St Martin's Press, 12 Vols.

Freud, Sigmund (1938) *The Basic Writings of Sigmund Freud*, A. A. Brill (trans.) New York: The Modern Library, Random House.

Freud, Sigmund (1939) *Moses and Monotheism*, New York: Vintage.

Freud, Sigmund (1949) *The Ego and the Id* [1923], Joan Riviere (trans.) London: Hogarth Press.

Freud, Sigmund (1950) *Totem and Taboo*, James Strachey (ed. and trans.) New York: W. W. Norton.

Freud, Sigmund (1953) "Delusions and dreams in Jensen's Gradiva", in James Strachey (ed.) Sigmund Freud, *The Standard Edition of the Complete Psychological Works of Sigmund Freud*, Vol. 9, London: Hogarth Press, pp. 2–95.

Freud, Sigmund (1953) "The interpretation of dreams" [1900], in James Strachey (ed. and trans.) *The Standard Edition of the Complete Psychological Works of Sigmund Freud*, Vol. 5, London.

Freud, Sigmund (1953) "Instincts and their vicissitudes", in *The Standard Edition of the Complete Psychological Works of Sigmund Freud,* James Strachey (ed. and trans.), Vol. 22, London, pp. 109–40.

Freud, Sigmund (1953) "Lecture XXXIII. Femininity", in James Strachey (ed. and trans.) *The Standard Edition of the Complete Psychological Works of Sigmund Freud,* Vol 22, London: Hogarth Press, pp. 112–35.

Freud, Sigmund (1953) "The psychical apparatus and the external world" (Ch. 8), in James Strachey (ed. and trans.), *"An Outline of Psychoanalysis, Part 3"*, *The Standard Edition of the Complete Psychological Works of Sigmund Freud,* Vol. 23, London: Hogarth Press, pp. 195–204.

Freud, Sigmund (1953–1974) *The Standard Edition of the Complete Psychological Works of Sigmund Freud,* James Strachey (ed.) London: Hogarth Press, 24 Vols.

Freud, Sigmund (1958) "A difficulty of psychoanalysis", in Sigmund Freud, *On Creativity and the Unconscious: Papers on the Psychology of Art, Literature, Love, Religion,* New York: Harper and Row, pp. 1–10.

Freud, Sigmund (1959) *Collected Papers,* New York: Basic Books, 5 Vols.

Freud, Sigmund (1959) "From the history of an infantile neurosis", in Sigmund Freud, *Collected Papers* 3, New York: Basic Books, pp. 473–605.

Freud, Sigmund (1960) *The Ego and the Id,* James Strachey (ed.), Joan Riviere (trans.) New York: W. W. Norton.

Freud, Sigmund (1961) *Beyond the Pleasure Principle,* in James Strachey (trans. and ed.) *The Standard Edition of the Complete Psychological Works of Sigmund Freud,* Vol. 18, London: Hogarth Press, pp. 1–66.

Freud, Sigmund (1961) *Civilization and its Discontents,* James Strachey (ed. and trans.) New York: W. W. Norton.

Freud, Sigmund (1962) "Screen memories", in James Strachey (ed.) *The Standard Edition of the Complete Psychological Works of Sigmund Freud,* Vol. 3, London: Hogarth Press, pp. 303–22.

Freud, Sigmund (1991) *On Metapsychology: The Theory of Psychoanalysis,* James Strachey (ed.) London: Penguin Books.

Freud, Sigmund (1995) *Three Essays on the Theory of Sexuality* (1905), James Strachey (ed.) *The Standard Edition of the Complete Psychogical Works of Sigmund Freud,* Vol. 7, London: Hogarth Press, pp. 123–245.

Freud, Sigmund (1995) "On transformations of instinct as exemplified in anal eroticsim", in James Strachey (ed.) *The Standard Edition of the Complete Psychological Works of Sigmund Freud,* Vol. 17, pp. 127–33.

Freud, Sigmund (2004) *Moses the man and monotheistic religion,* in J. A. Underwood (trans.) *Mass Psychology and Other Writings,* New York: Penguin Books, pp. 167–299.

Fujii, James (1993) "Death, empire, and the search for history in Natsume Sōseki's *Kokoro*", in *Complicit Fictions: The Subject in the Modern Japanese Prose Narrative,* Berkeley: University of California Press, pp. 126–50.

Fujita, Yukiko (1958) *Fujita yukiko no shitagi kyōshitsu.* Tokyo: Fujitayukiko yosai kenkyujo.

Fujita, Yukiko (1962) "Shitagi ga anata no sutairu o kimemasu", *Katei zenka* June: 25–32.

Fujitani, Takashi (1994) *Tennō no pājento,* Tokyo: NHK.

Fujitani, Takashi (1996) *Splendid Monarchy: Power and Pageantry in Modern Japan,* Berkeley: University of California Press.

Fukuda Kazuya (2004) "Kaisetsu", in Mishima Yukio, *Wakaki samurai no tame ni,* Tokyo: Bunshun bunko, pp. 269–76.

Furui Yoshikichi (1983) *Furui Yoshikichi sakuhin* 7, Tokyo: Kawade shobō.

Futabatei Shimei (1971) *Futabatei Shimei shū, Nihon kindai bungaku taikei* 4, Tokyo: Kadokawa shoten.

Gagnier, Regenia and Martin Delveaux (2006) "Towards a global ecology of the Fin de Siècle", *Literature Compass* 3(3): 572–87.

Garber, Marjorie (1992) *Vested Interests: Cross-Dressing and Cultural Anxiety,* New York: Harper Collins.

Gasché, Rodolphe (1994) *Inventions of Difference: On Jacques Derrida,* Cambridge: Harvard University Press.

Gay, Peter (1960/1989) "Sigmund Freud: A brief life", in Sigmund Freud, *The Ego and the Id,* James Strachey (ed.) Joan Riviere (trans.), New York: W. W. Norton, pp. xi–xxv.

Geertz, Clifford (1973) *The Interpretation of Cultures: Selected Essays*, New York: Basic Books.

Genette, Gérard (1980) *Narrative Discourse: An Essay in Method*, Ithaca, NY: Cornell University Press.

Gide, André (1973) "Journal of *The Counterfeiters*, translated from the French and annotated by Justin O'Brien", in *The Counterfeiters,* Dorothy Bussy (trans.), New York: Random House, pp. 399–451.

Gilman, Charlotte Perkins (1966) *Women and Economics: The Economic Factor Between Men and Women as a Factor in Social Evolution*, New York: Harper.

Gluck, Carol (1985) *Japan's Modern Myths: Ideology in the Late Meiji Period*, Princeton: Princeton University Press.

Gosling, F. G. (1987) *Before Freud: Neurasthenia and the American Medical Community, 1870–1910*, Urbana: University of Illinois Press.

Guattari, Félix (1992) *Chaosmosis*, Paul Bains and Julian Pefanis (trans.) Bloomington: Indiana University Press.

Goux, Jean-Joseph (1983) "Vesta, or the place of being", in *Representations* 1: 91–107.

Grosz, Elizabeth (1994) *Volatile Bodies: Toward a Corporeal Feminism*, Bloomington: Indiana University Press.

Hachijō, Takatake (1941) "Kokutai to kokka keitairon", *Nihon shogaku kenkyū* 12.

Hall, Robert King (ed.) (1949) *Kokutai no hongi: Cardinal Principles of the National Entity of Japan,* John Owen Gauntlett (trans.) Cambridge MA: Harvard University Press.

Hane, Mikiso (1982) *Peasants, Rebels and Outcastes: The Underside of Modern Japan*, New York: Pantheon Books.

Hara, Takeshi (2001) *Kashika sareta teikoku*, Tokyo: Misuzu shobō.

Harootunian, Harry (2001) "Review article: Hirohito Redux", *Critical Asian Studies* 33(4): 609–36.

Harootunian, H. D. and Masao Miyoshi (2002) "Introduction: the 'Afterlife' of area studies", in H. D. Harootunian and Masao Miyoshi (eds), *Learning Places: The Afterlives of Area Studies*, Durham: Duke University Press, pp. 1–18.

Harvey, Hannah B. and Karen Robinson (2007) "Hot bodies on campus: the performance of porn chic", in Ann C. Hall and Mardia J. Bishop (eds), *Pop-Porn: Pornography In American Culture*, Westport, CT: Praeger.

Hashikawa Bunzō (1978) "Shōwa ishin no ronri to shinri", in Hashikawa Bunzō and Matsumoto Hayashi, Isao, *Tōmei ningen: Okase!* Nikkatsu.

Hatanaka, Yoshiki (1985) "Sekai to hansekai no yume", *Bungakukai* 39(8): 302–7.

Haver, William (1996) *The Body of this Death: Historicity and Sociality in the Time of AIDS,* Stanford: Stanford University Press.

Hayashi, Isao (1978) *Tōmei ningen: Okase!* Nikkatsu.

Hayashi, Sharon and Anne McKnight (2005) "Good-bye Kitty, Hello war: the tactics of spectacle and new youth movements in urban Japan", *Positions* 13(1): 87–113.

Heath, Stephen (2003) "Notes on suture", in Slavoj Žižek (ed.) *Jacques Lacan: Critical Evaluations in Cultural Theory*, New York: Routledge, p. 10.

Herscher, Andrew (1997) "Everything provokes fascism: an interview with Slavoj Žižek", *Assemblage* 33: 58–63.

Hewitt, Andrew (1993) *Fascist Modernism: Aesthetics, Politics and the Avant-Garde*, Stanford: Stanford University Press.

Higgins, Lynne A. and Brenda R. Silver (eds) (1991) *Rape and Representation*, New York: Columbia University Press.

Hijiya-Kirschnereit, Irmela (1996) "Review of Roy Starrs" deadly dialectics: sex, violence and nihilism in the world of Yukio Mishima", *Journal of Japanese Studies* 22(1): 77–82.

Hijiya-Kirschnereit, Irmela (1998) "Response to Starrs" reply", *Journal of Japanese Studies* 24(1): 213–15.

Hill, Christopher (2007) "The body in naturalist literature and modern social imaginaries", *Tradition and Modernity: Comparative Perspectives*, 348–63, Beijing: Peking University Press.

Hill, Christopher L. (2009) *National History and the World of Nations: Japan, France, and the United States in the Second Imperial Wave*, Durham: Duke University Press.

Hirai Gen (2005) *Mikkī Mausu no puroretaria sengen*, Tokyo: Ōta shuppan.

Hirota Masaki (1990) *Sabetsu no shosō, Nihon kindai shisō* 2, Tokyo: Iwanami shoten.

Howe, Jeff (2003) "The two faces of Takashi Murakami", *Wired* 11(11). Online. Available at: http://www,wired.com/wired/archive/11,11/artist,html

"I killed two native villagers" [*Watshi wa futari no genchijin o koroshita*], *Josei sebun*, May 24–31, 1972, 207–9.

Igarashi, Yoshikuni (2000) *Bodies of Memory: Narratives of War in Postwar Japanese Culture, 1945–1970*, Princeton: Princeton University Press.

Igarashi, Yoshikuni (2002) "Yokoi Shōichi: When a soldier finally returns home", in Anne Walthall (ed.) *The Human Tradition in Modern Japan*, Wilmington, DE: Scholarly Resources, Inc.

Iguchi, Tokio (1999) " 'Joseiteki naru mono' mata wa kyosei (izen): Kobayashi, Yasuda, Dazai", in Hasegawa Kei, ed. *Tenkō no meian: Shōwa 10-nen zengo no bungaku*, Tokyo: Impakuto shuppan, pp. 95–109.

Iida Yūko *et al.* (1996) "*Kokoro* ronsō ikō", *Sōseki kenkyū*, no. 6.

Imamura, Shōhei and Kaneto Shindō (1988) "Gendai eiga to sei", in Shōhei Imamura (ed.) *Nihon eiga no tenbō*, Tokyo: Iwanami Shoten, p. 139.

Inoue, Shōichi (2002) *Pantsu ga mieru: shūchishin no gendaishi*. Tokyo: Asahi Shinbunsha.

Irigaray, Luce (1977) *Ce sexe qui n'en est pas un*, Paris: Minuit.

Irigaray, Luce (1985) *This Sex Which is Not One*, Catherine Porter and Carolyn Burke (trans.) Ithaca: Cornell University Press.

Irigaray, Luce (1992) *Elemental Passions*, Joanne Collie and Judith Still (trans.) New York: Routledge.

Irigaray, Luce (1993) *An Ethics of Sexual Difference*, Carolyn Burke and Gillian C. Gill (trans.) Ithaca: Cornell University Press.

Irigaray, Luce (1993) *je, tu, nous: Toward a Culture of Difference*, Alison Martin (trans.) New York: Routledge.

Irigaray, Luce (1993) *Sexes and Genealogies*, Gillian C. Gill (trans.) New York: Columbia University Press.

Irigaray, Luce (2002) *Between East and West: From Singularity to Community*, Stephen Pluhacek (trans.) New York: Columbia University Press.

Ishihara Chiaki (1997) *Hanten suru Sōseki*, Tokyo: Seidosha.

Ishihara Chiaki (2005) *Kokoro: Otona ni narenakatta Sensei*, Tokyo: Misuzu Shobō.

Ishikawa Jun (1989–90) *Ishikawa Jun zenshū* 1, Tokyo: Chikuma shobō.

Ishikawa, Jun (1990) *The Bodhisattva* William Jefferson Tyler (trans.), New York: Columbia University Press.

"It was Yokoi-san who killed my brother" [*Watashi no ani o koroshita no wa Yokoi san datta no ka*], *Josei Jishin,* May, 27, 1972, pp. 32–5.

Ito, Ken K (1997) "Writing time in Soseki's *Kokoro*", in Dennis Washburn and Alan Tansman (trans.) *Studies in Modern Japanese Literature: Essays and Translations in*

Honor of Edwin Mcclellan, Ann Arbor: Center for Japanese Studies, University of Michigan.

Itō, Mikiharu (1982) *Kazoku kokkakan no jinruigaku*, Minerva Shobo.

Ivy, Marilyn (1995) *Discourses of the Vanishing: Modernity, Phantasm, Japan*, Chicago: University of Chicago Press.

Iwano, Hōmei (1955) *Hōrō, Hōmei gobusaku*, Vol. 2, Tokyo: Shinchōsha, pp. 7–188.

Iwasa, Sōshirō (1986) *Seikimatsu no shizen shugi – Meiji yonjū nendai bungaku kō*, Tokyo: Yūseidō.

Jameson, Fredric (1979) *Fables of Aggression: Wyndham Lewis, the Modernist as Fascist*, Berkeley: University of California Press.

Jameson, Fredric (2006) "First impressions: review of Slavoj Žižek's *The Parallax View*", *London Review of Books,* September 7.

Johnson, Barbara (1987) "Apostrophe, animation, and abortion", in *A World of Difference*, Baltimore: Johns Hopkins University Press, pp. 184–99.

Johnston, William (1995) *The Modern Epidemic: A History of Tuberculosis in Japan*, Cambridge, MA: Harvard University Press.

Kaempfer, Engelbert (1727) *The History of Japan*, J. C. Scheuchzer (trans.) London.

Kaempfer, Engelbert (1777) *Geschichte und Beschreibung von Japan*, Hrsg, Dohm, C. W. Lemgo.

Kakegawa, Tomiko (1970) " 'Tennō kikansetsu' jiken: Nihon fashizumu chisei e no kōgeki", in Hashikawa Bunzō and Matsumoto Sannosuke (eds), *Kindai Nihon seiji shisōshi*, Vol. 2, Tokyo: Yūhikaku pp. 301–51.

Kakei, Katsuhiko (1913) *Kokka no kenkyū*, Shimizu Shoten.

Kamakura, Yoshinobu (2002) "Shizen shugi bungaku to Makkusu Norudau – 'Daraku ron' no yomare kata", *Kokubungaku gengo to bungei* 119(Nov.): 60–74.

Kamei Hideo (2002) *Transformations of Sensibility: The Phenomenology of Meiji Literature*, Michael Bourdaghs (ed.) Ann Arbor: Center for Japanese Studies, University of Michigan.

Kamoi, Yōko (1958) *Onna wa shitagi de tsukurareru.*

Kamoi, Yōko (1983) *Watashi wa roba ni notte shitagi o uri ni yukitai*, Horupu jiden senshū. Josei no jigazō; Tokyo: Horupu Shuppan.

Kanō, Mikiyo (1995) "Bosei fashizumu no fūkei", in Kanō Mikiyo (ed.) *Bosei fashizumu: haha naru shizen no yūwaku*, Tokyo: Gakuyō shobō, pp. 30–52.

Kantorowicz, Ernst (1957) *The King's Two Bodies: A Study in Medieval Political Theology*, Princeton: Princeton University Press.

Kaplan, Alice Yaeger (1986) *Reproductions of Banality: Fascism, Literature, and French Intellectual Life*, Minneapolis: University of Minnesota Press.

Karatani Kōjin (1988) *Nihon kindai bungaku no kigen*, Tokyo: Kōdansha.

Karatani Kōjin (1989) "One spirit, two nineteenth centuries", in Masao Miyoshi and H. D. Harootunian (eds) *Postmodernism and Japan*, Durham: Duke University Press, pp. 259–72.

Karatani Kōjin (1993) *Origins of Modern Japanese Literature,* Brett de Bary (ed. and trans.) Durham: Duke University Press.

Karatani Kōjin (1997) "Japan is interesting because Japan is not interesting", Lecture delivered in March. Online. Available at: http//www.karataniforum.org/jlecture.html (Accessed 19 November 2002).

Karatani, Kōjin (2002) *Nihon seishin bunseki*. Tokyo: Bungei Shunjō.

Katō Norihiro (2004) *Murakami Haruki Ierō pēji pāto 2*, Tokyo: Arechi shuppansha.

Kaufmann, Doris (2001) "Neurasthenia in Wilhelmine Germany: culture, sexuality, and the demands of nature", in Marijke Gijswijt-Hofstra and Roy Porter (eds) *Cultures of Neurasthenia from Beard to the First World War*, Amsterdam: Rodopi, pp. 161–76.

Kawamura Kunimitsu (1990) *Genshi suru kindai kūkan – meishin, byōki, zashiki rō, ariui wa rekishi no kioku*, Tokyo: Seikyūsha.

Kawamura Kunimitsu (2002) "Sōseki to shinkei suijaku – 'Kōjin' to sono shūhen kara", *Sōseki kenkyū* 15: 76–88.

Kawashima Takeyoshi (1963) *Ideorogī toshite no kazoku seido*, Tokyo: Iwanami shoten.

Kihira Tadayoshi (1938) *Waga kokutai ni okeru wa, Kokutai no hongi kaisetsu sōsho*, Tokyo: Kyōgakukyoku.

Kihira Tadayoshi (1941) *Waga kuni ni okeru ie to kuni*, Kokutai no hongi kaisetsu sōsho, Tokyo: Kyōgakukyoku.

Kin Yoshiharu (1998) "Nihon ni okeru seishin shitsugan gainen oyobi bunrui no jidai hensen", *Rinshō seishin igaku kōza,* Vol. 1, Tokyo: Nakayama Shoten, pp. 439–54.

Kinsella, Sharon (1995) "Cuties in Japan", in Lise Skov and Brian Moeran (eds) *Women, Media and Consumption in Japan*, London: Curzon Press, pp. 220–54.

Koga, Reiko (2004) *Korusetto no bunkashi*, Tokyo: Seikyusha.

Kojiki (1883) *Records of Ancient Matters*, Basil Hall Chamberlain (trans.), in *Transactions of the Asiatic Society of Japan*, Vol. 10 (Suppl), Yokohama: R. Meiklejohn.

Kojiki (1963) Tokyo: Iwanami Bunko.

Kojiki (1981) *Records of Ancient Matters*, Basil Hall Chamberlain (trans.) Rutland, Vermont: Charles E Tuttle.

Kolodny, Annette (1975) *The Lay of the Land: Metaphor as Experience and History in American Life and Letters*, Chapel Hill: University of North Carolina Press.

Komori Yōichi (1988) "Kokoro ni okeru hanten suru 'shūki' ", in *Kōzō toshite no katari*, Tokyo: Shin"yōsha, pp. 415–40.

Komori Yōichi (1993) "*Kokoro* ni okeru dōseiai to iseiai", in Komori Yōichi *et al.* (eds) *Sōryoku Tōron: Sōseki no Kokoro*, Tokyo: Shorin shobō, pp. 141–65.

Komori Yōichi (1993) "Nakagaki", *Sōryoku tōron: Sōseki no Kokoro*, p. 113.

Komori Yōichi (1998) *"Yuragi" no Nihon bungaku*, Tokyo: Nihon hōsō shuppan kyōkai.

Kōno Kensuke (1990) " 'Seishun' to iu tekusuto: Shimazaki Tōson Haru o megutte", in Satō Yasumasa (ed.) *Bungaku ni okeru nijūdai*, Tokyo: Kasama Shoin, pp. 123–44.

Kōno Seizō (1938) *Waga kokutai to shintō*, Kokutai no hongi kaisetsu sōsho, Tokyo: Kyōgakukyoku.

Kōnoshi Takamitsu (1986) *Kojiki no sekaikan*, Tokyo: Yoshikawa Bunkan.

Kōnoshi Takamitsu (1995) *Kojiki – tennō no sekai no monogatari*, Tokyo: NHK.

Konuma, Masaru (1973) "Hirusagari no jōji Koto-mandara."

Konuma, Masaru (1977) "Yumeno Kyūsaku no shōjo jigoku: Kasei no onna."

Kristeva, Julia (1980) *Desire in Language: A Semiotic Approach to Literature and Art*, Thomas Gora, Alice Jardine, and Leon S. Roudiez (trans.) Leon S. Roudiez (ed.), New York: Columbia University Press.

Kristeva, Julia (1982) *Powers of Horror: An Essay on Abjection*, Leon S. Roudiez (trans.) New York: Columbia University Press.

Kristeva, Julia (1984) *Revolution in Poetic Language*, Leon S. Roudiez (trans.) New York: Columbia University Press.

Kumashiro, Tatsumi (1979) "Akai kami no onna."

Lacan, Jacques (1972) *Ekuri*. Miyamoto Tadao (ed.), Tokyo: Kōbundō.

Lacan, Jacques (1973) *Le Séminaire de Jacques Lacan, Livre XI, Les Quatre Concepts Fondamentaux de la Psychanalyse*, J. A. Miller (ed.) Paris: Editions du Seuil.

Lacan, Jacques (1977) "The mirror stage as formative of the function of the I as revealed in psychoanalytic experience", in Alan Sheridan (trans.), *Écrits: A Selection*, London: Routledge, pp. 1–7.

Lacan, Jacques (1977) *The Four Fundamental Concepts of Psychoanalysis*, Alan Sheridan (trans.) London: Tavistock; New York: W. W. Norton.

Lacan, Jacques (1977) "The signification of the phallus", in Alan Sheridan (trans.), *Écrits: A Selection*, London: Routledge, pp. 281–91.

Lacan, Jacques (1977) "On a question preliminary to the possible treatment of psychosis", in *Écrits: a Selection*, London: Routledge, pp. 179–225.

Lacan, Jacques (1981) "Préface à l'édition japonaise des Écrits", *La lettre mensuelle de l'École de la cause freudienne* 3(3).

Lacan, Jacques (1982) "The meaning of the phallus", in Juliet Mitchell and Jacqueline Rose (eds and trans.), *Feminine Sexuality: Jacques Lacan and the École Freudienne*, London: MacMillan, pp. 74–85.

Lacan, Jacques (1988) *The Seminar of Jacques Lacan, Book II – The Ego in Freud's Theory and in the Techniques of Psychoanalysis 1954–5*, J. A. Miller (ed.) Cambridge: Cambridge University Press.

Lacan, Jacques (1993) "The quilting point", in Russell Grigg (trans.) *Seminar of Jacques Lacan, Book III: Psychoses 1955–1956*. New York: W. W. Norton.

Lacan, Jacques (1993) *The Seminar of Jacques Lacan, Book III: The Psychoses 1955–1956*, J.A. Miller (ed.) New York: W. W. Norton.

Lacan, Jacques (1997) *Écrits: A Selection*, Alan Sheridan (trans.) New York: W. W. Norton.

Lacan, Jacques (2001) *Autres Écrits,* Paris: Editions du Seuil.

Lacan, Jacques (2004) "Avis au lecteur Japonais", in J. A. Miller (ed.) *Le Séminaire de Jacques Lacan,* Vol. 11, Paris: Editions du Seuil, pp. 497–500.

Lacan, Jacques (2004) "*Postface au Seminaire XI*", in J. A. Miller (ed.) *Le Séminaire de Jacques Lacan,* Vol. 11, Paris: Editions du Seuil, pp. 503–7.

Lacan, Jacques (2004) *Le Séminaire de Jacques Lacan, Livre III, Les Psychoses*, J. A. Miller (ed.) Paris: Editions du Seuil.

Lacan, Jacques (2004) *Le Séminaire de Jacques Lacan, Livre X, L'angoisse*, 1962–1963, J. A. Miller (ed.) Paris: Editions du Seuil.

Lacan, Jacques (2005) *Le Séminaire de Jacques Lacan, Livre XXIII, Le Sinthome*, 1975–1976, J. A. Miller (ed.) Paris: Editions du Seuil.

Lacan, Jacques (2006) *Écrits: The First Complete Edition in English*, Bruce Fink (trans.) New York: W. W. Norton.

Lacan, Jacques (2006) "The mirror stage as formative of the I function, as revealed in psychoanalytic experience", in *Ecrits: The First Complete Edition in English*, pp. 93–100.

LaMarre, Thomas (2000) *Uncovering Heian Japan: An Archaeology of Sensation and Inscription*, Durham: Duke University Press.

Laplanche, Jean and Jean-Bertrand Pontalis (1988) *The Language of Psychoanalysis*, Donald Nicholson-Smith (trans.) New York: W. W. Norton (originally published in French as *Vocabulaire de la Psychoanalyse*, Presses Universitaires de France, 1967).

Levi-Strauss, Claude (1966) *The Savage Mind*, Chicago: University of Chicago Press.

Levy, Indra (2006) *Sirens of the Western Shore, The Westernesque Femme Fatale, Translation, and Vernacular Style in Modern Japanese Literature,* New York: Columbia University Press.

Long, Margherita (2006) "Nakagami and the denial of lineage: on maternity, abjection, and the Japanese outcast class", *Differences* 17(2): 1–32.

Lutz, Tom (2001) "Varieties of medical experience: doctors and patients, psyche and soma in America", in Marijke Gijswijt-Hofstra and Roy Porter (ed.) *Cultures of Neurasthenia from Beard to the First World War,* Amsterdam: Rodopi, pp. 51–76.

Machida, Kō (2003) "Official Machida Kou Website", Diary entry for 10 May. Online. Available at: http://www.machidakou.com/diary/diary-200305.html (Accessed 24 June 2007).

Maeda, Ai (1989) *Toshi no naka no bungaku,* Tokyo: Chikuma shobō.

Maltby, Richard (2003) "'A brief romantic interlude' Dick and Jane go to 3 1/2 seconds of the classical Hollywood cinema", in Slavoj Žižek (ed.) *Jacques Lacan: Critical Evaluations in Cultural Theory*, 10. London: Routledge.

Maruo Suehiro (1986) "Planet of the Jap" (Nihonjin no wakusei), in *Paranoia Sutā,* Kawade Shobō Shinsha, pp. 117–44.

Maruyama Masao (1992) *Chūsei to hangyaku: tenkeiki Nihon no seishinteki ichi,* Tokyo: Chikuma Shobō.

Marx, Karl (1963) *The Eighteenth Brumaire of Louis Bonaparte,* New York: International Publishers.

Massumi, Brian (1987) "Realer than real: the simulacrum according to Deleuze and Guattari", originally published in *Copyright 1*, Online. Available at: http://www.anu.edu.au/HRC/first_and_last/works/realer.html (Accessed 24 May 2008).

Matsushima, Toshiyuki (2000) *Nikkatsu Kabushiki Kaisha and Nikkatsu Roman poruno zenshi: meisaku, meiyū, meikantokutachi.* Tokyo: Kōdansha.

McClintock, Anne (1995) *Imperial Leather: Race, Gender, and Sexuality in the Colonial Contest,* New York: Routledge.

McGray, Douglas (2002) "Japan's gross national cool". *Foreign Policy* June/July: 40–54.

McKnight, Anne (2001) "Ethnographies of Modernity: Nakagami Kenji's Counter-history of Modern Literature (1968–1983)", PhD Dissertation, University of California, Berkeley.

Merivale, Patricia (1988) "Silences: Soseki Natsume's Kokoro and Canadian elegiac romance", in Kinya Tsuruta and Theodore Goosen (eds) *Nature and Identity in Candadian and Japanese Literature*, Toronto: University of Toronto and York University Joint Center for Asia Pacific Studies, pp. 127–41.

Merleau-Ponty, Maurice (1968) *The Visible and the Invisible*, Alphonso Lingis (trans.) Evanston: Northwestern University Press.

Metz, Christian (1982) *The Imaginary Signifier: Psychoanalysis and the Cinema.* Bloomington: Indiana University Press.

Miller, D. A. (1990) "Anal rope", *Representations* 32.

Miller, Jacques-Alain (ed.) (1988) *The Seminar of Jacques Lacan, Book II – The Ego in Freud's Theory and in the Techniques of Psychoanalysis 1954–5*, Sylvana Tomaselli (trans.), Cambridge: Cambridge University Press.

Minagawa Bunzō (1971) *Guamu-tō jūrokunen,* Tokyo: Chōbunsha.

Mishima Yukio (1968) *Taiyō to tetsu,* Tokyo: Shinchōsha.

Mitchell, Juliet (2003) *Siblings: Sex and Violence,* Cambridge: Polity Press.

Mitsuta, Ikuo (1986) "*Fugen*: naze Fugen na no ka?", in Miyoshi Yukio (ed.) *Nihon no kindai shōsetsu,* Vol. 2, Tokyo: Tokyo daigaku shuppankai, pp. 171–85.

Miyadai Shinji (1994) *Seifuku shōjo-tachi no sentaku.* Tokyo: Kodansha.

Miyakawa, Takeo (1994) "Saiwa sareta *Kokoro*", in Yōichi *et al.* (eds) *Sōryoku tōron: Sōseki no Kokoro*, Komori, Tokyo: Shōrin shobō.

Miyake, Yoshiko (1991) "Doubling expectations: motherhood and women's factory work under state management in Japan, 1930–1940", in Gail Lee Bernstein (ed.)

Recreating Japanese Women, 1600–945, Berkeley: University of California Press, pp. 267–95.

Miyamoto Moritarō (1997) "Seishin suijaku to bunmei – Natsume Sōseki to Uiriamu Jeimuzu", *Seiji keizai shigaku* 373(Sept.): 1–23.

Miyoshi, Masao (1996) *Accomplices of Silence*, Ann Arbor: University of Michigan Press.

Miyoshi, Yukio (1993) *Shimazaki Tōson ron*, Tokyo: Chikuma Shobō.

Mizumura, Minae (1997) "Resisting *Woman:* Reading Sōseki's Gubinjinso", in Dennis Washburn and Alan Tansman (eds) *Studies in Modern Japanese Literature: Essays and Translations in Honor of Edwin Mcclellan*, Ann Arbor: University of Michigan Press, pp. 23–37.

Moloney, James Clark (1953) "Understanding the paradox of Japanese psychoanalysis", *International Journal of Psycho-Analysis* 34: 291–303.

Monbushō (1937) *Kokutai no hongi*, Tokyo: Monbushō.

Mōri, Yoshitaka (2005) "Culture = Politics: the emergence of new cultural forms of protest in the age of freeter", *Inter-Asia Cultural Studies* 6(1): 17–29.

Morishige Satoshi (1976) "Tenchi kaibyaku shinwa no kōzō", in *Tenchi kaibyaku to kuni umi shinwa no kōzō,* Tokyo: Yūseidō.

Morishita Yūdō (1909) *Shinri ōyō nōshinkeisuijaku hitsujisaku*, Tokyo: Hakubunkan.

Morohashi, Tetsuji (ed.) *Dai kan-wa jiten,* Tokyo: Taishukan, 1955–60, 13 Vols.

Morris, Ivan (1964) *The World of the Shining Prince: Court Life in Ancient Japan*, New York: Knopf.

Mosse, George L. (1985) *Nationalism and Sexuality: Respectability and Abnormal Sexuality in Modern Europe*, Madison: University of Wisconsin Press.

Murakami, Haruki (1986) *Chūgoku yuki no surō bōto*, Tokyo: Chūkō bunko.

Murakami, Haruki (1991) *Dansu, dansu, dansu*, Vol. I, Tokyo: Kōdansha bunko.

Murakami, Haruki (1993) *Hardboiled Wonderland and the End of the World*, Alfred Birnbaum (trans.) New York: Vintage.

Murakami, Haruki and Kawai Hayao (1996) *Murakami Haruki, Kawai Hayao ni ai ni iku*, Tokyo: Shinchō bunko.

Murakami, Takashi (2001) *Summon monsters? Open the door? Heal? Or die?* Tokyo: Kaikaikiki Co., Ltd.

Murakami, Takashi (2001) "Takashi Murakami", Interview by Mako Wakasa, *Journal of Contemporary Art*, Online. Available at: http://www.jca-online.com/murakami.html (Accessed 13 February 2006).

Murakami, Takashi (2005) "Earth in my Window", in Murakami Takashi (ed.) *Little Boy: The Arts of Japan's Exploding Subculture*, New York: Japan Society; New Haven: Yale University Press, pp. 98–149.

Murakami, Takashi (2005) "Superflat trilogy", in Murakami Takashi (ed.) *Little Boy: The Arts of Japan's Exploding Subculture*, New York: Japan Society; New Haven, London: Yale University Press, pp. 150–63.

Muraoka Tsunetsugu (1962) *Kokuminsei no kenkyū*, Nihon shisōshi kenkyū V, Tokyo: Sōbunsha.

Nagahara Yutaka (1989) *Tennōsei kokka to nōmin*, Tokyo: Nihon keizai hyōronsha.

Nagahara Yutaka (2000) "Yūkan suru kioku", *Yurīka* 11(November): 218–29.

Nagai, Kafū (1993) *Jigoku no hana*, Tokyo: Iwanami Shoten.

Naganuma, Kenkai (1939) *Kokushi jō yori mitaru kokutai to kokumin seishin*, Tokyo: Kyōgaku sōsho tokushū, Vol. 13.

Nakagami, Kenji, Karatani Kōjin *et al.* (eds) (1996) *Nakagami Kenji zenshū*, Tokyo: Shūeisha, 1995–1996, 15 Vols.

Nakagami, Kenji (1999) *The Cape and Other Stories from the Japanese Ghetto*, Eve Zimmerman (trans.) Berkeley: Stone Bridge Press.

"Nakagami: Blind Spot Invisible Shame," *Writers on the Border* series, dir. Stephen Javor. Distributed by LA Sept, Tip TV, MV Films and Floating Island.

Nakajima, Izumi (2006) "Yayoi Kusama between abstraction and pathology", in Griselda Pollock (ed.) *Psychoanalysis and the Image: Transdisciplinary Perspectives*, Oxford: Blackwell, pp. 127–58.

Nasta, Susheila (ed.) (1991) *Motherlands: Black Women's Writing from Africa, the Caribbean, and South Asia*, London: The Women's Press.

Nathanson, Donald L. (1992) *Shame and Pride: Affect, Sex, and the Birth of the Self,* New York: W. W. Norton.

Natsume, Sōseki (1957) *Kokoro,* Edwin McLellan (trans.), Washington DC: Regnery.

Natsume, Sōseki (1965) *Wagahai wa neko de aru, Sōseki zenshū* 1, Tokyo: Iwanami Shoten.

Natsume, Sōseki (1966) *Kōjin,* in *Sōseki zenshū* 5, Tokyo: Iwanami Shoten, pp. 335–759.

Natsume, Sōseki (1985) *To the Spring Equinox and Beyond,* Kingo Ochiai and Sanford Goldstein (trans.) Rutland, VT: C.E. Tuttle.

Natsume, Sōseki (1986) "Danpen", in Miyoshi Yukio (ed.) *Sōseki bunmeiron shū,* Tokyo: Iwanami Shoten, pp. 308–24.

Natsume, Sōseki (1986) "Gendai Nihon no kaika", in Miyoshi Yukio (ed.) *Sōseki bunmeiron shū,* Tokyo: Iwanami Shoten, pp. 7–38.

Natsume, Sōseki (1995) *Kokoro,* in *Sōseki Zenshū,* Vol. 5, Tokyo: Iwanami.

Nehru, Jawaharlal (1967) *Towards Freedom*, Boston: Beacon Press.

Neocleous, Mark (1997) *Fascism*, Buckingham: Open University Press.

Nihon kokugo daijiten (2000–2) *Nihon kokugo daijiten,* 2nd edn., Tokyo: Shōgakukan, 13 Vols.

"Nikkatsu Roman poruno". Online. Available at: http://www.nikkatsu-roman poruno.com/jyanru/index.html

Nishimura, Shogoro (1971) *Danchizuma hirusagari no joji*. Nikkatsu.

Nixon, Mignon (2000) "Posing the phallus", *October* 92(Spring): 98–127.

Nochlin, Linda (1994) *The Body in Pieces: The Fragment as a Metaphor of Modernity,* London: Thames and Hudson.

Noguchi, Kinzaburō (1901) *Wafuku saihō kudensho tsūshin kyōjū*. Tokyo: Tokyo Saihō kyōjujo.

Noguchi, Takehiko (1988) "Junsui sanbun no tankyū", in Noguchi Takehiko, *Ishikawa Jun ron,* Tokyo: Chikuma shobō, pp. 54–98.

Nomura, Masaaki (1994) "Otoko to onna no shigarami o sarake dashita Roman poruno: Jūshichi nen no ayumi", in *Ano shīn o mōichido: Nikkatsu Romano poruno*. Tokyo: Kindai eigasha.

Nordau, Max (1993) *Degeneration*, Lincoln: University of Nebraska Press.

Nye, Joseph S. (2005) *Soft Power: The Means to Success in World Politics*. New York: Public Affairs.

Nye, Robert (1984) *Crime, Madness and Politics in Modern France: The Medical Concept of National Decline*, Princeton: Princeton University Press.

Ochi, Haruo (1985) *Sōseki to bunmei*, Tokyo: Sunagoya Shobō.

Ogden, Thomas H (1992) "The dialectically constituted/decentred subject of psychoanalysis I: the Freudian Subject", *International Journal of Psycho-Analysis* 73: 517–26.

Oguma, Eiji (2002) *Genealogy of Japanese Self-Images,* David Askew (trans.) Melbourne: Trans-Pacific Press.

Ohara, Kōyū (1978) *Momojiri musume: Pinku hippu gāru*. Nikkatsu.

Ōhashi, Yōichi (1996) "Kuiā fāzāzu no yume, kuiā neishon no yume: *Kokoro* to homosōsharu", *Sōseki kenkyū*, no. 6, pp. 46–59.

"Oh! Mōretsu". *Seinen eiga* 1969.

Ohtsuki, Kenji (1955) "The misunderstanding of Japanese psycho-analysis: a protest against the views expressed by Dr J. C. Moloney", *The International Journal of Psycho-Analysis* 36: 205–8.

Oka, Yoshitake (1982) "Generational conflict after the Russo–Japanese War", in Tetsuo Najita and Victor Koschmann (eds) *Conflict in Modern Japanese History: The Neglected Tradition*, Princeton: Princeton University Press, pp. 197–225.

Okamoto, Toshiko (2004) "Okamoto Tarō to 'Korosu na'," interview by Mizuguchi Yoshirō, *Shimin no iken 30 no kai* 86.

Ōkuma, Shigenobu (1906) "Seishin byō ni taisuru zakkan", *Shinkeigaku zasshi* 4(12): 614–25.

Oliver, Kelly (1995) *Womanizing Nietzsche: Philosophy's Relation to the "Feminine"*, London: Routledge.

Oppenheim, Janet (1991) *"Shattered Nerves": Doctors, Patients, and Depression in Victorian England*, New York: Oxford University Press.

Orr, James J. (2001) *The Victim as Hero: Ideologies of Peace and National Identity in Postwar Japan*, Honolulu: University of Hawaii Press.

Ōsawa, Masachi (2002) "'Zettai no hitei' e no yokubō", *Intercommunication* 41: 60–9.

Ōshima, Nagisa (1992) "Theory of experimental pornographic film", in Annette Michelson (ed.) *Cinema, Censorship, and the State: the Writings of Nagisa Oshima, 1956–1978*, Cambridge, MA: MIT Press, pp. x, 308.

Oshino, Takeshi (1994) "Isho no shohō: pen to noizu", in Komori Yōichi *et al.* (eds) *Sōryoku tōron: Sōseki no Kokoro*, Tokyo: Shōrinshobō, pp. 166–78.

Otomo, Rio (2006) "A Girl with the Amoebic Body and her Writing Machine", Paper presented to the 16th Biennial Conference of the Asian Studies Association of Australia, Wollongong 6/26–9, Online. Available at: http://coombs.anu.edu.au/SpecialProj/ASAA/biennial-conference/2006/Otomo-Rio-ASAA2006.pdf (Accessed 7 March 2007).

Oudart, Jean-Pierre (2003) "Cinema and suture", in Slavoj Žižek (ed.) *Jacques Lacan: Critical Evaluations in Cultural Theory*, 10, London: Routledge.

Ozaki Tetsuya (2003) "Kono sensō, kore kara no sensō", *Out of Tokyo* 59. Online. Available at: http//www.realtokyo.co.jp/japanese/column/ozaki59.htm (Accessed 1 October 2006).

Ozaki Tetsuya (2005) "Korosu na haku", *Out of Tokyo* 108. Online. Available at: http//www.realtokyo.co.jp/japanese/column/ozaki108.htm (Accessed 1 October 2006).

Paul, Robert A. (1996) *Moses and Civilization: The Meaning Behind Freud's Myth*, New Haven: Yale University Press.

Parker, Andrew; Russo, Mary; Sommer, Doris; Yeager, Patricia (eds) (1992) *Nationalisms and Sexualities*, New York: Routledge.

Partner, Simon (1999) *Assembled in Japan: Electrical Goods and the Making of the Japanese Consumer*, Studies of the East Asian Institute. Berkeley, CA: University of California Press.

Phillips, Adam (1996) *Terrors and Experts*, Cambridge: Harvard University Press.

Phillips, Adam (2004) "Close-ups", *History Workshop Journal* 57: 142–9.

Phillips, Adam (2006) *Side Effects*, New York: Harper Perennial.

Phillips, Mark Salber (2000) *Society and Sentiment: Genres of Historical Writing in Britain*, Princeton: Princeton University Press.

Phillips, Mark Salber (2004) "Distance and historical representation", *History Workshop Journal* 57: 123–41.

Porter, Roy (2001) "Nervousness, eighteenth and nineteenth century style: from luxury to labour", in Marijke Gijswijt-Hofstra and Roy Porter (eds) *Cultures of Neurasthenia from Beard to the First World War,* Amsterdam: Rodopi, pp. 31–49.

Prakash, Gyan (ed.) (1995) *After Colonialism: Imperial Histories and Postcolonial Displacements*, Princeton: Princeton University Press.

Radhakrishnan, R. (1992) "Nationalism, gender, and the narrative of indentity", in A. Parker *et al.* (eds) *Nationalism and Sexualities*, New York and London: Routledge.

Raglan, Ellie and Dragan Milovanovic (eds) (2004) *Lacan: Topologically Speaking*, New York: Other Press.

Raud, Rein (1999) "The Lover's subject: its construction and relativization in the Waka poetry of the Heian period", *Proceedings of the Midwest Association for Japanese Literary Studies 5: Love and Sexuality in Japanese Literature* (summer): 65–78.

Reber, Emily A. Su-lan (1999) "Buraku Mondai in Japan: Historical and modern perspectives and directions for the future", *Harvard Human Rights Journal* 12(Spring): 297–360. Online. Available at: http://www.law.harvard.edu/students/orgs/hrj/iss12/reber.shtml (Accessed 22 June 2008).

Reiter, Rayna (ed.) (1975) *Toward an Anthropology of Women*, New York: Monthly Review Press.

Ricoeur, Paul (1985) *Time and Narrative 2*, Kathleen McLaughlin and David Pellauer (trans.) Chicago: University of Chicago Press.

Riviere, Joan (1986) "Womanliness as a masquerade" (1929), in Victor Burgin, James Donald, and Cora Kaplan (eds) *Formations of Fantasy*, London: Methuen, pp. 35–44. (Originally published in *The International Journal of Psychoanalysis* (IJPA) 1929, Vol. 10.)

Rodríguez, Ileana (1994) *House/Garden/Nation: Space, Gender and Ethnicity in Post-Colonial Latin American Literatures by Women*, Robert Carr (trans.) Durham: Duke University Press.

Roelcke, Volker (2001) "Electrified nerves, degenerated bodies: medical discourses on neurasthenia in Germany, circa 1880–1914", in Marijke Gijswijt-Hofstra and Roy Porter (eds) *Cultures of Neurasthenia from Beard to the First World War,* Amsterdam: Rodopi, pp. 177–97.

Roji e: Nakagami Kenji no nokoshita firumu (2000), dir. Aoyama Shinji. Slow Learner, distributed by Kinokuniya.

Russell, Bertrand (1971[1921]) *The Analysis of Mind,* London: George Allen & Unwin.

Ryan, Marleigh Grayer (1965) *Japan's First Modern Novel: Ukigumo of Futabatei Shimei,* New York: Columbia University Press.

Saeki, Junko (1996) "Seibo wo kakomu dansei dōmei: *Botchan* ni Okeru Nanshoku teki Yōso". *Sōseki kenkyū*, no. 12, pp. 150–67.

Said, Edward (2003) *Freud and the Non-European*, London: Verso.

Saito, Tamaki (2009) "Sexuality of Otaku: Moe, phallic girls and Yaoi in light of psychoanalysis", in Ayelet Zohar (ed.) *PostGender: Gender, Sexuality and Performativity in Japanese Culture*, Cambridge: Cambridge Scholars Press.

Sakai, Naoki (1989) "Modernity and its critique: the problem of universalism and particularism", in H. D. Harootunian and Masao Miyoshi (eds) *Postmodernism and Japan*, Durham: Duke University Press, pp. 93–122.

Sakai, Naoki (1997) *Translation and Subjectivity: On Japan and Cultural Nationalism,* Minneapolis: University of Minnesota Press.

Sakai, Naoki and Jon Solomon (2006) "Addressing the multitude of foreigners, echoing Foucault", in Naoki Sakai and Jon Solomon (eds) *Traces 4: Translation,*

Biopolitics, Colonial Difference, Hong Kong: Hong Kong University Press, pp. 1–35.

Sakaki, Atsuko (1999) "The debates on *Kokoro*: a cornerstone", in *Recontextualizing Texts: Narrative Performance in Modern Japanese Fiction*, Boston: Harvard University Asia Center, pp. 29–54.

Sakuta Sōichi (1940) *Waga kokutai to keizai*, Kokutai no hongi kaisetsu sōsho, Tokyo: Kyōgakukyoku.

Sannosuke (ed.) (1970) *Kindai Nihon seiji shisōshi*, Vol. 2, Tokyo: Yūhikaku, pp. 209–31.

Santner, Eric (1999) "Freud's 'Moses' and the ethics of nomotropic desire", *October* 88(Spring): 3–41.

Santner, Eric (2001) "Miracles Happen: Benjamin, Rosenzweig, and the Limits of the Enlightenment", unpublished paper.

Sas, Miryam (1998) "Chambered Nautilus: the fiction of Ishikawa Jun", *Journal of Japanese Studies* 24(1): 35–98.

Satō, Hisayasu (1985) *Hitozuma korekutā*. Nikkatsu.

Satō, Izumi (2006) *Kokugo kyōkasho no sengoshi*, Tokyo: Keisōshobō.

Sawaragi Noi (1998) *Nihon gendai bijutsu*, Tokyo: Shinchōsha.

Sawaragi Noi (2002) *"Bakushinchi" no geijutsu*, Tokyo: Shōbunsha.

Sawaragi Noi (2003) "'Atarashii geijutsu' wa naze Iraku shinkō ni hannō shinakatta no ka?" *Gunzō* 58(7): 334–7.

Sawaragi Noi (2003) "Konnichi no Hansen undo", *Bijutsu techō* 55(835): 47–53.

Sawaragi Noi (2003) "Kono otoko o korosu na", *Gunzō* 58(8): 338–41.

Sawaragi Noi (2003) *Kuroi taiyō to akai kani – Okamoto Tarō no Nihon*, Tokyo: Chūō Kōronsha.

Sawaragi Noi (2005) "On the battlefield of 'superflat: subculture and art in postwar Japan'," in Murakami Takashi (ed.) *Little Boy: The Arts of Japan's Exploding Subculture*, New York: Japan Society/New Haven, London: Yale University Press, pp. 186–207.

Sawaragi Noi (2005) *Sensō to banpaku*, Tokyo: Bijutsu Shuppansha.

Schwartz, Joseph (1999) *Cassandra's Daughter: A History of Psychoanalysis*, New York: Viking.

Screech, Timon (1999) *Sex and the Floating World: Erotic Images in Japan 1700–1820*, London: Reaktion.

Sedgwick, Eve Kosovsky (1985) *Between Men: English Literature and Male Homosocial Desire*, New York: Columbia University Press.

Sedgwick, Eve Kosovsky (1990) *Epistemology of the Closet*, Berkeley: University of California Press.

Sedgwick, Eve Kosofsky (2003) *Touching Feeling: Affect, Pedagogy, Performativity*, Durham: Duke University Press.

Sedgwick, Eve Kosofsky and Adam Frank (eds) (1995) *Shame and Its Sisters: A Silvan Tomkins Reader*, Durham: Duke University Press.

Shapiro, Mary J. (1986) *Gateway to Liberty: The Story of the Statue of Liberty and Ellis Island*, New York: Vintage.

Sharp, Jasper (2008) "Pink thrills: Japanese sex movies go global". *Japan Times*, December 4.

Shimada Masahiko (1987) "Mishima ga yume de Watakushi ni kataru koto" in *Katarazu, utae*, Tokyo: Fukutake shoten, pp. 35–52.

Shingu Kazushige (2004) *Being Irrational: Lacan, the Objet a, and the Golden Mean*, M. Radich (trans.) Tokyo: Gakuju shoin.

Shimazaki, Tōson (2000) *Haru*, Tokyo: Iwanami Shoten.

Shirane, Haruo (2002) *Early Modern Japanese Literature: An Anthology, 1600–1900,* New York: Columbia University Press.

Shiratori, Shinichi (1976) *Kanjirun desu.* Nikkatsu.

" 'Shitagi nashi' ga ikenai: Nikkatsu poruno nado no tekihatsu keishichōga riyō setsumei". *Asahi shinbun*, January 30, 1972.

Silverman, Kaja (1992) "The Lacanian Phallus", *The Phallus Issue, Differences* 4(1): 84–115.

Sommer, Doris (1991) *Foundational Fictions: The National Romances of Latin America*, Berkeley: University of California Press.

Spivak, Gayatri Chakravorty (1988) "Can the Subaltern Speak?", in Cary Nelson and Lawrence Grossberg (eds) *Marxism and the Interpretation of Culture*, Urbana, University of Illinois Press, pp. 271–313.

Spivak, Gayatri Chakravorty (1994) "Can the Subaltern Speak?", in Patrick Williams and Laura Chrisman (eds) *Colonial Discourse and Post-Colonial Theory*, New York: Columbia University Press, pp. 66–111.

Spivak, Gayatri Chakravorty (1999) *A Critique of Postcolonial Reason*, Cambridge: Harvard University Press.

Spurr, David (1994) *The Rhetoric of Empire: Colonial Discourse in Journalism, Travel Writing, and Imperial Administration*, Durham: Duke University Press.

Starrs, Roy (1994) *Deadly Dialectics: Sex, Violence and Nihilism in the World of Yukio Mishima,* Honolulu: University of Hawaii Press.

Starrs, Roy (1998) Reply to review by Irmela Hijiya-Kirschnereit, *Journal of Japanese Studies* 24(1): 213–15.

"The stir from Yokoi's jungle confession" [Mitsurin no himitsu o kokuhakushita Shoicchan no dōyō], *Shūkan taishū* May 18, 1972, 142–3.

Strecher, Matthew (1998) "Beyond 'pure' literature: mimesis, formula, and the postmodern in the fiction of Murakami Haruki", *Journal of Asian Studies* 57(2): 354–78.

"The sudden cloud over the Yokoi myth" [Hayakumo kageri dashita "Yokoi-san shinwa"], *Shūkan bunshun*, May 22, 1972, 152–3.

Suga Hidemi (2003) *Kakumeiteki na, amari ni kakumeiteki na: "1968 nen no kakumei" shiron,* Tokyo: Sakuhinsha.

Suleri, Sara (1992) *The Rhetoric of English India*, Chicago: University of Chicago Press.

Suttmeier, Bruce (2007) "Seeing past destruction: trauma and history in Kaikō Takeshi", *Positions* 15(3): 457–86.

Suzuki Sadami (1988) "Fikushon no rasen undō: Ishikawa Jun no shuppatsu o megutte", *Yurīka* 20(8): 191–205.

Takamure, Itsue (1979) "Kamigokoro", in Takamure Itsue ronshū henshū iinkai, ed. *Takamure Itsue ronshū,* 253–7, Tokyo: Takamure Itsue ronshū shuppan iinkai.

Takechi, Tetsuji (1965) *Kuroi yuki.* Dai-san Productions, Nikkatsu.

Takeda Izumo (1990) *Ashiya dōman ōuchi kagami,* Tokyo: Kokuritsu Gekijō.

Takeda, Naoko (1997) *Shitagi o kaeta onna: Kamoi Yoko to sono jidai.* Tokyo: Heibonsha.

Taketomo Yasuhiko (1990) "Cultural adaptation to psychoanalysis in Japan, 1912–52", *Social Research* 57(4): 951–92.

Taki Kōji (1988) *Tennō no shōzō,* Tokyo: Iwanami shinsho.

Tanaka, Stefan (2004) *New Times in Modern Japan*, Princeton: Princeton University Press.

Tanizaki Jun'ichirō (1967) *Yoshinokuzu, Tanizaki Jun'ichirō zenshū,* Vol. 13, Tokyo: Chūō kōron, pp. 3–54.

Tanizaki Jun'ichirō (1991) *Two Novels: The Secret History of the Lord of Musashi and Arrowroot*, Anthony H. Chambers (trans.) San Francisco: North Point Press.

Tanno, Yuji (1970) *Harenchi gakuen.* Nikkatsu.

Taro, Kawasakishi (2005) *Okamoto Tarō Bijutsukan*, Tokyo: Nigensha.

Tayama, Katai (1972) "Futon", *Futon, Ippeisotsu*, Tokyo: Iwanami Shoten, pp. 5–84.

Tomioka Kōichirō (1995) *Kamen no shingaku: Mishima Yukio ron*, Tokyo: Kōsōsha.

Trachtenberg, Marvin (1986) *The Statue of Liberty*, New York: Penguin.

Trefalt, Beatrice (2003) *Japanese Army Stragglers and Memories of the War in Japan, 1950–1975,* New York: Routledge Curzon.

Theweleit, Klaus (1987) *Male Fantasies*, Vol. 1: *Women, Floods, Bodies, History*, Stephen Conway et al. (trans.) Minneapolis: University of Minnesota Press.

Theweleit, Klaus (1989) *Male Fantasies*, Vol. 2: *Psychoanalyzing the White Terror*, Erica Carter and Chris Turner (trans.) Minneapolis: University of Minnesota Press.

Tsuboi Hideto (1998) *Koe no shukusai: Nihon kindaishi to sensō*, Nagoya: Nagoya University Press.

Tsunoda Ryūsaku, Wm; Theodore De Bary and Donald Keene (eds) (1964) *Sources of Japanese Tradition*, New York: Columbia University Press.

Tsutsui, Edward G (1972) "Yokoi spoke only to me: The truth about his surviving alone", [*Yokoi san ga watashi dake ni katatta: hitori ikinokotta shinsō*], *Shūkan gendai*, February 17, pp. 20–5.

Tyler, William Jefferson (1990) "Introduction", in Ishikawa Jun, *The Bodhisattva*, New York: Columbia University Press, pp. xi–xv.

Tyler, William Jefferson (1990) "The Art and Act of Reflexivity in *The Bodhisattva*", in Ishikawa Jun, *The Bodhisattva*, New York: Columbia University Press, pp. 139–74.

Tyler, William Jefferson (1998) "Introduction", in Ishikawa Jun, *The Legend of Gold and Other Stories*, Honolulu: University of Hawaii Press, pp. xiii–xx.

Ueda Akinari, "Hankai (1970) A Translation from *Harusame Monogatari*", Anthony Chambers (trans.) *Monumenta Nipponica* 25(3/4): 371–406.

Uegaki, Yasuaki (1982) *Pinku no kāten.* Nikkatsu.

Ueno, Chizuko (1989) *Sukāto no shita no gekijō: hito wa dōshite panti ni kodawaru no ka.* Tokyo: Kawade Shobō Shinsha.

Ukai Satoshi (1997) "Nihirizumu ni tsuite", in *Tsugunai no arukeorojī*, Tokyo: Kawade shobō.

Uryū, Kiyoshi (1999) "Tōson no shinjidai ishiki to Haru", *Fukuoka kyōiku daigaku kiyō dai-ichi bu bunka hen* 48: 1–12.

Valentine, James (1990) "On the borderlines: the significance of marginality in Japanese society", in Eyal Ben-Ari, Brian Moeran, and James Valentine (eds) *Unwrapping Japan*, Manchester: Manchester University Press, pp. 36–57.

Van Deusen, E. H. (1869) "Observations on a form of nervous prostration (neurasthenia), culminating in insanity", *American Journal of Insanity* 25: 445–61.

Viglielmo, Valdo (1976) "*Kokoro*: a descent into the heart of man", in Kinya Tsuruta and Thomas E. Swann (eds) *Approaches to the Modern Japanese Novel*, Tokyo: Sophia University Press, pp. 168–73.

Vincent, J. Keith (1998) "Ōe Kenzaburō to Mishima Yukio no sakuhin ni okeru homofashizumu to sono fuman", *Hihyō kūkan* 2(16): 129–54.

Virilio, Paul (1976) *L'insécurité du territoire*, Paris: Stock.

Virilio, Paul (1984) *War and Cinema: The Logistics of Perception*, Patrick Camiller (trans.) London: Verso.

Virilio, Paul and Sylvère Lotringer (1983) *Pure War*, New York: Semiotext(e).

Vizzard, Jack (1970) *See No Evil; Life Inside a Hollywood Censor.* New York: Simon and Schuster.

Vlastos, Stephen (ed.) (1998) *Mirror of Modernity: Invented Traditions of Modern Japan*, Berkeley: University of California Press.

Wakakuwa, Midori (2000) *Sensō ga tsukuru joseizō*, Tokyo: Chikuma bungei bunko.

Walker, Janet (1979) *The Japanese Novel of the Meiji Period and the Ideal of Individualism*, Princeton: Princeton University Press.

Watanabe, Mamoru (1982) *Sērāfuku shikijō shiiku*. Nikkatsu.

Watanabe, Naomi (1992) *Tanizaki Jun'ichirō: gitai no yūwaku*, Tokyo: Shinchōsha.

Watanabe, Naomi (1995) "Nakagami Kenji zenshū kakukan no yomidokoro", *Subaru* 17(7): 30–46.

Watanabe, Naomi (1999) *Fukei bungakuron josetsu*, Tokyo: Ōta shuppan.

Watanabe, Naomi (2003) *Kakumo sensai naru ōbō: Nihon "68nen" shōsetsuron*, Tokyo: Kōdansha.

Watanabe, Naomi, Karatani Kōjin, Asada Akira, Suga Hidemi, and Nibuya Takashi (2000) Roundtable discussion, "Tennō to bungaku", *Hihyō kūkan* 2(24): 9–26.

Watarai Yoshiichi (2003) *Meiji no seishin isetsu – shinkei byō, shinkei suijaku, kamigakari*, Tokyo: Iwanami Shoten.

White, Hayden (1987) *The Content of the Form: Narrative Discourse and Historical Representation*, Baltimore: Johns Hopkins University Press.

Whitford, Margaret (ed.) (1991) *The Irigaray Reader*, Oxford: Blackwell.

Williams, Linda (1989) *Hard Core: Power, Pleasure, and the "Frenzy of the Visible"*. Berkeley: University of California Press.

Williams, Patrick and Laura Chrisman (1994) *Colonial Discourse and Post-Colonial Theory*, New York: Columbia University Press.

Woodhull, Alan S. (1978) "Romantic Edo Fiction: A Study of the Ninjōbon and Complete Translation of *Shunshoku Umegoyomi*", unpublished doctoral dissertation, Stanford University.

XYZ (anon) (1902) "Shinkei suijaku shō – sōkosha, bunshi, kanshi, gakusei shokun no ichidoku o yō su", *Taiyō* 8(7): 134–9.

Yabunaka Shun'an (1890) "Danjo seito no shinkei suijaku", *Jogaku zasshi* 204: 17.

Yamada Yoshio (1939) *Chōkoku no seishin*, Kokutai no hongi kaisetsu sōsho, Tokyo: Kyōgakukyoku.

Yamaguchi Tokio (2000) "Ishikawa Jun *Fugen* ron: sono hassō keishiki ga kanō ni shita mono ni tsuite", *Setsurin* 67–90.

Yamashita Etsuko (1988) *Takamure Itsue ron: haha no arukeorijii*, Tokyo: Kawade shobō shinsha.

Yamato Hōmei (2007) *Sōkyoku kashi kaisetsu: jiuta, sōkyoku*. Online. Available at: http://www2u.biglobe.ne.jp/~houmei/ kasi/0_hyousi.htm (Accessed 22 October).

Yamazaki Masakazu (1986) *Fukigen no jidai*, Tokyo: Kōdansha.

Yamazumi Masami (ed.) (1990) *Kyōiku no taikei*, Tokyo: Iwanami Shoten.

Yang, Daqing (2001) "The malleable and the contested: The Nanjing massacre in postwar China and Japan", in T. Fujitani *et al.* (eds) *Perilous Memories: The Asia-Pacific War(s)*, Durham: Duke University Press. pp. 50–86.

Yasko, Guy (1997) "Tōdai Zenkyōtō vs. Mishima Yukio: The cultural displacement of politics" in *The Japanese Student Movement 1968–70: The Zenkyōtō Uprising*, PhD Dissertation, Cornell University, pp. 156–210.

Yasuoka, Shōtarō (1976) "Shitagi buumu", in *Yasuoka Shōtarō essai zenshū*, Tokyo: Yomiuri Shinbunsha, pp. 133–6.

Yerulshami, Yosef Hayim (1991) *Freud's Moses: Judaism Terminable and Interminable*, New Haven: Yale University Press.

"Yokoi, don't make my son out to be a murderer!" [Yokoi-san watashi no musuko o satsujinsha ni shinaide], *Bishō* May 27, 1972, 547: 42–4.

Yokoi Shōichi (1974) *Asu e no michi*, Tokyo: Bungei shunjū.

Yokota-Murakami, Takayuki (1998) *Don Juan East/West: On the Problematics of Comparative Literature*, Albany, NY: State University of New York Press.

Yoshida Yutaka (1997) *Nihonjin no sensōkan: sengoshi no naka no henyō*, Tokyo: Aoki shoten.

Yoshimi Shun'ya (1995) *Koe no shihonshugi: denwa, radio, chikuonki no shakaishi*, Tokyo: Kodansha.

Yoshimoto, Midori (2005) *Into Performance: Japanese Women Artists in New York*, New Brunswick, NJ: Rutgers University Press.

Yuval-Davis, Nira and Floya Anthias (eds) (1989) *Woman-Nation-State*, London: Macmillan.

Zahlten, Alexander (2007) "The Role of Genre in Film from Japan: Transformations 1960s–2000s". Dissertation, University of Mainz.

Žižek, Slavoj (1989) *The Sublime Object of Ideology*, New York: Verso.

Žižek, Slavoj (1991) *Looking Awry: An Introduction to Jacques Lacan through Popular Culture*. Cambridge, MA: MIT Press.

Žižek, Slavoj (1993) *Tarrying With the Negative: Kant, Hegel, and the Critique of Ideology*, Durham: Duke University Press.

Žižek, Slavoj (1997) *The Plague of Fantasies*, New York: Verso.

Žižek, Slavoj (2000) *The Fragile Absolute – or Why is the Christian Legacy Worth Fighting for?* New York: Verso.

Žižek, Slavoj (2001) *The Fright of Real Tears*, London: BFI.

Žižek, Slavoj (ed.) (2002) "Afterword: Lenin's choice", to *Revolution at the Gates: Selected Writings of Lenin from 1917*, London: Verso.

Žižek, Slavoj (2003) *Jacques Lacan: Critical Evaluations in Cultural Theory*, 4 vols. New York: Routledge.

Žižek, Slavoj (ed.) (2003) "Introduction", in *Jacques Lacan: Critical Evaluations in Cultural Theory*, New York: Routledge.

Zohar, Ayelet (2005) "The seven genders of Japan", in *PostGender: Gender, Sexuality and Performativity in Contemporary Japanese Art*, ex, cat, Haifa, Israel, Tikotin Museum of Japanese Art, pp. 43–157.

Zohar, Ayelet (2007) "Strategies of Camouflage: Invisibility, Schizoanalysis and Multifocality in Contemporary Visual Art", PhD Dissertation, University of London.

Zohar, Ayelet (ed.) (2009) "Introduction: *Anti-Oedipus, Ajase* Complex and *PostGender*", in *PostGender: Gender, Sexuality and Performativity in Japanese Culture*, Cambridge: Cambridge Scholars Press.

Zohar, Ayelet (ed.) (2009) "The multiplicity of the phallus", in *PostGender: Gender, Sexuality and Performativity in Japanese Culture*, Cambridge: Cambridge Scholars Press.

Zwicker, Jonathan E. (2006) *Practices of the Sentimental Imagination: Melodrama, the Novel, and the Social Imagination in Nineteenth-Century Japan*, Cambridge, MA: Harvard University Asia Center.

8823blue. "Yami no naka no yōsei". Online. Available at: http://www12.ocn.ne.jp/~nacky/yousei/yousei09.html

Index

334 *Index*